Blender 3D Basics
Beginner's Guide
Second Edition

A quick and easy-to-use guide to create 3D modeling and animation using Blender 2.7

Gordon Fisher

BIRMINGHAM - MUMBAI

Blender 3D Basics Beginner's Guide
Second Edition

First published: June 2012

Second edition: August 2014

Production reference: 1190814

Published by Packt Publishing Ltd.
Livery Place
35 Livery Street
Birmingham B3 2PB, UK.

ISBN 978-1-78398-490-9

www.packtpub.com

Cover image by Gordon Fisher (phi3d@yahoo.com)

Credits

Author

Gordon Fisher

Reviewers

John W. Allie

Olivier Amrein

Michael Dunn

Jasper van Nieuwenhuizen

Brian Rocz

Commissioning Editor

Ashwin Nair

Acquisition Editor

Vinay Argekar

Content Development Editor

Anila Vincent

Technical Editors

Aman Preet Singh

Nachiket Vartak

Copy Editors

Roshni Banerjee

Sayanee Mukherjee

Karuna Narayanan

Alfida Paiva

Project Coordinators

Sanghamitra Deb

Priyanka Goel

Proofreaders

Paul Hindle

Clyde Jenkins

Bernadette Watkins

Indexers

Hemangini Bari

Mehreen Deshmukh

Rekha Nair

Tejal Soni

Production Coordinator

Shantanu Zagade

Cover Work

Shantanu Zagade

About the Author

Gordon Fisher got his start in computer graphics, working with industry pioneers at Information International, Inc. Since then, he has made 3D animation for clients including the U.S. Army, Ford Motor Co., the Dallas Cowboys, the Southeastern Conference, Costco, and Southwest Airlines.

He has been using Blender professionally since 2002, and has given classes on using Blender and using Python with Blender at Python conferences in Texas and Arkansas. His short film, Land and Sky, made with Blender, was shown at the Ozark Foothills Film Fest. His work has been displayed at the National Air and Space Museum.

He is the Creative Director for Point Happy Interactive and spends his spare time as a bicycling advocate and space activist. He has written articles about 3D modeling and animation for the American Modeler magazine and Digital Video Producer e-zine.

I would like to thank the people without whom this book would not exist. I would like to thank the staff at Packt Publishing, Ton Roosendaal, and the many Blender users around the world.

About the Reviewers

John W. Allie has been using Blender since 1999, when it wasn't even open source. He lives in New Haven, Connecticut, with his wife. Comics and other artwork can be found on his website http://www.johnwallie.com.

Olivier Amrein has been working on 3D for over 15 years. He is a CG generalist, interested in production aspects and workflows. Right now, he is working for RGBprod, a studio in Switzerland. He is a Blender Foundation Certified Trainer who loves all kinds of visual experiments.

He has been giving talks and workshops in Switzerland, the Netherlands, Brazil, Venezuela, and Russia. You can find more information about him at http://www.olivieramrein.com/.

> I would like to thank my wife, Qiongyao, and my two kids, Milla and Louis.

Michael Dunn is a Python developer at the University of Notre Dame and an aspiring 3D artist.

A sophisticated 3D studio such as Blender comes with a pretty steep learning curve. When he started to learn Blender, it was difficult to find good training materials for beginners—which made the learning process quite disheartening. So, it is with joy that he is able to contribute as a technical reviewer to *Blender 3D Basics Beginner's Guide* and hopes that it will help many other aspiring artists get off to a successful start with Blender.

Jasper van Nieuwenhuizen is a freelance animation professional with a special interest in the technical side of things. After graduating from an art school in 2004, he picked up Blender and has been using it ever since. Because he really enjoyed animation and 3D in particular, and wanted to learn as much as he could about it, he decided to go back to school. In 2010, he graduated in 3D Computer Animation and Visual Effects from Utrecht School of the Arts.

After this, he co-started the animation studio Fube, where he played his part in making commercials and an animated short film. During this time, he picked up Python and slowly evolved from a CG Generalist to a Technical Director, but still kept in touch with the artistic side of animation.

At the moment, he freelances under the name Lines of Jasper, and is involved in the startup of an animation collective. When he's not in front of his computer, he spends time with his family, grows vegetables on the balcony, and makes paper planes and robots. You can find more about him and his work at http://www.linesofjasper.com.

Brian Rocz received a BA in English from the University of Colorado, Denver, where he began studies in Math and Physics before transferring to the more subjective realm of literature and writing. His interest in 3D art grew out of his traditional art background, which, he admits, was left uncultivated and even less practiced. He has been using Blender for a number of years and is largely self-taught, though he cannot get away without saying that he owes a debt of gratitude to the Blender community for sharing their knowledge. He goes by the name Rocz3D in the digital space and on his website http://www.3dblenderstuff.wordpress.com.

www.PacktPub.com

Support files, eBooks, discount offers, and more

You might want to visit www.PacktPub.com for support files and downloads related to your book.

Did you know that Packt offers eBook versions of every book published, with PDF and ePub files available? You can upgrade to the eBook version at www.PacktPub.com and as a print book customer, you are entitled to a discount on the eBook copy. Get in touch with us at service@packtpub.com for more details.

At www.PacktPub.com, you can also read a collection of free technical articles, sign up for a range of free newsletters and receive exclusive discounts and offers on Packt books and eBooks.

http://PacktLib.PacktPub.com

Do you need instant solutions to your IT questions? PacktLib is Packt's online digital book library. Here, you can access, read and search across Packt's entire library of books.

Why subscribe?

- ◆ Fully searchable across every book published by Packt
- ◆ Copy and paste, print and bookmark content
- ◆ On demand and accessible via web browser

Free access for Packt account holders

If you have an account with Packt at www.PacktPub.com, you can use this to access PacktLib today and view nine entirely free books. Simply use your login credentials for immediate access.

Table of Contents

Preface

When researching, in preparation to write this book, we discovered that some Blender users try to learn Blender three times and give up twice before they become comfortable with Blender's effective, if unusual, interface. The editors at Packt and I decided that this was a problem that could be solved. The answer is to explain the basics in depth, give you practice so that your hands can learn Blender just as your mind does, and then you build on what you have learned. This isn't just a subject-by-subject reference book. It's a workbook to give you experience.

The theory behind *Blender 3D Basics Beginner's Guide Second Edition* is to start out simply and delve deeper and deeper into Blender in gradual stages, coming back to important topics several times. This book will start with an introduction to Blender and some background on the principles of animation, how they are applied to computer animation, and how these principles make animation better. Then you will be gently guided through the Blender interface, and introduced to using Blender with simple projects that cover the full process of modeling, lighting, camera work, and animation. Then you will continue to practice what you have learned and do more advanced work in all areas. Finally, you will bring it all together with an advanced project covering these subjects and edit animations made in this book; creating a video and a stereoscopic 3D animation. This may be a workbook, but it's a fun workbook with surprises, humor, and the projects build on each other, so it's not just a random series of exercises. When you are finished, you'll be prepared to show the world your skills.

Let's go!

What this book covers

Chapter 1, Introducing Blender and Animation, will help you to get your first hands-on use of Blender, a brief but very relevant bit of history of animation and computer animation and an overview of the basic principles of animation.

Chapter 2, Getting Comfortable Using the 3D View, includes some fun exercises that explore the usage of the Blender window system and the basic elements that are found in the 3D View window.

Chapter 3, Controlling the Lamp, the Camera, and Animating Objects, explains the basics of lights in Blender, good use of the camera, and making your first animation.

Chapter 4, Modeling with Vertices, Edges, and Faces, teaches you the fundamentals of 3D modeling, using Vertices, Edges, and Faces. You'll be introduced to Blender's library of premade objects and have fun bending and distorting Blender's lovely mascot, Suzanne.

Chapter 5, Building a Simple Boat, will teach you box modeling techniques. You will learn how to use them to make a small jon boat, give it a color, and make wooden seats. Then you will study the different lights that Blender has.

Chapter 5A, Lighting a Small Boat, will help you explore Blender's different lights. This chapter can be found online at https://www.packtpub.com/sites/default/files/downloads/4909OS_05A_Lighting_a_Small_Boat.pdf.

Chapter 6, Making and Moving the Oars, focuses on the oars for the boat. You will use more advanced modeling and animation techniques and discover how to create more complex keyframe animations.

Chapter 6A, Using Stereoscopic Cameras, gives you a brief introduction to setting up stereoscopic 3D cameras. This chapter can be found at https://www.packtpub.com/sites/default/files/downloads/4909OS_06A_Using_Stereoscopic_Cameras.pdf.

Chapter 7, Planning Your Work, Working Your Plan, teaches you to create templates to help you plan your modeling. You will get an introduction to modeling with Bézier curves, take a look at storyboarding and planning an animation, as well as being introduced to some charts and guides that help you plan your work.

Chapter 8, Making the Sloop, helps you to make the hull of the sloop using box modeling and subdivision surfaces. You will learn to make holes in objects with Boolean operations and create the ship's wheel with Spin Tools and DupliVerts.

Chapter 9, Finishing Your Sloop, explains how to use text and fonts in naming your sloop. Then you will assemble all the objects you made in this and the previous chapter, build some sails using NURBS surfaces, and add a few extras that have been provided in your download pack.

Chapter 10, Modeling Organic Forms, Sea, and Terrain, helps you build and paint an island and the ocean. You make trees for it, and assemble some prefab buildings, and also make a pier from four simple parts.

Chapter 11, Improving Your Lighting and Camera Work, focuses on professional lighting and camera techniques. You will also learn more about animation and ways to speed up performing test renders and improve the final rendering quality.

Chapter 12, Rendering and Compositing, covers assembling strips of animated sequences in the Video Sequence Editor to create a completed and edited animation with sound. You will use the node editor to assemble a 3D stereoscopic animation and get introduced to the cycles renderer, which adds even more realism and possibilities to a Blender scene.

What you need for this book

You need to download a copy of Blender available at `http://www.blender.org/download/get-blender/`. This book was written and tested on Blender 2.71. It should work with later versions of Blender as well, but we cannot guarantee it.

Who this book is for

This book was written to reduce the frustration that beginners who use Blender face, by offering a thorough introduction to the unique and powerful Blender interface, starting with simple projects and working up to more complex scenes and animations. It's intended to provide plenty of practice in using Blender, advice on things to keep in mind when doing 3D animation, and an exploration of Blender so that the students, when they finish the book, will have a solid background in using Blender and know enough that they can confidently participate in the worldwide Blender community.

This book also takes a peek into some arcane subjects such as the Cycles render engine, so that the reader will not be afraid, and will have a start on how to understand them. The student will have a sufficient solid basis in using Blender that they can continue and learn all of the higher functions of Blender including the physics engine, game engine, particles, armatures for character modeling, and more.

Conventions

In this book, you will find several headings appearing frequently.

To give clear instructions of how to complete a procedure or task, we use:

Time for action – heading

1. Action 1
2. Action 2
3. Action 3

Instructions often need some extra explanation so that they make sense, so they are followed with:

What just happened?

This heading explains the working of tasks or instructions that you have just completed.

You will also find some other learning aids in the book, including:

Pop quiz – heading

These are short multiple-choice questions intended to help you test your own understanding.

Have a go hero – heading

These practical challenges give you ideas for experimenting with what you have learned.

You will also find a number of styles of text that distinguish between different kinds of information. Here are some examples of these styles, and an explanation of their meaning.

Code words in text, database table names, folder names, filenames, file extensions, pathnames, dummy URLs, user input, and Twitter handles are shown as follows: "Copy the file to your `Image` directory."

New terms and **important words** are shown in bold. Words that you see on the screen, in menus or dialog boxes for example, appear in the text like this: "Go down to where it says **Normals**."

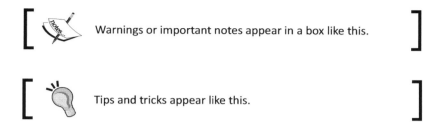

Warnings or important notes appear in a box like this.

Tips and tricks appear like this.

Reader feedback

Feedback from our readers is always welcome. Let us know what you think about this book—what you liked or may have disliked. Reader feedback is important for us to develop titles that you really get the most out of.

To send us general feedback, simply send an e-mail to feedback@packtpub.com, and mention the book title through the subject of your message.

If there is a topic that you have expertise in and you are interested in either writing or contributing to a book, see our author guide on www.packtpub.com/authors.

Customer support

Now that you are the proud owner of a Packt book, we have a number of things to help you to get the most from your purchase.

Downloading the example code

You can download the example code files for all Packt books you have purchased from your account at http://www.packtpub.com. If you purchased this book elsewhere, you can visit http://www.packtpub.com/support and register to have the files e-mailed directly to you.

Downloading color versions of the images for this book

For your convenience we have also provided a PDF that contains higher resolution color versions of the images used in this book. These can be extremely useful as you work through various stages of the project when working with materials or examining small detail changes as we tweak individual parameters. You can download the PDF from https://www. packtpub.com/sites/default/files/downloads/49090S_coloredimages.pdf.

Errata

Although we have taken every care to ensure the accuracy of our content, mistakes do happen. If you find a mistake in one of our books—maybe a mistake in the text or the code—we would be grateful if you would report this to us. By doing so, you can save other readers from frustration and help us improve subsequent versions of this book. If you find any errata, please report them by visiting http://www.packtpub.com/submit-errata, selecting your book, clicking on the **errata submission form** link, and entering the details of your errata. Once your errata are verified, your submission will be accepted and the errata will be uploaded to our website, or added to any list of existing errata, under the Errata section of that title.

Piracy

Piracy of copyright material on the Internet is an ongoing problem across all media. At Packt, we take the protection of our copyright and licenses very seriously. If you come across any illegal copies of our works, in any form, on the Internet, please provide us with the location address or website name immediately so that we can pursue a remedy.

Please contact us at copyright@packtpub.com with a link to the suspected pirated material.

We appreciate your help in protecting our authors, and our ability to bring you valuable content.

Questions

You can contact us at questions@packtpub.com if you are having a problem with any aspect of the book, and we will do our best to address it.

1
Introducing Blender and Animation

Welcome! It's a good guess that you are interested in learning how to create 3D animations or model 3D objects, maybe for use in games or 3D printing. You've chosen Blender 3D and you want to learn how to use it. This book is a good choice for learning Blender 3D. We did research on what hurdles new users faced and what were their frustrations with other training methods. So we will go step-by-step, learning how to use Blender comfortably to create animations, and do modeling, lighting, camera work, and much more. We will start out with simple steps and get comfortable at using the Blender interface, making and animating a rowboat and a sloop, and creating our own private island as shown in the following screenshot:

In this chapter, we will cover the following topics:

◆ A small introduction to Blender.

◆ Installing Blender and giving it a quick test.

◆ The top ten reasons to enjoy Blender 3D

◆ General animation and a glance at a few videos. The videos give us a quick introduction to animation.

◆ A few basic principles of animation.

◆ Watching some early computer graphics on how computer animators learned animation.

◆ Uses of 3D.

◆ The inner workings of Blender.

Welcome to the world of Blender 3D

The following is a screenshot of the *Big Buck Bunny* movie that was made using Blender:

The world of Blender is not an animated world as seen in films such as *Big Buck Bunny* or *Sintel* that was also made in Blender. It's the amazing community of people all over the world who use Blender. Artists, programmers, scientists, professionals, amateurs, teens, and retirees all use Blender, and now you will be one of the newest members of our community.

One thing that makes this community remarkable is the concept that since Blender is free, you pay for it by helping out the Blender community. There are many ways to give back to the community. You can recommend Blender to your friends, have fun helping other Blender users on websites such as www.blenderartists.org, critique their works, or pass along tips that you have learned. Blender is an open source software. Once you have mastered Blender, you can help create new functions for Blender itself or work with the Blender foundation team to make new cutting-edge examples of what Blender can do; for example, the films *Sintel*, *Tears of Steel*, and *The Gooseberry Project* were all created using Blender. There are as many ways to help the Blender community as there are Blender users and, most importantly, helping others will help you as a Blender user. Blender is not a solo sport, so join in!

Big Buck Bunny, Sintel, and Tears of Steel are animated films created by the Blender Institute

They were made with the dual purposes of improving Blender by bringing the best Blender users in the world together to push Blender to its limits, using its full capacity, and demonstrating to people what Blender is capable of. You can download Big Buck Bunny, Sintel, or Tears of Steel, or watch them at these locations:

Big Buck Bunny can be seen at http://www.bigbuckbunny.org/.

Sintel can be seen at http://www.sintel.org/.

Tears of Steel can be seen at http://mango.blender.org/.

Discovering Blender and animation

As Sintel, shown in the following screenshot, learned about her little Dragon, you will be learning a lot about how to use Blender. We will start out with some quick exercises to introduce you to the basics, and as you progress, you will be able to do more and more. As you study and practice, your hands will learn the Blender commands, freeing your mind to let it concentrate on modeling, lighting, camera work, and animation.

This book is about using Blender 3D; we will cover things that can help you build 3D objects for games, models, real-time simulations, 3D printing, and more. Blender began as an animation program, so it's good to start there.

However, there is more to animation than knowing which buttons to push while using Blender. Animators who are skilled at using the software but do not have a broader understanding of animation do not get the full use of the tools. They don't understand the culture or the history of animation or how animation principles have been used by masters such as Ub Iwerks, Chuck Jones, and Hayao Miyazaki, and therefore, they cannot profit from them. Thus, in this chapter, we will look at animation in general, and then computer animation specifically.

As you go through this book, you'll start by creating some simple animations such as moving the lights and camera in Blender. Once you are confident with this, you'll study the fundamentals of modeling and complete a simple modeling and animation project; finally, you will work on a more complex scene to expand your skills and get comfortable with the whole Blender production cycle.

There are many excellent books that teach you how to animate. In this book, we will focus on Blender and include pointers about animation that will help you educate yourself about animation in general and get the most from Blender.

Repetition is important when learning a skill. It takes repeated usage before your arms know what to do when the mind says "scale this box." So be patient. Play, learn, and have fun!

Learning Blender will literally change how you think

You'll be able to look at an object and think of several ways to create it. You will perceive everything differently. As you walk down a street, you will be imagining how you might model it or render it in Blender.

One thing to remember is that there are no buttons in Blender that say "Don't touch". As long as you back up your files and use the *Ctrl + Z* keys to undo any mistakes, not much is likely to go too wrong.

Now, it's time to begin our discovery of Blender. Using Blender is as simple or complex as you want it to be.

Let's begin simply. To start, we will open Blender and **render** a scene. Rendering is like taking a picture in Blender. When you take a picture in real life, you have a camera, some light, and something or someone you are taking a picture of.

In a Blender scene, there is a camera, a lamp, and something to render. When you render, Blender scans the scene from the camera's point of view. It notes which objects are where, and what lights are available. It figures out how each object will be lit, what the surface of the object looks like, what part of the object the camera can see, how big it should appear to the camera, and other factors, and then Blender creates a picture. It's pretty amazing.

We'll dip our toe into Blender, just so you can see that using Blender is not difficult and that you can do it. Then, we will do a little background study on animations so that you will understand what animators are trying to accomplish in Blender. Then, using what you have learned, you'll be ready to learn more about Blender.

Installing Blender

Go to `http://www.blender.org/` to download Blender for free. There is a **Download** button on the main menu, which will direct you to the location from where you can download the latest version of Blender for your system. Blender runs on Windows, Mac, and Linux. Follow the instructions and you should have Blender up and running quickly.

To use Blender, you need to first check that your machine has certain minimum system specifications so that it is capable of running Blender. Here's where to find your system information:

- On a PC that runs XP or Vista, click on the **Start** button at the lower left of the Windows screen, then go to **Programs | Accessories | System Tools | System Information**.

- On a PC that runs Windows 7, open **System Information** by clicking on the **Start** button. When the search box opens, type `System Information`, and choose **System Information** from the list of results.

- On a PC that runs Windows 8, at the bottom-left corner, tap or click on the Start button (Windows logo key) on the screen and choose **System** from the pop-up menu.

- On a Mac, click on the **Finder | Applications | Utilities | System Profiler** or **Finder | Applications | Utilities | System Information**.

- On a Linux machine, check the **System Settings | System Info**.

The following is what Blender needs in order to be able to run:

- System
    - Windows XP, Vista, 7, or 8
    - Mac OS X 10.6 or later
    - Linux

◆ Minimum hardware requirements

- ❏ A 32-bit Dual Core CPU with at least 2 GHZ and SSE2 support
- ❏ 2 GB RAM
- ❏ A 24-bit 1280x768 display
- ❏ A three-button mouse or trackpad
- ❏ An OpenGL-compatible graphics card with 256 MB RAM

◆ Recommended hardware requirements

- ❏ A 64-bit Quad Core CPU
- ❏ 8 GB RAM
- ❏ Full HD Display with 24-bit color
- ❏ A three-button mouse
- ❏ An OpenGL-compatible graphics card with 1 GB RAM

◆ Optimal (production-grade) hardware requirements

- ❏ A 64-bit Dual 8 Core CPU
- ❏ 16 GB RAM
- ❏ Two Full-HD displays with 24-bit color
- ❏ A three-button mouse and a graphics tablet
- ❏ Dual OpenGL-compatible graphics cards, quality brand with 3 GB RAM

Using a three-button mouse and the numeric keypad

After looking at the hardware specs, you may have noticed that Blender is designed to be used with a three-button mouse. Whether you are running a Mac and using a single-button mouse, or you have a laptop with a touchpad or trackpad, this is a great time to go to the store and buy a three-button optical or wireless mouse with a mouse wheel. They are not expensive. You shouldn't need anything special. I took one from a PC, plugged it into the USB port of a MacBook Air running Snow Leopard, and it worked fine. I polled a number of Blender users and they all said that using the three-button mouse was faster and easier than other devices.

If you are using a tablet with a higher end system, check your tablet documentation on how to reproduce right, middle, and left mouse-button clicks.

Also, if your computer does not have a numeric keypad built in, treat yourself to an external one. They are not expensive and will add a lot to your enjoyment of Blender, as well as improve your productivity.

Using Blender

Now that you have the latest version of Blender on your system, it's time to try it out.

Time for action – rendering your first scene in Blender

Although Blender is very powerful and has a lot of features, it's easy to get started using it. Blender has a default scene all set up for you to render. The following steps will help you render your first scene in Blender:

1. First, start your copy of Blender. You can either click on the **Blender** icon in the directory that you have installed it in, or use a shortcut or alias if you have created one. Blender will even run from a data stick, so you don't need to have it installed on a particular computer.

2. When you've started it, you should see something similar to the following screenshot. You will also see a splash screen in the center, with an attractive image made in Blender and some links.

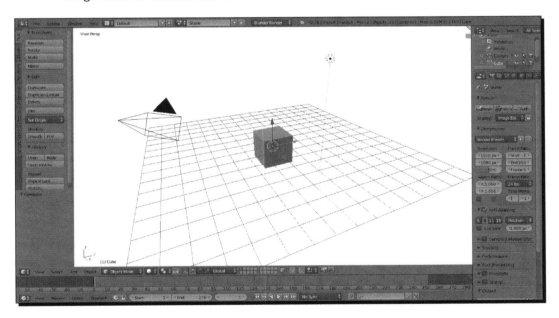

3. Move the cursor over the big central window. Click the mouse to close the splash screen.

4. Then, if you are running Windows or Linux, press the *F12* button on your keyboard.

5. If you have a Mac, click on where it says **Render** on the upper left, above the large 3D View window. Select **Render Image** from the drop-down menu. This is because Macs often have the *F1* and *F12* function keys already mapped to specific functions.

The following are the changes you should make to optimize your Mac for Blender. When you have made these changes, you will be able to use Blender in the same manner as Windows and Linux users, and you will be able to press the *F12* button to start rendering:

1. Go to **System Preferences**, select **Keyboard**, and then check **Use all F1, F2, etc. keys as standard function keys**. Don't worry, you can still get the regular functionality of the buttons by pressing the required button along with the *fn* function key.

2. Next, in **Keyboard Shortcuts** under **Dashboard & Dock**, uncheck the **Dashboard/F12** checkbox, so you can render by merely pressing *F12*.

3. Then, uncheck **Exposé Desktop/F11** under **Exposé & Spaces**. Now, you will be able to use the *F11* key to bring back your most recent rendered image.

4. Now, click on the left arrow at the top left of the **System Preferences** window to get back to the main **System Preferences** window. Now, select the **Exposé & Spaces** symbol in the top row above **Keyboard**. Select the **Exposé** button. Go down to the **Dashboard** section. Select the button that says **Middle Mouse Button** (**MMB**) when the menu pops up, and select the dash at the bottom of the pop-up menu. This will enable the MMB for use with Blender.

5. Finally, click on the left arrow at the top left of the **System Preferences** window to get back to the main **System Preferences** window. Select the mouse symbol next to **Keyboard**. Uncheck where it says **Zoom using scroll wheel while holding**. This will activate the control key while using Blender.

What just happened?

Congratulations! You've now rendered your first scene in Blender. You can see the scene to be rendered in the preceding image. The cube is easy to guess. The dot surrounded by dashed lines is the lamp. The four-sided cone with a triangle on top is the camera, and there is a reference grid beneath the cube.

When the scene is rendered, as seen in the following screenshot, Blender shows you what the camera would see. The cube is colored gray because you haven't chosen a color. There is only one lamp in the scene, and Blender calculates where the lamp is and where the sides of the cube are. The lamp is not an object like a light bulb, so it is not seen in the rendered image, but its light is used to set the brightness of the scene.

While it's rendering, Blender figures out what portion of the light would bounce off a particular side of the cube and into the camera lens. Some sides point away from the lamp, so they appear darker. The sides facing towards the lamp appear to be brighter. Blender even does a trick that you don't see at all. Blender figures out which parts of the cube the camera does not see, and to save itself from additional work, it doesn't render what cannot be seen.

Rendering this image was simple for you. Blender doesn't get any more difficult to use; you just learn more things to do with Blender. In the following chapters, we will break down the sections into easy-to-do steps using Blender.

Mac users, thank you for making changes to the interface of your Mac. Now, you can use the standard Blender commands. These will pay off by making the using of Blender much easier and fun. You can still access the Dashboard via the Mac menu bar.

Time for action – closing Blender

Now, let's close Blender and study some basics of animation. Steps for closing Blender are as follows:

1. Press the *Esc* key to close the render window and return to the 3D View window.

2. Press *Ctrl* + *Q* to quit Blender.

3. A dialog box will pop up, asking you to confirm that you want to click on **Quit Blender**; click on it to quit Blender.

What just happened?

When Blender renders a scene, it brings up a special render window over the 3D window. Pressing the *Esc* button closes this window, returning you to the 3D window. Pressing *Ctrl + Q* closes Blender 3D down completely. Congratulations! Everything else about learning Blender is just an elaboration on this.

Top 10 reasons to enjoy using Blender 3D

We all have our reasons for wanting to use Blender. The initial reason was that I wanted to teach a class on 3D animation at the Parks and Recreation center. I needed a 3D system that would fit the budget and that students could take home to use. Since then, I've also used it professionally, creating animations for an airline, a national football league team, banks, and more. With Blender, I made the first animated entry ever submitted to the Film in 48 Hours contest, and one Blender animation of mine was accepted in the Ozark Foothills Film Festival. I've even built a 3D printed model of a proposed lunar lander. Therefore, you never know how Blender will come in handy.

The top 10 reasons to enjoy using Blender 3D are given in the following table:

No.	Reasons
10	It's a fun hobby that will last all of your life.
9	You can use it to make a portfolio to get a job in games, films, advertising, and other fields.
8	You can start a home-based graphics, animation, or game business.
7	Blender has the largest user base and a great world-wide community.
6	You can express your artistic side and make things the way they should be.
5	It's fun to build your own worlds and have God-like power over them.
4	You can make games with the Blender Game Engine and make assets for them.
3	You can learn how to do computer programming with Python.
2	You can impress your friends by making animations for your civic social group or favorite team.
1	You can get coffee or a snack, or take a nap, while it's rendering and still be productive.

Getting a good background in animation

One of the best ways to learn animation is to study it from its beginning so that you can see for yourself how people learned about animation and improved what they could do. This was a lesson that was learned and then relearned when computer animation was introduced. So let's go back to the roots of animation and watch them grow, and then go back to the roots of computer animation and watch it get started.

Going back to the year 1922 on an animation field trip

We are going to go into the past, back to when animation was young. We are going there because there are general issues that everyone encounters when trying to put graphics into motion. Early animations were simple, so it is easiest to see the fundamental animation techniques done and also see examples of where it wasn't done so you can tell the difference.

Back then, like now, animators were under pressure; they had a short time to turn out a completed animation. They ran into issues such as what was required to tell a story believably, what kind of look to give it, how to make it easy to do, and how to complete it before their deadline. They also had to answer questions such as how to tell the story, how to get all the art work done, and how to photograph it with a camera. A lot of the answers they came up with are now universal.

First, we are going to look at a *Felix the Cat* animation called *Felix Turns the Tide* that was made a few years after World War I. It was one of the seventeen different Felix the Cat films made that year (which equates to approximately one animation every three weeks). It was a silent animation and cutting edge for its time but pretty primitive by modern standards, as you can see in the following screenshot:

From the thought balloon, borrowed from newspaper comics, you can see that animation hadn't come too far from its roots.

It's a good place to start because they had figured out the mechanics of making an animation, but they were just beginning to learn the language of animation. In this book, you will learn both the mechanics of a Blender animation and how to do it well. It's a learning experience we will share with these pioneers—so we're in good company!

Time for action – watching Felix Turns the Tide

Now, what you need to do next is find the animation and watch it. Next, you will think about certain aspects of what you have seen. There are no wrong answers. The important thing is to think about these concepts. Through these, you will understand more about animation principles and how they apply to Blender. Now, put yourself in the mind of someone living in 1922. World War I was just a few years ago. The first commercial radio stations were new. A person named Otto Mesmer did most of the animation work on Felix Turns the Tide. So put yourself in his place. You have a month to make it, and that is not enough time. How are you going to tell the story? Watch the animation, but go back and watch it again to see how he did it.

1. Search on the Web for the terms `Felix Turns the Tide + 1922`. YouTube, archive.org, or some other site should have the video. Archive.org may have a higher quality version. The *Felix Turns the Tide* movie was made in 1922 and stars *Felix the Cat*, who was the hottest animation star of the time.

2. Watch *Felix Turns the Tide*.

3. As you watch, look at Felix's movement. Does it look realistic or are we given a series of poses and a moment to see each one?

4. Look at the background. How did they stage the scenes? Think of the scene where he goes to say goodbye to his girlfriend, or when he hijacks the balloon. How is the camera used? Would you have used the camera in the same way?

5. Look at how they designed the animation to meet the audience's expectations. Audiences were used to the comic strips of newspapers, which used symbols such as speech balloons and musical notes to convey action. Do you see other places where the animation looks like a comic strip? Do modern animations use material from other genres that you are used to these days?

6. Look at how the sausages get to the battle by wireless. Do you think that modern audiences would accept this? Imagine you are remaking this animation in 3D using Blender for a modern audience. How would you handle getting the sausages to the battlefront?

What just happened?

Felix Turns the Tide sure isn't as complex as **Big Hero 6**, but it's surprising how well they used their limited tools and told a story. This was only six years after cel animation had been invented. Cel animation revolutionized early animation because it allowed you to put different parts of an animated frame on different transparent layers of plastic cellulose, so you didn't have to redraw the entire scene every frame. However, the animation was pretty stiff, and the motion went straight from pose to pose. Their use of the camera reflected the use of films at that time, plenty of long shots and long takes. They also borrowed the visual grammar from comics with things such as speech bubbles and dotted lines to indicate where they were looking.

Moving ahead a few years in time, to 1928

Animators are learning that their craft and technology is advancing. *Walt Disney* had lost its main character *Oswald the Lucky Rabbit* to *Universal Studios*. Universal also hired all of Disney's animators except *Ub Iwerks*, Disney's star animator. This was a serious blow to Disney. Therefore, Disney was desperate and they needed something to stay in business. In 1928, Walt Disney and Ub Iwerks created their first Mickey Mouse animation, *Plane Crazy*. It introduced both Mickey and Minnie. However, Disney could not find a distributor for it, so it did not get released. Their next Mickey Mouse movie, *Steamboat Willie*, was the first American animation with sound, and that opened up the market for Mickey. For us, since *Plane Crazy* was made as a silent film and retrofitted with sound, it showed how animators had perfected their skills in the period between 1922 and 1928 before the use of sound.

Time for action – enjoying Plane Crazy

Felix the Cat was pretty stiff. In the first Mickey Mouse cartoon, you can see that things had improved a lot in a short time and that they had discovered what made animation work. What differences do you see between the style of the Felix cartoons and those of Mickey? The following steps will guide you in understanding how revolutionary this animation is:

1. Search on the Web for the terms `Plane Crazy + 1928`. YouTube, archive.org, or some other site should have the video. This is a good example of silent animation at the dawn of sound. As you watch it, keep Felix Turns the Tide in mind and see how the two are different. In addition, look at the driver at **3:51**; is that Felix?

2. Watch it now. Don't be afraid to stop the action or look at some parts more than once.

3. Look at Mickey's movement. What differences do you see in how the characters move and look that allowed Iwerks to do a more subtle characterization with Mickey than the animators had done for Felix?

4. Look at the background. They are softer and lusher in *Plane Crazy* than they were in *Felix Turns the Tide*. Does this accomplish the purpose of highlighting the characters by contrast? How would you decide how much detail to put into a given background?

5. Look at how the camera is used. In what ways is *Plane Crazy* visually richer than *Felix Turns the Tide* and how does this help tell the story?

6. Look at how the things are squashed and stretched in *Plane Crazy*. How did Ub Iwerks distort things to make *Plane Crazy* more dramatic?

7. Look at how your expectations of what will happen are misdirected. How did Ub Iwerks manage to redirect your expectations so you were fooled, or does it allow him to add or remove something without you noticing?

What just happened?

Animation has improved quite a bit in these six years. Now, the basic principles of animation are codified and used with good results. Instead of a static, stage-like establishing shot, we enter the scene following a cow, from blackness into a farmyard filled with activity. Objects are contorted surrealistically. There is no way to foretell where the story is going and the camera is used to immerse you into what is happening. When Mickey is flying along the road, Disney puts you into the action, giving you a view from the plane's cockpit instead of showing you what the airplane is flying through, heightening the action, but also saving work by using just a few lines and some colored background to achieve a hair-raising ride.

Arriving in 1938, the animation industry is at a peak

By 1938, the animation industry is mature. Felix ceased production in 1936. Disney released *Snow White and the Seven Dwarfs* in December of 1937 and was beginning production on *Fantasia*. With the popularity of *Popeye*, *Fleischer Studios* had become the number two animation company and was working on *Gulliver's Travels*.

Time for action – sailing to Goonland

In 1938, Fleischer Studios did the Popeye cartoon *Goonland*. This is a good example of the state of animation as a mature art form. If you have questions about some of the terms, check the table in the *Animation Principles* section that follows. Animating well was a science by 1938 and was codified. As you watch Goonland, see what animation principles it employs. The following steps will help you focus on different parts of the animation that use different methods:

1. Search on the Web for the terms `Goonland + 1938`. YouTube, archive.org, or some other site should have the video.

2. Look at Goonland with an eye to what progress has been made since 1930. According to reviews on `www.imdb.com`, this has some of the best artwork of all the Popeye cartoons.

3. Look at how complex the motion is. In addition to the main character's motion, there is **secondary motion**. It can enhance or detract from the main motion. What places do you see where the secondary motion improves the scene?

4. Look at how objects move. **Arcs** make design and motion more interesting than straight lines. What places in the animation do they arc the motion to make it more interesting?

5. Look at when objects move. **Anticipation** and **follow through** help carry the motion.

6. Look for **exaggeration** of the motion. How does exaggeration help the feel of animation?

7. Notice how few **metaphors** are used. There are no eye-lines, no text balloons. Do visual metaphors like this still have a place in animation? Why or why not?

What just happened?

Goonland was made during the peak of 1930s animation. The principles of animation were well known and widely used. At the start, the secondary motion of clouds in the background is so dramatic that it almost makes you seasick. The anticipation of Popeye taking in an exaggeratedly deep breath prior to filling his sails with wind helps sell that it can be done. When he grabs the goony hair to disguise himself, it snaps and springs towards his hand. That is a follow through. There are fewer metaphors except when the goons fight and you see a cloud of fists and arms, or lines radiating from his face when Popeye sees his Pappy.

Animation principles

You have seen how animation developed over the space of 16 years. People learned techniques that aided in making an interesting and exciting animation. It didn't happen overnight, but when everything came together, the synergy of the techniques made animation come alive.

The following table lists techniques to think about and incorporate into your work as you learn to animate in Blender:

Technique	Benefit
Squash and stretch	Makes animated objects such as clay. A ball hitting a wall gets taller and narrower as it flattens on the wall momentarily, and then resumes its original shape. This punches up the motion and gives the viewer clues about the weight and rigidity of an object or character.
Anticipation	Anticipation prepares the audience for something that is going to happen. When Wile E Coyote goes off a cliff when chasing the Roadrunner, he pauses mid air before falling into a deep canyon and then he falls.
Staging	How is the action framed by the camera and what part of the image area is used? You want to present the action in the clearest and most dynamic manner.
Straight ahead action and pose to pose	Most 3D animations are pose to pose. You set keyframes of the most critical points of the animation and then Blender creates the motion between those points. However, you can modify this action so it flows on a curve and speeds up or down as it travels.

Technique	Benefit
Follow through and overlapping action	A baseball pitcher's arm doesn't stop instantly when the ball leaves his hand. That's follow through. The pitcher's arm moves rapidly, and his head moves much more slowly. That's overlapping action.
Slow in and slow out	Think of a drag racing car accelerating or an F1 car stopping in the pits. Motion rates do not change instantly. You need a period of transition.
Arcs	Arcing motion and curvy lines can be more attractive and powerful.
Secondary action	Motions that emphasize the main motions can add a lot to how interesting the motion is. Think of the motion of a woman's dress as she walks along.
Timing	The use of time in animation will affect pacing, characters, and the effect of an action. Events must happen at a believable rate but you can exaggerate time dramatically.
Exaggeration	Exaggerating size, timing, or motion makes it more interesting and accentuates what you want to be most important.
Solid drawing	This is applying basic drawing principles of form, weight, and volume to animations. For Blender, this becomes modeling, texturing, and moving the object to give it a proper feel of weight and mass.
Appeal	A character does not need to be as cute as Hello Kitty to have appeal, but the audience must have a way to relate to them and enjoy them. An object should also have pleasing proportions, and perhaps some sparkle to catch the eye or motion to add detail.
Misdirection	It can be used to change the plot, or guide the viewer's eyes, magician-like, so that they will not notice entrances, exits, or changes.
Contrast	How does the character or object being animated stand out from the background so your eyes know what to follow?

Learning from your animation heroes

One of the best ways to learn is to study what others have done; that is no surprise. If you wanted to be a soccer (football) star as a child, you probably watched Pelé on TV and imagined yourself scoring goals the same way.

Animation is the same. It's good to watch the animations that others have made. The following animations are a few recommendations that you can try to create:

◆ Oswald the Lucky Rabbit, Trolley Troubles

◆ Felix the Cat, Woos Whoopee

◆ Popeye the Sailor, The Paneless Window Washer

- Betty Boop, Minnie the Moocher
- Lotte Reiniger, The Adventures of Prince Achmed, made in Germany
- Jiri Trnka, Ruka (The Hand), considered the Walt Disney of Eastern Europe
- Ivan Ivanov-Vano, Blek end Uait, made in Russia, which may be disturbing to some
- Quirino Cristiani, El Mono Relojero, made in Argentina

Please remember that the times and values were different, and watch the animation and not their attitudes.

Time for action – making a folder of your animation heroes

You probably already have bookmark folders in your browser. Why not create one of your favorite animation heroes? The following steps will help you to make a folder for your animation heroes:

1. Think of who your animation heroes are.

2. Create a bookmarks folder in your web browser that will store the addresses of websites about your favorite animators or animations that you have seen.

3. Now, go online and look at some works that you know, whether it's Disney's Fantasia, South Park, or Plumiferos (Free Birds), which was the first feature length film made entirely in Blender.

4. Add a link to your folder whenever you find something you like.

5. You can find quite a number of interesting animations by just looking around on the Web. For example, Nina Paley's *Sita Sings the Blues* is a feature animation done by one person in Flash. It's pretty amazing. I also found *Snow-bo*, by Vera Brosgol and Jenn Kluska, and *Kenya* on www.weebls-stuff.com. There are many great Blender animations at www.blenderartists.org.

6. Come back and watch these animations repeatedly. You'll see something new each time.

What just happened?

You just gave yourself an animation reference library to enjoy and study. As you learn animation, you may want to come back to them as references, to see how they solved animation problems.

Starting to use computers for animation in the 1960s

The first interactive computer graphics project was carried out on the Whirlwind computer, which was used in an attempt to create a flight simulator for the military. Other early adopters were GM and Boeing who tried to use the computer to help them design automobiles and airplanes.

The history of interactive graphics began at the Massachusetts Institute of Technology (MIT) in 1961 with two big projects, one of which was called **Sketchpad**. It's shown in the next image that was provided by MIT. Sketchpad was created by *Ivan Sutherland*, and it was the forerunner of programs such as Blender. You can see Timothy Johnson using it to model what looks like a chair. To control it, he's using a light pen, the box with 40 buttons on it, and all the switches on the panel to his left. Blender also requires both hands to operate.

The other project was a game called **Spacewar!**, by *Steve Russell*, which was the first video game to be distributed.

Let's continue with our tour. We're going to look at a demonstration of Sketchpad. Then, we will look at Triple I, a company founded by three MIT professors to build advanced computer graphics display hardware, and we will see what their in-house 3D animation department was learning. Finally, we will look at the first short film from Pixar, where the animation and the computer animation industries met.

Beginnings of 3D animation in 1963

It's time to meet Blender's great-great-grandfather. Originally, TV screens were used by computers for short-term data storage, but it wasn't long before people tried to connect the screens to computers just to make graphics. The amazing thing about this is that one man came up with everything in 1961. Ivan Sutherland put this system called Sketchpad together. It was the first real-time interactive computer graphics system; all others are descended from it, including Blender.

Time for action – meeting Ivan Sutherland and Sketchpad

The video **Ivan Sutherland : Sketchpad Demo** is not an animation. It's a look at the interactive computer graphics program that was the prototype for all others, including Blender, and it gives you an idea of what primitive computer graphics were like. Follow these steps to watch the video and observe the variety of graphics that are being produced. While they may not look like modern animation, they have the same fundamental elements.

1. Search on the Web for the terms `Ivan Sutherland + Sketchpad Demo (2/2)`. YouTube, archive.org, or some other site should have the video.

2. Watch it now. This is the beginning of modern computer graphics.

3. What kind of graphics do you see? What kind of 3D animation is it doing?

4. What kind of input devices do they have?

5. They spoke about *master drawings* and *instances* of these drawings and the *data structures* that make them. Does this have anything to do with modern computer graphics?

6. They showed the Lincoln Labs TX-2 computer used by Ivan Sutherland. What do you think would win in a computing power contest, the TX-2 or your mobile phone?

What just happened?

We just saw the grandfather of all computer animation programs. Similar to early ink animations, it was all done with lines. They had the basic 3D transformations so they could rotate objects and display a quad view similar to the **Quad View** in Blender, but there was no shading. You probably noticed there was no standard keyboard or mouse, but there was a box with buttons, switches on the computer, and a lightpen that they used. The lightpen was a distant ancestor of a tablet or a touchscreen. The data structures were very important. Blender definitely uses versions of the master drawings and instances, as you will discover. And yes, your cell phone has much more computing power than the TX-2.

Going to the late 1970s, a few companies are doing 3D animation

By the late 1970s, a few companies are experimenting with video- and film-quality computer animation. One of the first was a company called *Information International, Inc.* or *Triple I*. At that time, they were doing some of the best animation in the world, which led to them being one of the teams that made the original *Tron*. Looking back, what is amazing is how simple the graphics are.

Time for action – seeing the Triple I demo 1976 – 1979

This video is a compilation of two different demo reels. You can tell the change by the soundtrack. Look at their approach to animation. This was bleeding-edge graphics in its time. The **Triple I** demo reel shows huge improvements in computer graphics. Objects have solid surfaces, colors, and highlights. Watch this demo reel and notice the improvements since Sketchpad. Compare it to modern computer animation to figure out what is missing:

1. Search on the Web for the term **Triple I (1976–1979)**. YouTube, archive.org, or some other site should have the video.

2. Watch it now and enjoy it.

3. Did you notice the equipment at the very beginning? Do you see the movie camera? How about the data tablet and the keyboard? Can you find the removable discs for data backup and the computer tape drives?

4. Just as we saw an improvement between Felix and Mickey, there's been a lot of advancement from Sketchpad to the Triple I demo reel. What changes do you see?

5. Notice the *teapot* on the table in one of the scenes? Have you seen it elsewhere?

6. Look at the geometry of the 3D models such as the ABC logo and the Mercedes Benz logo and the building. You can see that the sides are made of flat panels called polygons. What are some of the ways that they play with these polygons to make it more interesting?

7. Compare the animation here with the animation in Felix Turns the Tide. Both are primitive. Are there similarities in how they handle backgrounds? Is Triple I's plastic look equivalent to the line art in Felix because they couldn't do any better?

What just happened?

The first machine you saw was the *FR-80* graphics recorder, the most advanced film recorder of its time. Next, you can see a digitizing tablet and a keyboard terminal. The two low machines in the foreground are disk drives. The multi-platter disks had an enormous capacity of 200 MB. Backing up data has always been a problem for animators. What are some of the ways you can back up your work?

This is quite an improvement over the work in Sketchpad but still very stiff. The work on color, lighting, textures, and post processing was all being done for the first time. The animation was still being done by people trained at Cal Tech, not Cal Arts. What is amazing is that this was a professional demo reel. Now, it might not even get you a job as an intern. Back then, it was mind-boggling.

The teapot was created in 1975 at the University of Utah and has become like the mascot of computer graphics. This was a very early use of it, and in this case, it was testing curved surfaces and shading. The teapot makes many appearances in films, including in *Toy Story*.

Back then, there were no such things as geometric primitives. Each object was digitized vertex by vertex in a similar manner to what was done in Sketchpad. However, the use of the digitizing tablet allowed much more flexibility and precision. The Peter Fonda bust was made by taking aligned photographs of him, mounting the images on a digitizing tablet, and then inputting each vertex one by one, based on the images. It was the first CGI image of a human in a major motion picture.

Time for action – watching Triple I's 1982 demo reel

It's just a short time later. However, computer animation is starting to come of age. It's no longer a gimmick, and for the first time, professional art direction is being used. The **(Triple I) 1982 demo reel** is the beginning of computer animation being used in films and TV. Computer animation now had to compete with traditional photographic techniques and looks. Watch this demo and see whether they succeeded:

1. Search on the Web for the term `(Triple I) 1982 demo reel`. YouTube, archive. org, or some other site should have the video.

2. Watch it now and enjoy it.

3. Check out the magician Adam Powers. How do you think they animated him?

4. Does the KCET-TV animation compare well with modern motion graphics?

5. What is happening with the quality of modeling? How do the Star Wars X-wing fighters compare with the earlier Datsun car?

6. The Cindy character is the first whole body human character. Compare her and the Peter Fonda head?

What just happened?

In the first demo reel, the animation pretty much consisted of objects floating in space. In the 1982 demo reel, the background becomes an integral part of the scene, and in the Adam Powers section, we have a simple character animation and the first mo-cap animation.

Bringing on a creative director, *Richard Taylor*, Triple I's animation started to have filmic qualities; the KCET animation was an early example of good motion graphics.

The team consisted of the same people, with the addition of an Art Director. So we can see that using principles of graphic design is starting to make a difference.

Not only are the models becoming more detailed as with the X-wing fighters, but now they are getting shaded. The Cindy model was the first shaded representation of the human figure. Like their work, you may start out simple, but your work will get better and better.

Introducing Pixar in 1984, and everything comes together

In 1984, Pixar was the first place that combined computer animation technology with traditional animation techniques. While the modeling and rendering were not much better than anyone else at that time, the use of the twelve animation principles revolutionized computer animation. When it was introduced, other animators were in awe.

Time for action – adventuring with André and Wally B

This was Pixar's first animation. It was made in 1984. It was directed by *John Lasseter*, who had been a traditional cel animator at Walt Disney and was familiar with the standard animation principles. The modeling was very simple, and the storyline goes right back to the simplicity of Felix the Cat. So you can see, even successful and modern companies have learned from the old school, just as you're doing by reading this chapter. Here is where computer animators learned to use the same animation principles. Watch **The Adventures of André and Wally B** and observe how many of the principles that you can see are still in use:

1. Search on the Web for the term The Adventures of André and Wally B. YouTube, archive.org, or some other site should have the video.

2. Watch it now and enjoy it.

3. You learned about classic animation principles. What animation principles do you see being used?

4. Compare the color use and detailed backgrounds to what Triple I did.

5. Look at the trees, why are they all similar?

6. Compare how dynamic these characters are with Adam Powers by Triple I.

7. Often, animations have inside jokes. Did you notice the gloves on André's hands? Which other animated character wore gloves like that?

What just happened?

The Adventures of André and Wally B was a landmark film in a number of aspects. It took ten *VAX-11/750* super-minicomputers and a *Cray X-MP/48* supercomputer to render it out, and it was the first computer animation to use motion blur.

More importantly, it was the first computer animation to have used animation principles seriously. For example, in *Squash and stretch*—when Wally gets ready to chase André, he first squeezes front to back and then straightens out as he flies. Here is a list of the animation principles that were used in this film:

- **Anticipation**: Notice André's reaction as he first sees Wally B, but we don't.
- **Staging**: Notice the close up for their first encounter and then the long shot when Wally is chasing André.
- **Straight ahead action and pose to pose**: You can notice this when André is waking up.
- **Follow through and overlapping action**: Wally's feet are not attached, but they react to his motion. His wings move faster than his legs.
- **Slow in and slow out**: Note how André's eyes open and close as he is waking up.
- **Arcs**: When Wally goes to sting André, he does a barrel roll first.
- **Secondary action**: Wally moves in to threaten André, and André leans back in response.
- **Timing**: You can notice this when you see André quaking and then you see Wally for the first time.
- **Exaggeration**: You can notice this when Wally tweaks André's nose.
- **Solid drawing**: André and Wally seem to have real weight and mass.
- **Appeal**: Wally is cute.

The trees are an application of a master object and instance as invented by Ivan Sutherland. Their coloring sets the tone of the animation, and their smooth-rounded shapes contrast with the spiky-busy background. Those gloves on André's hands look suspiciously like Mickey Mouse's gloves.

You can see the difference between this and the Triple I animations. This animation was such a breakthrough that the Association of Computing Machinery had John Lasseter write a paper called *Principles of Traditional Animation Applied to 3D Computer Animation* for the July 1987 issue of Computer Graphics.

Have a go hero – educating yourself about 3D animation

There are a lot of great animations to look at. You can never watch too many. If you have time, watch any Pixar short films you can find. You might also want to check out the following films for a better idea of the range of animation that was happening back then. Do you see differences in the animation styles of the Americans, the Europeans, and the Japanese?

VintageCG on YouTube has a good collection of early computer animation. Some of the titles are:

◆ MAGI Synthavision demo reel (1982), this was Triple I's main competitor. Both worked on Tron.

◆ Sogitec Showreel (1985), this is a European competitor. They used some of the equipment that Triple I built, but had their own studios.

◆ Japan Computer Graphics Lab (1985) shows what the Japanese were doing at that time.

◆ Stanley and Stella in Breaking the Ice (1987), the first animation with flocking behaviors to control the birds and fish.

◆ Reboot Intro (1994), this was the first half-hour TV show that was entirely computer generated.

Your greater understanding of animation will increase your ability to create it.

Back to the present

So far, we've studied the roots of animation and of computers. It's good to see that the great started humbly, and to see how things improved as they practiced. This gives us inspiration. It's the journey we are all on. The changes from Adam Powers to The Adventures of André and Wally B are impressive, as animation professionals moved in and showed the computer boys what using the principles of animation could do for their computer-generated animations.

Using your 3D skills, what can you do with them?

There are a lot of different ways to use 3D. The following are a few ways you might want to use your Blender skills.

Creating 2D animations

It might seem odd, but if you watch animated shows such as Futurama and American Dad, in outdoor scenes or ones with cars, planes, and rockets moving in them, you can tell that they were originally created in 3D and were then colored to match the rest of the 2D animation. One director told me that his 2D animated show is all done in 3D but shot with a camera setting that flattens it out again. He finds it's faster to make it that way than with Flash or other 2D animation packages.

TV and videos

This is the market Blender was originally built for, back in the days when it was the in-house system at a Dutch advertising firm called *NeoGeo*. Blender is a good tool for local TV stations and advertisers because it can do a lot quickly and deliver quality results at a price that even the smallest TV station's manager will appreciate. Networks such as Azteca America have used Blender in some of their studios. Blender is good for schools and universities as well as personal video projects.

Films and pre-visualization

Blender has started to be used for feature films such as *Plumiferos* in Argentina and *The Naughty 5* from India. In addition, short films such as Sintel show that Blender has the capacity to do it. Hollywood has been known to use Blender for pre-visualizing a movie before it's made, to figure out how the movie will look when they make it. Pixar uses Blender for its intern program.

Stereoscopic 3D

This is a hot new trend in films. You need to have two cameras render the same scene from slightly different locations, just as if your eyes are slightly apart. However, the cameras have to work in sync with each other. Think of how your eyes shift if they were to go from threading a needle to looking at mountains in the distance. Blender can do this as well as any other 3D animation package.

Web animation

Blender is good for rendering complete animations or for making graphics to be used in Flash, gifs, or HTML 5 animations.

Games

Blender has its own *Game Engine*. Therefore, it's good for making your own games and showing what you can do. You can also export Blender files for use as assets with other game engines such as *Ogre*, *Unity*, and *CrystalSpace*. You can find out more at sites such as www.blenderartists.org.

Flight and driving simulators

The *Blender Game Engine* and Blender's *physics* packages make it possible to make your own flight and driving simulators.

Digital signage

Nowadays, we are seeing digital signs almost everywhere, from HD monitors in McDonalds to the building-sized signs in Las Vegas. With user-selectable resolution, you can make animations in Blender to whatever size you need, for whatever use. The files can then be uploaded to the Web and distributed to displays all over. This is a quickly growing market for advertising companies.

Displaying scientific data

Because the Python language allows using a scientific data set, anything from weather to a rocket to medical simulations can be animated. NASA uses Blender at some of its locations as does the National Radio Astronomy Observatory.

Legal evidence display

With animation for the legal system, the models are often simple though realistically proportioned. The clients are paying for accuracy, not fancy graphics. Blender's physics engine can help you make realistic animations. You can make car crashes, track bullets, and help when a crime comes to trial. It's an in-demand way to use your animation talents.

Architectural walkthroughs

Clients of a multi-million dollar project want to see what they are getting before they spend their money. This is a very specialized use of Blender and other 3D animation systems. You can give your clients either a high resolution video walkthrough or use the game engine to make it interactive.

Virtual reality

Blender can output a virtual reality .X3D file to create virtual reality on the Web that can be used interactively on most browsers.

Virtual sets

A set that you see behind the TV personality may not exist at all; it might be a set modeled and rendered in Blender.

Interactive instructions

The Blender game engine can be used to make interactive illustrations or lessons, or Blender can provide graphics for Flash or websites.

Showing what can't otherwise be seen

For anything from dinosaurs to the moons of Saturn, 3D is probably the best way to demonstrate what can't be seen directly. This can be used to show others the ideas in your head and the visions you see, taking them to places that are too small, too large, or too dangerous to visit in reality.

Creating a portfolio to get a job

If you do good work and can demonstrate it, many employers don't care what software you use. I know of one animator who perfected his Blender skills while serving in Iraq. He took what he did to the big studios and soon he was working on major Hollywood films. Get involved in animation social media groups. Check out other animators' portfolios.

Product development and visualization

Blender can be used to design and create real objects. Real copies can be made using 3D printers when you export your Blender files in an STL or X3D format. You can find out more about this in *Blender 3D Printing Essentials* by *Gordon Fisher*, which is published by *Packt Publishing*.

Pop Quiz – uses of Blender

Q1. Blender cannot be used for which of the following purposes:

1. Outputting a Flash animation
2. Creating games
3. Making a feature-length movie

Q2. Blender is not used by:

1. NASA
2. Restaurants
3. People like you

Summary

This first chapter was there to get you ready for Blender 3D.

You dipped your toe into Blender, opened it, rendered a scene, and closed Blender. You looked at the roots of animation, and the techniques that were developed to make animation producible and enjoyable. You got to see the beginning of computer animation and computer games and understand how the principles of animation apply to computer animation. You've got a top-ten list of cool things about Blender and some ideas on how you can use the skills that you will develop with this book.

In the next chapter, we will get you comfortable with working in Blender. We will discover the secrets behind all those windows, get an explanation of the basic geometry behind 3D animation, and learn how to use the 3D View window where most of the work in Blender is done.

Let's go!

2

Getting Comfortable Using the 3D View

In the previous chapter, you had a good introduction to animation and computer animation. You learned a little about how to make an animation come alive, and discovered that the animation principles are the same whether it's made in the old-fashioned way or with a computer. Now it's time to get into Blender itself.

In this chapter, you will learn about the following topics:

- ◆ The idea behind Blender's windowing system
- ◆ Manipulating and resizing the Blender windows
- ◆ 3D coordinates and measuring in 3D
- ◆ Learn how to navigate in the 3D View window
- ◆ Discover how computers create and use colors

Exploring the Blender 3D interface

In the early days of Blender, the developers took a different approach to their user interface, and time has proven that it is a very productive way to work. Instead of assigning fixed areas for certain tasks or creating a stack of windows, they decided on a flexible system of non-overlapping windows that could be resized interactively to give the user maximum control of their workspace.

When you start your copy of Blender as you did in *Chapter 1, Introducing Blender and Animation*, your screen will show a big central window surrounded by a number of boxes with text and buttons. There are five windows in total. I drew boxes around the windows so that you could see how the default Blender window is organized.

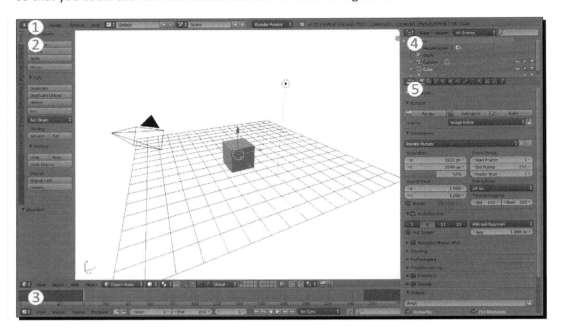

Breaking down the interface bit by bit will make it easy to understand. Remember, you don't have to understand how to use every single control to do a lot of great work with Blender. No one knows it all. You will go through it step by step giving you a strong foundation in using Blender.

You may notice that some of the colors of the 3D View window in the illustrations are different from your copy of Blender. The only difference is that some of the colors were changed so that the screen would show up better on the printed page. There is no change in function.

Using the three basic Blender controllers

The three basic Blender controllers are your **keyboard**, **NumPad**, and **mouse**. The keyboard is an obvious requirement. It is best if you have a built-in NumPad or alternate keys that can be used as a NumPad. Blender is designed to work with a three-button mouse. It is a standard Blender convention that the **left mouse button** is abbreviated (**LMB**), the **middle mouse button** is abbreviated (**MMB**), and the **right mouse button** is abbreviated (**RMB**).

Blender is a two-handed system, which means that you will need to use both the keyboard and mouse at the same time to do an operation. While this may seem a bit different from what you're used to, it's an effective way of working. Pretty soon, your hands will know just what to do. You won't waste time looking for tiny buttons on the edges of your screen every single time you want to change the angle that you are seeing or zoom into an object. This lets you work faster and maintain your focus on what you are trying to do, rather than getting distracted by the user interface. Practice is the key to using Blender well. Don't be afraid if things are a little slow at first; have patience. You will soon get a better understanding of Blender and your hands will know which keys to use.

Using the numeric keypad with Blender

Blender uses your computer's numeric keypad or NumPad to control what you see in the 3D View. If your computer does not have a numeric keypad, you have several options:

◆   Purchase a wireless or USB NumPad to use.

◆   Look closely and you may see something that looks like a NumPad near the *U, I, O, P* keys as seen in the next illustration. You'll have to consult your owner's manual to find out how to activate the NumPad instead of the keyboard. In my case, I press the *fn* button while pressing those keys. For me, the digits for the NumPad and the *fn* button are in blue. Your keyboard may differ.

◆ However, some computers, such as the MacBook Air, do not have a keypad at all unless you buy an external one. Blender will let you emulate a NumPad if you set it in **User Preferences**. I advise you to get an external keypad if at all possible, because Blender already uses the standard number keys for other functions, and there are Blender commands using the +, -, and . keys on the NumPad that are harder to perform if you emulate the NumPad. However, emulating the NumPad will get you through in a pinch.

Setting up Blender the way you want it

You will find the Blender interface to be very flexible. While this may take a little more time at first to feel comfortable, you will discover that it lets you set up Blender to be just the way you need it at any given moment. For now, most of our focus will be on the Blender windows, but I should mention the Blender **User Preferences**.

The **User Preferences** feature of Blender allows you to remap all the keys and mouse controls. It allows you to change the colors used in the display, the limit on your memory cache, the number of steps that Blender can undo, and hundreds of other settings. In this book, I'm going to try to keep changing **User Preferences** to a minimum so that you will be able to use Blender wherever you find it. However, after reading this book, you may want to modify your copy of Blender to reflect your own tastes.

Emulating the three-button mouse and NumPad

If you cannot obtain a three-button mouse and a NumPad, Blender does allow you to emulate them. There are checkboxes in the **Input** panel of the **User Preferences** window to emulate the three-button mouse and the NumPad.

Do the following steps only if you need to emulate the NumPad. Move your mouse to **File**, click on **File**, scroll down to **User Preferences**, and click on **User Preferences**. At the top of the new window, there is a row of buttons. Select **Input**, as shown in the following screenshot. On the left, there is a checkbox that says **Emulate NumPad**. Click on it. At the bottom of the window, there is a **Save User Settings** button. Click on it. Note that using the **Emulate NumPad** settings will not let you use commands that require the *, /, or . keys.

On a Mac with a single-button mouse, the mouse button maps to the **LMB**. To simulate the **MMB**, press the *Alt* key while pressing the mouse. To simulate the **RMB**, press the *command* key while pressing the mouse. Press the key before pressing the mouse button.

Emulating the keypad forces the regular numbers to respond as though they were the NumPad numbers. However, you won't be able to use the number keys for their regular functions.

Understanding how to use Blender windows

As you saw earlier, the main Blender window is divided into five smaller windows. There is one major difference between the Blender windows and those of other 3D animation systems. In Blender, a window can be any one of the 16 different kinds of editing windows. Think of them as tabs in your browser. As you can put any website in any tab, any of the Blender windows can hold any Blender content.

Time for action – playing with the Blender windows

Now, we are going to discover the structure of the windows:

1. Start Blender. In the largest Blender window, at the lower-left corner, there is a small button that looks similar to the button highlighted in the following screenshot. It has a white cube on it. This is the Current Editor Type button. Every window has this button, so you can change the type of editor that is in the window. The bar that the Current Editor Type button is on is called the **Header**.

2. In the main 3D View window, click on the Current Editor Type button with the LMB, and the Editor Type menu pops up with the 17 different kinds of editors that you can display in that window, as shown in the following screenshot:

3. Scroll up the menu, as shown previously, and select **Text Editor**. The window changes and it is now blank. The **Text Editor** is for you to enter text, such as production notes, text for text objects, python code, and other uses.

4. Now, go down to the window below the main window and click on the Current Editor Type button that has a clock on it with the left mouse button (LMB). The button is highlighted in the following screenshot. Again, the menu pops-up. Scroll up the menu and select the **Text Editor**, as shown in the preceding screenshot.

5. There are two windows on the right. Find the Current Editor Type buttons in these two windows. They will be at the top of the windows.

6. In each window, click on the LMB on the window button. Scroll up the menu and select the **Text Editor**. Text editors have their header at the bottom, so you will see the header pop up from the top to the bottom.

What just happened?

In Blender, any window can be any kind of window just like tabs in a browser. You just turned all the windows into text editors. This lets you see the basic structure of the Blender windows, as outlined at the beginning of the chapter, without getting confused with all the controls and buttons. The following image shows how Blender is laid out initially:

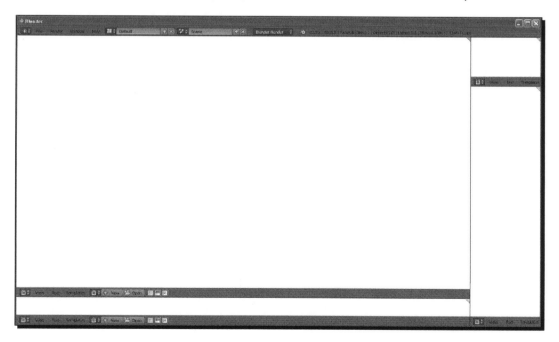

Time for action – resizing windows

Notice the black line between the Blender windows. This is shown in the following screenshot:

Blender windows can be resized as you need, so you can have any screen layout you want. Here is how to do this:

1. Move the cursor over one of these lines and you will see a double-headed arrow.

2. While the double-headed arrow is displayed, hold down the LMB and move your mouse perpendicular to the line. The windows on both sides of the line will resize.

3. If you selected a vertical edge between windows, now try it with a horizontal edge.

4. If you selected a horizontal edge between windows originally, now try it with a vertical edge.

What just happened?

You selected the line between two windows and moved it to resize the windows. Blender's windows do not overlap. If you make one bigger, the one next to it gets smaller. Unlike many window-based interfaces, you don't end up with a stack of windows that you have to search through to find in which window you were working.

Time for action – splitting the Blender windows

In addition to controlling the size of a window, you can create new windows. Unlike other systems, you are not limited to a set number of windows or a set layout.

1. Look at any of the windows; you will see three diagonal lines in the lower-left and upper-right corners of the window, as shown in the following screenshot. These control the creation and deletion of the window.

2. Put the cursor over the largest window and move it over the diagonal lines at the lower-left corner of that window.

3. Then, hold down the LMB as you move the cursor horizontally toward the center of the window, and then release the LMB when you have moved the window edge to replace one third of the old window.

4. Put the cursor over the center window that you just made. Move the cursor to the diagonal lines at the upper-right corner of that window. Then, hold down the LMB while you move the cursor horizontally toward the center of the window. Replace another one-third of the original window with the new window and release the LMB.

5. Put the cursor over the left-most window. Move the cursor over the diagonal lines at the lower-left corner of that window. Hold down the LMB and move the cursor up towards the center of the window to make a new window vertically. The screen layout should resemble the following screenshot:

What just happened?

You selected the diagonal lines in the lower-left corner of a window and moved the mouse horizontally. The window was split into two windows side by side. The new window is a duplicate of the first. Then, you repeated the steps using the diagonal lines in the upper-right corner and created another window. Finally, you discovered that windows can be split vertically as well. This flexibility in window layout gives you complete freedom in setting up Blender for greatest productivity, and it can be changed on the fly to reflect your needs at any stage of production. But don't worry, in the next section you will discover how to join these windows so you don't have too many open.

Time for action – joining the Blender windows

In addition to creating new windows, you can remove any window. Blender windows are easy to remove. The steps are as follows:

1. Bring the cursor over the upper-left window, and then the cursor over the diagonal lines at the lower-left corner of that window.

2. Hold down the LMB while you move the cursor down towards the window below it. The window below becomes darker and there is a light gray arrow pointing into that window.

3. Continue to hold down the LMB and move the cursor up to the original window; it becomes darker and has an arrow pointing into it, as shown in the following screenshot. Whichever window is darker and has the arrow will disappear when you release the mouse button.

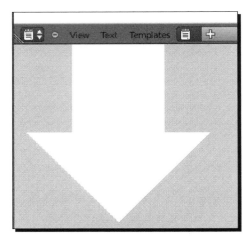

4. If you find you don't want the window to disappear, just move the cursor into another window besides those two. The arrow will go away and you can release the mouse button without any changes happening.

What just happened?

To join two windows, you selected the diagonal lines in the corner of a window and moved the cursor vertically toward the window next to it. Note that for one of the windows to be joined, both windows must share an entire side. There cannot be two windows on one side of their common edge and one window on the other side of the edge. If the windows do not share an entire side, you cannot remove one of them. Be assured that no matter what combination of windows you have open, this does not affect the scene on which you are working. No data is lost by closing a window.

Have a go hero – making windows with parallel edges

When the edges of two or more windows become aligned, they lock together and move as one. This can be useful, or you may want to break the alignment.

Try aligning two windows exactly. Move the edge between the two right-most windows until the edge is aligned with the edge between the three left text windows and the window below them. If the right edge is not aligned, then move the left edges up or down a little.

Let go and choose the edge again. How does it move?

Now, use your window adding and deleting skills to break this alignment.

Special window modifications

There are a number of other controls for windows. In general, it seems like there are usually two ways to do anything in Blender and you get your choice. In the following section, we will discuss some variations.

Making and removing windows the secret way

Blender made a secret method for windows to satisfy long-time users of Blender who are used to the old interface that was used in Blender versions 1.0-2.4.x. Move the cursor over the edge between two windows so you get the double arrowhead. Press the RMB to get a split/join menu. Move the mouse over the window that you want to split. Play around with it and discover how this method of splitting windows may be more powerful than the standard method.

Time for action – maximizing and tiling the window

Blender lets you **maximize** and **tile** the windows. The standard multiwindow display is considered tiled. Maximizing a window makes it fill the Blender window. The steps to do so are as follows:

1. Select a blank portion of the header of any window with the RMB. The secondary pop-up menu has a option for **Maximize Area**, as shown in the following screenshot:

2. Click on **Maximize Area** with the LMB now. There's only one window! Don't worry. The others are not gone. The window you maximized is just given the full display.

3. Right-click on the header again; the bottom selection will say **Tile Area**, and clicking on it with the LMB will show all of the windows again.

4. Note that there is a keyboard shortcut listed in the secondary menu, and it can also be seen in the previous screenshot. You can press *Ctrl* + up arrow to toggle between **Maximize Area** and **Tile Area**.

What just happened?

Blender gives you a lot of flexibility. If you need to, it allows any window to use the entire screen and you can quickly change it back to tiled windows when you are done. This is great when you need an extra big view of the 3D View window to select tiny parts or details.

Time for action – flipping the window header

As you have seen, the header is that bar at the top or bottom of each of the window. It has the Current Editor Type button on the left side and some other buttons, as you can see in the following screenshot:

You have seen the header positioned at the bottom and the top of a window. While some types of windows have top or bottom by default, you can set the header for any window the way you prefer. The steps are as follows:

1. Click the RMB on an empty area of the header of the main window. A menu will pop up that says **Header**. There is a secondary menu that says **Flip to Top**.

2. Select **Flip to Top** with the LMB.

3. Go to the header at the top. Select it with the RMB.

4. Select **Flip to Bottom**.

What just happened?

The header can be at the top or the bottom of the window. If it is at the bottom, you can flip it to the top. If it is at the top, you can flip it to the bottom. Set it the way you prefer.

Exploring the 3D View window – the heart of Blender

Finally, it's time to focus on the 3D View as shown in the following screenshot. It's the primary window where you will do most of your work.

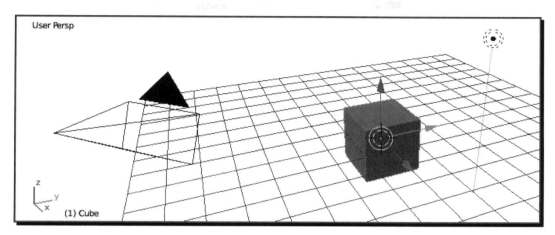

Keep your eye on the cursor. Whatever window the Blender cursor is over is the active window. For example, if you want to work in the 3D View, the cursor must be over the 3D View window; if you want to work in the **Timeline**, the cursor must be over the **Timeline** window.

Time for action – discovering your tools

The 3D View has three major control panels: the **Header**, which we have examined; the Tool Shelf on the left side, which says **Transform** at the top and has some tabs on the left; and the Properties Panel, which is hidden by default:

1. Close Blender and open it again.
2. With your mouse over the 3D View, press the *N* key. The Properties Panel appears. It has controls to change the location, rotation, and scaling of objects.
3. Press the *N* key again. The Properties Panel disappears.
4. Press the *T* key. The Tool Shelf disappears.
5. Press the *T* key again. The Tool Shelf reappears and contains many controls used when building objects.
6. When you have closed the Tool Shelf or the Properties Panel, note the small gray tab on the side of the 3D View window. If you click on that, the panel will reopen.

What just happened?

You looked at the Tool Shelf and Properties Panel, as shown in the following screenshot. You also learned how to toggle the Tool Shelf and the Properties Panel on and off.

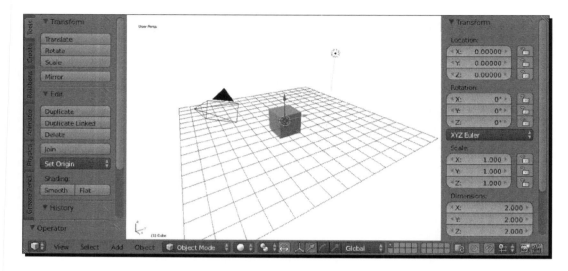

The Tool Shelf gives you control over the current object and the Properties Panel lets you set things like the location of the 3D Cursor and the location, rotation, and scaling of the current object. You will want to toggle them on and off depending on which controls you need and how well you need to see the objects in the 3D View window. It will be easy to remember the *N* and *T* keys, as you will use them frequently.

Understanding what you see in the 3D View window

The window looks pretty empty, but there is a fair amount in the default screen. It's got everything needed to render a scene. There are three kinds of things visible by default in the 3D view: **objects**, **text fields**, and **3D tools**. We will look at those now. Blender has 12 kinds of objects in total, which are listed in the table at the end of this section.

There are three objects in the default scene. The first is the default cube.

- ◆ The cube you see is a 3D mesh in the shape of a cube; you can use it or delete it. When Blender is opened, the cube is the active object, which means that it is the object currently being worked on.

- ◆ The four-sided cone with a triangle above it is the camera.

- ◆ The black dot surrounded by dotted lines with a line hanging down from it is a lamp.

- ◆ Only the cube will be seen when you render. The camera does not see itself, and the lamps will light the scene, though there is no physical light bulb to be rendered.

The text fields are on the left side of the 3D View, as seen in the previous screenshot. They give you current information about the scene:

◆ The upper text field tells what the view is. It shows where you are looking from and whether you have a Perspective (**Persp**) view or an Orthographic (**Ortho**) view.

◆ This view can be **Top, Bottom, Front, Back, Right**, or **Left** if you are looking from one of the major axes. There are also **Camera** and **User** views. **User** is whenever you are not on one of the major axes or taking the Camera's view.

◆ The lower text field has the current frame number in parentheses and tells which object is the active object.

There are four 3D tools:

◆ There is a reference grid to help you with orientation and size. It can be scaled and set for as many divisions as you want.

◆ In the lower-left corner there is a graphic with three lines (red, green, and blue) joined at one end and the letters **X**, **Y**, and **Z** nearby. This is the **3D axis** indicator, as shown on the left-hand side of the following graphic. It shows you where you are with respect to the center of the Blender world and gives you an indication of the direction:

   ❑ The red line shows the X axis.
   ❑ The green line shows the Y axis.
   ❑ The blue line shows the Z axis.

◆ At the origin, the center of the world in Blender, there are two controls—one is the **3D Cursor**. It's a red and white dashed circle with four black lines through it, and it is shown in the center of the following screenshot. This marks the location of where a new object will be made. It can be moved wherever you need it, as you'll discover later.

◆ The other 3D control at the origin is the **3D manipulator**, which is on the right-hand side in the following screenshot. It's a white circle with red, green, and blue arrows coming out of it and an orange dot in the center. It gives you control of rotating, translating, and scaling the active object in 3D.

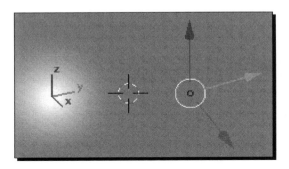

◆ There are twelve basic types of objects that can be shown in the Blender screen. You have already seen a few such as the lamp, camera, and mesh. The following table lists the twelve types of objects that Blender uses:

Object Type	Definition
Armature	This provides a framework to animate a character or complex model.
Camera	This records the image or animation when you render.
Curve	These are mathematical functions like Bézier curves and NURBS curves that Blender uses to create smooth rounded free-form shapes, such as the outline of a logo.
Empty	This is an object with only a location, rotation, and scale.
Force Field	This is used in physical simulations. It creates forces like wind, turbulence, and drag.
Lamp	This provides the light for a scene.
Lattice	This is a three dimensional grid that is used to guide the deformation of other objects.
Metaball	These are special spheres, tubes, and cubes that affect each other and can stretch toward each other and appear to merge.
Mesh	These are the standard shapes, such as cubes, spheres, cylinders, cones, monkeys.
Surface	These are also mathematical functions, and are composed of multiple curves that are used together for smooth, yet complex shapes like terrain.
Speaker	This allows you to put audio with a location, timing and volume in the scene.
Text	Use standard system fonts to create 3D letters and words.

Measuring things in 3D

3D stands for *3-dimensional*. Going back to school geometry, those dimensions are called **X**, **Y**, and **Z**. In Blender, X describes width, Y describes depth, and Z describes height. It is displayed as (**X**, **Y**, **Z**). The very center of things is at a point (0, 0, 0) called the *origin*. We describe the location of every object as a set of three values (X, Y, Z) in our Blender world by using numbers to show how far to the left or right it is (X), how far to the front or back it is (Y), and how far up or down it is (Z). We do this based on the **Front** view of the 3D world.

This following screenshot shows how those numbers appear from the front view:

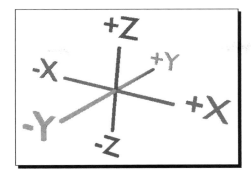

- Using your left hand, point to positive Z with your thumb, point to positive Y with your index finger, and point to positive X with your middle finger.

- As the value of X gets larger, it goes to the right. As the value of X gets smaller, it goes to the left. The numbers can be positive or negative.

- As the value of Y gets larger, it goes further away from you. As the value of Y gets smaller, it goes closer to you.

- As the value of Z gets larger, it goes up. As the value of Z gets smaller, it goes down.

- This applies to the world in the 3D View as well as the objects in it. The X, Y, and Z coordinates in the 3D world are called **global coordinates**. The X, Y, and Z coordinates that apply only to one object are called **local coordinates**. The reason for having local coordinates is that it makes it easier for you.

- Imagine that you take the default cube and you want to make it twice as wide as it is, but unfortunately it's been turned at a 53 degree angle with respect to the world. To do that correctly with global coordinates, you'd have to break out your math book and figure out the sines and cosines, because global coordinates are stuck to the world and turning something 53 degrees makes it harder to figure out what the scaling would be.

- However, with local coordinates, Blender remembers that the cube is 2 x 2 x 2 in local coordinates. Those coordinates only relate to the cube as it was made. So all you have to do is say okay, now the box is 2 x 4 x 2 in local coordinates. Blender will then handle turning it 53 degrees for you.

[Blender uses generic "Blender" units by default, but if you prefer you can specify Metric or Imperial units in the properties window.]

Navigating in the 3D View

Blender is a two-handed program. You need both hands to operate it. This is most obvious when navigating in the 3D View. When you navigate, you are changing your view of the world; you are not changing the world. There are three ways to navigate; you can rotate the scene so you see it from a different angle, zoom in or out to get closer or farther away, and pan (which is moving up and down or side to side in the scene).

Time for action – rotating the scene in 3D View

When modeling or animating, you frequently want to see differing angles of what you are working on. Rotating your view is often the best way to do this, try it by following the given steps:

1. Move the cursor over the cube in the 3D View. Press the MMB and move the mouse left and right.

2. Now try it again; start with the cursor near the center of the screen, press the MMB, and move the cursor up and down.

What just happened?

That isn't too difficult. Pressing the MMB and moving the mouse revolves your view around the origin.

Time for action – zooming the scene in 3D View

If you need to get a better overview of the scene or get a closer view, then zooming is what you need:

1. Move the cursor over the 3D View and push the *Ctrl* key.

2. Then, press the MMB and move the mouse up and down.

What just happened?

To zoom in and out of the 3D View, you press the *Ctrl* key and hold down the MMB while you move the cursor up and down over the 3D View.

Time for action – panning the scene in 3D View

The final way to move within the scene is panning, moving your view up and down and right and left. It helps you look at different parts of the scene. The steps are as follows:

1. Move the cursor over the 3D View, then press the *Shift* key. Press the MMB and move the mouse up and down.

2. Move the cursor over the 3D View, then push the *Shift* key. Press the MMB and move the mouse left and right.

3. Move the cursor over the 3D View, then push the *Shift* key. Press the MMB and move the mouse around as you like.

What just happened?

Pressing the *Shift* key and holding down MMB while you move the cursor in the 3D View pans the 3D View. Panning is moving your viewpoint horizontally or vertically. Very good; now you know how to navigate in the 3D View.

Have a go hero – navigating the scene in the 3D View

Now, try and maneuver the cube and grid into different angles. Try for dynamic-looking or weird angles, get a close up of the corner, or look along the edges. Use the rotate, zoom, and pan controls.

Navigating for those who have a mouse wheel

As I said before, Blender loves to give you a choice in how you do things. There is an alternate way to control rotating, zooming, and panning in the 3D View if you have a mouse wheel on your mouse. Here are the mouse wheel controls:

- Mouse wheel only: Zooms in and out of the scene
- *Shift* + mouse wheel: Pans up and down
- *Ctrl* + mouse wheel: Pans side to side
- *Shift* + *Alt* + mouse wheel: Rotates up and down
- *Ctrl* + *Alt* + mouse wheel: Rotates side to side

Using the NumPad to change the angle in 3D View

The controls we have studied are great to give you fine control over how you see the 3D View. However, sometimes you want to flip from a top view to a side view quickly or go back and forth. Also, in case you forget where you are in relation to an object, knowing which view you are looking from can help you get reoriented if you've gotten confused.

Blender has some good tools to help you. You use the NumPad to activate them. We will be pressing numbers on the NumPad; note that pressing numbers on the keyboard will not give the same results. You must use the NumPad.

Time for action – seeing the top view, front view, and right-side view

You will start by returning Blender to its default setup. To go back to the default scene. You don't have to quit as you did at the start of this chapter; there is another way. The steps are as follows:

1.   Move your cursor to the upper-left corner of the Blender window as shown in the previous screenshot. Left-click on **File**. A menu will drop down. Left-click on **New**. Another menu will appear asking you to **Reload Start-Up File**. Click on that and the default Blender file will be loaded.

2.   Press the 7 key on the NumPad. This gives you the **Top** view.

3.   Press the 1 key on the NumPad. This gives you the **Front** view.

4.   Press the 3 key on the NumPad. This gives you the **Right** side view.

What just happened?

You loaded a fresh copy of the default Blender scene and then used the NumPad to control from which direction you were viewing the scene. When you pressed the 7 on the NumPad, Blender displayed the **Top** view. When you pressed the 1 on the NumPad, Blender displayed the **Front** view and when you pressed the 3 on the NumPad, Blender displayed the **Right** view. Note that these changes are shown by the text field at the upper-left of the 3D View window, which will tell you from which direction you are viewing the scene.

Time for action – seeing the bottom view, and back view

Sometimes, you also need to look at an object or scene from the bottom, from behind, or from the left. The following keys will help you:

1. Press the *Ctrl* key and the *7* key on the NumPad. This gives you the **Bottom** view.

2. Press the *Ctrl* key and the *1* key on the NumPad. This gives you **Back** view.

3. Press the *Ctrl* key and the *3* key on the NumPad. This give you the **Left** view.

4. Now, press the *1*, *3*, and *7* keys on the NumPad, then press them while holding down the *Ctrl* key.

What just happened?

You know how to use the *1*, *3*, and *7* keys on the NumPad to change views. To see from the opposing angle of a view, you can press the *Ctrl* key and the number for the view on the NumPad. Pressing the *Ctrl + 7* key shows the **Bottom** view. Pressing the *Ctrl + 1* key shows the **Back** view and *Ctrl + 3* shows the **Left** view.

Seeing what the camera sees

Unlike some other systems, Blender only renders what a camera sees. You can find out what the camera is seeing by pressing the *0* key on the NumPad.

When you press the *0* key on the NumPad, Blender displays the **Camera** view. It also applies a gray mask called the passepartout to mark the limits of the image that will be rendered. The following screenshot shows the cube seen through the passe-partout on the left and the rendering of that scene on the right.

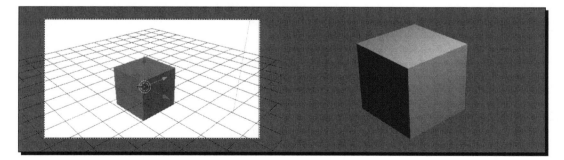

Time for action – verifying the Camera view

It's time to take a look at the Camera view and compare it with what the camera renders. Do you notice any differences?

1. Press the NumPad *0* key to get the Camera view.

2. Press the *F12* key to render the scene so you can see it.

3. Press the *Esc* key to close the rendering window.

4. Press the *F11* key to see the previously rendered view.

5. Press the *Esc* key again.

6. Alternate pressing the *F11* and the *Esc* keys and make sure that the Camera view is the same as the rendered scene. Do you notice any difference?

What just happened?

Just to be sure, after pressing the NumPad *0* key, you tried doing a test render to compare what is rendered in the camera with the **Camera** view. Of course, they looked the same. However, you also discovered that if you want to see a previously rendered image, then you press the *F11* key. Did you notice the difference in the shading between the 3D View and the rendering as shown in the previous screenshot? The lamp is to the right side of the camera in the scene. So in the rendered image, the darkest side is on the left, as it should be. However, in the 3D View window, the darkest side is on the right. This is because the default method of displaying objects in the 3D View is just a quick approximation. However, it's good enough for most tasks. You'll discover more accurate displays of lighting in the next chapter.

Time for action – rotating the view with the NumPad

In addition to displaying the scene from particular axes, Blender lets you use the NumPad to revolve around the center. The steps are as follows:

1. Press the *7* key on the NumPad to get the **Top** view.

2. Press the *4* key on the NumPad several times to rotate the view negatively on the Z axis.

3. Press the *6* key on the NumPad several times to rotate the view positively on the Z axis.

4. Press the *1* key on the NumPad to get the **Front** view.

5. Press the *4* key on the NumPad several times to rotate the view negatively on the Z axis.

6. Press the *6* key on the NumPad several times times to rotate the view positively on the Z axis.

What just happened?

Pressing the NumPad *7* key shifted your view to the Top view. This let you see how pressing the NumPad *4* key rotates the view counter-clockwise around the Z axis. Pressing the NumPad *6* key rotates the view clockwise. This is useful when you want to inspect an object carefully. It lets you rotate around the scene in 15 degree steps, and the motion is repeatable, so you can easily return to an earlier angle if you want. Pressing the *1* key on the NumPad did the same from the **Front** view.

Time for action – rotating the view in another direction with the NumPad

You can also rotate on other axes. However, these operate a little differently. The *2* and the *8* key rotate your view with respect to the view from which you start. The steps are as follows:

1. Press the *3* key on the NumPad to get the **Right** view.
2. Press the *2* key on the NumPad several times to rotate positively around the Y axis.
3. Press the *8* key on the NumPad several times to rotate negatively around the Y axis.
4. Press the *1* key on the NumPad to get the **Front** view.
5. Press the *2* key on the NumPad several times times to rotate positively around the X axis.
6. Press the *8* key on the NumPad several times to rotate negatively around the X axis.

What just happened?

Pressing the *3* key shifted your view to the **Right** view. Pressing the *2* key rotates the view so the front goes up. Pressing the *8* key rotates the view so the front goes down. Pressing the *1* key, you shifted your view to the **Front** view. Pressing the *2* key rotates the view so the front goes up. Pressing the *8* key rotates the view so the front goes down. The *2* and *8* keys are not connected to a particular axis the way the *4* and *6* keys are. Don't worry about memorizing all these. You can always try the numbers on the NumPad to remember what does what and there's a summary table which we'll see later in this chapter.

Time for action – zooming with the NumPad

The Blender NumPad also allows you to control the zoom. However, this may not work if you have Emulate NumPad enabled. If you do, skip to the next *Time for action – making the camera see what you do* section:

1. Press the + (plus) key on the NumPad several times to zoom in.
2. Press the - (minus) key on the NumPad several times to zoom out.

3. Press the . (period) key on the NumPad to center on the selected object and zoom into it. If you are using the NumPad emulator, this will not work; but you can select **View** on the 3D View header and find **View Selected** on the pop-up menu, as shown in the following screenshot:

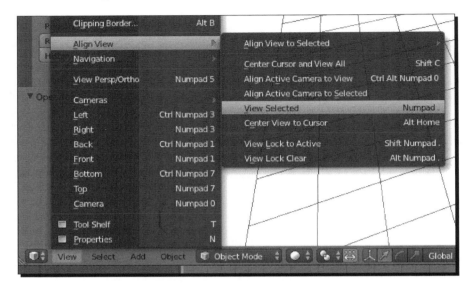

4. Press the *Home* key on the keyboard to zoom out to show the entire scene. This is not the *Home* key on the NumPad. Press *fn* + left arrow if you are using a Mac with no *Home* key.

What just happened?

Pressing the + key on the NumPad zooms into the scene by steps, and pressing the - key on the NumPad zooms out. To fill the view with the active object, you press the . key on the NumPad, which makes it easy to focus on what you are working. Pressing the *Home* key on the keyboard lets you see everything in the scene so that you can get your bearings, get an overview of the scene, or switch to working on a different object.

If you are emulating the NumPad, the regular plus and minus keys should work to zoom in and out. To equal the function of the NumPad period key, select the **View** from the 3D View header, and then choose **Align View** and **View Selected** from the pop-up menu.

Time for action – making the camera see what you do

As Blender only renders what the camera sees, it's useful to be able to point the camera on what you are working. The steps are as follows:

1. Use the keys on the NumPad to move your view to an angle that you like.

2. Press the *Ctrl* key, the *Alt* key, and the *0* key on the NumPad at the same time to make the camera match the view you had of the scene.

 If you accidently press *Ctrl + 0* without pressing the *Alt* key and the screen seems to be blank, then press *Ctrl + Z* to undo this command and return to where you were. You just turned the cube into the camera.

3. Press the *7* key on the NumPad to get the **Top** view.

4. Press the *0* key on the NumPad to get the **Camera** view.

What just happened?

You got a little practice in using the NumPad to move the view. Then, when you press the *Ctrl* key, the *Alt* key, and the *0* key on the NumPad at the same time. Blender matches the camera's view to the current view, as seen in the following screenshot. Pressing the *7* key moves you to the **Top** view, so that you can see that when you press the *0* key on the NumPad to get the **Camera** view, that it matches the angle you had selected.

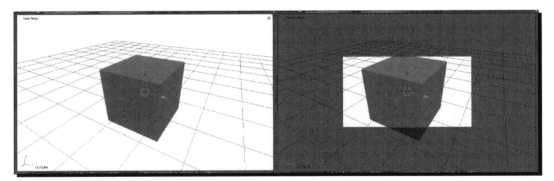

Understanding Perspective and Orthographic views

Blender has two ways to display the 3D View. If you've taken any art courses, you are probably familiar with what perspective is. In Perspective, all parallel lines stretch off to the horizon and finally appear to meet at a single point. This is pretty much what our eyes see. If you look at the left side of the illustration in the following screenshot, you can see what's happening with the grid.

Orthographic is slightly different. It comes from the world of **Computer Aided Drafting** (**CAD**). With Orthographic projection, all parallel lines are shown as being parallel, as shown in the right side of the illustration in the following screenshot. Games like Sim City also use an Orthographic view.

Perspective is what you want to see when you are checking to see how a scene will look in your 3D image or animation. However, coming from CAD, the Orthographic view is better when you are modeling an object. When you use a front, side, or top view, all parallel points are right behind each other, which makes it easier to grab them and move them precisely.

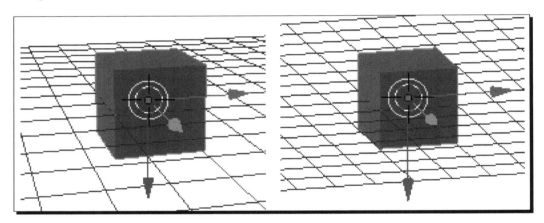

Time for action – toggling between the Perspective and Orthographic views

Now, you will discover how to change between Perspective and Orthographic view. The steps are as follows:

1. Press *1, 8, 8, 4*, and *4* on the NumPad to get a nice angle on the cube.
2. Press the *5* key on the NumPad.
3. Press it again.
4. Press the *5* key several times and observe how the view changes.

What just happened?

When you press the *5* key on the NumPad, the 3D View switches between Perspective and Orthographic views as in the previous illustration.

Have a go hero – playing with Perspective and Orthographic views

Now it's time to play. Using what you have learned about navigating in the 3D view, experiment by finding different angles to view the scene, and shifting between Perspective and Orthographic views and see how they compare. Be sure to try views like top, left, and, front, as well as use the *2*, *4*, *6*, and *8* keys to gently rotate the scene. Otherwise, you can use your mouse if you wish.

Displaying the Quad View and Full Screen

You've seen that you can adjust Blender windows just about any way you want. However, when you are modeling, sometimes it's handy to have a quick way to see several sides of an object at once. Blender has a special view for this called the Quad View.

Time for action – toggling the Quad view

The Quad View is a special view with the camera, front, top, and right side views. I especially like it for setting up lighting.

1. Press the *Ctrl* key, the *Alt* key, and the *Q* key at the same time.
2. Press the *Ctrl* key, the *Alt* key, and the *Q* key again.
3. With the 3D View in Quad View, press the *5* key on the NumPad.
4. Press it again. What change do you see?

What just happened?

When you press the *Ctrl* key, the *Alt* key, and the *Q* key, Blender toggles the Quad view on and off. The Quad view gives you three Orthographic views and the Camera view, while the Ortho views do not change. When you press the *5* key on the NumPad, the camera window does toggle between the **Ortho** and **Persp** views.

Navigating in the 3D View

Here is a handy reference table that you can use while you practice. You've now mastered how to navigate in the 3D View window in Blender:

Keys	Navigation
Pan, zoom, and rotate with the mouse	
MMB	Rotate View
Shift + MMB	Pan View
Ctrl + MMB	Zoom View
Ctrl + *Alt* + Q	Quad View toggle
Pan, zoom, and rotate with the mouse wheel	
Mouse wheel only	Zoom in or out
Shift + mouse wheel	Pan up and down
Ctrl + mouse wheel	Pan right and left
Shift + *Alt* + mouse wheel	Rotate up and down
Ctrl + *Alt* + mouse wheel	Rotate right and left
NumPad	
Preset viewing angles and stepping views	
0	Camera view
Ctrl + *0*	Set camera view to current object
Ctrl + *Alt* + *0*	Set camera view to current view
1	Front view
Ctrl + *1*	Back view
2	Rotate front up
3	Right side view
Ctrl + *3*	Left side view
4	Rotate counter-clockwise
5	Perspective/Orthographic toggle
6	Rotate clockwise
7	Top view
Ctrl + *7*	Bottom view
Shift + *7*	Aligns view with active camera.

Keys	Navigation
NumPad zooming commands	
8	Rotate front down
-	Zoom out
+	Zoom in
.	Zoom to current object; this can also be done done via the **View** switch on the 3D View header and by choosing **View Selected** from the pop-up menu
Home	Display whole scene
Miscellaneous NumPad keys	
9	Redraw
/	Local view and cursor/previous view toggle; this can also be done by clicking on the **View** switch on the 3D View header and choosing **View Global/Local** from the pop-up menu

Making pictures with computers

Now that you are a little familiar with the 3D View, it's good to understand a bit about the 3D world contained within it and how the computer knows what to display.

When you looked at the 3D View, what did you see? A camera? A box? A grid? No, you saw pixels, thousands of them. A pixel is a single little colored rectangle on your computer screen, as shown in the magnification of the following picture. Pixels are what digital TVs, mobile phones, game consoles, and computer screens use to display anything you see. The following picture is 640 pixels wide and 287 pixels tall. The magnified area shows you what an area of 21 pixels wide by 16 pixels tall would display. When it is shrunk to the scale of the main picture, they seem to blend together to make a picture.

These pictures are what Blender creates to make animations and still images, and Blender also uses pictures like this as backgrounds and to create textures.

You can see that each pixel is a tiny rectangle of color. However, how does a computer know which color to make the rectangle? That's what we'll look at now.

Understanding how a computer uses color will help you to do the following:

 ◆ Select colors for objects and lights
 ◆ Understand how to use colors in combination
 ◆ Make adjustments to your renderings so that the final colors look exactly right

Making colors with a computer

As you may know, if you dig deep into a computer, you will get to a point where everything the computer knows is either a zero or a one. Like a little light switch, it's either on or off. In the computer, each little switch is called a **bit**.

So, imagine you have eight little light switches in a row. Each one can turn on or off as a light. By flipping different switches, you can light them up in 256 different combinations: four lights on, four lights off; or two lights on, three lights off; three lights on, and so on.

In the computer, a group of eight switches is called a **byte**. The computer uses this block of eight switches to store a number between 0 and 255, that is, 256 different numbers. That's why you will see the number 256 popping up a lot. These bytes can be used to store color information and they enable Blender to create millions of different colors.

Making millions of colors with just red, green, and blue

It's also important to understand how your eye works if you want to know why computers display colors the way they do.

Your eyes have two different kinds of receptors; **rods** that see only black and white but tell you about how bright an object appears to be and **cones** that tell you how much red, green, or blue light you are seeing. Your brain mixes all this information together, so you think you see shades of yellow, dark magenta, turquoise, beige, and raspberry; but it's really just combinations of red, green, and blue light.

Computers were designed to match how your eyes see by telling the display to show red, green, and blue light of differing amounts. Like a box of crayons, the more colors you have, the better you can color. How many colors a given picture can show is called its **color depth**.

The greater the number of colors there are, the greater the color depth a picture will have. Frequently, you will see pictures that have two colors, 256 colors, or 16.2 million colors.

◆ In the simplest pictures (such as the leftmost in the preceding screenshot), there would be just two colors, black or white.

◆ More complex ones could have 256 different gray values from black to white, such as the second image from the left.

◆ A simple color picture might have only 256 different colors such as the third image from the left.

◆ With a true color image, like the one on the right, you can have 256 different shades of red, 256 shades of green, and 256 shades of blue. You mix all of those together and you can display 16.2 million different colors. As each of the red, green, and blue channels have 8 bits or little switches each, we add them up and call it a 24-bit image. This gives you subtle nuanced colors.

◆ Some formats, such as the JPEG 2000 can have 16 bits per channel, making a 48-bit image, which can display trillions of colors—far more than your eyes can see, but it's useful for applications such as astronomy and medical imaging.

Pop quiz – learning about Blender windows

See, Blender windows are pretty easy. You open them, you close them, and change their size. You can put whatever editor you want in any window. Let's review some basics about Blender windows:

Q1. How do you make a new Blender window?

1. Click the LMB on the diagonal lines and drag it toward the window next to it.

2. Click the LMB on the edge and drag perpendicular to the edge.

3. Click the LMB on the diagonal lines and drag it toward the center of the window.

Q2. What are pixels?

1. Employees of Pixar

2. Colored rectangles that make up a digital picture

3. Small Celtic fairies

Q3. If a cube is at the location (−5, 5, 0), where is it in relation to the origin (0, 0, 0)?
Use your left hand to help.

1. To the left, farther away from you than the origin, and at the same height

2. To the right, nearer to you than the origin and below

3. To the left, nearer to you than the origin and above

Q4. Which key do you press to zoom in on the active object?

1. *Shift* + MMB

2. *Ctrl + Alt + 0*

3. The . (period) on the NumPad

Summary

You learned that Blender is not as intimidating as it seemed at first. In this chapter, you learned about the structure of Blender's windows and why they are that way. You learned how to resize them to make them as you want them. You found out how a computer measures things in a 3D world. You learned to use the mouse, the mouse wheel, the keyboard, and the NumPad to navigate in the 3D View window. You discovered how the computer makes colors.

In the next chapter, we're going to have fun. It will be lights, camera, and action as we discover the basics of using light, how to control the camera, and make our first animation.

Let's go!

3

Controlling the Lamp, the Camera, and Animating Objects

You have learned how to use the Blender window and the 3D View window. Now, you will use the principles you have learned about animation, and make use of what you know about modifying windows and navigating in 3D View.

In this chapter, we will cover the following topics:

- ◆ Study how light affects the scene
- ◆ Practice placing lights in different locations
- ◆ Change the light's colors
- ◆ Use multiple lights
- ◆ Learn about using global and local coordinates
- ◆ Discuss composing an image with the camera
- ◆ Move, rotate, and scale the camera
- ◆ Make keyframes for an animation
- ◆ Preview your first animation and render it
- ◆ Use Graph Editor to improve the animation
- ◆ Learn how to save files and use backup files

This chapter introduces you to using Blender as your own movie studio. We will start with a simple project, and in further chapters, expand on this so you will be comfortable doing animation or just lighting your models to show them off to their best advantage.

Placing lamps in the scene

Lamps are how Blender controls the light in a scene. There is no physical light bulb or lamp stand needed, so you can put a lamp wherever you want it, and it won't be seen in the image, apart from the light it casts. The light of the lamp can be of any color.

Time for action – moving the lamp

Until now, you've just changed your view of the scene. Now, it's time to alter the scene itself. Move the lamp and see how this affects the cube:

1. To start, either open Blender or select **New**. You will see the familiar 3D View.

2. Press *F12* to render the scene.

3. Observe how the cube looks.

4. Press the *Esc* button to close the render window.

5. Place the cursor over the lamp. Hold the RMB down and begin to drag the mouse. When the lamp begins to move, you may release the RMB. Move the lamp to the left so that it is not only between the camera and the cube but also above them, as shown in the next image. Press the LMB to release the object. If you press the RMB again, it will cancel the movement.

6. Press *F12* to render the scene.

7. Observe how the cube looks. The left side is much lighter as you can see in the following screenshot:

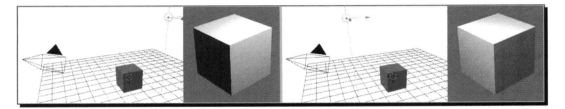

8. Press the *Esc* button to close the render window.

What just happened?

You rendered the cube to see how it looks, as shown on the left-hand side of the previous screenshot. Then, you used the RMB to move the lamp and rendered the cube again to see how the lighting has changed, as shown on the right of the previous image. You also learned that you can move an object simply by grabbing it with the RMB.

Time for action – moving the lamp close to the cube

Now, it's time to use a different method to move an object. By performing the following steps, you will demonstrate that the lamp is a point of light radiating out:

1. Press the *1* key on the NumPad to get the front view.
2. Put the cursor over the lamp.
3. Press the RMB to select the lamp.
4. Press and release (tap) the *G* key.
5. Use the mouse to move the lamp down until it is in level with the cube and is right next to it, as shown in the next screenshot. Press the LMB to release the lamp.
6. Press the *7* key on the NumPad to get the top view.
7. Tap the *G* key.
8. Use the mouse to move the lamp up so that it is next to the cube and at the same level as the center of the cube. Press the LMB to release the lamp.
9. Press *F12* to render the scene.
10. Observe how the cube looks. It should look as shown in the following screenshot.
11. Press the *Esc* button to close the render window.

What just happened?

Earlier, you saw that moving the lamp affects how the scene is lit. This time, when you did a render, with the lamp right next to the cube, you created a hotspot that is visible on the cube, as shown in the following screenshot. You did not see the lamp itself though. It also shows that you have to be careful about where you place the lamp, unless you specifically want to show the hotspots, which can look nice, adding a highlight to the edge. This is shown in the following screenshot:

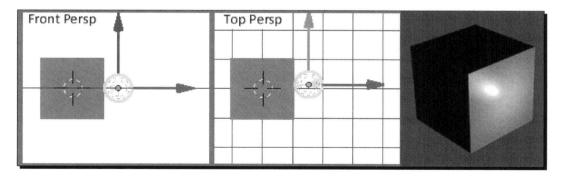

You learned another way to move an object. You learned that once you select an object with the RMB, in addition to dragging it, you can also use the *G* key (grab) to move it. Once you have selected it, it can be moved repeatedly. I use it often, because if the object is close to other objects, selecting with the RMB can sometimes be difficult. If you have already selected it, then pressing the *G* key lets you move it without the risk of selecting something else accidentally.

For your reference, the file `49090S_03_putting the lamp close to the object 1.blend`, which has been included in the download pack, shows the position of the lamp when it is close to the cube. The file `49090S_03_putting the lamp close to the object 2.blend` shows the position of the lamp when it is in level with the cube.

Time for action – moving the lamp far away

There is another way to move an object, which you will explore now. Notice the change in how the cube looks when you move the lamp close to the camera:

1. Press the *1* key on the NumPad to get the **Front** view.

2. Press the *Home* key. On a Mac without a *Home* key, press the *fn* and left arrow key. This will show you all the objects in the scene.

3. Check in the upper-left corner of the 3D View window to make sure that you are in the **Front Ortho** view. If it says **Front Persp**, press the *5* key on the NumPad to get the orthographic view.

4. Observe the red and blue arrows that stick out of the lamp.

5. Put the cursor over the blue arrowhead. Hold the LMB down and move the lamp up until it is in level with the camera, as shown in the left section of the following screenshot. Note that when you select the arrowhead, the arrows disappear and are replaced by a line that shows you the direction you can move in. Release the LMB when it's in level with the center of the camera.

6. Press the *7* key on the NumPad to get the top view.

7. Use the red and green arrowheads to move the lamp near the camera, as shown in the center section of the following screenshot.

8. Press *F12* to render the scene.

9. Observe how the cube looks.

10. Press the *Esc* button to close the render window.

What just happened?

This time, the lamp is farther away, so the lighting seems dimmer and the highlights are more muted, as with a real lamp. You switched to the Orthographic view to make it easier to align the lamp and the camera. You also learned a third way to move an object. You learned that once you select an object with the LMB, you can use the 3D manipulator to move it. Using the 3D manipulator restricts motion to a single direction. The red handle controls the motion in the *X* axis, the green handle controls the motion in the *Y* axis, and the blue handle controls the motion in the *Z* axis, as shown in the following screenshot:

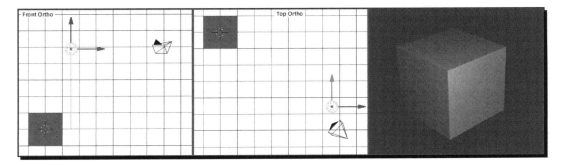

 For your reference, the file `49090S_03_moving the lamp far away 1.blend` shows the position of the lamp when it is close to the camera. The file `49090S_03_moving the lamp far away 2.blend` shows the position of the lamp when it is in level with the camera.

Checking the lighting without rendering

This is a good start. Did you know that you can check the lighting without rendering?

Time for action – observing how the lighting looks without rendering

Sometimes, you want to get an idea of how a scene looks without rendering. You can do this with the **Viewport Shading** menu, as explained in the following steps:

1. On the header at the bottom of the 3D window, there is a blank white circle, as highlighted in the following screenshot.

2. Click on the white circle with the LMB, and a menu appears.

3. Scroll up to the circle with the checkerboard and the word **Texture**.

4. Press the LMB.

5. Move the lamp close to one corner of the cube, as shown in the following screenshot.

6. Press *1* on the NumPad to see the front view.

7. Move the lamp close to the cube.

8. Press *0* on the NumPad to see the view from the camera.

9. Move the lamp. What happens? The difference is illustrated on the left and right of the next screenshot.

What just happened?

You changed the **Viewport Shading** method from **Solid** to **Texture**, and shifted to **Top View** to move the lamp close to the cube. Then, you switched back to **Camera View** so that you could get the camera's view of the lighting to change as you move the lamp around, as shown in the following screenshot:

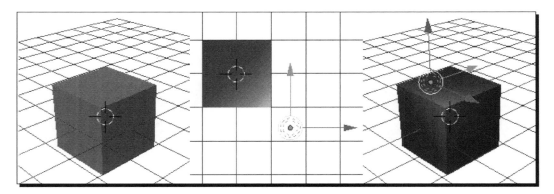

For your reference, the file 49090S_03_see how the lighting looks1.blend shows the position of the lamp when it is close to the cube and ready to move back and forth. The file 49090S_03_see how the lighting looks2.blend shows the position of the lamp when it has been moved interactively.

Adding color to the lamp using the Properties window

The Properties window is, by default, the lower window on the right-hand side (window number 5 of the following image). This is different from the Properties Panel in the 3D View, which is displayed and hidden with the *N* key, which I will refer to as the 3D View Properties panel.

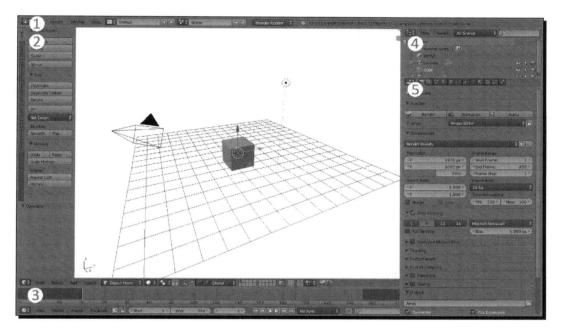

The Properties window is the second-most-used window in Blender. Clicking on one of the buttons on the header will display a panel with a set of controls and buttons. These panels control the following:

- Rendering
- Scene
- World
- Object
- Constraints
- Object data
- Material
- Texture
- Particles and physics

Each panel in the Properties window is divided into a series of subpanels. The subpanels are divided by horizontal lines. They have a title in the upper-left corner of the subpanel and a downward-pointing triangle that can be used to close or open the subpanel.

Time for action – adding color to Lamp

White light is great, but with a full spectrum from which to choose, why restrict yourself? Now, you will learn to set a lamp to any color you wish. Use the following steps to add color to **Lamp**:

1. If the **Lamp** is not selected, select it with the RMB.

2. Pull the edge between the 3D View window and the Properties window to the left until you can see all of the buttons in the Properties window header. Move the mouse over the header of the **Properties** window. Select the button that has the glowing dot with four arrows coming out of it, with the LMB so the button is highlighted in blue, as shown in the next screenshot.

3. This is the **Object data** button for the lamp. When you select the **Object data** button instead of the button with the still camera on it, notice that the entire **Properties** window changes.

4. The **Properties** window is divided into panels and subpanels. When you selected the **Object data** button, you opened the **Object data** panel. Move the cursor down to the subpanel labeled **Lamp**. Click on the white box with the LMB. It is the Light Color button. A color wheel pops up, as shown in the following screenshot:

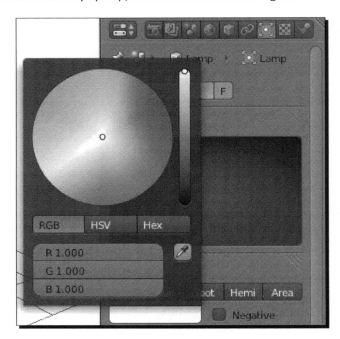

5. Click on the red area of the color wheel with the LMB, somewhere near the edge of the circle. Note that the Light Color button just below the color wheel is now a shade of red. Move the cursor to an open area within the Lamp subpanel to close the color wheel.

6. Press *F12* to render the cube.

7. Observe how the cube looks.

8. Press the *Esc* button to close the render window.

What just happened?

With the lamp selected, you started to learn about using the **Properties** window. Clicking on the LMB on the **Object data** button brought up the **Object data** panel. You opened the color wheel and changed the color of the lamp to red. In the 3D View window, the cube became a red color. When you rendered the cube, the red light colored the cube red. Nothing happened to the actual color of the cube.

Remember our discussion of colors in *Chapter 2, Getting Comfortable Using the 3D View*, where we talked about there being 256 levels of red, green, and blue. Look at the digital readout of the RGB colors just below the color wheel. The maximum value is 1.0. For convenience, Blender expresses the 256 levels for a given color for the red, green, and blue channels as percentages of 256. You changed the color from white to red, and after you changed it, Red was a value close to 1.0 while Green and Blue were near zero. The color you see depends on both the color of the object and the color of the light because Blender copies the real world.

 For your reference, the file `49090S_03_adding color to the lamp.blend` shows the lamp when it has been colored using the **Properties** window.

Using multiple lamps for better lighting

The best way to see the effect of lighting is to have more than one lamp.

Time for action – adding a second lamp

Now, you'll learn to copy objects in a Blender scene and see how multiple lamps improve the look:

1. Press *1* on the NumPad to get the front view. Look at the upper-left corner of the 3D View to make sure that the 3D View is in the **Ortho** mode. Press *5* on the NumPad if it isn't in the Ortho mode.

2. Move the lamp to the major horizontal grid line above the cube.

3. Press *7* on the NumPad to get the top view.

4. Move the lamp up until it is just to the right of the cube and level it with the center of the cube, as shown in the following screenshot:

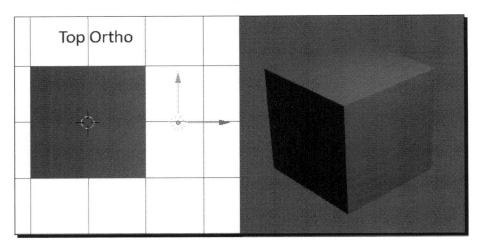

5. Press *F12* to render the cube.

6. Observe how the cube looks.

7. Press the *Esc* button to close the render window.

8. With the lamp selected, press the *Shift* key and the *D* key together, to make a copy of the lamp.

9. Move the cursor. The new lamp moves while the original stays put. Move this lamp so that it is centered below the cube, as shown in the following screenshot:

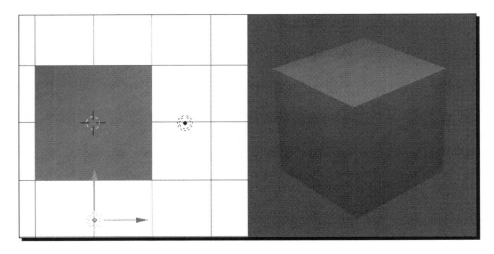

10. Press *F12* to render the cube.

11. Observe how the cube looks.

12. Press the *Esc* button to close the render window.

13. Now, go to the **Properties** window, and using the color wheel, change the color of the new lamp to green.

14. Press *F12* to render the cube.

15. Has the cube changed? It should look like the image on the right of the following screenshot:

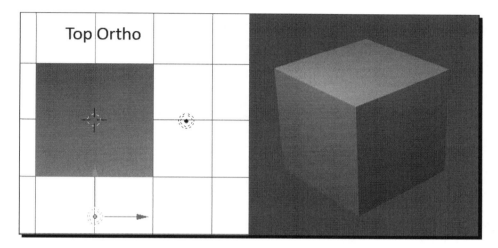

What just happened?

The previous screenshot shows what you did. First, you rendered the cube to remind yourself of how the lighting looked. By pressing *Shift* + *D* (duplicate), you created a copy of the first lamp and moved it. Then, you rendered the scene again and you could see that the lighting on the cube was more even. Then, you changed the light color of the second lamp to green, and as expected, one side of the cube shows green. But, why is the top of the cube yellow? We will discover that now.

For your reference, the file 49090S_03_adding a second lamp1. blend shows the lamp when it has been colored and moved into position. 49090S_03_adding a second lamp2.blend shows the position of the lamp when it has been copied and moved. 49090S_03_adding a second lamp3.blend shows the red and green lamps in position.

Now that you are getting into material where color matters, if you don't have the colored e-book version, colored images of these illustrations are available as a part of the download pack.

Light color mixing

We mentioned about the three colors that a computer displays and the 256 levels of each color earlier. The diagram on the left side of the following image will give you a slightly better idea of how light colors mix. We can get the following colors if we mix a few:

♦ When you mix red and blue, you get magenta
♦ When you mix blue and green, you get cyan
♦ When you mix green and red, you get yellow
♦ When you mix red, green, and blue, you get white, because white is the result of all colors mixed

In the previous section, with a red lamp on one side of the cube, that side was colored red. With the green lamp on the second side, it was colored green. Because the top was lit by both lamps, the light was mixed and the color was yellow. The Venn diagram on the left-hand side of the following illustration shows this.

With your 256 shades of each color, you can mix light more subtly than that. For example, if you have 100 percent red and 50 percent green, you get orange. The color wheel on the right here shows you basic combinations with RGB values written out for use in Blender in the form of (R, G, B). 100 percent becomes 1, 50 percent becomes 0.5, and so on.

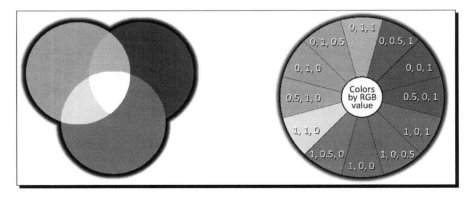

Time for action – setting colors

The following steps will guide you while setting the colors:

1. Go to the **Properties** window, and using the sliders at the bottom of the color wheel panel, change the color of the lamp to 1.0 Red, 1.0 Green, and 0.0 Blue. What color is shown in the Light Color button?

2. Now, change the color of the lamp to 1.0 Red, 0.0 Green, and 1.0 Blue. What color is shown in the Light Color button?

3. Now, change the color of the lamp to 0.0 Red, 1.0 Green, and 1.0 Blue. What color is shown in the Light Color button?

4. Now, change the color of the lamp to 0.5 Red, 0.0 Green, and 1.0 Blue. What color is shown in the Light Color button?

Have a go hero – experimenting with multiple lamps

You now know how to change lamp colors. Play around with moving the lamps and changing the colors.

The following screenshot shows a couple of lighting setups that I came up with and diagrams of where I put the lamps. See what you can do. The first way I tried, putting all the lamps on one side of the cube, is shown in the following screenshot:

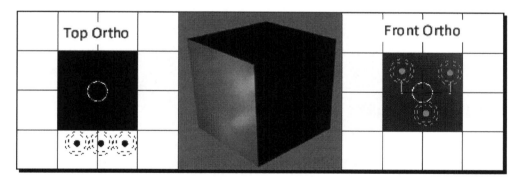

On my second try, as shown in the following illustration, I used each lamp to color a single side of the cube from different angles and distances:

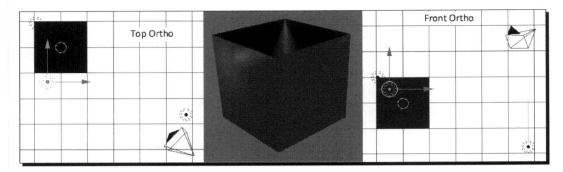

See in what way you can use light to color the different sides of the cube. Does the result look good? Put both lamps on one side of the cube. See what colors you can mix. Try three lamps as described in the first example.

In addition to mixing colors with the red, green, and blue values, you can also mix them using **HSV (Hue, Saturation, Value)**. Hue selects the color. Saturation selects how much color is mixed with white. Value selects how dark or light it is.

Spend a little time playing with this. There is a lot you can do. See if you can create a mood just using color.

For your reference, the file 4909OS_03_experimenting with multiple lamps1. blend shows the three lamps on one side of the cube as I set them up, and 4909OS_03_ experimenting with multiple lamps2.blend shows the three lamps on varying sides of the cube.

Thinking about a career in lighting

Some animation professionals called Lighting Technical Directors build entire careers just working with lighting color. A quick look through job ads found positions for a 3D Lighting Artist for Games, a Lighting Artist, and a Senior Lighting Artist. Click on the URL http://www.3drender.com/jobs/TD.htm to know what Jeremy Birn, Technical Director at Pixar, has to say about what a Technical Director does.

Here is a link to a good discussion of real world lighting for 3D, http://en.wikibooks. org/wiki/Blender_3D:_Noob_to_Pro/Understanding_Real_Lights.

You will explore standard lighting methods and setup later.

Saving your work

Now that you are doing more exciting work, it's always a good idea to save what you have done.

Time for action – saving a file

Now, it's time for the most important command in Blender, saving the work that you have done. The following steps will show you how to save a file:

1. In the upper-left corner of the Blender window, select **File** and choose **Save As** from the drop-down menu. This opens **File Browser**, as shown in the following screenshot:

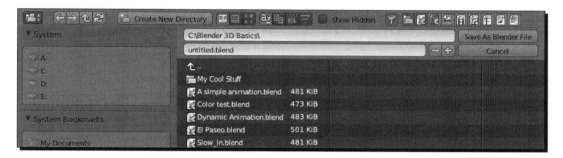

2. Click on the LMB where it says `untitled.blend`, as shown in the previous screenshot. The background behind the word `untitled.blend` becomes darker and you can edit the name now. When you have named the file, press *Enter*.

3. If you wish to increment the filename, that is, to have files named `animation1.blend`, `animation2.blend`, and so on, move the cursor over to the upper right corner of the window and click on the plus sign. Before you press the **Save As Blender File** button, make sure that you are in the right directory.

4. To go up a directory, click on the upward pointing bent arrow at the top of the list of files. To go into a directory, click on the icon that looks like a cardboard file folder, similar to the **My Cool Stuff** folder in the previous screenshot.

5. Once you are in the right place, click on the **Save As Blender File** button.

What just happened?

Blender does not use the computer's filing interface. It has its own. You named the file. You learned about incrementing the name numerically, which is very important for keeping different versions of a project saved in case you have to go back to an earlier version. You learned how to go through the directory structure and save the file.

Always have a backup file

Computers being what they are, it's always good to have a backup file. You have learned to save files on your own, but you wouldn't be the first person to get working in Blender and discover that the hours flew by and you forgot to save the file on which you are working. If that should happen, remember the upcoming tip.

The auto backup feature

Blender helps you with this by automatically making a backup file often. The default time is every five minutes. These files are tucked away in your Documents and Settings folder. The filename is a number with a .blend extension. It will be in the directory, Documents and Settings\"Your user name"\Local Settings\temp. Of course, your username is whatever name the computer has for you as a user. This will be slightly different for Mac and Linux users, so pay attention to where the installation program loads it.

After you have used Blender a little, you may notice files labeled .blend1 and .blend2. Blender creates these when you save over a file that has already been saved. The old copy of the .blend file becomes .blend1, and if there is a .blend1 copy, it becomes .blend2. They can be used by renaming the .blend1 or .blend2 file to a .blend extension. So, if you made a mistake and then hit **Save**, .blend1 and .blend2 are your friends.

Controlling the camera

In *Chapter 2, Getting Comfortable Using the 3D View*, I discussed the global *X*, *Y*, and *Z* axes and the local *X*, *Y*, and *Z* axes. Using the camera helps us to see the difference in a slightly more vivid way. The following screenshot shows how to manage the Global and Local axes:

Time for action – using the global axis and local axis

We discussed the global and local axes. It's kind of an abstract concept until you use it. Now, we'll learn how to use it:

1. Select **New** in the **File** menu. Then, select **Reload Start-Up File** from the pop-up menu.

2. With the cursor over the camera, click the RMB to select it. Note that the *Z* axis (in blue) in the 3D manipulator is straight up. You can press *5* on the NumPad to toggle to the **Ortho** mode to confirm that the *Z* axis is pointing up.

3. Move the mouse over the **Orientation** selector in the **3D View** header, outlined in the previous screenshot. By default, it is labeled **Global**. Click on the **Orientation** selector. Move the mouse up the **Orientation** pop-up menu and select **Local** with the LMB. Note that the direction the *Z* axis is pointing changes as you switch from global coordinates to local coordinates. The blue arrow now points through the camera lens.

4. Change from **Local** back to **Global** and back several times, noting the change in direction. In **Local** mode, tilt your head so that the blue arrow is up and the axes will look familiar.

What just happened?

By changing the value of the Orientation selector, you can choose whether you are working with the global or local axes. Why is this important? The global *Z* axis is up and down. The local *Z* axis for the camera points toward the lens of the camera and away from the scene. This allows you to move the camera in or out, to get closer or farther from your subject just by moving along the camera's local *Z* axis without worrying about how the camera is rotated in space.

Moving objects, faster and easier

You got a start on moving objects by learning three ways to move the light. Now, you will refine your techniques for greater speed and control.

Time for action – moving an object in one plane in the global mode

Sometimes, you want to move an object freely, and sometimes, it's better to move it along one axis. Here's a way to move it, by specifying the axis by letter:

1. Load a new file into Blender.
2. Select the camera with the RMB. Press the *G* key to grab it. Now, move your mouse.
3. Now, tap the *Z* key and move the mouse.
4. Now, tap the *X* key and move the mouse.
5. Now, tap the *Y* key.
6. Press the RMB to let go of the camera.

What just happened?

You discovered that you can restrict the axis that you move by pressing the *G* key and then pressing the key of the axis in which you wish to move. This gives us similar control as using the 3D Manipulator.

Time for action – moving an object in one plane in the local mode

We talked about global and local axes. Now, you see the difference in action. You tap an *X*, *Y*, or *Z* key once to specify moving along a global axis; you tap them twice to specify moving along a local axis:

1. With the camera selected, press the *G* key to grab it.
2. Now, tap the *Z* key twice and move the mouse.
3. Now, tap the *X* key twice and move the mouse.
4. Now, tap the *Y* key twice and move the mouse.
5. Press the LMB to let go of the camera.

What just happened?

You discovered that when you press the *G* key, you can restrict the motion to the global *Z* plane by pressing the *Z* key once. If you press the *Z* key two times in a row, the motion is restricted to the local *Z* plane. The same applies to the *X* plane and the *Y* plane.

Have a go hero – controlling the location with numbers

Not only can you control whether you move, rotate, and scale an object along the required axis with keys, but you can also tell Blender with what values to do it. Try it.

Get the Right Ortho view and select the cube. Press the *G* key, then the *Y* key, and then the *2* key. This moves the object two units in the Y direction. If you like the changes, then press the *Enter* key. If you don't like the change, press the *Esc* key and it will go back to where it started. Try it in other axes and with other distances. This is great when you are trying to locate things with precision.

Seeing through the lens

You may have found it frustrating to not be able to control the camera when you press render. You're going to fix that now. You'll study the basics of getting the best use of the camera lens and a little bit of the vocabulary of camera motion.

Time for action – setting up Blender so you can see what the camera sees

Quite often, you may need to have more than one view of the scene visible at one time. Blender is great that way because you can break up the 3D View window as you like. In this case, we want to see what the camera is seeing as well as having our standard view of the scene. The following steps will help you set up Blender as you like:

1. Select **New** in the **File** menu.
2. Create a new 3D View window horizontally as you learned in *Chapter 2, Getting Comfortable Using the 3D View*.
3. With the cursor over the right-hand 3D View, press *0* on the NumPad to get the camera view.
4. Press *T* to close the **Tool Shelf** in the right 3D View window. It should look similar to the following illustration.
5. Now, save the file as Two 3D Views.blend.

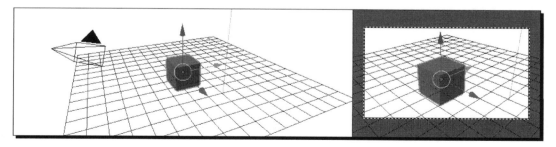

What just happened?

This last exercise was to create a basic Blender file that you can use multiple times. It has the standard 3D View window as well as a 3D View window locked to what the camera sees. This will give you the flexibility of moving around in the scene as you please, and you can manipulate things while observing how they appear to the camera.

 For your reference, the file `49090S_03_Two 3D Views.blend` has the double 3D View setup as shown previously.

Using the camera as a canvas

In *Chapter 1, Introducing Blender and Animation*, we discussed how animation progressed from the static posing of Felix the Cat to the lively compositions of Mickey Mouse. You saw how it happened again in the early days of computer animation. These rules that enabled good composition were first conceived by painters, amplified by filmmakers, and later applied to animation.

Understanding the rules of composition

There are three basic rules of composition of which to be aware. They are as follows:

- The rule of thirds
- Using positive and negative space
- Using a limited palette

Applying the rule of thirds for well-balanced scenes

With the rule of thirds, you visually break down an image into thirds vertically and horizontally, as done in the left side of the following graphic. A grid has been placed over the left image to show you where the thirds of the image are.

Placing the points of interest along the lines that mark the intersections of the thirds gives you a visual sense of flow that just placing the point of interest in the center of the image would not.

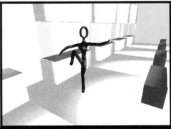

Here, on the left, the subject was posed with the rule of thirds in mind. In the right portion of the image, the subject was posed in the center. In the left portion of the image, you are drawn into the scene. You get a stronger feeling of presence. For more information, here is a link that explores the rule of thirds in more depth, `http://www.digital-photography-school.com/rule-of-thirds/`.

 For your reference, the file `49090S_03_rule of thirds.blend` was used to create the left-hand image shown previously.

Using positive and negative space to put the focus on the action

The positive space is the area occupied by the subject of the image. In this case, it is the dancing figure and the benches. The negative space is everything else. As simple as that is, there is always a delicate dance going on between the two that can add or subtract from the composition. They can complement or clash, but which of these outcomes you want depends on what you are trying to do. Therefore, there is no right or wrong, but you must consider the effect that the background has on the foreground.

In the following photo, the subject is the man looking at the bicycle, the positive space. Most of the background consists of flat paving stones; there is little detail in them. This is the negative space. It opens up the image, contrasting the amount of detail in the man and the bicycle, and directs your attention to the man. Within the negative space, the strip at the edge of the water reinforces the direction of the man's motion and echoes the top tube of the bicycle, so there is a lot of harmonious diagonal motion. Moreover, there is an informal breaking of the image into thirds vertically. The bicycle is the lowest, the men are the center, and the gondolas are the top. The men and the bicycle occupy the center third horizontally, with negative space on either side.

Scott McCloud investigated this subject well in his book *Understanding Comics*. I recommend that you read it. Here is another link that also explores positive and negative space, `http://artinspired.pbworks.com/w/page/13819678/Positive-and-Negative-Space`.

 If you are reading the printed version of this book, refer to the colored images in your download directory.

Using a limited palette for better results

A long time ago, painters discovered that using all colors possible didn't work as well as having a limited palette of fewer colors. In the image of the dancer shown previously, all the tones are in the range of reds and blues; there are no yellows or greens. This helps to unify the image. Though, often, painters will bend the rules by having one small bit of opposing color or a saturated red (pure red, not mixed with white) to draw your eye to the focal point of the image. The preceding image is a good example. Most of the image is in yellows and oranges. In this case, it is the white helmet with the spot of red that draws your attention to the bicycle, similar to the way the man's attention is on the bicycle, and there is only a little blue that is on the girls in the corner, which helps to set them apart. They are not part of the man's attention, although they help with the flow of the image, by counter-balancing the figure in the lower left.

If you watch movies carefully, you may notice that some of the scenes have very limited palettes, where the director wants to use blue to emphasize the coldness of the actions within the scenes, and the next scene may be all oranges or greens. Here is a link to more on limited palettes, `http://channeling-winslow-homer.com/a-rational-palette-index-to-chapters/chapter-one-2/chapter-two-eye-candy-avoiding-monotomy/chapter-three-mixing-convenience/chapter-four-saturation-costs/five-is-the-saturated-palette-what-we-want/six-the-extremely-limited-palette/`.

Employing Blender's camera composition guides to make your work look better

To help you with your composition, Blender includes a series of camera composition guides, including one that outlines the rule of thirds.

Time for action – investigating the camera composition guides

Blender has composition guides to help you display within the camera's finder. The following steps will guide you while investigating the camera composition guides:

1. Select the camera with the RMB.

2. Look in the Properties window header and find the image of the movie camera, with its two film magazines, in the Properties window header, as shown in the following image. This is the **Object data** button for the camera. Click on it with the LMB.

3. At the top-right of the **Display** subpanel, there is a button labeled **Composition Guides**. Select that button.

4. Choose **Thirds** from the pop-up menu. Now, you see guidelines in the Camera view. This will make laying out your scenes easier.

5. You can have several scenes at one time and choose whichever you like. See what kinds there are and do a search on those terms to find out more about them.

What just happened?

The composition guides are great tools. You learned to access them. They help you to plan your camera work. The Center and Center Diagonal guides are pretty obvious. You have seen the thirds. Golden divides the screen into proportions of the Golden Ratio (1.618). The Golden Triangles have a diagonal line and then two lines perpendicular to it and running through the corners. The Harmonious Triangles have the diagonal line, but the lines crossing it start at the corners and run to 0.618 of the length of the far side.

Understanding the fundamental camera moves

There are six fundamental camera moves, namely moving in and out (dolly), side to side (truck), up and down (boom), tilting right and left (roll), up and down (tilt), and swiveling right and left (pan). They are illustrated in the following screenshot:

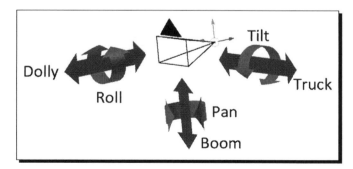

More specifically, in Blender terms, these are as follows:

◆ **Dolly**: This moves the camera towards or away from the scene along its local *Z* axis

◆ **Roll**: This turns the camera on its local *Z* axis

◆ **Boom**: This moves the camera up and down on its local *Y* axis

◆ **Pan**: This turns the camera on its local *Y* axis

◆ **Truck**: This moves the camera sideways along its local *X* axis

◆ **Tilt**: This turns the camera on its local *X* axis

Rotating and scaling the camera and other objects

Blender has a very consistent user interface. The commands for manipulating a camera also work on other objects such as the cube or the lamp. You've got a good idea of the ways to move an object by pressing the *G* key. Rotating and scaling are almost the same, except that you press the *R* key to rotate the active object and the *S* key to scale it.

Using keyboard commands to grab, rotate, and scale objects

You can get a lot of control with just the keyboard too. There is a sequence for giving keyboard commands.

First, you type which operation you want to do. Next, you type in which axis to do it. Then, type in the number for distance, rotation, or scaling. In future, for actions, I will indicate a sequence of commands like this by separating the keystrokes with commas, asking you to type *G*, *X*, *1*, and *Enter* to move an object in the direction of the *X* axis, or *R*, *Y*, *2*, and *Enter* to rotate 2 degrees around the *Y* axis.

Moreover, as you saw earlier in the chapter, if you type the *X*, *Y*, or *Z* axis twice in a row, you work on the local axis, and not the global axis.

Time for action – moving, rotating, and scaling objects

You've learned the commands to move, rotate, and scale objects. Have some fun doing it just with the keyboard to help train your fingers, following these steps:

1. Press the *Home* key to see the entire scene.
2. With the camera selected, type *G*, *Z*, *1*, and *Enter*. Watch the camera view as you type in the number.
3. Type *G*, *Z*, *Z*, *1*, and *Enter*.
4. Select the cube with the RMB. Press *R*, *Y*, *45*, and *Enter*.
5. Type *S*, *X*, *2*, and *Enter*. Then, type *S*, *2*, and *Enter*.

What just happened?

This was a pretty brief exercise, but you got a chance to see the strength of using the keyboard to move, scale, and rotate objects. If you know how much change you need, or need to make a precise change, this is a great way to do it. You found the difference in motion along a global axis and a local axis. You rotated and scaled an object and discovered that when you scale an object without saying which axis, then the object is scaled along all three axes.

Making an animation

It's time to make an animation. Animation adds a fourth dimension to 3D. Besides the *X*, *Y*, and *Z* axes, there is time. In animation, time is broken into **frames**, a sequence of individual images, similar to the frames of a movie. These images are shown one after another. The speed at which they are shown is usually expressed as **frames**. As a rule of thumb, web animations such as animated gifs and banner ads can play at between 7 and 15 **frames per second (fps)**; a film plays at 24 fps and a video plays at 30 fps (NTSC) or 25 fps (PAL). Blender renders at 24 fps by default.

Look at the window directly below the 3D window. By default, that window is used for the **Timeline window**. The Timeline window lets us know how far along in an animation we are. Look at the following screenshot:

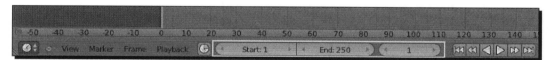

The Timeline window consists of the following components:

- The three large grey buttons, outlined in the preceding graphic, give you the most important information.

- By default, Blender allows you 250 frames in which you can create an animation. It starts on frame 1, it ends on frame 250, and the third button shows you the frame that Blender is currently on, which by default is frame 1.

- To change the frame, you can press the LMB over the number in the button on the right and type in a different number, or use the two small arrows at either end of the button to change the value.

- If you look at the center of the previous image, you see numbers going from left to right. There is a little green vertical line just to the right of 0. This is the **current frame indicator**. It shows you the frame you are on, and you can drag the current frame indicator to change the frame as well.

Earlier, you set up a Blender file with two 3D View windows. Now, you need it to do your animation. So, let's load the file.

Time for action – loading a file

Loading a file is pretty simple, but essential if you are working on a project that you need to interrupt or make changes to. This is shown as follows:

1. Loading a file is very similar to saving one.

2. Select **File** from the upper-left corner of the Blender window and then choose **Open** from the drop-down menu. The **File Browser** opens, and as you roll the mouse over the files, the one you are over is highlighted. Find Two 3D Views.blend.

3. Press the LMB to select it. Click the LMB on **Open Blender File**, as shown in the following screenshot:

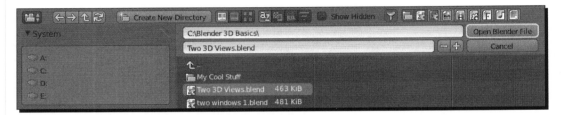

What just happened?

You loaded a file. It's very similar to saving a file. You're saving yourself from a little work and promoting a standardized work environment by reusing the dual 3D View setup that you saved earlier.

Time for action – making a simple animation with keyframes

In animation, keyframes are the beginning and end of a transition. This transition could be a movement, rotation, or scaling of an object. It can also be a change in the color of an object, the brightness of the light, or almost anything that you can set in Blender. The animation is a sequence of keyframes. So let's start by making a simple animation:

1. If the cube is not selected, select it with the RMB.

2. With the cursor over the left-hand side of the 3D View window, press the *I* key, (*I* for Insert), to insert a keyframe. A menu will appear, as shown in the next screenshot.

3. Select **Location** and press the LMB.

4. In the Timeline window below the 3D View window, drag the green current frame indicator right until it is over 20. As you do that, the current frame text fields in the lower left of the 3D Views will change, as will the current frame button in the Timeline window.

5. Grab the green 3D manipulator in the left-hand 3D View with the LMB and move the cube along the *Y* axis. Watch the other 3D View so you can see how it looks on the camera. Release the LMB when the cube is where you want it.

6. With the cursor over the left-hand 3D View window, press the *I* key. A drop-down menu will appear. Select **Location** and press the LMB.

7. Notice that in the center of the green current frame indicator, there is a yellow line at frame 1. This shows that frame 1 has a keyframe.

8. Move the current frame indicator in the Timeline window between 20 and 1 and back to 20 to see the cube's motion. Moving through the frames like this is called **scrubbing**. When you do this, you can also see that there is a yellow line at frame 20, which indicates that frame 20 also has a keyframe.

9. Select the large button in the Timeline window that is marked **End**. Click on **250**. The number will move to the left and you can type in 20 and press *Enter*. Now, the animation will end at frame 20.

10. To see a preview of the animation in the 3D View, put the cursor over the 3D View window and press the *Alt* key and the *A* key simultaneously. This will be written as *Alt + A*. Press *Esc* to stop it from playing.

11. Save your file to a unique name so you can remember it.

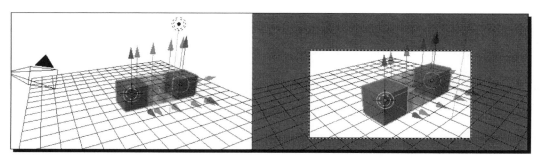

What just happened?

Congratulations! You are now a computer animator. You created a keyframe that tells the computer where the cube is on frame 1. Then, you created another keyframe to tell the computer where the cube is on frame 20. The computer then figured out how to move the cube at frames 2 to 19 so that the cube would appear to move smoothly.

A keyframe tells the computer what the *state* of an object on a particular frame is. In this example, the first keyframe tells the computer that the state of the cube's location on the Y axis is 0 at frame 1. The second keyframe tells the computer that the state of the cube's location on the Y axis is about 5 at frame 20. Blender allows us to animate almost any property of the object. A property is any one of the attributes of the object such as location, rotation, scaling, or color, and much more.

Finally, you learned how to preview the animation.

For your reference, the file `49090S_03_a simple animation.blend` has our first animation.

This is a pretty simple animation; one cube isn't much for Blender to calculate. However, as you go through this book, the models and animations will get more complex. You will get tips and recommendations on how to optimize your rendering and previews.

Making an animation preview run smoothly

You can preview the animation in the 3D View in any display mode. Remember though, that the computer has to calculate all of this in real time. If, in the future, a large scene does not play smoothly as a texture display, try previewing it as a solid or wireframe display, which Blender can do much faster.

Rendering your animation

Now, it's time to see what you have done. You need to render it so you can see the light, the motion, and the objects. Now is the time for that quick snack or cup of coffee I talked about in *Chapter 1, Introducing Blender and Animation*. This is your moment. But hurry right back; the Blender renderer is pretty quick and there isn't much in this scene to render.

Time for action – rendering the animation

You've seen how you can render a single frame by pressing the *F12* key, and look at it by pressing the *F11* key. Rendering an animation is very similar as explained in the following steps:

1. Press the *Ctrl* key and the *F12* key to start the rendering.

2. Look at the text across the top of the frame where the image is being rendered. It tells you which frame is being rendered, how long the previous frame took to render, how many vertices and faces there are, how much memory was needed, and other things. This text is for your information only; it doesn't show up in the final images or animation, as shown in the following screenshot:

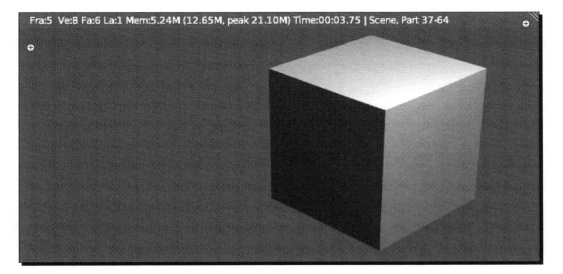

3. When the animation has finished rendering, press the *Esc* key to close the render window. Then, press the *Ctrl* key and the *F11* key. In a moment, you should see your animation. Notice how the lighting changes and how the speed of the cube varies.

4. Press the *Esc* key when you are done looking at your animation.

What just happened?

You learned how to render your animation by pressing the *Ctrl* + *F12* keys, and how to view it using the *Ctrl* + *F11* keys.

Controlling motion in Graph Editor

Now, let's look at what motion looks like to Blender, and see how we can control the motion and other transitions using F-Curves.

Time for action – exploring Graph Editor

Graph Editor displays the data associated with every single keyframe. It lets you adjust the keyframes and the transitions between them easily, as explained in the following steps:

1. Move the cursor over the Timeline window and down to the **Current Editor Type** button.

2. Press the LMB, scroll up the menu to **Graph Editor**, and press the LMB again.

3. Move the cursor to the edge between Graph Editor and 3D View until you see the double-headed arrow. Press the LMB and drag the border between the windows up until you can see the curving line as shown in the following screenshot. Release the button when you have moved the edge enough.

4. Use *Shift* + MMB to move the graphs so that they are centered in the window. Now, use the *Ctrl* + MMB buttons to scale the display of the graph so it fits comfortably in the window as shown in the following screenshot.

5. Click on the Graph Editor window with the LMB. Then, while holding down the LMB, move the mouse right and left. The current frame indicator line will move, and if you look in the 3D View, your cube is moving as well.

What just happened?

Now, the bottom window is Graph Editor, not Timeline. It looks similar, but it displays the mathematical curves that control the motion. By moving the current time indicator line, you can change which frame you are on. On the left-hand side of the Graph Editor window is a panel that allows you to select which motion curves you are working with. You also discovered that you can use the same commands to navigate in Graph Editor as in 3D View.

[For your reference, the file 49090S_03_exploring the Graph Editor.blend shows the curve in Graph Editor.]

Introducing the F-Curve

The curve in the Graph Editor window is called an F-Curve. The orange lines with orange circles at the end are how you control the curve. The orange dot at the center is the control point. It represents the keyframe. The orange circles at the end are the control handles with which you control the curve. These allow you to control how your object goes from one keyframe to another. There are three ways to do this:

♦ **Linear interpolation**: This goes in a straight line from one keyframe to another, as shown in the left side of the following screenshot.

♦ **Constant interpolation**: This keeps the value constant until the next keyframe as shown in the center of the following screenshot.

♦ **Bézier interpolation**: This gives you the most control because it allows you to control the path between keyframes very flexibly, as shown on the right side of the following screenshot. The Bézier (pronounced as *beh-zee-yay*) curve is named after the French engineer Pierre Bézier, who used them to design automobile bodies for Renault.

The Bézier interpolation is the default method in Blender, so we'll look at that in more detail. The various interpolations are shown in the following screenshot:

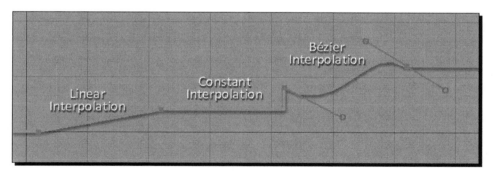

You choose which way you want to interpolate by selecting **Key** on the Graph Editor header, then choosing **Interpolation Mode** from the pop-up menu, and then choosing one of the three interpolation modes.

 For your reference, the file 49090S_03_introducing the f-curve. blend shows the three interpolation methods.

Linear interpolation is great when you need nice mechanical transitions between keyframes, for example if you were rotating the hands of a clock and want the hands to rotate at a constant speed. Constant interpolation is used when you want to shift from one state to another, like the escape mechanism that controls the unwinding of a clock spring.

Blender's consistent interface makes it easier for you

The same commands used to move objects in 3D View can be used to move keyframes in Graph Editor.

Modifying motion with the Bézier curve controls

As you saw in the preceding illustration, Linear interpolation goes in a straight line from one keyframe to another, without changing the speed of its motion, but the Bézier Interpolation is much more free-form. With the control handles, you can control the rate of acceleration or deceleration of an object as well as its motion.

Time for action – working with a Bézier curve

Bézier curves are very powerful. Blender uses them for modeling as well as for the F-Curves that control animation. Here is how to control them:

1. In Graph Editor, the current frame indicator is the vertical line with a box at the bottom. Move it left and right to scrub along the timeline of the Graph Editor. Watch the motion of the cube in 3D View.

2. Now, select the left dot on the upper Bézier handle, with the RMB, and move it up as shown in the next screenshot.

3. Press the LMB to release the handle. The curve will go upwards. Move the current frame indicator back and forth again and watch the motion of the cube. The Bézier handles can be moved with all the same controls as keyframes and objects.

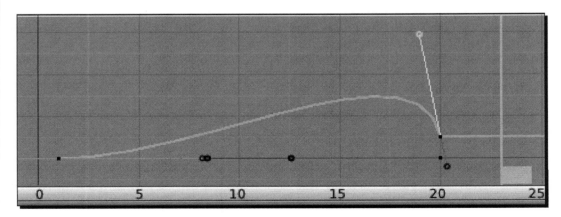

4. With the cursor over either the Graph Editor or 3D View, press *Alt + A* to play the animation and *Esc* to stop.

What just happened?

You scrubbed the current frame indicator along the timeline of Graph Editor to see that the 3D views reflect how you are controlling the graph editor. Then, you modified the motion curve by moving the Bézier handle to change the curve without changing the actual keyframe. This changed the motion of the cube. It now moves farther away from the camera and comes back. The return is much more dynamic than the trip out, and it stops suddenly without much slow out. You can see this reflected in the Bézier curve in the Graph Editor window.

For your reference, the file 4909OS_03_working with a Bezier Curve.blend shows how to change the motion of the cube using the curve handle.

Practice is the only way you will learn all the Blender commands. It may help to write out a list of the commands that you only use occasionally so that you can find them quickly. The following information box contains a list of the keyboard shortcuts for the **Timeline** window:

Moving the current frame indicator with keystrokes

Pressing the *right arrow* key goes one frame forward.

Pressing the *left arrow* key goes one frame back.

Pressing the *up arrow* key goes to the next keyframe.

Pressing the *down arrow* key goes to the previous keyframe.

Pressing the *Shift + right arrow* key goes to the end of the animation.

Pressing the *Shift + left arrow* key goes to the beginning of the animation.

Pressing the *Shift + up arrow* key goes 10 frames forward.

Pressing the *Shift + down arrow* key goes 10 frames back.

If you accidentally press the *Ctrl* button while pressing an arrow key, you will see a different screen layout. Press *Ctrl* and the opposite arrow key to get back.

Time for action – adding squash and stretch to the animation

We learned how using squash and stretch adds to how dynamic an animation feels.
It's easy to do, and just takes a little extra time and a keyframe or two, as shown in
the following steps:

1. Use the arrow keys to move the current frame indicator in the Graph Editor back to
   frame 1.

2. Place your cursor over the 3D View window and check that the cube is still
   selected. If it isn't, select it with the RMB. Press *I*. Press the LMB on **LocRotScale** to
   simultaneously create keyframes for location, rotation, and scaling. Look in Graph
   Editor to see the new curves.

3. Go to frame 20 and make another keyframe in 3D View with **LocRotScale**.

4. In Graph Editor, move the current frame indicator to frame 17. In 3D View,
   press *I*. Scroll up the menu to where it says **Scaling**. Make a keyframe for
   Scaling only.

5. Move the current frame indicator to frame 19. Move the mouse over 3D View,
   press *S* and *Y*, and then move the mouse to scale the cube in Y so that it is longer.
   Press the LMB to affirm the scaling. Press *I* to make a keyframe for **Scaling**.

6. Press *Alt + A* to preview the animation.

7. Save this Blender file. Use the incrementing feature that we discussed earlier to save
   it to a unique filename.

What just happened?

You have created your first example of stretching using multiple keyframes. This may seem to
be a roundabout way to put in the keyframes, but it was efficient at putting the effect when
we wanted it.

First, you modified the keyframes you had already made in frames 1 and 20. This ensured
that the **Location**, **Rotation**, and **Scaling** values were locked down, as shown in the following
screenshot. This let you make further keyframes in the location, rotation, and scaling
channels without worrying whether you are altering the starting and ending values.

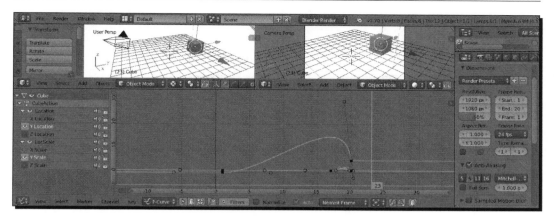

Then, in the middle of the cube's motion, you added a scaling keyframe to keep the scaling constant until you were ready to start stretching the cube. You went a couple of frames later, when you wanted the cube stretched to its maximum. You stretched it in Y, and then made a keyframe that recorded how you stretched the cube. The final keyframe already had the scaling set to be the same as it was originally, so the cube stretches and bounces back. You can see all the keyframes and curves in the preceding screenshot. Note the large curve controlling the motion and the smaller curve controlling the scaling in the preceding screenshot.

For your reference, the file 49090S_03_making the animation more dynamic.blend shows how squash and stretch was created with the Bézier curves.

Doing more with the Bézier curve handles

The Bézier curve handles are pretty flexible controls. Let's find out more about what they can do.

Time for action – refining the use of the Bézier curve handles

Ironically, you can sometimes get more control by restricting the motion. You'll try limiting the motion of the control handles to a particular axis, and you will set the control point so that only one control handle moves at a time:

1. In Graph Editor, zoom into the keyframe on frame 19 where you stretched the cube, select one of the handles with the RMB, press the *G* key to grab it, and move it around with the mouse. Tap the *Y* key. Move the cursor around and observe how this affects the movement.

2. Press the *X* key. Move the cursor around and observe how this affects the movement. Press the RMB to release the curve handle without making a change.

3. Now, select the control point in the center of the control handle.

4. Press the *V* key. Select **Free** from the drop-down menu, as shown in the following screenshot. Pick one of the control handles and move the cursor around and observe how this affects the curve.

What just happened?

You discovered that pressing the *X* or *Y* key locks the handle motion to that direction. Pressing the *V* key and selecting **Free** allows you to control each handle of the control point individually.

> Different handle types give you a different control over a control point.
>
> **Free** handles are independent.
>
> **Vector** handles point to the previous or next handle.
>
> **Aligned** handles lie in a straight line and give a continuous curve.
>
> **Automatic** chooses the length and direction to ensure the smoothest result.
>
> **Auto Clamped** restores the default handle settings.

Here's a page with a lot of good information about using control points and control handles on the F-Curve, http://wiki.blender.org/index.php/Doc:2.6/Manual/ Animation/Editors/Graph/FCurves.

Have a go hero – experimenting with control handles to adjust motion

You've seen a lot of ways to set keyframes now. Play with them in both 3D View and Graph Editor.

Remember that in Graph Editor, you can move not only the control handles but also the control points themselves, changing the value and the time of each keyframe. Change values in **Rotation**, **Location**, and **Scaling** of the cube. Try out the **Vector**, **Aligned**, **Automatic**, and **Auto Clamped** settings as well.

Selecting which channel to work on

Things look pretty straightforward right now. However, imagine that you have 20 objects all moving at the same time. It's good to be able to control which animation channels you see.

Time for action – adding keyframes in Graph Editor

3D View is not the only place in which you can add keyframes. Graph Editor actually gives you much better control while adding and manipulating keyframes. In 3D View, select the camera. The steps to add keyframes in Graph Editor are as follows:

1. Using the arrow keys, move the current frame indicator to frame 1.

2. With the cursor over Graph Editor, use *Ctrl* + MMB to zoom Graph Editor out so that you can see at least -10 to 10 on the vertical scale on the left side of Graph Editor. Look at the left side of Graph Editor. It's blank.

3. With the cursor over 3D View, press the *I* key and make a **Location** keyframe.

4. In Graph Editor, there are three colored lines, red, blue, and green, just like the 3D axis indicator. Since you have just made a **Location** keyframe, these are F-Curves for locations in X, Y, and Z. Use *Ctrl* + MMB to zoom in until you can see the red and blue lines clearly.

5. Use the arrow keys to move the current frame indicator to frame 21. Note that you can see orange dots at frame 1 on these lines. They are the keyframes you just made.

6. Click on the orange dot on the blue line with the RMB. This selects the Z Location F-Curve.

7. In the 3D View window, press *G* and *Z*, and use the mouse to move the camera down. Press the LMB to release the camera.

8. With the cursor over Graph Editor, press the *I* key. A menu pops up. Scroll down the menu to choose **Only Selected Channels** as shown in the following screenshot:

9. Click the LMB to create a keyframe. Notice that keyframes have only been created on the selected channel, in this case, the camera's Z location channel, and they are created on the frame where the current frame indicator is.

10. Move the current frame indicator to frame 11.

11. In the 3D View window, press *G* and *Y*, and use the mouse to move the camera. Press the LMB to release the camera.

12. Scroll the current frame indicator back and forth between frames 1 and 21.

What just happened?

You moved the current frame indicator and made a keyframe for the camera's location as you have done before. Then, you moved to frame number 21 and discovered that you could make a keyframe in Graph Editor. However, making keyframes in Graph Editor gives you different choices compared to when making them in 3D View.

In 3D View, if you make a location keyframe, it is automatically made in all three F-Curves: location X, location Y, and location Z. If you choose a single or several curves in Graph Editor and choose **Only Selected Channels**, a keyframe is made only on the active curve(s). If you choose **All Channels**, a keyframe is made on every channel of the selected objects.

Then, you moved to a different frame and moved the camera. However, when you scrubbed the current frame indicator in time, that movement disappeared because you never made a keyframe for it.

It's always good to think about whether you need a keyframe to control the motion, and only create a keyframe if you need it.

Time for action – controlling the F-Curves with the Channel Selection Panel

With several objects for Location, Rotation, and Scaling F-Curves, Graph Editor is likely to get cluttered. You need a way to choose which F-Curves you are seeing. It also helps if you can lock an F-Curve so you don't adjust it when you don't intend to use the Channel Selection Panel, as given in the following steps:

1. In the 3D View window, move the cursor over the Cube and select it with *Shift* + RMB. Note that in Graph Editor, you can see that there are now channels displayed on the left for both the Cube and the Camera, as shown in the following screenshot.

2. On the left side of Graph Editor, press the LMB on the triangle next to the **Location** channel of **Camera** so it points down, as shown in the following screenshot:

3. The **X Location**, **Y Location**, and **Z Location** channels for **Camera** appear.

4. Click several times on the eye symbol next to **Z Location** of **Camera** with the LMB and watch the F-Curve for **Z location** as you click. Scrub the current frame indicator back and forth and watch the 3D View window. Do it when you can see the eye and do it when you cannot see the eye.

5. Click on the eye icon of **CameraAction**, **Z Location** with the LMB so that you can see the F-Curve in Graph Editor. Then, press the LMB over the loudspeaker symbol to the right of it. Scrub the current frame indicator back and forth and watch the 3D View window. Do it when you can see the sound emitting out of the loudspeaker and do it when you cannot see the sound emitting out of the loudspeaker.

6. Press the LMB over the loudspeaker so that the F-Curve is not grayed out. Then, press the LMB over the lock symbol to the right of the loudspeaker so that the lock is locked. Look at the F-Curve. Note how the F-Curve is a dashed line.

7. Move the current frame indicator to frame 26. With the cursor over the Graph Editor window, press the *I* key to make a keyframe and choose **All Channels** from the menu.

8. Inspect the location of the *X*, *Y*, and *Z* axes of the F-Curves at frame 26.

What just happened?

On the left-hand side of Graph Editor, there is **Channel Selection Panel**, as shown in the previous screenshot. It lets you control which channels you can see and work on. The eye controls visibility of the F-Curve in Graph Editor. The loudspeaker controls whether the F-Curve is used in the scene. The lock controls whether you can make changes to the F-Curve. Finally, you saw what putting a keyframe on all channels does. In this case, it made keyframes on every channel for all objects except for the Z Location channel, which you had locked.

Time for action – controlling channel display with the header

Sometimes, you want to be able to see the channels for all the objects when working on one. There is a button that will let you display the F-Curves for all visible objects:

1. In 3D View, click on **Camera** with the RMB.

2. In the Graph Editor header, there is an arrow button that is highlighted in the next screenshot. Click on it with the LMB.

3. Do it several times and watch Graph Editor and the Channel Selection Panel.

What just happened?

The arrow button toggles between whether only the F-Curves related to the currently-selected objects are displayed or whether the F-Curves for all visible objects are displayed. The ghost next to it allows you to display the F-Curve of objects that are not displayed.

Copying, pasting, and deleting keyframes

In addition to creating and modifying the Bézier curve control points, you can move, copy, paste, and delete them.

Time for action – copying and pasting keyframes

Keyframes, just like about everything in Blender, can be copied and reused. In the following steps, you will learn to copy a keyframe and place it elsewhere in an F-Curve:

1. Make sure that the arrow button in the Graph Editor header is darkened, so that only the channels related to selected items are displayed.

2. Select the cube in 3D View.

3. In **Graph Editor**, click on the triangle next to the **CubeAction** channel to open it and repeat with the **Location** channel. Click on the word **Y Location** in the menu to select the F-Curve. Select the keyframe for the Y Location at frame 20 with the RMB.

4. Press *Ctrl* + *C* to copy the keyframe.

5. Move the current frame indicator to frame 14. Press *Ctrl* + *V* to paste the keyframe.

6. Press *X* to delete the keyframe you copied. Press *Ctrl* + *Z* to undo the deletion.

What just happened?

You discovered how to copy and paste keyframes in Graph Editor. The key combinations, *Ctrl + C* and *Ctrl + V*, are for the same commands on PC and Linux machines, and are used to copy and paste. Then, you deleted the keyframe. The key *X* is the key to press to delete things in Blender. Finally, you discovered that *Ctrl + Z* undoes the last command.

Keyframes for properties

You can move the lights and camera and make keyframes for them, just as you did for the cube. In fact, Blender allows you to set keyframes for almost every property. You sure didn't see them in the drop-down menu, so where are they?

Time for action – keyframes for lights

Next, we'll make keyframes for light color specifically, when in the Properties window using the following steps:

1. Move the current frame indicator to frame 1.

2. Select the lamp in 3D View with the RMB. Select the **Object data** button in the header of the Properties window. It's the button with the lamp, highlighted with the blue background in the following screenshot:

3. Down in the **Lamp** subpanel, there is the white Light Color box that you used in order to change the lamp color earlier. Move the cursor over that box and press *I* to insert a keyframe. There is no menu, but the white box gets a border. In Graph Editor, you now see a control curve for the lamp.

4. In Graph Editor, move the current frame indicator to frame 20.

5. In the **Lamp** subpanel of the Properties window, use the color wheel to make the light a different color. The white box changes color. When you like the color, with the cursor over the box, press the *I* key to insert another keyframe. You will see the new keyframe appear in Graph Editor as well.

6. Ensure that the 3D View window is set to **Texture mode**, so you can see the color change.

7. Press *Alt + A* to preview the animation.

What just happened?

You discovered that not all the keyframes are created in 3D View or Graph Editor. You also discovered that many properties can be animated. You learned how to set keyframes for the color of the light and how to observe it while previewing it by putting 3D View into the Texture mode.

 For your reference, the file 49090S_03_keyframes for lights.blend shows the keyframes created for changing the light color.

Have a go hero – adding more keyframes

You have done very well. You can control the cube, the camera, and the light. You can make keyframes, you can copy objects, and you can control the length of the animation by following these steps:

- Using these skills, create three animations, one of 30 frames, one of 60 frames, and one of 90 frames in length
- Use the camera composition guides to help you plan your shots

When you are satisfied with each animation, save the Blender file with a unique name. Take your time and have fun.

Pop quiz – working in time and space

Let's take a moment to review what you've learned about working in time and space:

Q1. How do you move 10 frames forward in the timeline?

1. By pressing the *left arrow*.
2. By pressing *Shift + up arrow*.
3. By pressing *Shift + right arrow*.

Q2. While the image of the dancer obeys the rule of thirds, what might be done to it to improve the visual flow?

1. Put something in the foreground to bridge the gap between the end of the bench and the dancer's foot.
2. Show the horizon in the background.
3. Make the wall in the background green.

Revisiting the commands

Here is a table with many of the commands you learned in this chapter.

 Remember, do not type the *comma* or + keys listed here The + key means to push the keys at the same time. The *comma* means to push the keys one after another.

Key	Function
Object Manipulation	
RMB	This selects an object.
Shift + RMB	This selects a new item while keeping previously-selected items selected.
G	This grabs an object to move it.
S	This scales an object.
R	This rotates an object.
G, X	This grabs an object and moves it along the *X* axis.
G, Y	This grabs an object and moves it along the *Y* axis.
G, Z	This grabs an object and moves it along the *Z* axis.
S, X	This scales an object along the *X* axis.
S, Y	This scales an object along the *Y* axis.
S, Z	This scales an object along the *Z* axis.
R, X	This rotates an object around the *X* axis.
R, Y	This rotates an object around the *Y* axis.
R, Z	This rotates an object around the *Z* axis.
G, X, 1	This moves an object one unit along the *X* axis.
S, Z, 2	This scales an object along the *Z* axis to twice its former size.
R, Y, 180	This rotates an object 180 degrees around the *Y* axis.
X	If tapped while moving, rotating, or scaling, this restricts the operation to the *X* axis.
Y	If tapped while moving, rotating or scaling, this restricts the operation to the *Y* axis.
Z	If tapped while moving, rotating, or scaling, this restricts the operation to the *Z* axis.
Shift + *A*	This opens up the **Add object** menu.
Shift + *D*	This duplicates an object.

Key	Function
Rendering	
F12	This renders the current frame.
F11	This displays the last rendered frame.
Ctrl + F12	This renders an entire animation.
Ctrl + F11	This displays a rendered animation.
Esc	When over a rendered image, this closes the image display.
Files	
Shift + Ctrl + S	This opens **File Editor** for saving files.
F2	This opens **File Editor** for saving files.
Graph Editor Commands	
MMB	In Graph Editor, this pans the view.
Mouse wheel	In Graph Editor, this zooms in the view.
Shift + MMB	In Graph Editor, this pans the view.
Ctrl + MMB	In Graph Editor, this zooms in the view.
Right arrow	This moves one frame forward.
Left arrow	This moves one frame back.
Up arrow	This goes to the next keyframe.
Down arrow	This goes to the previous keyframe.
Shift + right arrow	Go to the end of the animation.
Shift + left arrow	This goes to the beginning of the animation.
Shift + up arrow	This moves 10 frames forward.
Shift + down arrow	This moves 10 frames back.
I	This opens the keyframe menu or creates a keyframe if no menu is needed.
V	This sets the keyframe handle type.
V, F	Free handles are independent.
V, V	The Vector handles point to the previous or next handle.
V, A	The Aligned handles lie in a straight line and give a continuous curve.
V, U	This automatically chooses the length and direction to ensure the smoothest result.
V, C	This restores the default handle settings.
Shift + D	This creates a duplicate.
Ctrl + C	This copies the selected content.
Ctrl + V	This pastes the copied content.

Key	Function
X	This deletes objects, keyframes, and so on.
Delete	This deletes objects, keyframes, and so on.
General	
Ctrl + Z	This undoes the previous operation.
Home	This zooms to show you all the objects in Graph Editor or 3D View.
Ctrl + left arrow	This shifts to a different default screen layout.
Ctrl + right arrow	This shifts to a different default screen layout.
Ctrl + up arrow	This toggles the current window's full screen/regular screen.

A more complete list of keyboard shortcuts can be found at
`http://blendertips.com/hotkeys.html`.

Summary

Wow, that was quite a chapter. In this chapter, you studied how light affects the scene. You practiced setting the lights in different locations and changed the light colors as well as experimenting using multiple lights. You learned about using global and local coordinates to control objects and learned to move, rotate, and scale objects. We discussed composing an image within the camera. You learned about keyframes, made several animations, and learned about using Graph Editor to adjust F-Curves. You also learned how to save your work.

In the next chapter, you will start modeling objects. You will get under the hood and find out what a mesh object is made of. You'll be able to control every last point, edge, and face. You will discover Blender's menu of pre-made objects. You'll meet Suzanne, Blender's very lovely mascot, and have fun stretching and twisting her. You'll learn how to use grouping to make it easy to do what you want and then you'll be ready to start making your own models.

Let's go!

4

Modeling with Vertices, Edges, and Faces

Well, that was quite a chapter. You learned how to control the camera and other objects. You learned the basics of using lights. You created animations by making and adjusting key frames. You learned how to save and load files.

In 3D, every model from futuristic cities to prehistoric dinosaurs depends on what we will study in this chapter. The vertex, edge, and face provide the foundation for all the mesh models. You will be learning how to construct and manipulate them and fix problems pertaining to them. This will give you the background you need to build objects in Blender. You will use your knowledge of operating the 3D View window to make it easier.

You will learn the following topics:

◆ Using **Object Mode** and **Edit Mode** for modeling

◆ Selecting and manipulating vertices, edges, and faces

◆ Blender's basic geometric solids for modeling

◆ Blender's data structure that underlies the model

◆ Analyzing and fixing modeling problems

◆ You will be meeting Blender's official mascot Suzanne, and then stretching and bending her while learning to change centers of scaling, rotation, and motion

◆ Grouping vertices to make modeling easier

◆ Creating vertices, edges, and faces from scratch

Using Object Mode and Edit Mode

Until now, when you worked in the 3D View, you were in **Object Mode**. When you moved, rotated, or scaled an object, you did it to the entire object. This chapter is going to focus on **Edit Mode**. We will be working at the subobject level of a Mesh object, translating, scaling, and rotating vertices, edges, and faces. You may not build much in this chapter; the exercises will be quick practice with vertices, edges, and faces, but you will be training your hands in what to do so that your mind can focus on building in later chapters.

Time for action – going into Edit Mode

The difference between **Object Mode** and **Edit Mode** is a little confusing at first. You look at the cube, and it's hard to tell which mode you are in. However, don't worry; you'll quickly get the hang of it:

1. Open Blender. Zoom in to the cube so that it fills up most of the 3D View. You are going to look at it in more detail.

2. Now, press the **Tab** key. Press it several times. Note the changes in the 3D View and the changes in the 3D View header.

What just happened?

You opened Blender and zoomed in to the default cube. Then, you pressed the *Tab* key to go into **Edit Mode**. This mode lets you modify parts of an object; that is, the vertices, edges, and faces. You should have noticed three major differences: the cube is alternated between grey and orange, the header has changed, and the Tool Shelf has changed.

In **Object Mode**, there is an orange border around a gray cube. In **Edit Mode**, you see dots at every corner of the cube, and all the edges of the cube are highlighted in orange. I exaggerated the border and the dots in the next screenshot so that you can see the difference more easily.

In the header, the text on the Interaction Mode Selector button changes from **Object Mode** to **Edit Mode**, and some of the buttons change. The buttons in the Tool Shelf change as well. Observe the Interaction Mode Selector button highlighted on the left-hand side of following screenshot; it tells you which mode you are in:

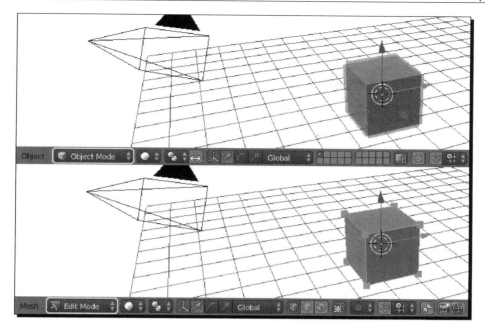

Investigating vertices, edges, and faces

Vertices, edges, and faces are the basic building blocks of the 3D mesh objects. A vertex is a point in space. The plural of vertex is vertices, pronounced (ver-tuh-sees), and is used when talking about two or more points in space. You describe a point by the X, Y, and Z coordinates, as we discussed in *Chapter 2, Getting Comfortable using the 3D View*. An edge is a line that connects two vertices. A face is the flat area or plane between three or more vertices, outlined by edges that connect those vertices. It is also referred to as a polygon. The following graphic shows them all together:

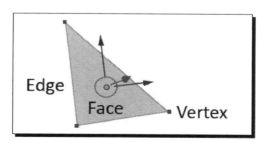

In the next illustration, I will show the default cube so that you can see how the vertices, edges, and faces are used in a solid object. For illustration purposes, I went into **User Preferences** and made the vertex and the dot in the center of the face display larger than normal.

On the left-hand side of the screenshot, you can see the vertices shown as small squares and a bordered round dot that represents the center of the cube. The cube has eight vertices. The four lighter ones are the selected vertices. The black ones have not been selected.

In the center screenshot, only the edges are shown, and there are 12 of them. Each of the lighter edges goes between two of the selected vertices.

The faces are shown in the screenshot on the right-hand side. The cube has a dot in the center of each face and in the edges of that face. There are six faces. Only the lighter face with a lighter edge and lighter face dot are associated with the selected vertices.

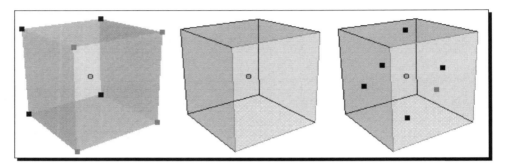

Time for action – choosing the best display mode

The **Viewport Shading** menu is in the header of the 3D View window. It lets you choose between the different methods of shading the objects displayed. While you may want the **Texture** display when you need to show an object's appearance, quite often, the **Solid** and **Wireframe** views will be best for modeling:

1. Use the *Tab* key to get into **Edit Mode** in 3D View, if you have not done so already. If you are unsure, look at the Interaction Mode Selector button on the header near the left-hand side of the 3D View window. It tells you what mode you are in.

2. Move the cursor to the **Viewport Shading** menu, as seen in the next screenshot. It's the same one that you used to change the mode to the **Texture** when you were playing with the lighting.

3. Now, select the **Wireframe** mode. What is different about the 3D View?

What just happened?

You changed the **Viewport Shading** in the 3D View to **Wireframe**. Now, the cube is transparent, and you can see all the vertices and edges. When you are working in **Edit Mode**, this is often the easiest way to work. The differences are deeper than just visual. In **Wireframe**, you can see and select all the vertices, edges, and faces. The **Solid** mode lets you choose all the vertices, edges, and faces, or just the ones facing you.

Time for action – working with vertices, edges, or faces

In the 3D View header, to the right of where you choose whether you are in the **Global** or the **Local** mode, there are three boxes, as shown in the following screenshot:

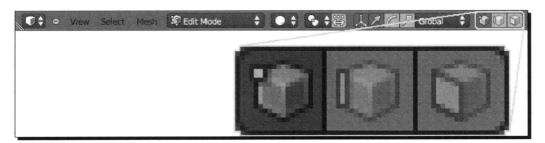

The left one has an orange dot next to a cube. It is the **Vertex Select Mode** button. The center one has an orange vertical line next to a cube. It is the **Edge Select Mode** button. The right one has an orange parallelogram on a cube. It is the **Face Select Mode** button. They control whether you are selecting vertices, edges, or faces. Let's learn more about these:

1. If you are not already in **Edit Mode**, put the cursor over the 3D View and press the *Tab* key.

2. Press the Vertex Select mode button on the 3D View header.

3. In the 3D View window, click on one of the vertices of the cube with the RMB. Press the G key and move the vertex. Press the RMB to release the vertex where it began.

4. Press the G key and move the vertex. Press the LMB to release the vertex where you have moved it.

5. In the 3D View header, click the LMB over the Edge Select Mode button—the box with the orange vertical line.

6. In the 3D View window, click on one of the edges of the cube with the RMB. Press the G key and move the edge. Press the RMB to release it where it began.

7. Press the G key and move the edge. Press the LMB to release the edge where you have moved it.

8. In the 3D View header, click on the LMB over the Face Select Mode box with the orange parallelogram.

9. In the 3D View window, click on the center of one of the faces of the cube with the RMB and move the face. Press the RMB to release it where it began.

10. Press the G key and move the face. Press the LMB to release the edge where you have moved it.

What just happened?

You selected a vertex and moved it; then, you selected an edge and moved it; finally, you selected a face and moved it. You discovered how to choose to work on vertices, edges, or faces. You found that you can use the same controls to move vertices, edges, and faces that you use to move whole objects. You discovered that ending the move with the RMB releases the movement back to where it was, and ending the move with the LMB releases the movement to where you moved it.

Have a go hero – rotating and scaling edges and faces

Now, try rotating and scaling the faces and the edges; you can use the same commands. Instead of G, press R to rotate or S to scale.

Selecting multiple vertices, edges, and faces

It's easy to select one vertex. However, when you are working with many vertices, you will want tools to make it easier to select them together rather than selecting them one by one. The following diagram illustrates some of the selection tools that you'll check out next; they are the border selection tool, the circle selection tool, and the lasso selection tool.

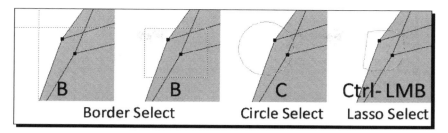

Selecting all vertices

Selecting all vertices is probably the method you'll use most frequently. It's often used to clear the current selection so that you can choose a different set of vertices.

Time for action – pressing A to select all

Press the *A* key to select all the vertices; this is one of the easiest selections available. It selects all the vertices or deselects them if they are all selected:

1. Click on the **Vertex Select Mode** button in the 3D View header button with the LMB so that you can work with vertices.

2. Press the *A* key several times.

What just happened?

Pressing the *A* key either selects or deselects everything. You worked with vertices, but this applies to edges, faces, and objects as well. If you look just above the 3D View window on the right-hand side, Blender shows you how many vertices you have selected as you do it.

Selecting vertices with Border Select

The Border Select mode allows you to select the vertices, edges or faces in a rectangular area. It's a very easy and flexible method.

Time for action – pressing B for border selection

The border selection works similar to the **Marquee** tool in Flash or Photoshop, stretching a border around the vertices you want to select:

1. Press the *A* key once or twice so that everything is deselected.

2. Move your cursor above and to the left of the cube.

3. Press the *B* key. Notice that the cursor has dotted lines coming out of it—crossed lines as on the left-hand side of the previous illustration.

4. Hold down the LMB while you drag the cursor down and to the right. Any vertices within the border will be selected when you release the LMB. Just select the vertices on the left-hand side.

5. Press the *B* key again. Make another selection, but start at the bottom-right and move to the top.

6. Now, press the *B* key, move over the vertices you have already selected, and press the MMB as you drag the cursor.

What just happened?

The *B* key starts border selection. You hold down the LMB while you drag the cursor. All the vertices within the border get selected. Each time you do the border selection, vertices are added to the vertices already selected. It doesn't matter which way you go as long as you create a box around the vertices that you want to select. If you hold down the MMB while doing this, you deselect the vertices.

Selecting with the Circle Selector

The Circle Selector is used like a paint brush; this makes it good for complex or detailed selection.

Time for action – pressing C for circle selection

The Circle Selector gives you a circular cursor to use in selecting vertices, edges, faces, and objects. The selection with the circle selector is cumulative. So, using it adds to the vertices that have been selected:

1. Press the *A* key once or twice to deselect everything.

2. Press the *C* key. Notice the circle around the cursor. Tap the LMB over the vertices to select them. You can also hold down the LMB and move the mouse to select more vertices.

3. To stop the selection, use either the RMB or the *Esc* key.

4. Press the *C* key again. Hold down the MMB while moving over the vertices selected earlier.

What just happened?

You learned about using the *C* key to initiate the selection of vertices by holding down the LMB and dragging the cursor, or clicking the LMB. You learned to press the RMB or the *Esc* key when you are done. Pressing the MMB instead of the LMB after pressing the *C* key deselects vertices.

Selecting with the Lasso Selection

The Lasso Selection is a versatile tool that lets you start anywhere you want and trace a path around the vertices, edges, or faces you want.

Time for action – pressing Ctrl + LMB for Lasso Selection

Unlike the other selection methods, the Lasso Selection tool is not started with a key command, but requires a combination of a key command and the mouse button.

1. If needed, press the *A* key once or twice so that everything is deselected.

2. Press the *Ctrl* button and hold it down. Hold the LMB down, and drag the cursor around the screen. When you have put the border around the vertices you want to select, release the LMB.

3. Press the *Ctrl* button and the *Shift* button and hold them down. Hold down the LMB while you drag the cursor over the vertices you have already selected.

What just happened?

You learned to do a lasso selection by holding down the *Ctrl* button and the LMB while moving the cursor around the vertices that you want to select. Pressing the *Shift* button and the *Ctrl* button while holding down the LMB deselects anything within the lasso area.

A warning about *Ctrl* + LMB

You need to be careful to not hold down the *Ctrl* key, and just click and release the LMB without moving the cursor. This will extrude the selected vertices. However, if it happens, you can easily undo it by pressing *Ctrl* + *Z*.

Creating Blender's primitives

You've done well in learning how to select vertices, edges, and faces. As a change up, let's start out by looking at the ready-made objects that Blender has, which you can use as a start for modeling. In *Chapter 2, Getting Comfortable using the 3D View*, I listed the different kinds of objects that Blender handles. Now, you will create them yourself. The premade ones are called Blender's primitives. You make them in the 3D View. They will be created wherever the 3D Cursor is.

Time for action – making a primitive object

Well, you're not really creating a primitive object; Blender will make it for you. However, now is a good time to look quickly at what is available:

1. Open Blender, or select **New** from the **File** menu. You already have our first primitive object, the cube.

2. Press *Ctrl* + MMB, and use the mouse to zoom in close to the cube so that you can see it well.

3. Press the *X* key to delete the default cube. A dialog box pops up asking you if it is **OK** to delete the object. Select **Delete**.

4. Now, you can make a new object. Press the *Shift* key and the *A* key at the same time. The **Add** menu will pop up, as seen in the following screenshot. There are quite a few kinds of objects that you can add, from **Mesh** and **Metaball** to **Text** or **Camera**.

5. So, to start making a mesh object, move the cursor over **Mesh**; then, move the cursor to the right and select **Plane** with the LMB.

6. You just made a plane. It can be a building block for a larger object, used as the ground or the surface of the ocean.

7. Look over in the lower half of the Tool Shelf. You will find additional controls to make primitive objects, as seen in the next screenshot. Right now, the subpanel title is **Add Plane**.

8. Put the cursor over the **Radius** button. Hold down the LMB and move the mouse to the left and right. Release the LMB to set the scaling.

9. Next, click on the **Align to View** checkbox a few times and see what happens.

10. Press the *X* key to delete the plane.

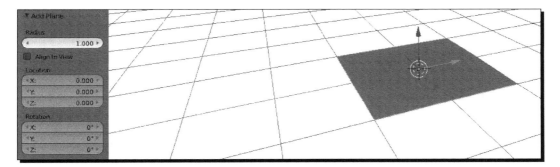

11. Press *Shift* + *A* to open the **Add** menu, and select **Circle**. Look at the Tool Shelf on the left-hand side of the 3D View; there are buttons that will let you add vertices, change the size of the circle, and select how to fill the interior of the circle.

12. Try them out. With the cursor over the **Vertices** button, press the LMB and hold it down while you move the mouse to the left or right. Move the number of vertices down to **3**. Change the **Radius**.

13. The **Fill Type** option allows you three choices on how to fill the circle, as shown in the following screenshot. You can have no fill, fill in the circle with a single ngon polygon, or fill the circle with a Triangle Fan around the center point, which looks like a pie, with a center vertex and triangles spreading out to the edges of the circle.

14. Change the number of vertices to about **11**. Set **Fill Type** to **Triangle Fan**. Press the *Tab* key to get into **Edit Mode** and see what the Triangle Fan looks like. Press the *Tab* key again to return to **Object Mode**.

15. Press the *X* key to delete the circle. If you want, make another circle and try out different settings. Delete them when you are done.

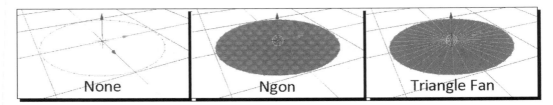

None   Ngon   Triangle Fan

16. Press *Shift + A* to open the **Add** menu, and select the **UV Sphere**. The UV Sphere looks similar to the longitude and latitude lines on a globe.

17. In the Tool Shelf, you will find buttons to change how many segments and rings the UV Sphere has and its size. Change the number of **Segments**. Change the number of **Rings**. See how they change the appearance.

18. Press the *X* key to delete the UV Sphere.

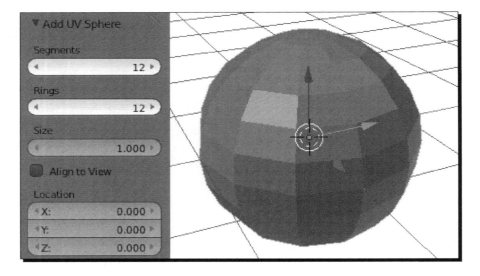

19. Press *Shift + A* to open the **Add** menu, and select **Icosphere**. The **Icosphere** is a mathematical solid as is the cube.

20. Put the cursor over the **Subdivisions** button in the **Add Icosphere** subpanel of the Tool Shelf, as shown in the next screenshot. Press the LMB and move the mouse to the left and right. Watch what happens to the smoothness of the Icosphere.

21. Set the subdivisions to **1**. With the subdivisions set to **1**, the Icosphere is an icosahedron. Play with the location and rotation settings in the **Add Icosphere** subpanel.

22. Press the *X* key to delete the Icosphere.

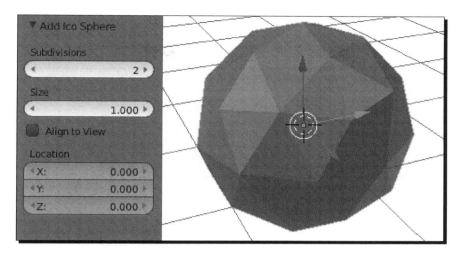

23. Press *Shift + A* to open the **Add** menu, and select **Cylinder**. In the **Add Cylinder** subpanel of the Tool Shelf, you can select how many vertices you want around the perimeter of the cylinder, as seen in the next screenshot. You can choose the radius of the cylinder, and you can choose the depth (or height) of the cylinder.

24. Clicking on the **Cap Fill Type** button allows you three ways to cap the end of the cylinder: **Nothing**, **Ngon**, or **Triangle Fan**. Pick your choice.

25. Press the *X* key to delete the Cylinder.

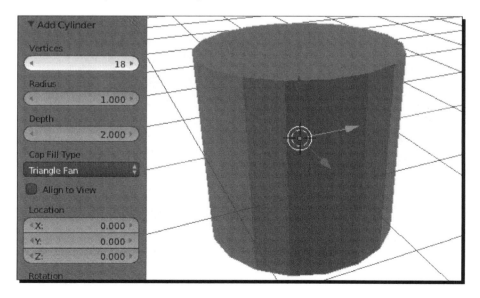

26. Press *Shift + A* to open the **Add** menu, and select the **Cone**, which is another mathematical solid. Like the cylinder's cap, the **Base Fill Type** can be **Nothing**, **Ngon**, or **Triangle Fan**.

27. Play with **Radius 1** and **Radius 2**, as shown in the following screenshot.

28. Press the *X* key to delete the **Cone**.

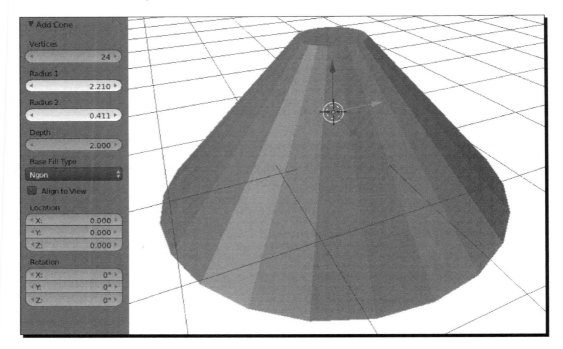

29. Press *Shift + A* to open the Add menu, and select the Grid.

30. Use the buttons in the **Add Grid** subpanel of the Tool Shelf to control the number of **X Subdivisions** and **Y Subdivisions** it has, as seen in the following screenshot:

31. Change the size of the grid.

32. Go into **Edit Mode** to see the grid; then, return to **Object Mode**.

33. Press the *X* key to delete the grid.

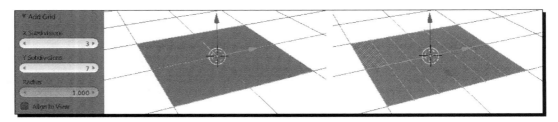

34. Press *Shift + A* to open the **Add** menu, and select **Torus**, which is also a mathematical solid. The **Torus** has more controls than other objects.

35. You can control the values of **Major Radius** and **Minor Radius** and the number of **Major Segments** and **Minor Segments**, as seen in the next screenshot.

36. Make one, play with the settings, and delete it. Do this several times.

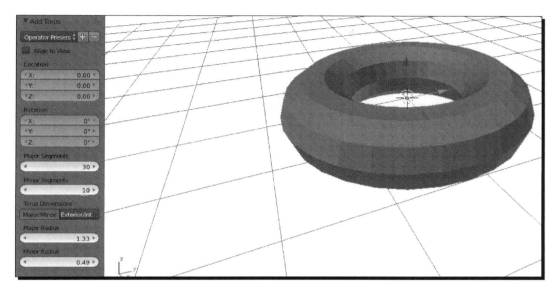

What just happened?

You started off by deleting the default cube and using the *Shift + A* command to open the **Add Object** menu. In this chapter, you are working with the mesh objects, so you went to the **Mesh** object submenu. You tested the list of geometric primitive objects that come with Blender, including cones, cylinders, spheres, and so on, to understand their properties and how to control them in the Tool Shelf.

Introducing Suzanne

You may have noticed that when testing the geometric primitives, we skipped over **Monkey**. The monkey is named Suzanne. The monkey really isn't a geometric solid like the other shapes, and it really isn't a monkey either. That's Blender for you.

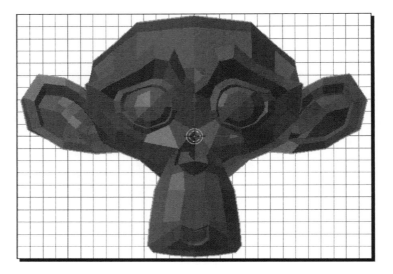

Suzanne is actually a chimpanzee, not a monkey, and she was named after Suzanne, the orangutan, in the movie *Jay and Silent Bob Strike Back*. She is often used to test materials, animation, lighting, and almost anything you want. In this way, she is Blender's version of the **Utah Teapot** that is seen in the next screenshot. The Teapot was made in 1975 at the University of Utah to test out things such as mapping, texturing, and shadows and has been seen in *Toy Story*, *The Simpsons*, and many other animations.

Blender users tend to be a bit irreverent, so there have been a number of variations of Suzanne, including aliens and the three-eyed monsters. Now, you are going to join this tradition and do some hideous and unnatural experiments on her.

 For your reference, the `4909_04_making—a primitive object.blend` file, which has been included in the download pack, has Suzanne all ready for her close up.

Making precise selections

While the tools you have studied are a great start, when you are making detailed models, picking vertices is a challenge sometimes. So, here are some more techniques to help you.

Time for action – making back-facing geometry accessible

When you are using the Texture or Solid shading, Blender lets you control whether you can see and modify vertices, edges, and faces that point away from you. This can be a help or a hindrance depending on what you are doing. So, it's good to be able to have it set the way you want it:

1. Open a new file. Delete the default cube. Press *Shift + A* and choose **Mesh**; then, choose **Monkey**.

2. Press *1* on the NumPad to get the front view. Press *5* on the NumPad to get the Ortho View. Press the *Tab* key to get into the Edit Mode.

3. Press *A* to deselect all the vertices.

4. Press *B* and move the LMB to use the border selection tool to select all of the vertices. Don't rotate the view; you just want to select them as seen from the front.

5. Press *X*. A menu pops up. Select **Vertices**.

6. Press the MMB and rotate the view so that you can see Suzanne from the side.

What just happened?

Good question. You did Border Select on all the vertices and then deleted the selected vertices. So, why is anything left? As you can see in the following screenshot, it turns out that when you view the scene in the Solid Mode, the faces, edges, and vertices that are facing away from you are hidden so that they can't be selected. Let's do something about it.

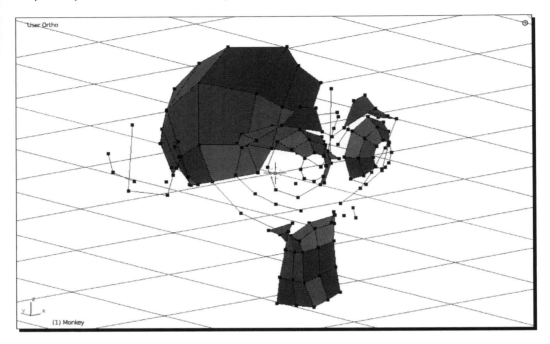

Time for action – controlling the visibility of vertices

As horrible as this looks, it's not bad. Only selecting the visible vertices gives you one way to control the vertices on which you are working. It's a tool, but it's no good unless you have control over it:

1. Press *Ctrl + Z* to undo deleting Suzanne's vertices.
2. Press *1* on the NumPad to select the **Front View**.
3. Now, look at the 3D View header. There is a button that controls the visibility of the hidden and back-facing vertices, edges, and faces. It is highlighted on the right-hand side of the following illustration. It is just to the right of the three buttons that control whether you are working on vertices, edges, or faces. Left-click on it so that it turns light grey. You'll notice that you can see more edges within Suzanne.

4. Press *A* to deselect all the vertices.

5. Use the Border Select tool to select all of the vertices.

6. Press *X*. A menu pops up. Select **Vertices**.

What just happened?

Okay, everything worked as expected. You selected all the vertices, deleted them, and everything disappeared. This time, the hidden, back-facing, and the front-facing vertices were selected. Controlling whether you display the hidden and back-facing vertices can save time when you make your selections. It's good to know about it, just in case you find yourself wondering why some vertices aren't getting selected. You can check to see if that button is set properly.

Time for action – selecting vertex by vertex

While most of the time, you can select the vertices you need with just a couple of border selections and a circle selection, sometimes, you need a particular vertex or vertices. The same rules apply to selecting individual objects, vertices, edges, or faces.

1. Press *Ctrl + Z* to undo deleting Suzanne's vertices.

2. Press *A* to deselect all the vertices.

3. Move the cursor over one of Suzanne's vertices. Click the RMB to select one vertex.

4. Now, hold down the *Shift* key and select the other vertices with the RMB.

5. While holding down the *Shift* key, select a vertex that you have already selected.

What just happened?

This is probably the simplest way to select vertices, edges, and faces. It is also the most laborious, as you can only choose one at a time. However, if you use the other methods to select the majority of vertices and finish off with the vertex-by-vertex selection, it gives you the best control. Holding down the *Shift* key lets you accumulate the selected vertices. Clicking on a vertex that is already selected, deselects it.

Time for action – fine-tuning the circle selection tool

You can adjust the size of the circle to tailor it to your needs. You can use the + and – signs on the NumPad. If you are emulating the NumPad, you will have to do this with a mouse wheel:

1. Press *C* to activate the Circle Selection tool.
2. Select some of the vertices.
3. Now, press the + (plus) sign on the NumPad several times.
4. Select more vertices.
5. Now, press the – (minus) sign on the NumPad several times.
6. Select more vertices.
7. If you have a mouse wheel, roll it forward and select more vertices. Roll it backwards and select more vertices.
8. Press the RMB or *Esc* key when you are finished selecting.

What just happened?

That's right. You can adjust the size of the circle selection tool. When you make it tiny, you can work in almost as detailed a way with the circle selection tool as with the vertex-by-vertex RMB selection method. As you can drag the mouse when using the circle selection tool, you can work faster. You can increase the size of the circle to enormous and select a lot of vertices at once, such as border selection, making it a very flexible tool. If you have a mouse wheel, you can use it to make the circle larger or smaller while selecting.

Time for action – hiding the vertices you aren't working on

One of the keys to working with a complex object is hiding the vertices that you don't want to work with. In this way, it makes things simpler visually, and you don't select the wrong vertices by accident:

1. Press *A* to deselect all the vertices.
2. Select some of the vertices using whatever commands you want.
3. Press *H*.
4. Select some more vertices.

5. Press *G*, then *X*, and move the cursor to move your selected vertices in *X*.

6. Press *Alt + H*. If nothing happens, open **Mesh** on the header, scroll up the menu to **Show Hide**, and then choose **Show Hidden**.

7. Press *Shift + H*.

8. Press *Alt + H*.

What just happened?

You selected some of the vertices. Then, you hid the selected vertices by pressing the *H* key. You selected more vertices and moved them. Then, you showed the hidden vertices with the *Alt + H* command.

Despite the fact that the vertices had been selected prior to being hidden, they were not affected when you selected other vertices and moved them. Blender does not move the hidden vertices.

Then, you pressed *Shift + H*, which hides all vertices that are not selected. When you pressed *Alt + H* again, they reappeared. Hidden vertices that are redisplayed with *Shift + H* are displayed as selected vertices. These display commands work not only with edges, faces, and vertices, but also with complete objects.

Time for action – modifying objects made by other people

As great a modeler as anyone can be, no one has the time to make all the models they use. So, sometimes, you will use a model that someone else has made. Sometimes, you will need to go in and make minor changes. This exercise will also give you a chance to practice your selection skills:

1. Press *Ctrl + Z* until Suzanne is whole again, and the vertices that you moved are back in their original places. Press *A* to deselect all the vertices.

2. Zoom in to Suzanne's right eye (on your left-hand side). Keep the front view.

3. Make sure that you can see the hidden vertices by toggling the visibility selection button on the 3D View header if necessary.

4. Select the vertices of Suzanne's right eye using the circle selection tool. Note that as seen in the following screenshot, the eyes extend beyond the sockets. Do not select the vertices from her skin. Remember that if you have to shift the view within the 3D View while you are selecting, press *Esc* or the RMB to stop the selection. Then, adjust the view with *Shift* + MMB or *Ctrl* + MMB, and press *C* again to continue selecting.

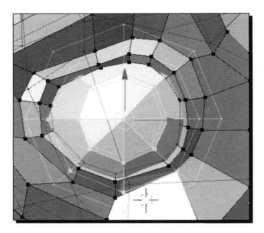

5. Be very careful which vertices you select. Suzanne's eyes have eight sides; it's like a spider web. Don't select any vertices that aren't part of this pattern.

6. Are you sure you got them all and only the vertices of the eye? Zoom in and look very closely.

7. Another way you can test this is by moving the vertices you have selected, and see if there are any surprises. Press *3* on the NumPad to get a side view. Press *G*, then *Y*, and drag the vertices with the cursor.

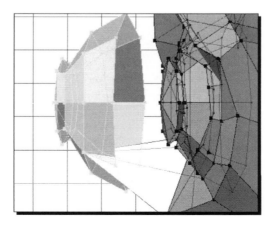

8. Press the RMB to return the vertices to their original position.

What just happened?

Well, you carefully selected just the vertices in the eight-sided pattern of the eye. Then, you zoomed in to double-check your work. When you tested this by moving the eye in *Y*, the eye should have moved without bringing any of the head with it. However, it appears as though some of the head has come too, as you can see in the previous screenshot. I have two theories about what is wrong. I think that it could be either that the faces of the eye and the skin share a vertex, or there are two vertices in exactly the same place. Now, you have to figure out exactly what the problem is and resolve it, which is what we will do next.

 For your reference, the `4909_04_practical modeling1.blend` file, which has been included in the download pack, has Suzanne with her eye vertices selected. `4909_04_practical modeling2.blend` has the eye pulled out with the skin attached.

Time for action – fixing Suzanne's eye

Small mistakes happen to the best of modelers. It's good to know how to look at the file and figure out what the problem is so that you can modify the object and fix the problem:

1. Save a copy of the Suzanne file using the **Save As** command in the **File** menu, but increment it, as you learned in the previous chapter, so that you have the original and a copy that is at the current state. This is just to preserve your work, in case you need to go back.

2. The first thing to check is whether there are two vertices in the same location.

3. Press *G*, then *Y*, and move the eye out in front of Suzanne's face again. While you move it, press the *Ctrl* button. Make sure that it is far enough from front of her face that the eye does not overlap her skin at all. This time, press the LMB to drop it there.

4. Press *A* to deselect all the vertices.

5. Using the vertex select, click the RMB several times on the vertex that seems to be in both the eye and head. Do you see changes similar to the ones shown in the following two screenshots?

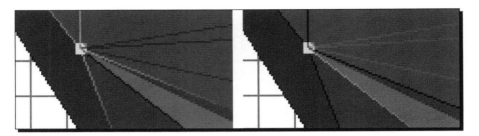

6. As you can see in the preceding screenshot, you seem to have selected a single vertex, but the highlighted edges extending from it seem to go in two different patterns. One selects edges for the eye as on the left-hand side, and one selects edges for the skin as on the right-hand side. So, it appears that there are two vertices in the same place.

7. Keep selecting that vertex till you have selected the one that connects to edges on the skin, as seen in the previous right-hand side screenshot.

8. Next, rotate your view so that you are looking up at Suzanne from the lower right, as shown in the following screenshot:

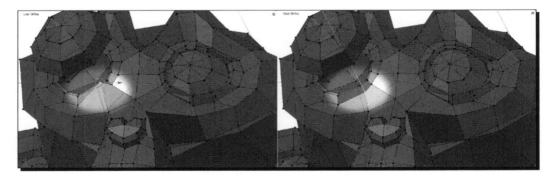

9. Press *G*, then *Y*, and move the vertex towards the face until the rim around her eye is pretty much even, as seen on the right-hand side of the previous screenshot.

10. Click on the LMB to drop the vertex in that location.

11. Press *3* on the NumPad to switch to the side view again.

12. Press *A* to deselect all the vertices. Select all the vertices of the eye. Press *G* and then *Y* to move them. Press the *Shift + Ctrl* buttons while you are moving them. Move them till they are even with the vertices of the other eye.

13. Click on the LMB to drop them in place. You may want to zoom in for the final placement.

What just happened?

Well, you found that even the pros goof up once in a while, so a mistake is no big deal. You learned how to analyze a problem with a model and make corrections to it. Well done!

You wisely saved a backup copy of your file, just in case things went wrong during the repair. Next, you moved the eye along the *Y* axis to investigate why the skin and the eye were stuck together. As you pressed the *Ctrl* key while you moved the eye, it moved in increments of 0.01, so moving it back into place later on was easy.

By clicking on the vertex a number of times and noting that the highlighted edges that radiate out changed, you discovered that there were two vertices in the same place. If there had only been one vertex, which was used by both the eye and skin, then the edges would not have changed in appearance as you continued to click.

Knowing what was wrong, you were then able to select the skin's vertex and move it back into place. While you were doing this, you discovered some more ways to control the motion of the cube with smooth increments, while you move it.

Finally, you moved the eye back in place by aligning it with the other eye. Since you used the *Shift + Ctrl* key when moving the eye, it fell back right into its original place. If you have any other irregularities that happen during modeling, I know that you'll figure out how to fix them.

For your reference, the 4909_04_untangling suzannes eye1.blend file, which has been included in the download pack, has Suzanne with her eye vertex selected. The 4909_04_untangling suzannes eye2.blend file has Suzanne with the skin vertex selected. The 4909_04_untangling suzannes eye3.blend file has the skin vertex being moved back into place.

Organizing your work by grouping

Well, you've separated the eye from that one vertex. However, the scary thing is that if you need to work on the eye again, you'll probably have to separate them again. Wouldn't it be nice if you didn't have to go through the work of selecting them again? There is a way to preserve your selections; it's called **grouping**.

Time for action – grouping vertices

Grouping is pretty simple. Once you have selected the vertices, you go to the Properties window, create a group, and assign the vertices to the group:

1. Select the Object Data button on the Properties window header. It's outlined and has a triangle with vertices and edges, as shown in the following screenshot.

2. Use the LMB to click on the plus sign in the **Vertex Groups** subpanel. This creates a vertex group named **Group**.

3. Click the LMB over the word **Group** in the button, and when the background turns black, change the word **Group** to **Eye - R** and press *Enter*.

4. Now, left-click on **Assign** to assign the vertices you selected in the previous *Time for Action* section, to the **Eye - R** group.

5. Save the file with a unique name.

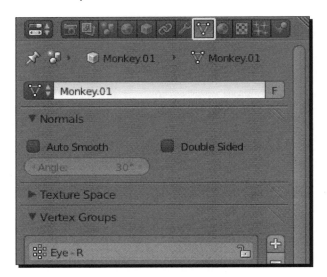

What just happened?

You opened up the **Object Data** panel in the Properties window and created a group to save the information about which vertices are in Suzanne's eye. By saving the group, you won't have to select it again while modeling. For this reason alone, it's good to make grouping a routine part of your modeling methods.

However, grouping also provides you with other benefits. It organizes your object for use in the future, when you may have forgotten completely about what happened while you were making the object. It makes it easier for others who may also be using the object that you make. This is very handy if you are distributing your models for other gamers, for an animating team for a 48-hour film project competition, or selling them on the web.

One of the best benefits of grouping comes when you are making an object for animation. Take a moment, and raise your eyebrows a couple of times. Then, think about animating Suzanne's eyebrows. A vertex can be in more than one group, and you can specify how strongly a vertex is weighted towards a particular group. If you had some vertices near Suzanne's eye, they could be part of an eyelid group and strongly weighted, and they could also be part of the eyebrow group, but slightly weighted. If you raised Suzanne's eyebrow group, those vertices will move a little, just as your eyelids move a little when you raise your eyebrows.

 For your reference, the `4909_04_grouping vertices.blend` file, which has been included in the download pack, has Suzanne's right eye grouped.

Have a go hero – selecting the other eye

As it happens, the other eye has the same problem. One of the vertices for the eye is in the same place as one of the vertices for the skin. Figure out a way to select the eye, without selecting the vertex for the skin. There are at least two ways to do it. Then, make a group for it named `Eye - L`. Save your file; you are going to use it later in the chapter.

Time for action – scaling and rotating groups of vertices

Many times, you want to make part of an object taller or wider and then turn it in a different way. Blender provides some visual manipulator tools that you may enjoy using:

1. Press *1* on the NumPad so that you are looking at Suzanne from the front. Press *A* to deselect all the vertices.

2. Select most of her ears with the Border Select tool as seen here. Go close to her head but not into it. Make sure that the selections are identical on both sides.

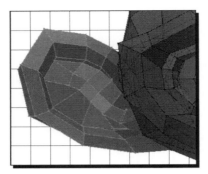

3. Create a group called `Ears`, and assign the vertices to it. Save the file with a unique name.

4. You have used the 3D Manipulator for moving. Now, let's use it for scaling.

5. When in **Edit Mode**, there are three buttons on the 3D View header, as shown here: an arrow, a curve, and a square with a line along the diagonal. The arrow is the translation manipulator, the curve is the rotation manipulator, and the square with the diagonal is the scaling manipulator. In 3D, translation refers to moving something from one place to another.

6. To the left of these three buttons is one with three lines of red, blue, and green. It controls whether the 3D Manipulator is visible or not.

7. Select the scaling manipulator button (square with a diagonal) on the header.

8. Press *6* on the NumPad three times to rotate the view of Suzanne about 45 degrees so that you can see her side. Press *8* on the NumPad to rotate the view of Suzanne 15 degrees so that you can see her from a higher angle.

9. Put the cursor over the green manipulator handle, press and hold the LMB, and use the mouse to make the ears thinner. If you don't like what has happened, you can release the scaling by pressing either the *Esc* key or the RMB, while holding the LMB down. When you like the results, release the LMB key.

10. Use the blue handle of the 3D Manipulator to scale her ears so that they look f like bat ears, as shown in the following screenshot.

11. Use the red handle to make the ears wider.

12. Now, select the rotation manipulator button on the header.

13. Play with the blue, green, and red handles to rotate Suzanne's ears.

What just happened?

We are being cruel to poor old Suzanne, heh heh heh! You used the blue, green, and red handles of 3D Manipulator to scale her ears into grotesque shapes and then used the 3D manipulator to rotate them into improbable positions.

> For your reference, the 4909_04_scaling and rotating groups. blend file, which has been included in the download pack, has Suzanne's ears extended like a bat.

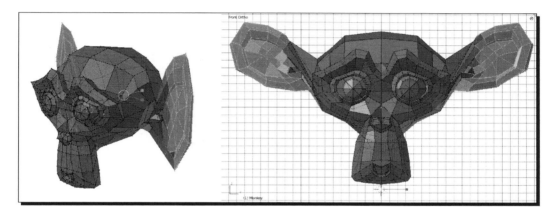

Controlling the center of scaling and rotation

We're finally having fun with Blender, but it's good to be able to control your scaling more precisely.

Time for action – controlling the center of scaling

The **3D Cursor** is a very handy tool. You can use it to set a temporary center for motion, rotation, scaling, and use it to define the center of an object in whatever location you want. Now, you are going to use it as a center for scaling:

1. Load the file of Suzanne that you saved after grouping her eyes. Make sure that you are looking at Suzanne from the front view.

2. Deselect all the vertices.

3. Use the circle selection or the Lasso tool to select the vertices in Suzanne's ears.

4. When you have Suzanne's ears selected, use the LMB to click on the second button to the left of the mode selector in the 3D View header, as seen in the following screenshot. A **Pivot Point** menu pops up. It lists the ways you can set the center of scaling and rotation. Select 3D Cursor with the LMB.

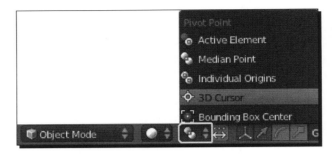

5. First, start by making sure that the 3D Cursor is in the center of the Blender world.

6. Press *Shift + S* to bring up the **Snap** menu, as shown in the following screenshot. Select **Cursor to Center**.

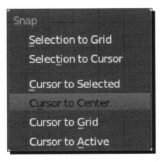

7. In our previous Time for Action section, you were using the 3D Manipulators. We don't need them now, so click on the button to the left of the translation Manipulator button, the one with the red, green, and blue lines, and lighten it so that you do not see a 3D Manipulator in the 3D View window.

8. Now, click on the LMB between Suzanne's eyes to put the 3D Cursor there.

9. Move your cursor a little distance away from the 3D Cursor for better control. Press the *S* key and move the mouse. Notice how the ears scale. Press the *Esc* key or the RMB to release the ears without moving them permanently.

10. Use the LMB to click on the right of Suzanne's ears. Once again, move your cursor away from the 3D Cursor.

11. Press the *S* key and move the mouse. Press the *Esc* key or the RMB to release the ears without moving them permanently.

12. Use the LMB to click below Suzanne's chin. Once again, move your cursor away from the 3D Cursor.

13. Press the *S* key and move the mouse. Notice how the ears scale. Press the LMB to accept the change, or press the *Esc* key or the RMB to release the ears without moving them permanently.

14. Use the LMB to click between Suzanne's eyes.

15. Press the *R* key and move the mouse. Notice how the ears rotate. Press the LMB to accept the change, or press the *Esc* key or the RMB to release the ears without moving them permanently.

16. Now, use the LMB to click on Suzanne's nose.

17. Press the *R* key, then *X*, and use the mouse to rotate Suzanne's ears. While you do this, also experiment with pressing the *Ctrl* button, the *Shift* button, and both at the same time. You saw how they affected your moving Suzanne's eye and how they affected twisting Suzanne's ears.

18. Press the LMB to accept the change, or press the *Esc* key or the RMB to release the ears without moving them permanently. Doesn't Suzanne look cute with puppy ears, as shown in the following screenshot?

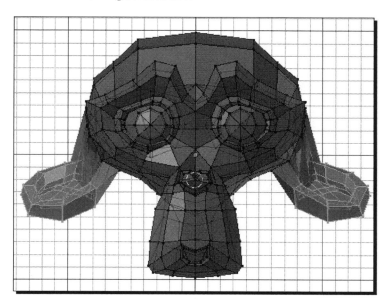

19. Press the *Tab* key to get back into **Object Mode**.

What just happened?

Well, Suzanne is quite the clown. By moving the center, you can get quite a bit of control on how things scale and rotate. You also discovered that the *Ctrl* and *Shift* buttons work on rotations as well as translation.

The point of this exercise has been to show you the power of using the 3D Cursor in modeling vertices, edges, and faces, and give you a little more experience in modeling in the Edit Mode. Choosing the center of scaling or rotation properly makes modeling easier. A simple example would be a support pier for a bridge over a valley. You could tuck your basic pier object right under the bridge and put the 3D Cursor at the top of the pier. Go into Edit Mode, choose the bottom vertices of the pier, and scale them in z until they hit the valley floor. You won't have to measure the height of the pier. Another example would be if you were making the cylinder of a gun with six chambers, you could model a section that has only one chamber. Then, you duplicate that section and rotate the copy to make an additional chamber. Then, you repeat the duplication and rotation four more times. It's easy if you choose the proper center of rotation and press the *Ctrl* button while rotating it to control the rotation of each copy precisely.

For your reference, the `4909_04_controlling center of scaling.blend` file, which has been included in the download pack, has Suzanne's ears scaled up with the center of scaling at her chin.

Have a go hero – how bizarre can you make Suzanne?

Using the location, scaling, and rotation controls on vertices, edges, and faces, see what you can do for Suzanne or to Suzanne, as the case may be.

Understanding what lies behind vertices, edges, and faces

You are progressing well. You've learned to navigate in the Blender world. You've learned to translate, rotate, and scale objects in the Blender world. You've learned to open the object and translate, rotate, and scale vertices, edges, and faces. You're really digging into Blender.

It's good to understand how Blender sees your scene as well. The following graphic illustrates how the information is arranged in Blender. What you see are little boxes connected together, and this is how Blender is organized:

1. So, the Scene is just a little box of information called a data block with a few bits of information about what objects it is connected to. It has a link to each object.

2. The object is just a box called a data block. It has little information about the faces, edges, vertices, and other things that it is connected and linked to.

3. As you have probably guessed, each face is a data block with a little information about, say, which texture it is connected to and a link to the data block of that texture. The process goes on.

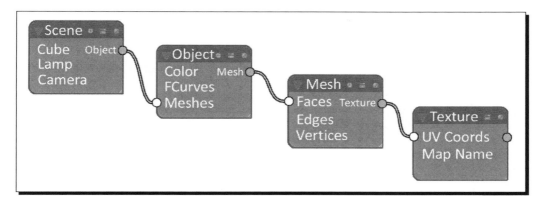

This structure has important benefits. You can make a texture once, and any mesh that needs that texture uses it. When you make a change to the texture, all the mesh objects that use that texture show that change. If you move or rotate an object, it tells all the faces what is happening. You don't have to keep track of it.

Keep this structure in mind as you study Blender. It will help you understand Blender, and toward the end of the book, in the Node Editor, you will meet some tools that look much like the connections here.

Building vertices, edges, and faces from scratch

We've seen how you can manipulate the number of vertices, edges, and faces in an object by setting mathematical values. However, sometimes to get what you want, you need to make them yourself, and that's what this section is about. For flexibility and power, nothing can touch this technique, and it introduces you to the methods used to modify and refine your objects.

Time for action – making faces out of vertices and edges

The most fundamental unit of a mesh object is the vertex. So, now, you are going to make a vertex, and when you make a second one, the two will be connected by an edge. Then, you continue until you have enough vertices for a face:

1. Load a new file.

2. Press 7 on the NumPad to get the **Top View**. Press 5 on the NumPad to get the Ortho View.

3. Press the *Tab* key to get into Edit Mode.

4. Click the 3D Manipulator button in the 3D View header, as highlighted in the following screenshot, so that the 3D Manipulator icon does not show in the 3D View.

5. Press *A* two times to make sure that all vertices are selected. Press *X*, and then select **Vertices** from the popup menu to delete them.

6. Look in the lower-left corner of the 3D View window. It still shows that the active object is the cube. Only the data block of the cube remains. It has no connections to any vertices, edges, or faces. You deleted them. However, to delete the cube itself, you would still need to press *X* while in **Object Mode**. Please don't do that.

7. Hold down the *Ctrl* key, and click the LMB somewhere to the left and above the 3D Cursor to create a vertex.

8. Press *Ctrl* + LMB three more times in different locations moving in a clockwise direction around the 3D Cursor.

9. Use *Shift* + RMB to select the first vertex in addition to the last vertex. Press *F* to join them.

10. Use *Shift* + RMB to select the lower-right vertex in addition to the first and last vertices. Press *F* to make a face, as shown on the left-hand side of the following illustration.

11. Press *Shift* + RMB again to deselect the lower-left vertex, as seen in the center of the screenshot. This will deselect it. Next, select the upper-right vertex. Press *F* to make the other face, as seen on the right-hand side of the next screenshot:

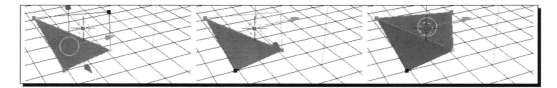

What just happened?

You started with a fresh file, went into **Edit Mode**, and immediately deleted all of the vertices, leaving only the data block as a placeholder. This is because Blender needs an object to toggle between **Edit Mode** and **Object Mode**. You made four vertices and edges between them using *Ctrl* + LMB. You controlled the position of the vertices within the top view. As you cannot judge the depth from the top view, Blender put them all on the same z depth as the 3D Cursor.

Then, you joined the first and last vertices together, by selecting them and pressing the *F* key. Finally, you made a face by selecting three vertices and pressing *F*. The *F* key makes both edges and faces, depending on how many vertices you are connecting. When it does make a face, the front of the face it made faces you, and the back of the face faces away from you.

Finally, you saved yourself a little selecting work by unselecting one vertex, selecting another one, and then pressing *F*. This was quicker than selecting all the vertices every time you want to make a face.

> For your reference, the `4909_04_making faces.blend` file, which has been included in the download pack, has the vertices and one face created.

Time for action – making a face from an edge

This short exercise will introduce you to what some 3D modelers have called the most powerful tool available to modelers, the humble extrusion.

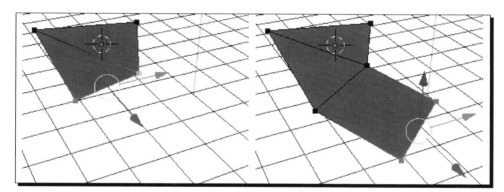

1. Select two vertices along the bottom side of the shape you made, as shown on the left-hand side of the preceding screenshot.

2. Tap the *E* key, and then move the mouse to create another face as shown on the right-hand side of the preceding screenshot.

What just happened?

We discovered that if you press the *E* key when you have two vertices selected in **Edit Mode**, then Blender will create a new face. This is called an **extrusion**. You built a face, and extruded another from it. This is often how modelers create objects, such as automobiles, which often have fluid lines and no definite edges for much of their surface. Making faces and extruding them, you can make just about anything.

 For your reference, the 4909_04_making a face from an edge.blend file, which has been included in the download pack, has the face being created from an edge.

Pop quiz – making selections

Q1. Which key do you press to do Border Select?

1. *A*
2. *B*
3. *C*

Q2. How do you deselect with the circle selection tool?

1. *C* + MMB
2. *C* + RMB
3. *C* + LMB

Q3. Which of these methods could you have used to solve the last *Have a go hero* section, and select all the vertices of Suzanne's eye without selecting that skin vertex? Experiment on Suzanne to test what works.

1. Use the Circle select mode with the circle made as small as possible
2. Select the edges instead of the vertices, then change to the vertex selection mode
3. Select the faces instead of the vertices, then change to the vertex selection mode

The key-function table

This table has functions you have learned and some you may find useful.

Key	Function
Mode	
Tab	Pressing the *Tab* key toggles between the Edit mode and the Object mode
Ctrl + Tab	When you are in **Edit Mode**, this opens the **Mesh Select Mode** menu, allowing you to choose to work in vertex, edge, or face mode
Selection	
A	Select/deselect all
B	Border select, use LMB while selecting
B	Border deselect, use MMB while deselecting
C	Circle select, use LMB while selecting
C	Circle deselect, use MMB while deselecting
Ctrl + LMB	Lasso select
Ctrl + Shift + LMB	Lasso deselect
+	Numpad plus sign used while doing circle select increases the size of the circle
-	NumPad minus sign used while doing circle select decreases the size of the circle
H	Hides selected vertices
Alt + H	Redisplays hidden vertices as selected vertices
Shift + H	Hides unselected vertices
L	Selects linked vertices
Transformation controls	
Shift	When used with the G, R, or S keys, it limits the transformation to small increments
Shift + Ctrl	When used with the G key, it limits the movement to increments of 0.01
Shift + Ctrl	When used with the R key, it limits the rotation to steps of 1 degree.
Shift + Ctrl	When used with the S key, it limits the scaling to steps of 0.01
Ctrl	When used with the G key, it limits the motion to steps of 0.1
Ctrl	When used with the R key, it limits the rotation to steps of 5 degrees
Ctrl	When used with the S key, it limits the scaling to steps of 0.1
Shift	Press the S key, then *Shift* + X, and you can scale on both the Y and Z axes at the same time

Key	Function
Shift	Press the *S* key, then *Shift* + *Y*, and you can scale on both the *X* and *Z* axes at the same time
Shift	Press the *S* key, then *Shift* + *Z*, and you can scale on both the *X* and *Y* axes at the same time
Shift	Choosing manipulators on the 3D View edit mode header allows you to display more than one manipulator in the 3D View at one time
Shift	Choosing vertex, edge, and face selection on the 3D View edit mode header allows you to select several edit modes at once, that is, faces and vertices.
Shift + *S*	Brings up the **Snap** menu
Faces	
F	When two vertices are selected, it creates an edge, and when more than two vertices are selected, it creates a face.
E	Extrudes a face from two vertices or an edge, and it can be used on multiple edges as well.
I	Insets a new face into the center of a selected face.

Summary

That was good. You learned a lot about the basic skills needed to create and work with vertices, edges, and faces. You will be using these skills in the following chapters to build quite a variety of objects. You learned the difference between the **Object Mode** and **Edit Mode** and learned to select and manipulate multiple vertices, edges, and faces. You were introduced to Blender's geometric primitives.

You learned a lot about the basic skills needed to create and work with vertices, edges, and faces. You were introduced to Blender's mascot—Suzanne. You got a bit of experience in troubleshooting a model, seeing how much difference changing the center of rotation and scaling can make in the model.

You learned how to group vertices, edges, and faces. You discovered the basic structure of Blender and learned how to make vertices, edges, and faces from scratch.

Congratulations!

You have covered the basics. You understand the tools, and it's time to get started with the application of what you have learned to a real project. It seems that as the world is two-thirds ocean and everyone has a river, lake, or sea near them, a nautical theme would be appropriate. So, in the next chapter, you'll begin by building yourself a seaworthy little boat, launch it, and sail it through various kinds of light.

Let's go mateys.

5

Building a Simple Boat

It's time to get out your hammers, saws, and tape measures, and start building something. In Chapter 4, Modeling with Vertices, Edges, and Faces, you focused on the basics of building objects: how to adjust vertices, edges, and faces; how to create edges and faces from vertices; different ways to select vertices, edges, and faces; and how to group vertices so that you can organize your work.

In this chapter, you're going to put your knowledge of building objects to practical use, as well as your knowledge of using the 3D View to build a boat. It's a simple but good-looking and water-tight craft that has three seats, as shown in the next screenshot.

You will learn about the following topics:

◆ Using box modeling to convert a cube into a boat

◆ Employing box modeling's power methods, extrusion, and subdividing edges

◆ Joining objects together into a single object

◆ Adding materials to an object

◆ Using a texture for greater detail

Turning a cube into a boat with box modeling

You are going to turn the default Blender cube into an attractive boat, similar to the one shown in the following screenshot. First, you should know a little bit about boats. The front is called the **bow**, and is pronounced the same as bowing to the Queen. The rear is called the **stern** or the **aft**. The main body of the boat is the hull, and the top of the hull is the **gunwale**, pronounced *gunnel*.

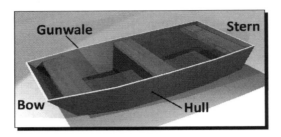

You will be using a technique called **box modeling** to make the boat. Box modeling is a very standard method of modeling. As you might expect from the name, you start out with a box and sculpt it like a piece of clay to make whatever you want. There are three methods that you will use in most of the instances for box modeling: **extrusion**, **subdividing edges**, and **moving**, or **translating vertices**, **edges**, and **faces**.

Using extrusion, the most powerful tool for box modeling

Extrusion is similar to turning dough into noodles, by pushing them through a die. It's the same as the way you made a face out of an edge in *Chapter 4, Modeling with Vertices, Edges, and Faces*. Then, Blender pushed out the edge and connected it to the old edge with a face. While extruding a face, the face gets pushed out and gets connected to the old edges by new faces.

Time for action – extruding to make the inside of the hull

The first step here is to create an inside for the hull. You will extrude the face without moving it, and shrink it a bit. This will create the basis for the gunwale:

1. Create a new file and zoom into the default cube.

2. Select **Wireframe** from the **Viewport Shading** menu on the header, as discussed in *Chapter 4, Modeling with Vertices, Edges, and Faces*.

3. Press the *Tab* key to go to **Edit Mode**.

4. Choose **Face Selection** mode from the header. It is the orange parallelogram, as seen in *Chapter 4, Modeling with Vertices, Edges, and Faces.*

5. Select the top face with the RMB.

6. Press the *E* key to extrude the face, then immediately press *Enter*.

7. Move the mouse away from the cube. Press the *S* key to scale the face with the mouse. While you are scaling it, press *Shift + Ctrl*, and scale it to 0.9. Watch the scaling readout in the 3D View header.

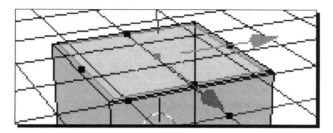

8. Press the NumPad *1* key to change to the Front view and press the *5* key on the NumPad to change to the Ortho view. Move the cursor to a place a little above the top of the cube.

9. Press *E*, and Blender will create a new face and let you now move it up or down. Move it down. When you are close to the bottom, press the *Ctrl + Shift* buttons, and move it down until the readout on the 3D View header is **1.9**. Click the LMB to release the face. It will look like the following screenshot:

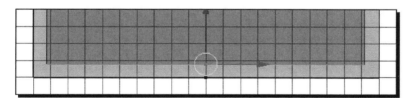

What just happened?

You just created a simple hull for your boat. It's going to look better, but at least you got the thickness of the hull established. Pressing the *E* key extrudes the face, making a new face and sides that connect the new face with the edges used by the old face. You pressed *Enter* immediately after the *E* key the first time, so that the new face wouldn't get moved. Then, you scaled it down a little to establish the thickness of the hull. Next, you extruded the face again. As you watched the readout, did you notice that it said **D: -1.900 (1.900) normal**? When you extrude a face, Blender is automatically set up to move the face along its normal, so that you can move it in or out, and keep it parallel with the original location.

For your reference, the 4909_05_making the hull1.blend file, which has been included in the download pack, has the first extrusion. The 4909_05_making the hull2.blend file has the extrusion moved down. The 4909_05_making the hull3.blend file has the bottom and sides evened out.

Using normals in 3D modeling

What is a normal? The normal is an unseen ray that is perpendicular to a face. This is illustrated in the following image by the red line:

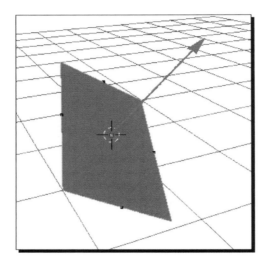

Blender has many uses for the normal:

◆ It lets Blender extrude a face and keep the extruded face in the same orientation as the face it was extruded from

◆ This also keeps the sides straight and tells Blender in which direction a face is pointing

◆ Blender can also use the normal to calculate how much light a particular face receives from a given lamp, and in which direction lights are pointed

 Modeling tip

If you create a 3D model and it seems perfect except that there is this unexplained hole where a face should have been, you may have a normal that faces backwards. To help you, Blender can display the normals for you.

Time for action – displaying normals

Displaying the normal does not affect the model, but sometimes it can help you in your modeling to see which way your faces are pointing:

1. Press *Ctrl* + MMB and use the mouse to zoom out so that you can see the whole cube.

2. In the 3D View, press *N* to get the Properties Panel.

3. Scroll down in the Properties Panel until you get to the **Mesh Display** subpanel.

4. Go down to where it says **Normals**.

5. There are two buttons like the edge select and face select buttons in the 3D View header. Click on the button with a cube and an orange rhomboid, as outlined in the next screenshot, the **Face Select** button, to choose selecting the normals of the faces.

6. Beside the **Face Select** button, there is a place where you can adjust the displayed size of the normal, as shown in the following screenshot. The displayed normals are the blue lines. Set **Normals Size** to 0.8. In the following image, I used the cube as it was just before you made the last extrusion so that it displays the normals a little better.

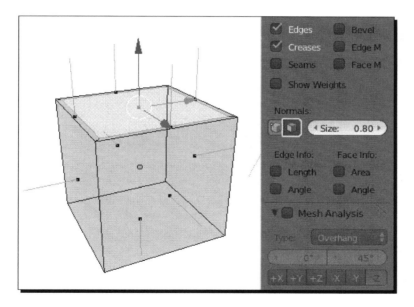

7. Press the MMB, use the mouse to rotate your view of the cube, and look at the normals.

8. Click on the **Face Select** button in the **Mesh Display** subpanel again to turn off the normals display.

What just happened?

To see the normals, you opened up the Properties Panel and instructed Blender to display them. They are displayed as little blue lines, and you can create them in whatever size that works best for you. Normals, themselves, have no length, just a direction. So, changing this setting does not affect the model. It's there for your use when you need to analyze the problems with the appearance of your model. Once you saw them, you turned them off.

For your reference, the `4909_05_displaying normals.blend` file has been included in the download pack. It has the cube with the first extrusion, and the normal display turned on.

Planning what you are going to make

It always helps to have an idea in mind of what you want to build. You don't have to get out caliper micrometers and measure every last little detail of something you want to model, but you should at least have some pictures as reference, or an idea of the actual dimensions of the object that you are trying to model. There are many ways to get these dimensions, and we are going to use several of these as we build our boats.

Choosing which units to model in

I went on the Internet and found the dimensions of a small jon boat for fishing. You are not going to copy it exactly, but knowing what size it should be will make the proportions that you choose more convincing. As it happened, it was an American boat, and the size was given in feet and inches.

Blender supports three kinds of units for measuring distance: **Blender** units, **Metric** units, and **Imperial** units. Blender units are not tied to any specific measurement in the real world as Metric and Imperial units are. To change the units of measurement, go to the Properties window, to the right of the 3D View window, as shown in the following image, and choose the **Scene** button. It shows a light, a sphere, and a cylinder. In the following image, it's highlighted in blue. In the second subpanel, the **Units** subpanel lets you select which units you prefer. However, rather than choosing between **Metric** or **Imperial**, I decided to leave the default settings as they were.

As the measurements that I found were Imperial measurements, I decided to interpret the Imperial measurements as Blender measurements, equating 1 foot to 1 Blender unit, and each inch as 0.083 Blender units. If I have an Imperial measurement that is expressed in inches, I just divide it by 12 to get the correct number in Blender units.

The boat I found on the Internet is 9 feet and 10 inches long, 56 inches wide at the top, 44 inches wide at the bottom, and 18 inches high. I converted them to decimal Blender units or 9.830 long, 4.666 wide at the top, 3.666 wide at the bottom, and 1.500 high.

Time for action – making reference objects

One of the simplest ways to see what size your boat should be is to have boxes of the proper size to use as guides. So now, you will make some of these boxes:

1. In the 3D View window, press the *Tab* key to get into **Object Mode**. Press *A* to deselect the boat.

2. Press the NumPad *3* key to get the side view. Make sure you are in Ortho view. Press the *5* key on the NumPad if needed.

3. Press *Shift + A* and choose **Mesh** and then **Cube** from the menu. You will use this as a reference block for the size of the boat.

4. In the 3D View window Properties Panel, in the **Transform** subpanel, at the top, click on the **Dimensions** button, and change the dimensions for the reference block to 4.666 in the **X** direction, 9.83 in the **Y** direction, and 1.5 in the **Z** direction. You can use the *Tab* key to go from **X** to **Y** to **Z**, and press *Enter* when you are done.

5. Move the mouse over the 3D View window, and press *Shift + D* to duplicate the block. Then press *Enter*.

6. Press the NumPad *1* key to get the front view.

7. Press *G* and then *Z* to move this block down, so its top is in the lower half of the first one.

8. Press *S*, then *X*, then the number 0.79, and then *Enter*. This will scale it to 79 percent along the X axis. Look at the readout. It will show you what is happening. This will represent the width of the boat at the bottom of the hull.

9. Press the MMB and rotate the view to see what it looks like.

What just happened?

To make accurate models, it helps to have references. For this boat that you are building, you don't need to copy another boat exactly, and the basic dimensions are enough. You got out of **Edit Mode**, and deselected the boat so that you could work on something else, without affecting the boat. Then, you made a cube, and scaled it to the dimensions of the boat, at the top of the hull, to use as a reference block. You then copied the reference block, and scaled the copy down in X for the width of the boat at the bottom of the hull as shown in the following image:

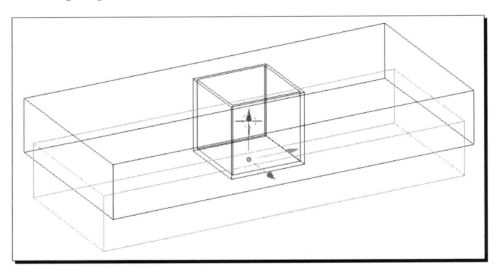

Reference objects, like reference blocks and reference spheres, are handy tools. They are easy to make and have a lot of uses. For your reference, the 4909_05_making reference objects.blend file has been included in the download pack. It has the cube and the two reference blocks.

Sizing the boat to the reference blocks

Now that the reference blocks have been made, you can use them to guide you when making the boat.

Time for action – making the boat the proper length

Now that you've made the reference blocks the right size, it's time to make the boat the same dimensions as the blocks:

1. Change to the side view by pressing the NumPad *3* key. Press *Ctrl* + MMB and the mouse to zoom in, until the reference blocks fill almost all of the 3D View. Press *Shift* + MMB and the mouse to re-center the reference blocks.

2. Select the boat with the RMB. Press the *Tab* key to go into **Edit Mode**, and then choose the **Vertex Select** mode button from the 3D View header.

3. Press *A* to deselect all vertices. Then, select the boat's vertices on the right-hand side of the 3D View. Press *B* to use the border select, or press *C* to use the circle select mode, or press *Ctrl* + LMB for the lasso select, as discussed in *Chapter 4, Modeling with Vertices, Edges, and Faces*.

4. When the vertices are selected, press *G* and then *Y*, and move the vertices to the right with the mouse until they are lined up with the right-hand side of the reference blocks. Press the LMB to drop the vertices in place.

5. Press *A* to deselect all the vertices, select the boat's vertices on the left-hand side of the 3D View, and move them to the left until they are lined up with the left-hand side of the reference blocks, as shown in the following image:

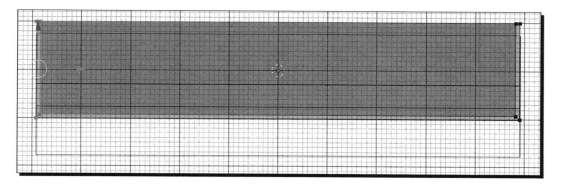

What just happened?

You made sure that the screen was properly set up for working by getting into the side view in the **Ortho** mode. Next, you selected the boat, got into **Edit Mode**, and got ready to move the vertices. Then, you made the boat the proper length, by moving the vertices so that they lined up with the reference blocks.

 For your reference, the 4909_05_proper length.blend file has been included in the download pack. It has the bow and stern properly sized.

Time for action – making the boat the proper width and height

Making the boat the right length was pretty easy. Setting the width and height requires a few more steps, but the method is very similar:

1. Press the NumPad *1* key to change to the front view. Use *Ctrl* + MMB to zoom into the reference blocks. Use *Shift* + MMB to re-center the boat so that you can see all of it.

2. Press *A* to deselect all the vertices, and using any method discussed in *Chapter 4, Modeling with Vertices, Edges, and Faces*, select all of the vertices on the left of the 3D View.

3. Press *G* and then *X* to move the left-side vertices in *X*, until they line up with the wider reference block, as shown in the following image. Click the LMB to release the vertices.

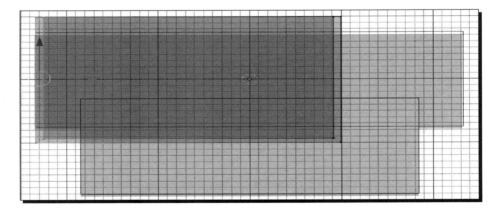

4. Press *A* to deselect all the vertices. Select only the right-hand vertices with a method different from the one you used to select the left-hand vertices. Then, press *G* and then *X* to move them in *X*, until they line up with the right side of the wider reference block. Press the LMB when they are in place.

5. Deselect all the vertices. Select only the top vertices, and press *G* and then *Z* to move them in the Z direction, until they line up with the top of the wider reference block.

6. Deselect all the vertices. Now, select only the bottom vertices, and press *G* and then *Z* to move them in the Z direction, until they line up with the bottom of the wider reference block, as shown in the following image:

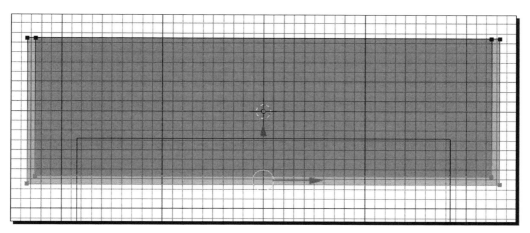

7. Deselect all the vertices. Next, select only the bottom vertices on the left. Press *G* and then *X* to move them in X, until they line up with the narrower reference block. Then, press the LMB.

8. Finally, deselect all the vertices, and select only the bottom vertices on the right. Press *G* and then *X* to move them in the *X axis*, until they line up with the narrower reference block, as shown in the following image. Press the LMB to release them:

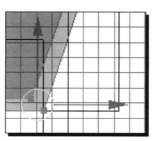

9. Press the NumPad *3* key to switch to the **Side** view again. Use *Ctrl* + MMB to zoom out if you need to. Press *A* to deselect all the vertices. Select only the bottom vertices on the right, as in the following illustration. You are going to make this the stern end of the boat. Press *G* and then *Y* to move them left in the *Y axis* just a little bit, so that the stern is not completely straight up and down. Press the LMB to release them.

10. Now, select only the bottom vertices on the left, as highlighted in the following illustration. Make this the bow end of the boat. Move them right in the *Y axis* just a little bit. Go a bit further than the stern, so that the angle is similar to the right side, as shown here, maybe about **1.3** or **1.4**. It's your call.

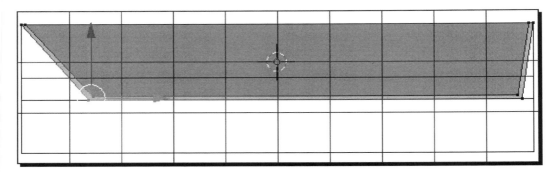

What just happened?

You used the reference blocks to guide yourself in moving the vertices into the shape of a boat. You adjusted the width and the height, and angled the hull. Finally, you angled the stern and the bow. It floats, but it's still a bit boxy.

For your reference, the 4909_05_proper width and height1. blend file has been included in the download pack. It has both sides aligned with the wider reference block. The 4909_05_proper width and height2.blend file has the bottom vertices aligned to the narrower reference block. The 4909_05_proper width and height3.blend file has the bow and stern finished.

Time for action – adding curves to the boat's lines by subdividing

You've discovered two of box-modeling's most powerful methods: extrusion and moving vertices. Now, it's time to discover the third one: subdividing. Now, the hull will begin to look like a boat after you perform the following steps:

1. Press *A* to deselect all vertices.

2. Select **Edge Select mode** on the 3D View header.

3. Press *B* to do a Border select to select the edges of the sides of the boat, but not the bow or the stern, as shown in the following image:

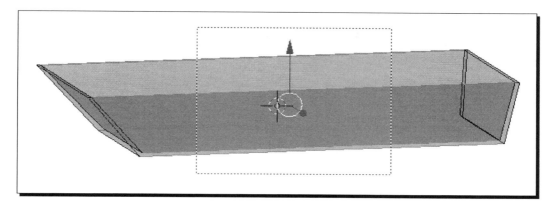

4. Press *W* to get the **Specials** menu. Select **Subdivide** with the LMB.

5. On the left, in the **Tool Shelf**, a subpanel is labeled **Subdivide**. Make sure that the arrow next to the word **Subdivide** is pointing down. Change **Number of Cuts** to **3**. Blender will cut each of the edges into three as shown in the following image. Press *A* to deselect the edges. Now, you can see the new edges better.

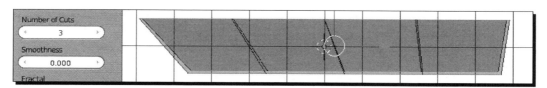

6. Change to the **Vertex Select** mode in the 3D View header.

7. Select the vertices of the bow on the left.

8. Press the NumPad *7* key to change to the Top view. Press the *Ctrl* + MMB, *Shift* + MMB, and the mouse to zoom and pan, so that you can see the whole boat.

9. Scale the vertices in the X direction, so that the outside of the front of the hull is about as wide as the narrow reference block, as shown in the next illustration.

10. Deselect all the vertices. Now, select the next set of vertices as shown in the following image. Scale them in X to give the boat a bit of a curve.

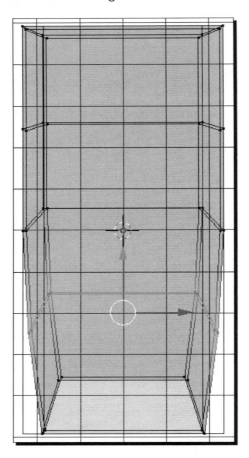

11. Deselect all the vertices. Select the vertices on the stern, and scale them a little in X to add a bit of curve to the stern.

12. Press the NumPad *1* key to get the front view. Press the *Tab* key to get into **Object Mode**. Press *A* to deselect the boat. Select the two reference blocks with the RMB for the first one, and then press *Shift* + RMB for the second.

13. Press *M* to bring up the **Move to Layer** menu, as shown in the following image. There are twenty small buttons in groups of five. The upper left square is dark. Click the LMB on the square just to the right of the dark square. This will move the reference cubes to layer two, out of view.

14. Save the file and give it a unique name.

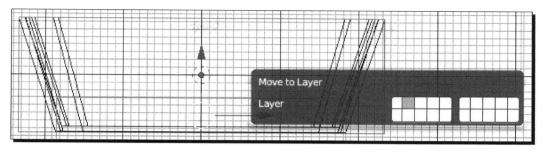

What just happened?

Now, you have put a little art into your modeling. There were no hard measurements to set the width of the boat to, so you just had to use your artistic flair. You subdivided the sides of the hull by 3, and scaled the vertices to give the boat a little curve. You finished off with a discovery about Blender's layers. The Blender layers let you control the visibility of objects.

 For your reference, the 4909_05_adding curve1.blend file has been included in the download pack. It has the sides subdivided. The 4909_05_adding curve2.blend file has the sides curved as seen from the top. The 4909_05_adding curve3.blend file is the completed hull.

Have a go hero – adding curves to the hull

It's the smaller details that often make the difference. Can you use what you know to add some curve to the profile of the boat and point the bow?

As you can see in the next image, the boat has a little curve in its hull on the bottom and a very subtle one on the top. Try doing that for your boat.

Move the vertices to give it some nice lines, similar to the ones in the following image. When you are happy with them, be sure to rotate the view, and check the boat from all sides to make sure she looks good from all angles.

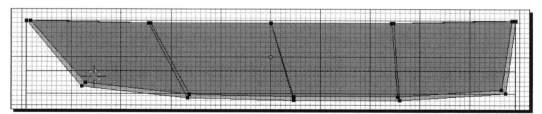

The finished boat should look something similar to the following image. Well done!

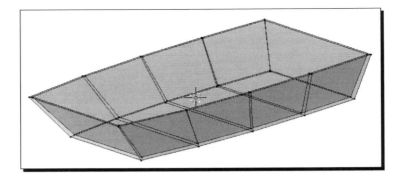

Next, use the subdivide command to point to the bow. The boat will move through the water a little faster if you subdivide the hull end-to-end and add a bit of a *V* shape to the bottom of the hull, and a point to the bow. The next image will give you a hint.

Get the front view, and set the **Mesh Select** mode to **Edge Select**. Select only the edges that run across the center of the boat. Subdivide them and then move the vertices. Save the file when you are happy with the boat.

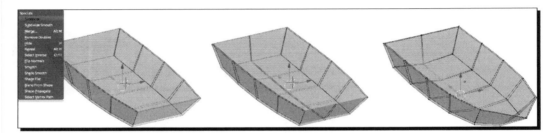

Using clean building methods

The way you built this model was very solid. Some of the salient features of the boat are as follows:

- Since the hull is a single piece, there are no holes in it. This is known as **water tight**, which is good for a boat.
- Since it has no holes, you can use it with the water functions of the physics engine, so the boat will float or it can be filled with water.
- Objects for 3D printers must be water tight like this.
- It also makes it nice and clean for use in the game engine.
- The number of faces was kept to a minimum, so the rendering time will be short.

Choosing between quadrilaterals and triangles

In *Chapter 4, Modeling with Vertices, Edges, and Faces*, we briefly discussed that a face usually has three or four edges. Because of the way you created it, this boat is made entirely of quadrilaterals or four-edged faces. Quadrilateral faces are preferred because they subdivide nicely, as you saw when making the sides of the boat. If you are making a model that is controlled by an armature, such as a model of a person or an animal, they deform better.

There is one problem with quadrilateral faces though. You have to ensure that the quadrilateral face is flat. We talked about normals earlier, and how a normal is a line perpendicular to the face. If you are not careful with a quadrilateral face, it may not be flat. Then Blender won't be able to figure out what the normal for the face is, and won't know how to render it properly.

Imagine a flat floor, and you are trying to sit on a four-legged chair that has one leg that is a bit too short. You will always be rocking a bit. Quadrilaterals that are not flat, or non-planar as they are called, are similarly irritating. That's where triangular faces are easier as the normal is a line that is perpendicular to the face. If you are not careful with a quadrilateral face, it may not be flat. Then, Blender won't be able to figure out what the normal for the face is, and won't know how to render it properly. When Blender gets a quadrilateral face that is non-planar, it divides the face into two triangles, and calculates the normal for each triangle, sometimes with poor results. Now, it's time to check this out.

Time for action – making a non-planar polygon

Take a moment to check out what I just said and make a non-planar polygon by following these steps:

1. Create a new file. Get into **Edit** mode.
2. Select the upper vertex of the cube nearest to you, move the vertex about half-way down the cube, and a little to the right, then render it.
3. You haven't added any faces to the cube, but what do you notice about the top face and the right side?

What just happened?

When you moved the vertex, some of the faces became non-planar. When you rendered it, you could see how Blender then divided the non-planar face into two triangular faces.

Time for action – adding a seat to the boat

Congratulations! You made a boat out of quadrilaterals. Let's continue modeling with quadrilaterals. The next step is to add seats to the boat. You'll see that you can have an object where not all the parts are connected:

1. Open the jon boat file. I'm using the flat bow version, but you can use a flat or pointed bow as you prefer. Press the NumPad *3* key to get the side view. Make sure you are in Ortho view.

2. Press *Shift + S*, and select **Cursor to Center** from the menu.

3. In the 3D View header, turn off the 3D manipulator display. It has the red, green, and blue axes. Make it light gray.

4. Move your cursor close to the top of the boat, to the location shown in the following image, and then click the LMB to move the 3D Cursor up:

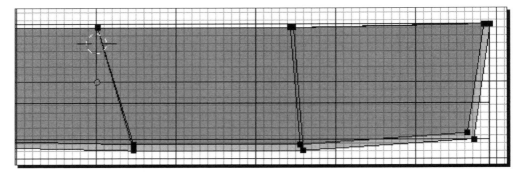

5. Make sure that the boat is in **Object Mode**. Press *Tab* to change it, if it is not.

6. Press *A* to deselect the boat if needed.

7. Use *Shift + A* to make a new cube. If the Properties Panel of the 3D View is not already open, press **N** to open it.

8. Press the NumPad *7* key to get the **Top** view.

9. In the **Transform** subpanel, look where it says **Dimensions**. Set the **Y** dimension to 1. Set the **Z** dimension to 0.166. Use the *Tab* key to go between **Y** and **Z**.

10. In the **Viewport Shading** menu, select **Solid**.

11. Press *S* and then *X* to scale the cube in X, until it just meets the inner sides of the boat. The seat I made was 4.320 wide in X. Your width may vary.

12. Press the MMB, and rotate your view around the boat. Check that the seat is not poking out through the boat or floating between the inner sides of the hull, as shown in the next image. If it is, press *S* and then *X*, and use the mouse to scale it a little. Press the LMB when done.

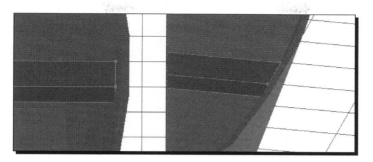

13. Press *F12* to render the boat as I did in the following image. The ends of the seat should just touch the inner hull of the boat as shown in this image. Press *Esc* when you are done looking at the boat.

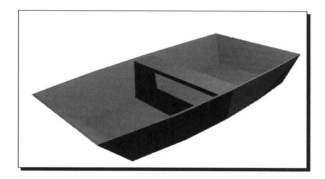

What just happened?

First, you chose a center point for the seat, by moving the 3D Cursor. Then, you deselected the boat to make a different object. Next, you made a cube and scaled it in the X, Y, and Z directions, so that it became a seat for the boat. Finally, you did a quick sample render to see what you made, as in the previous image.

For your reference, the `4909_05_boat_adding seat.blend` file has been included in the download pack. It has the first seat completed.

Time for action – making the other seat

The first seat was pretty straightforward. The second seat is in the bow, and to fit it in, the front edge of the seat is a little narrower than the back edge. So, you'll copy the first seat, and modify the copy:

1. Change to the **Top** view. Zoom out until you can see the entire boat.

2. Select the Viewport Shading menu from the 3D View header, and set the shading to **Wireframe** again.

3. Change to **Edit Mode**.

4. Select all of the vertices.

5. Press *Shift + D* to duplicate them. Move the mouse downward, and press the MMB to lock the motion to that direction. Move the new vertices to the front section of the boat.

6. Look at how much of a gap you see between the ends of the center seat and the hull. You will want to give the new seat about the same gap between the ends of the seat and the hull. Scale the vertices in the X direction so that the rear edge of the front seat is the proper width. For best control, move the mouse to the farthest corner of the 3D View before you start scaling. Press *S*, then *X*, and scale the new seat.

7. Deselect all the vertices.

8. Now, select only the vertices on the front of the seat.

9. You want to make the angle of the side of the front seat match the angle of the hull. Press *S* and then *X* to scale these in *X*, so that the sides of the front seat are parallel with the angle of the hull, as shown in the following image:

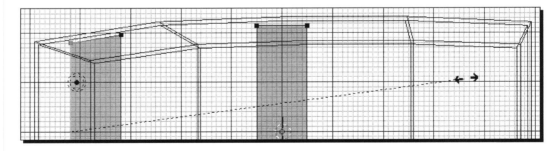

10. In the **Viewport Shading** menu, select **Solid**. Press the *Tab* key to exit **Edit Mode**.

11. Press the MMB and rotate your view around the boat. Check that the seat is not poking out through the boat or floating between the inner sides of the hull. If it is, press the NumPad *7* key, return to **Edit Mode** and **Wireframe** shading, then scale the vertices of the front seat again and repeat the previous step.

12. Press *F12* to render the boat. Press *Esc* when you have examined the boat.

13. Save the file with a unique name.

What just happened?

Working in **Edit Mode**, you duplicated the seat and moved it to the bow. You also learned that you can move in a certain axis, by starting the motion in that direction and then pressing the MMB to restrict the motion to that axis. You scaled the seat in X, and then scaled the front edge of the seat in X. Since you duplicated the vertices to make the new seat in **Edit Mode** instead of duplicating the seat in **Object Mode**, both seats are a single object, which will make it easier for you to add textures to it. Well done! You've built a boat similar to the left-side image, and you've simultaneously learned the basics of modeling with Blender.

Have a go hero – adding a third seat

Add a third seat in the aft of the boat, as shown in the preceding image on the right.

The steps are about the same as for making the seat in the bow. Change **Viewport Shading** to **Wireframe** to make it easier. Then, save the file to a unique name.

 For your reference, the 4909_05_boat_making the other seat1.blend file has been included in the download pack. It has the second seat. 4909_05_boat_making the other seat2.blend has three seats completed.

Making modeling easier with Blender's layers function

A short while ago, you used the **Move to Layer** menu to hide the reference blocks so that you could render the boat. Blender's layers are a powerful tool and something that deserves a bit more study. Perhaps you may have used layers in Photoshop or AutoCAD. Blender's layers work differently:

◆ In Blender, layers are similar to cubbyholes that you can put objects in, and hide them or show them.

◆ Something on the top layer won't necessarily render on top of something on another layer. You cannot link them together, or move a layer as you can in Photoshop.

◆ An object may be in more than one layer at a time.

◆ An object in a layer that is active can be moved, modified, or rendered. An object in a layer that is not active, may not.

◆ Layers cannot be accessed in **Edit Mode**.

There are 20 layers in Blender. You can use any or all of them. You can select them with the 20 buttons in the 3D View header in **Object Mode**, as shown in the next image. They are called the **Layer Visibility Controls**. The button for layer one is on the upper left, the button for layer 10 is on the upper right, the button for layer 11 is on the lower left, and the button for layer 20 is on the lower right. Buttons that are dark indicate the layers that are displayed. Buttons with a dot in the center show layers that contain objects. The yellow dot means that the currently active object is in that layer.

Time for action – introducing layers

It's time for a little introduction to using Blender's layers. Here, you will be learning how to use them with the keyboard.

If you are using the NumPad emulator setting rather than pressing the numbers on your keyboard, use the Layer Visibility Controls as just discussed, and select the layer that corresponds with the keyboard number:

1. Select the **Viewport Shading** menu on the 3D View header, and make sure the shading is set to **Solid**.

2. Use the MMB to rotate the scene, so you can see the top of the boat. Make sure you are in **Object Mode**.

3. Press the *5* key on the number row of your keyboard, not on the NumPad. If you are emulating the NumPad, select layer 5 from the Layer Visibility Controls.

4. Press the *2* key on your keyboard.

5. Press the *1* key on your keyboard.

6. Press the *Alt* key and the *7* key simultaneously. Note how the dark color on the Layer Visibility Control shifts to layer 17. NumPad emulators select layer 17.

7. Press *Shift + A* and choose mesh and then monkey from the pop-up menus.

What just happened?

When you press the number keys on the keyboard, Blender displays the corresponding layer. With key *5*, you saw nothing because there was nothing in layer 5. Pressing key *2* showed the reference blocks, which you had moved to layer 2. Pressing key *1* gets you back to layer 1, where you have been working. Keys *1* to *0* display layers 1 to 10. To get layers 11 to 20, press the *Alt* key and a number key. When you opened layer 17 with the *Alt* and the *7* key, and made a monkey, a dot appeared in layer 17 to let you know that there was now an object on that layer. The dot is yellow, because the monkey is the active object.

Time for action – using layers for controlling rendering

Layers don't just control what you can see while modeling. They also control what is rendered:

1. Press the *Shift* key, and hold it while you press the LMB over the layer 1 box in the Layer Visibility Control.

2. Press *F12* to render the scene. Press *Esc* when you have seen the rendering.

3. Press *Ctrl + MMB*, and zoom back until you can see the lamp. Use the RMB to select the lamp.

4. Press *M* to get the **Move To Layer** menu.

5. Select **Layer 5** on the menu with the LMB. Then, move the mouse away from the menu.

6. Press *F12* to render the scene. Press *Esc* when you have seen the rendering.

7. Press the number *5*. NumPad emulators select layer 5.

8. Press *M* and *1*.

9. Press *1* and *Shift + Alt + 7*. NumPad emulators choose layer 1. Then, press *Shift* and choose layer 17.

10. Press *F12* to render the scene. Press *Esc* when you have seen the rendering.

11. Use the RMB to select the monkey. Press *X* to delete it.

What just happened?

Just as the *Shift* key lets you select multiple objects, using the *Shift* key when selecting layers lets you select multiple layers to display or render. Pressing the *M* key brings up the **Move To Layer** menu. You can choose which layer to move to by picking the layer off the menu or by pressing the number of the layer on the keyboard.

You rendered the scene with the lamp on an active layer, then moved the lamp to another layer and rendered the scene again. You saw that if the lamps are not on an active layer, then they will not illuminate the scene. You moved the lamp back to layer 1 and then selected layer 1 and layer 17 as active layers. When you did the rendering, you saw both the boat and the monkey because both layers were active. The monkey got deleted later because it is no longer needed.

Coloring the boat to add realism

The proper use of colors makes an object seem more real. It's time to learn a bit more about how to apply color and textures to the model you have made. There are two kinds of decoration you can do: **Materials** and **Textures**. Materials assign a color to the faces of an object. They tell Blender how shiny or dull the surface is, how transparent it is, and other qualities. Textures allow you to add a design to the surface, and not just colors and pictures, but patterns of roughness, bumps, and shapes as well. First, you will add a material to the boat, and then you will add a texture to the seats.

Time for action – coloring the hull and the gunwale

Your boat is a pretty simple object. The entire hull can be one color, but it's nice to give the gunwale a different color to accent the top and provide more definition:

1. Make sure you are working in **Layer 1**.
2. If you have the Properties Panel in the 3D View closed, open it with the *N* key.
3. Select the camera with the RMB.
4. Press *0* on the NumPad to change to the **Camera** view.
5. Move the camera back by pressing the *G* key and then tapping the *Z* key twice. Then, move the mouse so that the camera dollies out along its local Z direction until the whole boat shows up.
6. Change to the **Top** view.

7. Select the lamp with the RMB. In the Properties Panel of the 3D View window, set the lamp's **Location** so that X is equal to **-1.900** and Y is equal to **-6.800**.

8. Press *Shift + D* to copy the lamp. Move it a little with the mouse so that you can see that you are working on the second lamp. Set the location of the second lamp to X= **4.400** and Y= **0.200**.

9. Change to the **Right** view and zoom into the boat.

10. Select the boat with the RMB and press *Tab* to go into **Edit Mode**.

11. Choose **Wireframe** in the Viewport Shading menu on the header, and then choose **Face Select Mode** on the 3D View header.

12. Press *A* once or twice to deselect all faces.

13. Put the cursor below the boat and to the left. Press *B* for border select. Select the bottom and the side faces, but not the top ones.

14. Go to the Properties window on the right, and select the materials button in the header, as shown in the previous image. It has a shiny chrome ball on it. When you do, it will become highlighted in blue, as shown in the previous image. You may need to slide the header to the left with the MMB to see it.

15. After you have selected the **Material** button, enlarge the Properties window by dragging the edge to the left, until the button with the text **Mat**, as shown in the following image, becomes **Material**. You will need to enter text into this button. If your **Material** panel is pretty much blank, press the button labeled **New**.

16. In the expanded button labeled **Material**, rename **Material** to **Hull**, which is bordered in yellow in the previous image. Click on the word **Material**, type in Hull, and then press *Enter*.

17. In the **Diffuse** subpanel of the Properties window, click on the white Diffuse Color box, and use the color wheel menu to change the color to a dark green. You can use the mouse and the color wheel, or type in the values below. I used R=**0.015**, G=**0.24**, and B=**0.054**. You can use the *Tab* key to move between the **R**, **G**, and **B** buttons. Then, move the cursor outside of the color wheel menu to continue after you have chosen the color.

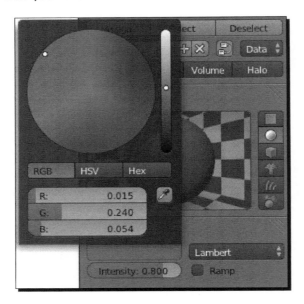

18. To assign the color to the selected vertices, click on the **Assign** button. It is located at the top of the **Material** panel, just above where you entered the word `Hull`. If you do not see it, make sure that you are in **Edit Mode** and not **Object Mode**. The button is not visible in **Object Mode**.

19. Render it. The boat is all green. Press *Esc* to show the 3D View window after viewing.

20. Choose **Select** on the 3D View header. Choose **Inverse** from the pop-up menu.

21. In the Properties window, add a new material slot by clicking the LMB on the plus sign, across from the word **Hull**, as shown in the next image.

22. Click on the button that has a plus sign and the word **New** on it, as shown in the following image, to create a new material. Name the new material **Gunwale**.

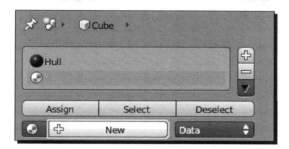

23. Press the LMB over the color bar in the **Diffuse** subpanel. The color wheel will appear as shown in the next image. Make the Gunwale material light green. I used R=**0.850**, G=**1.000**, and B=**0.500**.

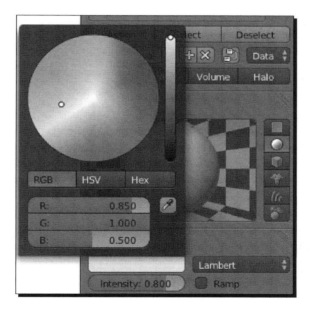

24. Left-click on the **Assign** button, as shown in the row of three light gray buttons in the illustration before the last, to assign the material to the selected vertices.

25. Now render it. It should look similar to the following image. Press *Esc* when you have finished looking at it.

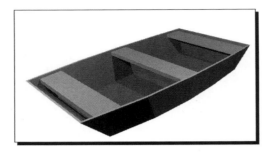

26. Save the file and give it a unique name.

What just happened?

First, you spent a little time setting up the scene to display the materials well. You moved the camera to where it would see the entire boat, and put modeling lamps on both sides of the boat too, so nothing would be too much in shadow.

Then, you selected the faces of the sides and the bottom of the hull. You took the default materials slot, made a material for it, and colored the material green. Finally, you assigned that material to the hull of the boat. Next, you inverted the selection, so you had only the faces on the top of the hull selected. Then, you made a new materials slot, gave it a name, and set its color to light green. You assigned that material to only the faces on the top of the hull.

For your reference, the 4909_05_boat_color the hull.blend file has been included in the download pack. It has the materials added to the hull and gunwale.

Time for action – adding a texture to the seats

Now, you've added a material to the boat. Next, you will add a wood texture to the seats and learn a new panel in the Properties window:

1. Press *Tab* to go into **Object Mode**, and select the seats with the RMB.

2. Add a new material slot as you did when you made the Hull material. Name it **Seats**.

3. Go up to the header of the Properties window, and select the **Textures** button. It has a red and white checkerboard on it, and it is next to the **Materials** button. It's highlighted in blue, as shown on the top of the next image.

4. Add a new texture by clicking on the button called **New**, as shown at the bottom of the following screenshot:

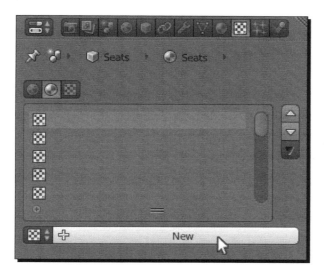

5. Where the **New** button was, it now says **Texture**. Click on the word **Texture**, and change it to **Seat Texture**. Press *Enter* when you are done.

6. Go to the `Chapter 5/Images` directory of the download pack, and choose `4909_05_37.png`. The images may be in with the Blender code. `4909_05_37.png` is a wood texture. Copy the file to your `Image` directory.

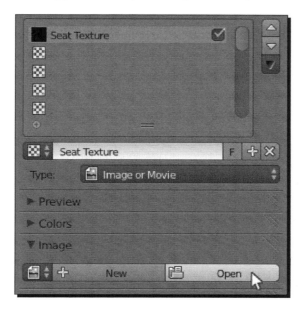

7. In the Properties window, just below where you named the texture, it says **Type:**. Click on the dark button to the right of **Type:**. A menu comes up. Select **Image or Movie**.

8. A subpanel appears that is labeled **Image**. At the bottom of the subpanel, it says **Open**, as shown in the previous image. Select the **Open** button, and you will get the Blender file browser. Find `4909_05_37.png` in your `Images` directory.

9. In the Properties window header, select the **Materials** button.

10. Press *F12* to render the scene. Your boat now has wooden seats. Press the *Esc* button when you are done admiring your work.

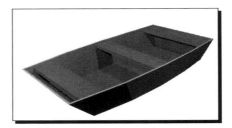

11. Save the file and give it a unique name.

What just happened?

You added a textured material to the boat seats. First, you created a new material slot and a material to put into it. Then, you opened up the texture panel to add the texture. You chose an **Image or Movie** texture, and chose a wood-grain texture from the download pack. Since you added the material to the entire object, you did not have to get into **Edit Mode** to assign the material, and you saved the file just in case something goes wrong with the next step.

 For your reference, the `4909_05_boat_add texture to seats.blend` file has been included in the download pack. It has the materials added to the hull and gunwale, and the texture added to the seats.

Time for action – naming objects and joining them

Next, you will select the seats, and then add the boat to your selection. Then, you can join the two objects into a single object:

1. On the header of the Properties window, select the Object button. It has the orange cube. It's highlighted in blue in the following image.

2. Use the button shown at the bottom of the following graphic, in the Properties window, to change the name to Seats. Type it in and press *Enter* when you finish.

3. Select the boat. Change the name to `Boat`.

4. Save the Blender file.

5. Select the seats again with the RMB. Then, press the *Shift* key when selecting with the RMB to also select the boat.

6. Press *Ctrl + J*.

7. The seats and the boat are now a single object. Now look at what the name is.

8. Look at the **Material** panel in the Properties window. Note that the properties of all three materials are listed, since both objects have been joined.

9. Save the file to a unique name.

What just happened?

You selected the seats and named them. Then, you selected the boat, named it, and saved the file just in case you want to go back and make changes later.

Then, you selected both the seats and the boat and used the command *Ctrl + J* to join the two objects. The first object selected is joined into the last object selected. Finally, you saved the finished boat to its own file.

> You can refer to the bonus chapter *Chapter 5A, Lighting a Small Boat*, that is available for download at `https://www.packtpub.com/sites/default/files/downloads/4909OS_05A_Lighting_a_Small_Boat.pdf`. It has the boat completed and named.

Using basic lighting

In addition to building your boat, you really want to display it in its best light. As a bonus, I have provided a special section that introduces you to using the variety of lights that Blender provides and helps you understand the basics of how to use them. They will be covered again in this book in greater detail, but I recommend that you check out the bonus chapter, *Chapter 5A, Lighting a Small Boat*.

It will add another layer to your learning and help you in later chapters.

Pop quiz – extrusion, subdivision, moving vertices

Q1. When you press the *W* key in Edit mode, what operation will you be doing next?

1. Extrusion
2. Subdivision
3. Moving vertices

The key-function table

This table has some good key functions to help you in your work that we may not have had time to discuss in this chapter:

Key	Function
Z	Toggles between the **Wireframe** and **Solid** mode in **Viewport Shading**.
Ctrl + Tab	**Edit Mode** brings up the **Mesh Select Mode** menu to select vertices, edges, or faces.
Tab	In three part buttons, such as X, Y, and Z locations or R, G, and B colors, it can be used to jump from one button to the next.
Alt + Tab	Jumps from one button to the previous one.
Shift	When using **Move to Layer**, holding the *Shift* button when selecting multiple layers allows you to move the selected object to all of the selected layers.

Summary

In this chapter, you put your knowledge of building objects to a practical use, and built a boat. It was also a good practice in using the controls of the 3D View, keyboard shortcuts, and buttons, including the buttons on the header, in the Tool Shelf, and in the Properties Panel.

You studied box modeling to create the boat from the default cube, and used box modeling's most powerful methods: extrusion, subdividing edges, and moving vertices, to reshape the cube into a hull. You learned about joining objects together, so that the boat and the seats can be used as a single object. You got your first taste of creating a material to make the boat look more realistic, and added a wooden texture to the seats.

In the next chapter, you will make some oars and oarlocks to move the boat with. You will extend your ability with more powerful modeling techniques. You will animate the boat, the oars, and the oarlocks as a coordinated unit, so that the oars appear to propel the boat.

Let's go!

6

Making and Moving the Oars

*In the previous chapter, you put your knowledge of building objects as well as
3D View to practical use. You made a small boat and added materials and then
explored different ways of lighting.*

*In this chapter, you will expand your modeling skills and all that you have
learned about animation in order to take things to the next level. You'll learn
some cool modeling techniques, and animate the boat and the oars.*

In this chapter, you will cover:

- Creating oars and oarlocks to move the boat
- Controlling the smoothness of a surface
- Appending objects to the scene to reuse previously made objects
- Creating child-parent relationships to group objects for animation
- Using kinematics to organize animation
- Employing animation cycles to save work
- Using camera tracking to follow the boat's motion

Let's start by making the oar.

Modeling an oar

We'll do a little more precise modeling with the oar. We'll be flipping groups of vertices
around to make rich details while keeping the polygon count as low as possible. First,
you need to know more about what you are making.

Getting a scale from an image

It's good to be able to make an object of the size you want it to be. As I used a real boat as the basis on which to build the boat model, a picture of an oar will help make a realistic oar, and as you'll discover, you can get quite a bit of information from it.

For a reference image, I went to a website and grabbed an image of an oar similar to the one shown in the following screenshot:

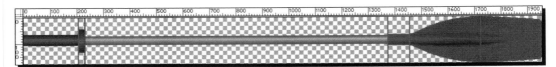

Now, I had to figure out the size of the oar. The specs on the website had the length of the oar and the width of the blade, which was enough information for me to scale things in the image and get the following basic measurements:

- I trimmed down the image until it was just the oar and got an image that was 1954 x 178 pixels in size. I knew that the oar was 6 feet long. Moreover, the boat was modeled at 1 foot, that is, one Blender unit. Therefore, I divided six by 1954 and got a scaling factor of 0.003. This means every pixel was 0.003 Blender units long.

- Then, all I had to do was measure the length of a part in pixels and convert that to Blender units. It's easy to measure the pixels in an image using the rulers and guides in a paint program, as seen in the previous illustration.

- For example, the grip, which was 195 pixels long in the image, got multiplied by 0.003, and this meant that the grip was 0.6 units long.

- I measured them all and made a list of my measurements. I also took note that, on the website, one customer complained that the shaft of the oar was just a bit too small for his oarlocks. Therefore, in my measurements, I slightly boosted up the radius of the shaft a bit.

Measurements of the oar

If you want to experiment, here are the measurements from the preceding figure; they may differ a little from the instructions:

Part	X dimension (taken from the top of the oar)	Y dimension
Picture	5.862	0.643
Grip	0.613	0.130
Grip guard	0.06	0.271

Part	X dimension (taken from the top of the oar)	Y dimension
Shaft	3.385	0.1
Oar shaft	0.242	0.130
Oar top	0.790	0.536
Oar blade end	0.672	0.395

Creating an oar from a cylinder

Once all the measurements are made, it's time to begin. The shaft itself is simple, so there are two basic parts, the grip and the blade, that need the most work.

Time for action – making the shaft of the oar

Starting the oar is pretty easy. In *Chapter 4, Modeling with Vertices, Edges, and Faces*, you looked at the basic shapes that are present in Blender; this is where you will begin:

1. Open Blender.
2. Press *X* to delete the default cube.
3. Press *Shift + A* and select a cylinder from the pop-up menu.
4. In the **Add Cylinder** section of **Tool Shelf** set **Vertices** to 12, **Radius** to 0.083, and **Depth** to 4.2. You can use the *Tab* key to jump between the **Vertices**, **Radius**, and **Depth** buttons. Set the **Cap Fill Type** to **Ngon**. This will make the oar handle and shaft as seen in the following screenshot. Press *Enter* after setting the values.

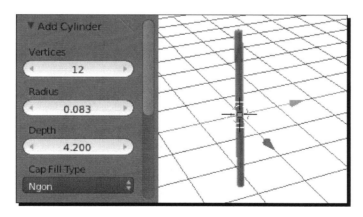

5. Now, you have the handle to the right length.
6. Press the *Tab* key to get into **Edit Mode**.

7. Press the NumPad *1* key to set the view to **Front** and then press the NumPad *5* key to set the view to **Ortho**.

8. Zoom into the cylinder.

9. Make sure that the **Limit selection to visible** button is light gray in the 3D View header, as shown by the highlighted button on the right-hand side in the following screenshot, so that you select all the edges and not just the visible ones:

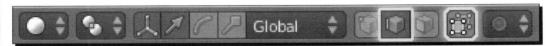

10. Choose the **Edge Select** mode from the 3D View header; it's the highlighted button on the left-hand side of the previous screenshot, with the cube and the vertical line.

11. Press *A* to deselect all the edges. Press *B* and then draw the marquee border across the middle of the cylinder. Do not select the ends. If you have questions about using the border select, check *Chapter 4, Modeling with Vertices, Edges, and Faces*, to refresh yourself.

12. Press *W* to get the **Specials** menu and choose **Subdivide**. In the **Tool Shelf**, set the number of cuts to 2, as shown in the following screenshot:

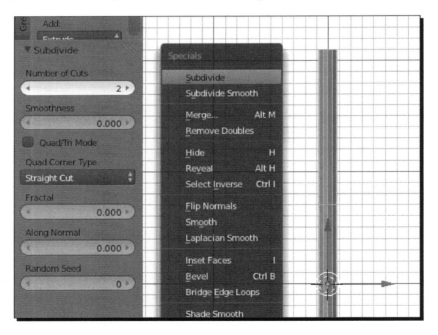

What just happened?

You created a cylinder, modified it to the required size, and divided it into three parts to create the edges needed to make the grip and guard.

Time for action – making the grip and guard

Now, you are going to use the box-modeling tools, which you learned in *Chapter 5, Building a Simple Boat*, moving vertices, scaling, and subdivision to create the grip and guard for the oar:

1. Press *A* to deselect all the edges. Press *B* to select a border. Select the upper set of the horizontal edges that you just created.

2. Zoom in so that the edges that you selected are at the bottom of 3D View and that the top of the cylinder is at the top of the 3D View window, as seen on the left-hand side of the following screenshot. Move the mouse so that it is level with the selected edges.

3. The reference grid in the background will help you judge how far to go. Each section of the main grid in the background is 0.1 Blender units. The grip is about 0.6 units in length, therefore, when you move the selected edges, the inner edge of the grip will be six boxes from the top.

4. Press *G*, and use the mouse to move the edges up. When you start moving the edge, press the MMB briefly to lock the motion to the *Z* axis. Move them until they are 0.6 Blender units or six boxes from the end of the oar, as seen on the left-hand side of the following screenshot. For best control, press the *Ctrl* key while you move. Press the LMB to release it.

5. Deselect all the edges.

6. Press *Ctrl* + MMB and use the mouse to zoom out so that you can see the lower set of horizontal edges that you created. Select these edges. Put your cursor on the edges.

7. Press *G*, and move the edge back up. Press the MMB briefly as you move them up to lock the motion to the *Z* axis. Press the LMB to release it.

8. Move them close to the upper set of edges. Hold the *Ctrl* key while moving them. Move it up until it is one grid mark below the upper edge you just moved.

9. Zoom in until the smaller grid appears.

10. Press *G*. Press the MMB briefly, as you move the edges up to lock the motion to the *Z* axis, and using the reference grid in the background, use the mouse to move the edges until there are four small boxes below the upper set of edges. Hold the *Ctrl* key while moving them for precise control. Press the LMB to release it.

11. Now, you have the edges in the right place to make the grip. Next, you will make the guard.

12. Zoom in and recenter 3D View on the area between the edges you just moved.

13. Press *A* to deselect all the edges. Press *B* and use the border select tool to select only the vertical edges that are between the two edges that you just adjusted and moved, as shown at the center of the following screenshot.

14. Press *W* to get the **Specials** menu, and choose **Subdivide**. Set the number of cuts to 2.

15. Press *A* to deselect all the edges. Press *B* and use the border select tool to select the horizontal edges that you just made with the **Subdivide** command and the vertical edges between them.

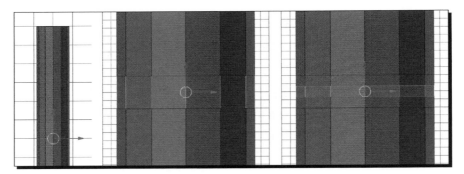

16. Move the mouse away from the cylinder; this will give you the most subtle control of your scaling. Press *S* and use the mouse to scale the edges until the guard section is 0.07 Blender units larger in radius than the main oar shaft, as seen on the left-hand side of the following screenshot, that is, seven of the small grid units. Press the LMB to release it.

17. Press *S* and *Z* and use the mouse to scale them on the *Z* axis. Scale them up until they just cover the first set of edges you made, as seen on the right-hand side of the following screenshot. Press the LMB to release it.

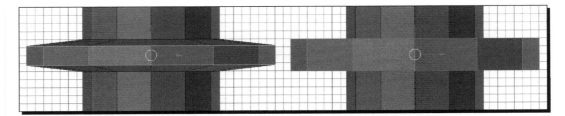

What just happened?

You have created the oar. First, you made a cylinder and gave it the proper length and radius. Twelve sides were chosen, and because these oars will not be seen very closely, this is enough detail.

Then, the side edges were subdivided to make some vertices to create the grip guard. They were moved into position, and then you subdivided that space again to make the guard itself. Next, the guard was scaled out to the proper radius and then scaled in the Z axis so that the side walls of the guard are parallel.

In addition, you learned another way to control motion: by starting to move the edges in one direction and then pressing the MMB to lock the motion to the most similar axis. It works with edges, vertices, sides, and objects.

For your reference, the `4909_06_Oar Grip1.blend` file has the cylinder with the first two subdivisions, `4909_06_Oar Grip2.blend` has the vertical edges selected, `4909_06_Oar Grip3.blend` has the next two subdivisions, `4909_06_Oar Grip4.blend` has the guard scaled up, and `4909_06_Oar Grip5.blend` has the guard scaled in the Z axis.

Making a round shaft into a wide flat blade

Making the grip and guard was pretty straightforward. Now, it's time for some fancier techniques that will help you understand how powerful the basic methods of extrusion, subdividing edges, and moving vertices, edges, and faces can be, as discussed in *Chapter 5, Building a Simple Boat*.

Time for action – making the base of the blade of the oar

Now, you need to make the plastic part of the oar. This will require more detail, so you will be using both extrusion and subdivision to make this transition between parts of the oar. The following steps will help you to make the base of the blade of the oar:

1. Zoom out so that you can see most of the oar.
2. Move to the bottom end of the oar. Rotate the view so that you can see the bottom of the oar.
3. Press A to deselect all edges. Switch to the **Face Select** mode in the **3D View** header. Select the face at the bottom with the RMB, and press X to delete it. Choose **Faces** from the pop-up menu.
4. Change to the **Front Ortho** view. Zoom in to the bottom of the oar.

5. Switch to the **Edge Select** mode in the **3D View** header. Make sure that the **Limit Selection to Visible** button is still turned off. Use the border select tool to select the edges at the bottom of the oar.

6. Press *E* and then press *Enter*.

7. Scale the edges so that they spread out to the next major grid line, as shown in the middle portion of the next screenshot. This will be the beginning of the oar blade.

8. If you think that you goofed up and need to redo an extrusion, use *Ctrl + Z* to undo the step(s), and be sure to go one step past the extrusion. A double extrusion will add unnecessary vertices to the model and may cause problems that are hard to figure out.

9. Press *W* to subdivide the edges. Set the number of cuts to 1. The shaft is simple, but you will need more detail to make the oar blade.

10. Pan the view towards the topside so that the bottom of the oar is near the top of the 3D View window. Move your cursor to the top as well.

11. Press *E* and move the new extruded edges below the three major grid sections or 0.3 Blender units down as shown on the right of the next screenshot. As you did a few steps earlier, press the MMB to lock your motion to the *Z* axis and use the *Ctrl* key as you move it down, so you can see how far you've gone.

12. Note that now, as seen on the right-hand side of the following screenshot, the blade has 24 sides around and the shaft has only 12:

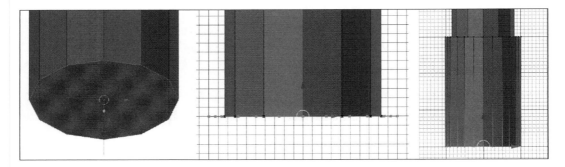

What just happened?

You started making the blade of the oar. The blade of the oar requires more detail than the grip did, so the edges were subdivided. Then, the shaft was extruded to the point where the blade of the oar appeared.

For your reference: the file `4909_06_Oar Blade1.blend` has the center vertex on the end of the shaft being deleted, `4909_06_Oar Blade2.blend` has the blade shaft being created by scaling out the vertices, `4909_06_Oar Blade3.blend` has the edges moved into place and subdivided, and `4909_06_Oar Blade4.blend` has the beginning of the blade.

Time for action – making the blade

Now it's time to make the oar blade. The modeling will be a little more complex, so pay close attention to these steps:

1. Zoom out a little and move the bottom of the oar to the top of 3D View. Move the mouse to the top of 3D View. Have at least eight major grids below the bottom of the oar.

2. Press *E*, and move the new edges down 0.8 Blender units, eight of the grid sections. Press the MMB after starting your motion to restrict the motion to *Z*. Use the *Ctrl* key while moving the edges for more precision.

3. Zoom in to the bottom of the oar. Choose the **Vertex select** mode. Press *A* to deselect all vertices. Press the RMB to select the left vertex, and then *Shift* + RMB to select the right vertex on the sides at the bottom, as seen in the following screenshot:

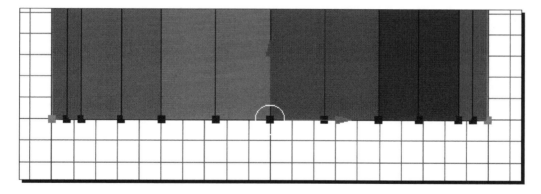

4. You don't need to rotate the view, but after selecting the vertices, zoom back out so you can see three or more large grid lines on either side.

5. Press *S*, *X*, and use the mouse to scale them in the *X* axis. Scale them out by one and a half grid units as shown in the next screenshot on the left-hand side. Press the LMB to release it.

6. Rotate the view so you can see the bottom of the oar.

7. Deselect all the vertices. Select the vertices that are still in a circle, as shown in the right screenshot:

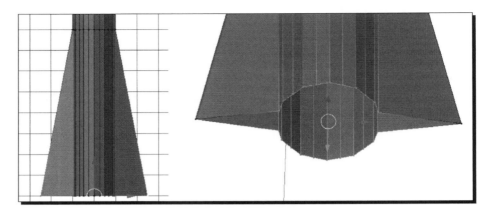

8. Press *S*, *X*, enter the value 0.37, and press *Enter* to scale them along the *X* axis to 37 percent of their original width, as shown in the following screenshot:

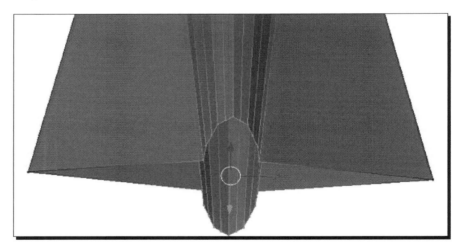

9. Next, the tip of the shaft needs a point. First, you will make the right side of the point. Change the view to the **Right-Side** view.

10. In the **3D View** header, two buttons to the right of the **Edit Mode** button is the **Pivot center** button. By default, the image on the button is two overlapping balls for the **Median Point** pivot point. Left-click on the button and select **3D Cursor** from the pop-up menu.

11. Press *A* to deselect all the vertices. Press *C* to use the circle selection tool to pick the vertex that is immediately to the right of the center vertex. Press the RMB when it is selected.

12. Press *Shift + S* and choose **Cursor to Selected** from the menu.

13. Press *C* to use the circle selection tool to select all the other vertices to the right of the center vertex in addition to the one you already selected, as seen in the left-hand side of the following screenshot. Then, press the RMB to end your selection.

14. Press *R* and *X*, enter the value -90, and press *Enter*. This is shown in the middle part of the next screenshot.

15. Press *S* and *Y*, enter the value 0 (zero), and press *Enter*. This ensures that all the vertices are flat along the *Y* axis with respect to the others.

16. Now, you will be making the left side of the point.

17. Press *A* to deselect all the vertices. Use the **Circle** selection to pick the vertex that is immediately to the left of the center vertex.

18. Press *Shift + S* and choose **Cursor to Selected** from the menu.

19. Select the vertices to the left of the center vertex. This includes the one next to the 3D Cursor.

20. Press *R* and *X*, enter the value 90, and press *Enter*.

21. Press *S* and *Y*, enter the value 0 (zero), and press *Enter*. This ensures that all the vertices are flat with respect to the others, as shown in the following screenshot:

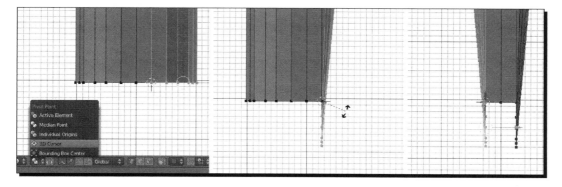

22. Finally, you need to make the bottom edge of the oar.

23. Change to the **Front** view. Pan the view so that the bottom of the oar is at the top of the 3D view. Make sure that there are eight grid units visible below the oar.

24. Select all the vertices at the bottom.

25. Place your cursor just above the bottom edge of the oar.

26. Extrude the vertices, and move the bottom edge down another eight grid units as seen in the left-hand side of the next screenshot. Remember the MMB and the *Ctrl* button.

27. In the **3D View** header, set the **Pivot Point** button to **Median Point**.

28. Press *S* then *Z*, enter the value 0 (zero), and then press *Enter* to flatten the bottom of the oar.

29. Press *S* then *X*, enter the value 0.85, and then press *Enter* to taper the bottom of the oar.

30. Rotate the view so that you can see the bottom of the oar.

31. Press the *F* key to make a face at the bottom of the oar, as shown in the center of the following screenshot.

32. Press the *Tab* key to get out of **Edit Mode**. The oar is done. Good work!

33. In the top-right corner of the **Blender** window above the **Properties Window**, there is a small window called the **Outliner Window**, as seen on the right-hand side of the following screenshot. Clicking on **Camera** will select the camera.

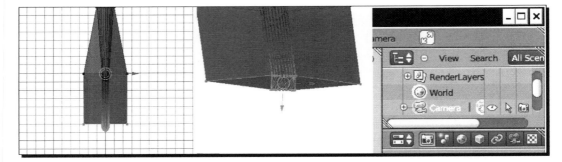

34. Press the NumPad *0* key to change to the **Camera** view in the 3D View.

35. Move the camera so that the oar is completely visible.

36. Render it and save the file with a unique name.

What just happened?

You made an oar. Well done! To make the blade, you extruded the end edges. You took two of the vertices at the end to make the blade and scaled them out in the *X* axis. Then, in a nifty trick, you squeezed the other vertices in the *X* axis to make them narrower and then rotated them 90 degrees to make a cool-looking point for the oar shaft; you then flattened them to the surface of the blade by scaling them to zero in the *Y* axis so that the point would be flat. Then, you repeated the steps on the other side. After that, you extruded the points again to make the end of the oar and scaled all the vertices to zero in the *Z* axis so that the bottom end of the oar was flat. Finally, you capped the end of the oar and rendered it out to see what you made.

For your reference, the 4909_06_Oar Blade5.blend file has the blade shaft extruded, 4909_06_Oar Blade6.blend has the blade rotated in the 3D View, 4909_06_Oar Blade7.blend has the two blade vertices selected, 4909_06_Oar Blade8.blend has the blade vertices scaled out, 4909_06_Oar Blade9.blend has the end of the shaft scaled in the *X* axis, 4909_06_Oar Blade10.blend has the vertices selected to make the pointed tip of the shaft, 4909_06_Oar Blade11.blend has the pointed tip completed, 4909_06_Oar Blade12.blend has the blade extruded to the full length, and 4909_06_Oar Blade13.blend has the end of the oar flattened.

Controlling how smooth the surface is

As you may have noticed in the render, the grip and shaft do not look smooth at all. You might want it to look a little nicer. Fortunately, Blender allows you to control how smooth or flat faces appear. By default, the surfaces are flat. You must set them as smooth surfaces if you want them to be smoothed. This tells Blender to consider the normals of the adjacent faces when reading the normal for a particular face.

Time for action – controlling flat and smooth surfaces

By default, the surfaces are flat. However, you want the rounded surfaces to be smooth. Selecting the faces is the main task. Making them smooth once you have them selected is easy. The following steps will guide you to control the flat and smooth surfaces:

1. Press the NumPad *1* key and adjust the 3D View window so that you can see the grip and guard.

2. Select the **Oar** and get into **Edit Mode**.

3. Choose the **Face Select** mode from the **3D View** header.

4. Press *B* and use **Border Select** to choose the faces of the grip, as seen in the left-hand side of the following screenshot. Do not select the end of the grip.

5. Next, use **Border Select** to select the faces on the perimeter of the grip guard, as shown in the center of the next screenshot. Do not select the faces of the sides.

6. Now, select the faces of the oar shaft, the top perimeter of the blade, and where the shaft tapers down within the blade, as shown on the right-hand side of the following screenshot:

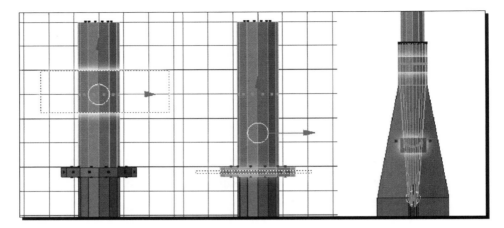

7. In the tool shelf on the left-hand side of the 3D View window, click on the **Shading/UVs** tab with the LMB. Look at the **Shading** subpanel and find the **Smooth** button in **Faces:**; then, click on it with the LMB.

8. Press the *Tab* key to get into **Object Mode**. Zoom out. Select the lamp; then, change the lamp to a **Hemi** lamp as you changed lamps in the bonus chapter *Chapter 5A, Lighting a Small Boat*. Press *F12* to render the image.

What just happened?

You selected faces where the surface should be smooth from face to face and assigned them to have smooth shading.

Other sections of the oar, such as the end of the grip, flat sides of the grip guard, end of the oar blade, and flat sides of the blade, should be flat because they are flat surfaces.

The difference between smooth and flat surfaces is that when calculating a smooth surface, Blender considers the normals of adjacent faces as well as the normal of the face it is rendering. With flat surfaces, Blender only needs to calculate the normal of that face without considering other faces.

 The 4909_06_Oar Blade14.blend file has the basic oar with the surfaces smoothed.

Have a go hero – tidying up the details

Modeling, like other arts, is often something where you decide on changes as you go along. Here are some suggestions to improve the oar:

1. The outside edge of the oar blade needs some curve in the top section. Add it.

2. Make a group for the grip, a group for the shaft, and a group for the blade, as shown in *Chapter 4, Modeling with Vertices, Edges, and Faces*. The oar needs to be colored. Add materials to them as seen in the right-hand side of the following screenshot. Use the groupings you just created to make it easier.

3. Find the **Object** button (the orange cube highlighted as shown in the following screenshot) in the **Properties Window** header; press it and rename the object to **Oar** in the box, as shown in the following screenshot:

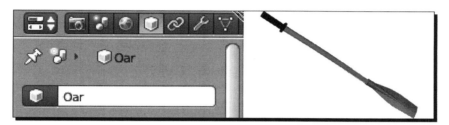

4. Save your .blend file with the oar.

> The 4909_06_Oar Blade15.blend file consists of the oar with all details tidied.

Making the oarlock

The oarlock is small but important. It connects the oar with the boat, and when animated, it will be used for the rotation keyframes for the *Z* axis. To make it, you will start with a torus.

Time for action – making the oarlock

This will be a change of methods. However, with some deletion of faces, copying them, moving them, and extruding them, you will soon have an oarlock:

1. Open a new file in Blender.
2. Press *X* to delete the default cube.

3. Make a cylinder. In the **Tool Shelf**, set the radius to 0.083 like the shaft of the oar, as seen in the following screenshot:

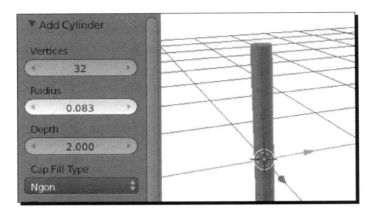

4. Change to the **Top** view, **Ortho** mode, and zoom in to the cylinder.

5. Press *A* to deselect the cylinder. Press *Shift + A*, and select **Mesh** and then **Torus** from the drop-down menu.

6. In the **Tool Shelf**, set the **Major Segments** to 18 and the **Minor Segments** to 12; then, set the **Major Radius** to 0.13 and the **Minor Radius** to 0.035. This is shown in the following screenshot:

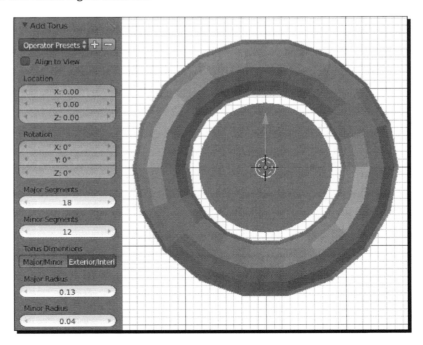

7. Press the *Tab* key to get into **Edit Mode**. Choose the vertex select mode from the **3D View** header.

8. Make the **Limit selection to visible** button on the **3D View** header light gray so that you can select all the vertices.

9. Deselect all the vertices. Press *B* for the border select tool to select the vertices above the center of the torus, as shown in the next screenshot.

10. Press *X* and select the vertices from the pop-up menu.

11. Press *B* for the border select tool to select the top ring of vertices. Press *E* to extrude vertices and start moving them up. Move them up to the next major grid line or to 0.100. Don't forget to use the MMB and the *Ctrl* key.

12. Extrude them again and go up 0.0500, as shown in the center of the next screenshot.

13. Press *F* to fill the top ends with polygons.

14. Press *A* to deselect all the vertices. Press *B* for the border select tool to select the vertices from one of the ends.

15. Move the cursor up to the top of the torus.

16. Press *Shift + D* to copy the selected polygons.

17. Move it below the oarlock as shown on the right-hand side of the following screenshot. Use the *Shift + Ctrl* buttons in the final placement to make sure it is centered below the torus.

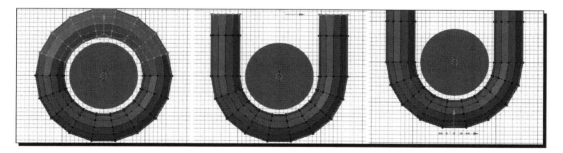

18. Press *E*, enter the value *-0.4*, and press *Enter* to extrude the cylinder end into a shaft 0.4 units long, as shown on the left-hand side of the next screenshot. This will become the oarlock pin.

19. Press *B* for the border select tool and select all the vertices in the oarlock pin. Bring them into a group named Pin. This will help if you have to go back to adjust the pin's height.

20. Press *G* and *Y*, and use the mouse to move the pin up in the *Y* axis until the top is level with the central portion of the metal of the oarlock, as shown in the center of the next screenshot. Press the LMB to release it.

21. Press *A* to deselect all vertices. Press *B* for the border select tool to select only the vertices at the top of the oarlock on the left-hand side.

22. Press *S*, *X*, enter the value 0.5, and then press *Enter*.

23. Press *G* then *X*, and use the mouse to move the selected vertices in the *X* axis so that the left-hand side is vertical, as shown on the right-hand side of the following screenshot. Press the LMB to release it.

24. Press *A* to deselect all the vertices. Press *B* for the border select tool to select only the vertices at the top of the oarlock on the right-hand side.

25. Press *S*, *X*, enter the value 0.5, and then press *Enter*.

26. Press *G* then *X*, and use the mouse to move the selected vertices in the *X* axis so that the right-hand side is vertical. Press the LMB to release it.

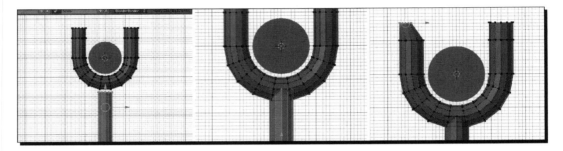

27. In the **Properties** window, select the **Object** button (orange cube) in the header. In the subpanel below, rename the object as Oarlock.

28. Save the file.

What just happened?

First, you made a cylinder of the same radius as your oar, for scale. To make the oarlock, you started by making a torus that would fit around the oar's shaft. Then, you removed half of it and extruded the ends up to create a U shape. You made a copy of one of the ends and moved it below the torus to create the oarlock pin and then extruded the pin. You grouped the extrusion to avoid having to search for the vertices if you ever need to work on the oarlock in the future, and then, you moved the oarlock pin up so that both pieces appear to be one. Finally, you shrank the top ends of the oarlock to make it easier for the oar to be located into the oarlock.

For your reference, the 4909_06_Oarlock1.blend file has the torus with the top half removed, 4909_06_Oarlock2.blend has the top of the oarlock extruded, 4909_06_Oarlock3.blend has the shaft started, 4909_06_Oarlock4.blend has the shaft in place, and 4909_06_Oarlock5.blend has the oarlock completed.

Assembling the boat, oars, and oarlocks

Well done! You've made the boat, an oar, and an oarlock. Now, it's time to assemble everything and animate them all. We'll open the boat and then add the oar and oarlock by appending them to the file. This section will introduce you to a new concept: parent and child objects. Imagine a mother and child holding hands. Both are independent, but the mother controls the child's actions. 3D objects can control each other in a similar way.

Time for action – loading all of the models together

You have the boat, the oar, and the oarlocks all done. Now, it's time to assemble them together:

1. Load the final version of the boat you built, or if you want, you can load 4909_05_boat_test the lights.blend from the download pack.

2. Press *A* to deselect everything.

3. Select **Layer 3** by pressing *3* or using **Layer Visibility Controls**.

4. Choose **Wireframe** from the **Viewport Shading** menu on the **3D View** header.

5. Select the **File** menu, and go to **Append** in the drop-down menu.

6. Find the directory that you stored the oarlock in, or you can use 4909_06_Oarlock5.blend from the download pack. Select **Object** from the next menu. Then select **Oarlock** from the final menu. Press the **Link/Append from Library** button in the upper-right corner of the window.

7. Select **Oarlock** with the RMB. In the **Properties** window, name the Oarlock, **Oarlock–R**. Press *Enter* after naming.

8. Find the directory that you stored the oar in, or you can use 4909_06_Oar Blade15.blend from the download pack. Choose **File** and then select **Append** from the drop-down menu. Select **Object** from the next menu, and then select **Oar** from the final menu. Press the **Link/Append from Library** button in the upper-right corner of the window.

9. Select the oar with the RMB. Name the oar, `Oar-R`. Press *Enter* after naming.

10. Press the *Home* key to see the entire oar. Press *R, Z*, enter the value *90*, and press *Enter* to rotate the oar so that the blade is parallel to the oarlock shaft, as shown on the left-hand side of the next screenshot.

11. Zoom in so that you can see the oarlock.

12. Press *Shift* + the RMB to select the oarlock. Note that the oar is a lighter color than the oarlock. This is because the oarlock is the active object. Press *Ctrl + P* to parent the oarlock to the oar. Choose **Set Parent to Object** in the pop-up menu.

13. Select only the oarlock and move it around to check that the oar moves when you move the oarlock. Press *Esc* or the RMB to let it go to the original position. If the oar doesn't move with the oarlock, go back a step and try to parent the oarlock to the oar again. Remember to select the oar first.

14. Make sure that only the oarlock is selected. Press *R, X*, enter the value 90, and press *Enter* to rotate the oarlock into the correct orientation. The oar will follow the oarlock, as seen on the right-hand side of the following screenshot:

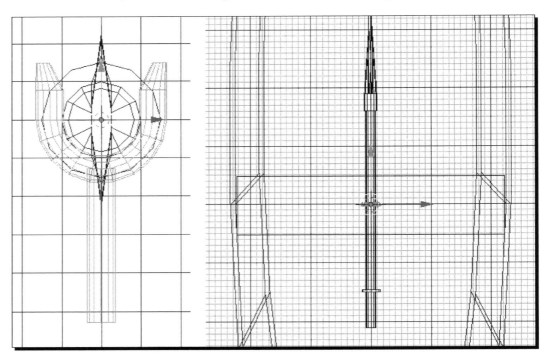

15. Press *Shift + 1* to display both layer 3 and layer 1. Alternatively, use *Shift* + LMB over layer 1 in **Layer Visibility Controls**.

16. Change to the **Right** view. Zoom in until you see the smaller grid.

17. Press *G* then *Z*, and then move the oarlock up with the mouse so that the top of the oarlock pin is above the gunwale. Press the LMB to drop it in place.

18. Press *G* then *Y* to move the oarlock 1.2 units to the right, as shown in the following screenshot. Press the LMB to release it.

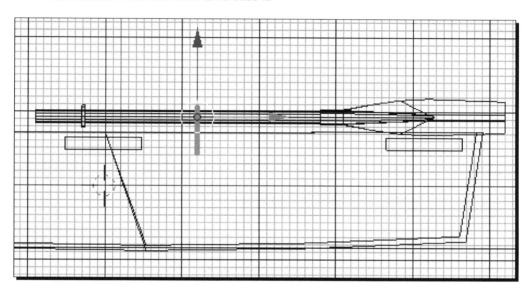

19. Set the **3D View Viewport Shading** button to **Solid**.

20. Press *Ctrl* + NumPad *1* to change to the **Back** view. Press *G* and then *X*, and use the mouse to move the oarlock to the right, so that it is next to the gunwale. Make sure it doesn't stick through the boat to the outside, as shown on the left-hand side of the following screenshot. Press the LMB to release it.

21. Press *R, Z*, enter the value 90, and press *Enter* to rotate the oarlock.
The oar, as a child of the oarlock, will rotate along with the oarlock.

22. Press *Shift* + RMB and select the oar in addition to the oarlock.

23. Press *Shift + D* and then press *Enter* to duplicate them. Use the mouse to move the duplicates to the opposite side of the boat; press the MMB to keep motion to the *X* axis. Move the new oarlock till it pokes out at the side of the boat; then, move it back a little so that it doesn't show.

24. Press *R*, *Z*, enter the value `180`, and press *Enter* to rotate the oarlock as shown on the right-hand side of the following screenshot.

25. Select the oar you just made with the RMB and name it `Oar-L`. Press *Enter* after naming.

26. Select the oarlock you just made with the RMB. Name it `Oarlock-L`. Press *Enter* after naming.

27. Now, select the boat in addition to the oarlock. Press *Ctrl* + *P* to parent the boat to the oarlock. Choose **Set Parent to Object** in the pop-up menu.

28. Select the other oarlock with the RMB, and then select the boat with *Shift* + RMB. Press *Ctrl* + *P* again.

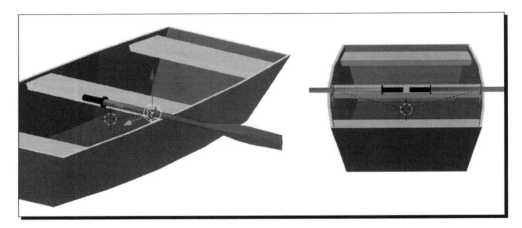

29. Select only the boat with the RMB and test rotate it to make sure all the parenting is correct and that the oar locks and oars follow the boat. Press *Esc* or the RMB to release the boat back to its original position.

30. Select **Layer 3**. Press *B* and select the oars and oarlocks. Press *M* and move them to **Layer 1**. Select **Layer 1**. Save the file to a unique name.

What just happened?

You just loaded the boat, oar, and oarlock into a single file. You made some minor adjustments to the oar and oarlock. You parented the oarlock to the oar and then moved the oarlock into place and rotated it properly. You tested the parenting to make sure that the oar follows the oarlock. After duplicating the oarlock and oar, you parented the boat to both oarlocks. Notice that when you copied both the oarlock and oar, the parenting relationship between the objects was copied as well. Well done! If the parenting did not succeed, just press *Ctrl* + *Z* to undo what you did and retry it.

For your reference, the 4909_06_ boat_assembled1.blend file has the boat, oar, and oarlock in one file; 4909_06_ boat_assembled2. blend has the oarlock parented to the oar, and the properly oriented oar; 4909_06_ boat_assembled3.blend has the oarlocks in position; and 4909_06_ boat_assembled4.blend has the boat parented to the oarlocks and oars.

Have a go hero – adding some blocks to put the oarlock in

You put the oarlocks in the proper place, but for it to look the best, it would help if there were wooden blocks around the oarlock pin. Select the boat; then, in **Edit Mode**, add a block around the oarlock pin and copy it to the other side. Give the block the same texture as the hull of the boat. Save the file when you are done. The blocks can be seen in the following screenshot:

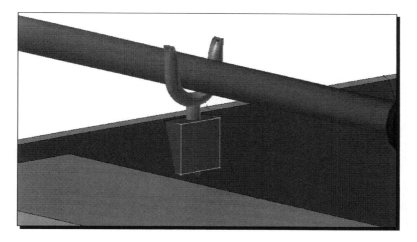

Animating the boat

It is said that *an animator is an actor with a pencil*. The point remains true even though you are using Blender instead of a pencil. A good animator is also a good actor. This is true even for something as simple as rowing the boat.

Think about rowing the boat. Basically, you dip the oars into the water, move the blades backwards with respect to the boat until the stroke is done, then lift up the oars and move them back to the starting position. So, how long is this motion going to take?

Rowing is not just a mechanical action. People will row differently depending on their purpose and attitude.

All animators should own a stopwatch. You can get an inexpensive one online or at a local store. If you don't have one, you can use a clock or an online stopwatch that you might find at sites such as `http://www.online-stopwatch.com/`. However, none are as convenient or as accurate as a real stopwatch.

Time for action – timing a stroke

The best way to figure out how long an action takes is to do it and time it. In the following steps, you'll do a rowing stroke to see how long the animation should be set, where you can lean forward and backward:

1. Hold your arms out and hold your stopwatch in one hand.

2. Start the stopwatch and immediately lean backwards as though you are pulling oars against the water. This is called the *drive* phase of the stroke.

3. At the end of the stroke, move your hands down to lift the oars out of the water and lean forward. These are known as the *extraction* and *recovery* phases.

4. Then, move your hands back up to the starting point to dip the oars back into the water. This is the *catch* phase.

5. Do this three times and then stop the stopwatch. Write down the time it took.

6. Repeat the timing two more times. Hopefully, all three readings will be about the same. Take the average of these three readings and then divide this time by three to get the length of time a single-stroke cycle takes.

7. Now, start the stopwatch and just pull backward. Stop the stopwatch when you finish pulling backward. Write down the time. Do it three times.

What just happened?

You just did your first bit of acting. By rowing three strokes each time, you got a better average of how long a single stroke should take. By repeating it three times, you know how consistent you are being. My average for the three strokes was 5.8 seconds for three repetitions or 1.93 seconds for each stroke.

However, you also want a little bit more information about the stroke. That's why you timed just the drive stroke. I was surprised that just the drive stroke was 0.85 seconds. It seemed short, but it leaves 1.08 seconds to raise the oar and move back to the starting position.

Now there is one caveat here

Few of us have a rowboat and a lake at our desk to be sure of our timing. Therefore, as an additional reference, I found some rowing videos for you to watch:

◆ **Row Exercise**: Competitive Rowers,
`http://youtu.be/_6JhKZMVL_g`

◆ **Tupan**: Man rowing a homebuilt skiff in a relaxed manner,
`http://youtu.be/6Xc9lLccEf0`

◆ **Old Wharf Dory Rowing 1**: Maneuvering and turning,
`http://youtu.be/Z5wTN0zBFx0`

When I timed the row-exercise video, the timing was similar to what I had done, so I was happy with my timing.

Have a go hero – figuring out how long it takes you to row the boat

Using the information you got when you acted out rowing the boat, figure out how many frames it will take to do the two parts of the rowing cycle. Assume a video speed of 30 frames per second.

Parenting and kinematics

Earlier, you chose the oarlock and parented it to the oar. You also found that you could move the oar around just by moving the oarlock. The oar follows the oarlock just like a child holding their parent's hand.

In *Chapter 3, Controlling the Lamp, the Camera, and Animating Objects*, we talked about global axis and local axis. Now, each oar has a global axis, a parent boat axis, the parent oarlock axis, and a local axis for the oar itself. It may seem confusing if you describe it, but by seeing the boat and the oars, it becomes more intuitive.

Kinematics describes how objects control the motion of other objects. You will use two basic kinds of kinematics in animation: forward kinematics and inverse kinematics. They are described as follows:

◆ **Forward kinematics** is what you will use with the rowboat. The motion of the boat controls the motion of the oarlock, and the oarlock controls the oar.

◆ **Inverse kinematics** is like your hand and shoulder. You focus on moving your hand in relation to your shoulder, and this moves your arm, elbow, and forearm automatically.

Time for action – animating the oarlock and oar

Now that you have the timing, you can animate the oarlock and oar using the information you got from your timing:

1. In the 3D View window, shift to the **Top** view. In the timeline window, drag the **Current Frame Indicator**, the green vertical line in the **Timeline** as seen in the next screenshot, to go to frame **1**.

2. Set the **Pivot Point** to **Median Point**. Make sure you are in the **Object** mode. Now, select the **Oarlock-R**.

3. Press *R, Z*, enter the value 45, and press *Enter*.

4. Move the cursor over the 3D View window and press the letter *I* to set a **Rotation** keyframe at frame **1**. Then, move the timeline to frame **58** and set another **Rotation** keyframe. It will look like the image on the left-hand side of the next screenshot. You can either drag the **Current Frame Indicator** or type in the number of the frame in the button to the right of **End**.

5. Move to frame **26**.

6. Press *R, Z*, enter the value -90, and press *Enter*. Press *I* to set a rotation keyframe.

7. Repeat this for the other oarlock so that they move in sync with each other. With the cursor over the Timeline window, press the down arrow to go to the previous keyframe at frame 1. Select **Oarlock-L**, press *R, Z*, enter the value -45, press *Enter*, and set a rotation keyframe at frame 1. Move to frame **58** and set another rotation keyframe.

8. Move to frame **26**. Press *R, Z*, and enter the value 90, and press *Enter* and set a rotation keyframe. It will look like the center portion of the image shown in the next screenshot.

9. In the 3D View window, change the view to the **Right** view.

10. Move to frame 1.

11. Select **Oar-L**. Press *R, Y, Y*, enter the value 45, and press *Enter* to dip the oar in the water, as shown on the right-hand side of the following screenshot. This rotates the oar on its local *Y* axis. Now, make a rotation keyframe.

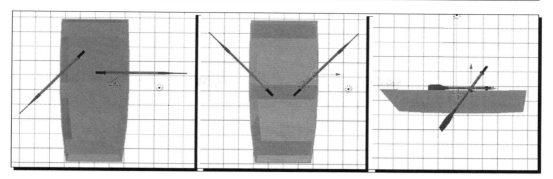

12. Select the other oar. Press *R, Y, Y*, enter the value 45, and press *Enter* to dip the oar in the water. Make a rotation keyframe.

13. Go to frame **26**. Make rotation keyframes for both oars.

14. Go to frame **58**. Make rotation keyframes for both oars.

15. Go to frame **30**. Select an oar. Press *R, Y, Y*, enter the value -40, and press *Enter* to make a keyframe for that oar, as seen on the right-hand side of the previous screenshot.

16. Select the other oar. Press *R, Y, Y*, enter the value -40, and press *Enter* to make a keyframe.

17. Go to frame **53**. Select an oar. Press *R, Y, Y*, enter the value -40, and press *Enter* to make a rotation keyframe for that oar.

18. Select the other oar. Press *R, Y, Y*, enter the value -40, and press *Enter* to make a rotation keyframe.

19. Scrub the **Current Frame Indicator** in the **Timeline** window to test the animation.

20. Save the file with a unique name.

What just happened?

You set up an animation cycle for the oarlocks and oars. The oarlocks rotate and move the oars forward and backward by forward kinematics. You set up the drive stroke from frame 1 to frame 26 (that is 0.85 seconds) and the recovery stroke from frame 26 to frame 58. Rotating the oars on their local *Y* axes dips the blades in the water and raises them. First, you set up the keyframes at the ends of the drive stroke. Then, you added keyframes for the other extreme of the oar stroke. You placed them a few frames before and after the ends of the drive stroke for the catch and extract phases of the rowing cycle.

 For your reference, the 4909_06_boat_animated1.blend file has all the keyframes for the oarlock and oar.

Animation cycles

In *Chapter 3, Controlling the Lamp, the Camera, and Animating Objects*, you experimented with copying keyframes. Here, you put that knowledge to use by creating a rowing cycle. As you may have noticed, the keyframes at frame 1 and frame 58 are identical. Therefore, you are going to copy the keyframes from frame 26 through frame 58 and move them in time to create a rowing cycle.

Time for action – copying keyframes to make a rowing cycle

Everybody likes to save work. Now that you have made a single rowing cycle, you can just copy it and move the copy down the timeline for a smooth flowing animation using the following steps:

1. Use the **Current Editor Type** button at the lower-left corner of the **Timeline** window, which is below 3D View, to change **Timeline** to **Graph Editor** in the window. Move the top edge of the window up vertically so that you can use the Graph Editor more easily.

2. Using the RMB and *Shift* + RMB, select both oars and both oarlocks.

3. Use *Ctrl* + MMB and *Shift* + MMB so that you can see all the F-Curves, as shown in the next screenshot.

4. With the cursor over the Graph Editor, press *A* to deselect all the keyframes. Use **Border Select** to choose all the keyframes between frame 26 and frame 58, as shown in the following screenshot. You can see that all the keyframes from frame 26 onward are highlighted.

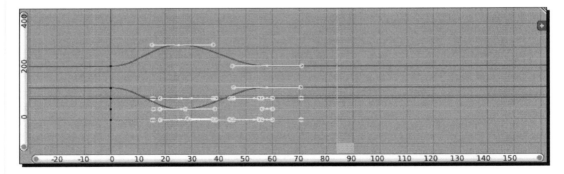

5. Move the current frame indicator to frame 84 in the Graph Editor. You can see what frame you are on in the lower-left corner of the 3D View window.

6. Press *Shift + D* to copy the keyframes. Move the mouse to the right to start moving the new keyframes, and then press the MMB to restrict the motion to that direction.

7. Move them until the copies of the keyframes that were at frame 26 are over frame 84. Press the LMB to release the keyframes, as shown in the following screenshot:

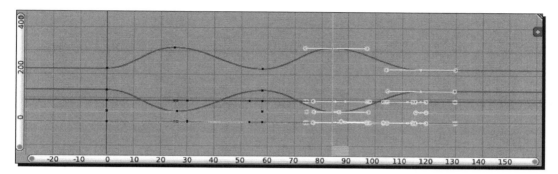

What just happened?

Well done! You made an animation cycle. Did you notice how much less work it took to copy the keyframes than it did to make the original rowing stroke? Animation cycles are a secret that animators have used since *Felix the Cat*.

The cycle that started at frame 1 finished at frame 58 with identical keyframes, so the rowing cycle is 58 frames long. To repeat the cycle, move copies of the cycle 58 frames farther along the timeline. So, when you copied the keyframes from frames 26 to 58 and moved them, frame 58 became similar to frame 1. When you add 58 to 26, the result is 84. Therefore, you dragged copies of keyframes at 26 to 58 and set them down at 84 to 116 to duplicate the cycle.

Have a go hero – adding more cycles

Make additional cycles by pasting the new frames starting at frame 142 and again at frame 200. You can really start to see the cyclic nature of the motion, as shown in the following screenshot. You can see the oscillation of the oarlocks in blue and the dipping of the oar in green.

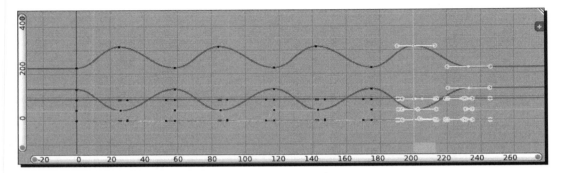

Moving the boat

It looks somewhat silly for the boat to stay still while the oars flail quickly. It's time to get your craft moving.

Time for action – moving the boat in sync with the oars

When you row, you dip the oar in the water and push the boat forward using the oar as a lever. The boat coasts while you are moving the oars back. You are going to create a marker to track this motion. When the oar is in the water, the marker will give you a location for the oar tip. When the oar is out of the water, the width of the marker will show you how far to move the boat while it's coasting:

1. Press the NumPad *3* key to get the **Right** view. Make sure you are on frame **1**. Use the **Current Editor Type** button in the lower-left corner of **Graph Editor** to change **Graph Editor** to **Timeline**.

2. Move your cursor below the boat. Press the LMB.

3. Deselect all the objects and make a cube. Move the cube so that the left corner is just below the blade of the oar, as shown on the left-hand side of the next screenshot.

4. Select the boat and make a location keyframe. Do not make a keyframe for the cube.

5. Move the time to frame 26.

6. Select the boat and move it on the *Y* axis so that the oar lines up over the left corner of the cube. Make a location keyframe for the boat, as shown in the following screenshot:

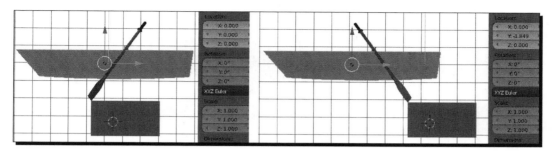

7. Press *N* to open the **Properties** panel. Observe the **Y:** location's values at frame 1 and frame 26.

8. Mine were **0** and **-3.82**. That's how far the boat moved when being rowed. Assume that it goes about the same distance while coasting but give it a few frames extra, as it will be slower.

9. Select the cube. Change its *Y* dimension to `3.82` or the distance your boat went. This is equal to the distance the boat will coast. Move the cube so that the right-hand side of the cube touches the bow of the boat, as seen on the left-hand side of the next screenshot.

10. Go to frame **58**. Select the boat. Move the boat in the *Y* axis until the bow of the boat touches the left-hand side of the cube, as shown in the following screenshot. Press the LMB when you are done and make a location keyframe.

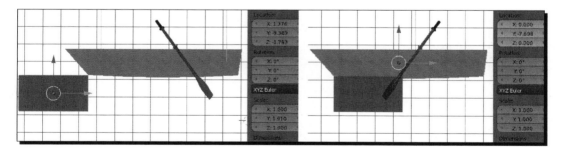

11. Select the cube and move it so that the left corner is under the oar again. Don't make a keyframe for the cube. It is just a reference object.

12. If you find you've made a keyframe for the cube, open the Graph Editor and delete the keyframe. Remember what you learned about selecting particular action channels in *Chapter 3, Controlling the Lamp, the Camera, and Animating Objects*, to make it easier. You can use the arrow button next to the **F-Curve Editor** button in the **Graph Editor** header to select active F-Curves.

13. Twenty-six frames past 58 is frame 84. In the **Timeline**, move to frame 84. Move the boat again in the *Y* axis until the oar is over the left corner of the cube, as seen in the previous graphic on the right-hand side. It doesn't have to be exact. A little variation is good. It makes it more believable. Make a location keyframe.

14. Go to the frame where the oar dips into the water again. Move the cube so that its right-hand side is touching the bow. Move the boat in the *Y* axis until the bow is touching the left-hand side of the cube. Make a location keyframe. Move the cube so that its left corner is by the tip of the oar.

15. Move the current time indicator in the frames until the oar has completed its drive stroke. Move the boat in the *Y* axis so that the tip of the oar is next to the left-hand side of the cube. Make a location keyframe.

16. Continue this cycle of keyframing the boat's motion as long as your oar strokes continue, as shown in the following screenshot. Mark the oar when it is in the water and mark the bow when the boat is coasting.

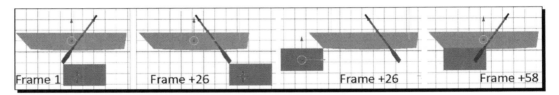

17. Now, press *Alt + A* to watch the animation preview. Press *Esc* when you are done watching it.

18. Save the file with a unique name.

What just happened?

When the oar's stroke is set, you know how far the boat should go with each stroke. You started creating motion keyframes for the boat. Making the keyframes for when the oars are in the water is the easy part. The art is figuring out how long to coast and how far you go when coasting.

If you watched the rowing videos, you know that there is a wide range of expression there. Are you racing, are you purposefully going to a favorite fishing hole, or just enjoying the freedom of being on the water, say with the morning mists curling up from the surface? These would be what you might try to express in a rowing cycle.

For your reference, the `4909_06_boat_animated2.blend` file has the oarlock, oar, and boat motion.

Have a go hero – rowing your boat

As you saw in the videos, rowing a boat is not just a mechanical motion; it can be very expressive. This is your chance to expand on what you have done.

Modify your rowing cycles and the motion of your boat to express different situations. Here are some suggestions:

- If the cycle seems a bit clumsy, change the timing of when the oar keyframes happen so that the catch and extract phases are smoother. You need to show only the *Y* axis rotations for the oars and zoom in to them so that you can see the rotation.

- Race your boat.

- Make slow, relaxed strokes that let the boat coast a lot.

- Turn the boat in circles.

- Create some buoys in the water and maneuver the boat around them.

- Get cartoony and exaggerate the speed and rowing; you can even raise the bow up and down in response to the drive strokes.

Save your file with a unique name when you are done.

Tracking the boat with the camera

Now, let's follow the boat with the camera. It's pretty easy!

Time for action – tracking the boat

It's pretty natural that if you are watching a boat go by, you turn your head to follow it. The camera is no different. The **Track to Constraint** command lets you do just that. The following steps will help you to track the boat:

1. Select the camera with the RMB.

2. Press the *Shift* key and the RMB to select the boat.

3. Press *Ctrl* + *T* to get the tracking menu. Select **Track to Constraint**.

4. Press the NumPad *0* key to get the camera's view.

5. Press *Alt + A* to preview the animation. Press *Esc* when you are done watching it.

6. Save the file with a unique name.

What just happened?

Tracking is very similar to parenting. Select the camera and then select what you want to track. Press *Ctrl + T* and select **Track to Constraint**, and the camera will follow the object you want to track.

 For your reference, the 4909_06_boat_animated3.blend file has the camera tracking the boat.

Have a go hero – tracking with a light

If you've seen an ice skater, you've probably seen them tracked by a spotlight. Now it's time for you to try your hand at tracking an object in motion.

Change the light to a spotlight and track the boat's motion. The commands are the same as for the camera.

 For your reference, the 4909_06_boat_animated4.blend file has the camera and the spotlight tracking the boat.

Making stereoscopic 3D animation

That tracking was pretty cool. What if you could do it in stereo just like *Avatar* or *Men in Black 3*? Blender has got you covered. Check out the bonus chapter *Chapter 6A, Using Stereoscopic Cameras*, that can be downloaded from https://www.packtpub.com/sites/default/files/downloads/4909OS_06A_Using_Stereoscopic_Cameras.pdf. You'll learn how to make two different kinds of stereo camera rigs and use them to record stereo pairs of images.

Pop quiz – pivot points and parents

Q1. Which of the following do not describe available pivot points?

1. Average Location
2. Median Point
3. 3D Cursor

Q2. When choosing two objects to make a parent/child relationship, which object do you select last?

1. Child
2. Parent
3. Either

The key-function table

Here is a table of keyboard commands and their functions:

Key	Function
MMB	Press it after starting to move, scale, or rotate an object and it locks the motion, scaling, or rotation to the nearest axis
Ctrl + *Z*	Undoes a step
Ctrl + *Shift* + *Z*	Redoes a previous step undone with *Ctrl* + *Z*
F	Creates a face from selected vertices
Alt + *F*	Makes faces from selected vertices
Shift + *Alt* + *F*	Done after using *Alt* + *F*, this makes a nicer set of faces
Tab	When using a multiset button, such as *X*, *Y*, *Z*, or *R*, *G*, *B*, it allows you to move quickly between the buttons
B	Does a border select in the Graph Editor
Ctrl + *P*	Child a group of selected objects to the last object selected
Ctrl + *T*	Sets an object(s) to track the last chosen object
Ctrl + NumPad *0*	Sets the active object as the active camera

Summary

In this chapter, you learned how to create oars and oarlocks to move the boat with, and discovered some tricks to make subtle shapes, such as where the shaft tapers into the oar. You found out how to control the smoothness of a surface. You learned to append objects to the scene so that you can combine and reuse objects. You created child-parent relationships to group objects for animation. You used kinematics to organize your animation. You learned to use animation cycles to save work. You tracked objects in motion with a camera, spot lamp, and camera rig.

As you have been making the boat, you may have been wondering how you can plan out your work, how you can use plans from the real world to model, and how you can organize these files to make it easier to work, and so that you can find them later. This is what the next chapter will help you with, and we'll get started with your main project, creating and animating a nautical scene.

Let's go!

7

Planning Your Work, Working Your Plan

In the last chapter, you enhanced your understanding of animation. You assembled the boat, parenting the different objects together and animating them. You learned about children, parents, and kinematics. You explored tracking and expanded that knowledge into doing stereoscopic rendering.

With this good foundation, it's time to take a moment and start planning your big project. You need to understand the conventions that will help you keep track of what you do and where you put what you have done to make it easier for you to achieve what you want.

In this chapter, you will examine the following:

- ◆ Setting up a template in Blender to guide your modeling
- ◆ Using the template to help model the mast, boom, gaff, and bowsprit
- ◆ Using Bézier Curves to model the rudder, keel, and tiller
- ◆ Learning better ways to help keep your projects organized, such as:
    - ❑ Planning your animation
    - ❑ Creating a story
    - ❑ Using storyboards to plan what you are going to do
    - ❑ Using animatics to get the timing right before you animate

◆ Using charts and guides to help you create your animation in the following ways:

    ❑ Safe Title/Safe Action/Lower Third guides

    ❑ Timing diagrams

    ❑ Exposure sheets and Bar sheets

◆ Using the sound track to guide animation timing

Let's get started.

Using templates to model

Well, first you need to have a good idea of what you want to make. This is your next project, a comfy little sloop, as shown in the following screenshot:

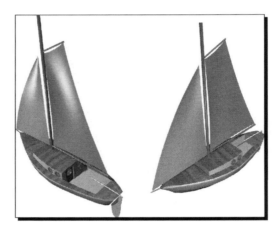

You will need something to help you tell what size the object you are building will be. There are many ways to get the measurements you need. You've already tried some of these methods.

Quite often, you can find plans on the net on websites such as `http://www.boatdesign.net/plans/index.htm`. You can also measure the object yourself. Once, to build a model of an electric guitar, I went to the Carvin guitar factory, took my caliper micrometer and rulers to measure the dimensions of one of their Ultra V guitars, and made some accurate drawings to guide my modeling.

In the plans for the sloop, as shown in the next screenshot, you will see a top view and a side view, and to the very right of the side view, the number **6** is present between two dashes to indicate the scale of the drawing. In this case, the lines above and below **6** show the scaling for six Blender units. I decided that a front view was not necessary because all the details can be figured out from the side and top views.

Time for action – adding a template

Now, get started by putting up the templates so that they can be seen within 3D View, executing the following steps:

1. Open a new file in Blender.

2. Press *3* on the NumPad to get the **Right** view in 3D View and press the *5* on the NumPad for the Ortho view.

3. Press *N* to display the **Properties** panel in 3D View.

4. Scroll down to the **Background Images** subpanel of 3D View's **Properties** panel, as seen in the next screenshot.

5. Click on the triangle that is to the left of the subpanel to open it.

6. Check the checkbox by the text **Background Images**, so that the background image can be displayed.

7. Click on the **Add Image** button.

8. Click on the **Open** button and load the image 4909_07_01.png from this chapter's Images directory in the download pack.

9. Click on the dark **All Views** button next to **Axis:**, and select **Right** from the pop-up menu, as shown in the following screenshot:

10. Press *7* on the NumPad to see the **Top** view in 3D View.

11. Click on the **Add Image** button in the **Background Images** subpanel of 3D View's **Properties** panel. Scroll down and you will see the subpanel where you just added the first template. Below this, there's another subpanel that says **Not Set**, in the upper-left corner. This is the panel you want. You will have to add another template.

12. In the **Not Set** subpanel, select the **Open** button and load the image 4909_07_02.png from the download pack.

13. In the pop-up menu beside **Axis:**, change **All Views** to **Top**. Notice that **Not Set** has been replaced with **4909_07_02.png**.

14. Check that the templates are in place by pressing *7* on the NumPad followed by *3* on the NumPad, and repeat the process.

What just happened?

You just added two templates, one for the **Right** view and another for the **Top** view. You also created two new subpanels in the **Background Images** subpanel with quite a few control buttons.

Have a go hero – inspecting the templates

Before you use the templates, it's a good idea to inspect them to make sure that they are all in scale with each other. If you are copying from plans, there should be some indication of the scale somewhere on the plans. What you may need to do is take the plans that you find into a photo-editing program and adapt them to your needs, adding, subtracting, or modifying details. You don't really want details in the plans that you are not going to make.

Sometimes, the images that you get on the Web are not necessarily scaled accurately relative to each other. You may need to make sure that the projections are of the same scale as each other so that details in a front view are of the same scale as they are on a side view. Also, make sure that the details for the side view are of the same size as they are on the top, the details in the front are as wide as they are in the top view, and so on, as explained in the following points:

♦ Look at the graphics 4909_07_01.png and 4909_07_02.png in a paint program. The file name with 01 is the side view and 02 is the top view. They are shown in the subsequent screenshots.

♦ Put the two graphics in a single graphic and make the top view semi-transparent.

♦ Rotate the top view image 90 degrees clockwise. Then, move it so that the graphics overlay, and you can see how the two views compare in size and detail. The 4909_07_02.png file was originally made so it would lie over the 4909_07_01.png file, but it was then rotated 90 degrees for use in Blender.

- You want to see if the length of the ship is the same in both images; check that the front and rear edges of the cabin and the cockpit match up as well.

 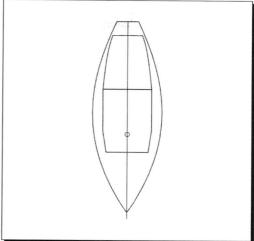

All the graphics for templates used together should be of the same width. Blender uses the width of the graphic as a basis to scale the graphic.

The following illustration has the names of the major components with which you will be dealing as you make your sloop in the next three chapters:

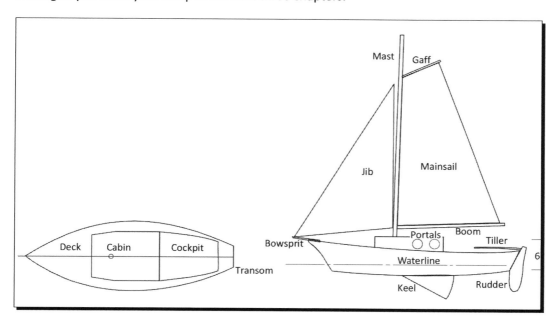

Time for action – scaling and aligning the template

The next step is to make sure that the template is properly scaled to the Blender scene, so that the units marked on the template are equal to the number of units in the Blender scene.

To do this, you have to set the cube to the size of 6 Blender units. Next, you have to adjust the template to the dimension marks—the two lines above and below the number 6 on the side-view template—and align them with the top and bottom of the cube. The following steps will guide you through this process:

1. In 3D View, select the cube. Scroll to the top of 3D View's **Properties** panel so you can see the **Transform** subpanel. Set the **Dimensions:** values as the following: **X:** to 6.00, **Y:** to 6.00, and **Z:** to 6.00, the same way that you set the dimensions of reference blocks in *Chapter 5, Building a Simple Boat*.

2. Press NumPad *3* to display the **Right** view.

3. Scroll down to the **Background Image** subpanel of 3D View's **Properties** panel.

4. Look in the panel, where it says **4909_07_01.png**, as shown in the next screenshot.

5. Change the size of the background image by setting the value of **Size:** to 25. This makes the width of the template 50 units wide or 25 units on either side of the axis. The height of the template is adjusted proportionately.

6. Above the **Size:** button in the panel, as shown in the following screenshot, set the **Y:** value to 18:

7. Zoom out in 3D View until you see the entire image of the sloop, with the cursor over 3D View. Press *G, Z, 3,* and then press *Enter* to move the cube up 3 units in the Z axis. Look at the template. Press *G* and move the cube in the X axis until you reach the number **6** with the two dimensioning marks, above and below, as shown in the next screenshot. Make sure that the top and bottom of the cube line up with the marks. If they are in line with the marks, you can skip the next three steps.

8. If the marks above and below the number **6** do not match with the top and bottom of the cube, you will need to adjust the **Size:** in the **4909_07_01.png** subpanel until they do. To do this, make an adjustment of the **Size:** of the background image, then move the cube so that it is centered between the dimensioning marks.

9. Repeat this until the dimensioning marks on the template fit the top and bottom of the cube. Then, make sure that the cube is selected; in the **Transform** subpanel of 3D View's **Properties** panel, set the cube's location **Z:** value to 3.

10. Finally, in the **Background Images** subpanel of the 3D View's **Properties** panel, adjust the template's **Y:** value until the dimensioning marks lie over the top and bottom of the cube once again. Well done!

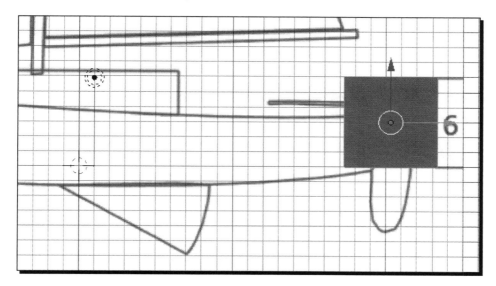

11. In the **Background Images** subpanel of the **Properties** panel, select the subpanel for the 4909_07_02.png image, as shown in the following screenshot.

12. Change **Size:** of the template image to 25. If you had to adjust the size of the first image, change it to your final size.

13. Press 7 on the NumPad for the **Top** view. You want to make sure that the template is centered. If it is not centered, adjust it in **X:** so that the centerline of the boat template lies over the Y axis.

14. Save the file with a unique name.

What just happened?

By adjusting the size of the background image, you scaled it to an object of known size, which in this case is a reference block of 6 Blender units. This helped scale your background image properly. You changed the X axis offset of the template so that the waterline of the sloop is at the origin of the scene. Then, the **Top** view template was scaled to the same size to keep both templates in registration. Now, you have two templates to guide you in building the sloop. Well done!

 For your reference, the file 4909_07_templates_set_up.blend has both templates and the six-unit reference block.

Time for action – building the mast

It's now time to start building the sloop. Since you have the template in the Blender file, you can build each object to the template and be confident that they will all fit together when you are done. The following steps will guide you to build the mast:

1. Press *3* on the NumPad to get the **Right** view. Make sure you are in Ortho mode. Use *Shift* + MMB to center your view on the mast, and press *Ctrl* + MMB to zoom into the mast so that the width of the mast in the template covers a third of 3D View.

2. Press *Shift* + *S* and select **Cursor to Center** from the menu. This makes sure that the 3D Cursor is centered with respect to the *X* axis, so your mast will be centered in the sloop.

3. Place your cursor over the center of the mast in the template. Press the mouse button to put the 3D Cursor there. Press *Shift* + *A*, select **Mesh**, and then select **Cylinder** from the menu to make a cylinder.

4. Press *S* and use the mouse to scale the cylinder so that it is about the same diameter as the mast, as shown in the following screenshot. Press the mouse button to release the scaling.

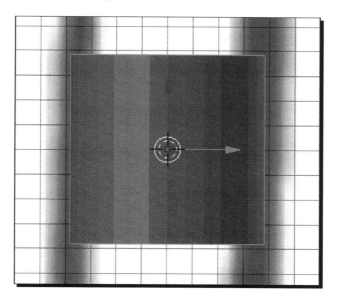

5. Press the *Tab* key to go into **Edit Mode**.

6. Make sure that the **Limit Selection to Visible** button on the **3D View** header is light gray so that you select both the front- and back-facing vertices.

7. Press *A* to deselect all the vertices, and then press *B* to start the **Border** select. Select the bottom vertices.

8. Zoom out so you can see the bottom of the mast in the template. If you need help moving the view around within the scene, check out *Chapter 2, Getting Comfortable Using the 3D View*, to refresh your memory.

9. Press *G* and use the mouse to move the selected vertices to the bottom of the mast. Press the LMB to release the move.

10. Press *A* to deselect all vertices. Then, select the top vertices and move them to the top of the mast.

11. Zoom in to the top of the mast. Then, press *S* and scale the top vertices a little smaller to match the template more closely. Use the mouse to release the scaling.

12. In the **Properties** window, to the right of the 3D View window, select the **Object** button from the header (the orange cube). Name the object **Mast** and press *Enter*.

13. With the cursor over the 3D View window, press the *Tab* key to return to **Object Mode**.

14. Press the *Home* key on your keyboard to see the entire scene again. This is not the *Home* key on your NumPad. If you are using a Mac, press *fn* + left arrow key.

What just happened?

Well, you just made the mast. Pretty easy as it turns out. You scaled the cylinder to the right diameter. Then, by moving the top and bottom vertices independently, you copied the slight angle of the mast and gave it a small bit of taper, just like the template.

Have a go hero – making the boom, gaff, and bowsprit

Now, try it again with different parts. As you make the parts, make sure you get into **Object Mode** after making them and before making a new part. Otherwise, the parts will be stuck together as part of a single object, just as the seats of the boat were in *Chapter 5, Building a Simple Boat*. It is easiest if you rotate the part so that it is at about the same angle as the object on the template that you are making before you scale it and go into **Edit Mode**. Here are some points to remember:

- The boom is the pole at the bottom of the mainsail
- The gaff is the pole at the top
- The bowsprit is the pole that sticks off of the bow of the sloop
- Make them and name them
- Save the file with a unique name

For your reference, the file `4909_07_sloop - mast.blend` has the mast started, and `4909_07_sloop - mast_boom_gaff_bowsprit.blend` has the mast, boom, gaff, and bowsprit completed.

Modeling with Bézier Curves

In *Chapter 3, Controlling the Lamp, the Camera, and Animating Objects*, we discussed the use of Bézier Curves as F-Curves to control motion. Blender uses Bézier Curves to model as well. They are good to make objects with smooth curves.

One big difference between the curves used to control motion and the curves used to model is that the latter can move along the *X*, *Y*, and *Z* axes instead of just the timeline axis; therefore, they can be used with much more flexibility.

Making an object with a single Bézier Curve

Most of the time, Bézier Curves are used like cookie-cutters to describe a shape which is then extruded. These may even have holes in them so that you can make very complex shapes. However, you will start with a simple one.

Time for action – making the rudder with a Bézier Curve

The controls for the Bézier Curves work in a similar manner as the controls for the F-Curve. You have a control point that represents a particular location in space and two control handles that control how the curve approaches and departs from the control point. Check *Chapter 3, Controlling the Lamp, the Camera, and Animating Objects*, if you need a reminder on how they work. Use the following steps to create the rudder:

1. Select the scaling reference cube. Press *M*, *2*, and *Enter* to move it to layer 2 so that it won't be in your way.

2. Press *Shift* + *S* and select **Cursor to Center** from the menu. Use *Shift* + MMB to center your view on the top of the rudder, and use *Ctrl* + MMB to zoom in to the rudder. Check the screenshot provided earlier in the chapter if you don't remember what the rudder is. Put your mouse cursor to the top-right corner of the rudder, as shown in the next screenshot. Use the mouse to move the 3D Cursor to that spot.

3. Press *Shift + A*, and select **Curve**, and then **Bezier**, as shown in the following screenshot:

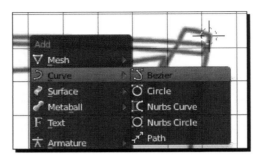

4. In the **Add Bezier** subpanel of the Tool Shelf, click on the **Align to View** checkbox.

5. Press the *Tab* key to get into **Edit Mode**. Use the RMB to select the left-hand control point. Move it to the left-hand top corner of the rudder and click to drop it in place. Move the right-hand control point to the right-hand top corner of the rudder.

6. Move the mouse cursor to where the curve at the back of the rudder changes direction as shown in the right side of the next screenshot, and press *Ctrl* + LMB to make the new control point.

7. Move the cursor to the bottom of the rudder. Make a control point. Make one point where the rudder meets the bottom of the hull, as shown in the right side of the following screenshot:

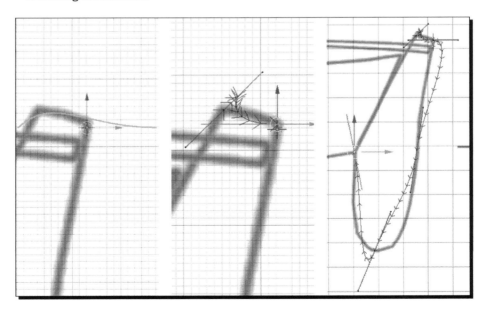

8. Select the first control point again using *Shift* + RMB. Press *F* to join the first and last control points together.

9. Zoom in and make sure that each control point is centered over the outline of the rudder in the template. Move the control points if necessary. Don't worry about where the curve or the handles go, just get the control points in place. Zoom back out when you are done.

10. Press the RMB to select the right-hand control handle for the control point at the bottom of the rudder, then move the control handle about 90 degrees clockwise so that the path follows the shape of the rudder more closely.

11. Then, select the other control handle and move it horizontally so that the curve follows the rudder outline, as shown in the left portion of the next screenshot.

12. At the place where the rudder contacts the bottom of the hull, select the upper control handle of the control point. Press *V* and select **Vector** from the pop-up menu.

13. Between the top two control points are two control handles, as shown in the center portion of the next screenshot. Select both control handles, press *V*, and select **Vector** from the menu.

14. Zoom in to the top of the rudder. Press *G*, and then move the two controls and handles at the top of the rudder up just a little so that there is a gentle arch on the top of the rudder.

15. Move the lower control handle of the top-right control point so that the curve aligns with the outline of the rudder on the template.

16. Rotate the control handles in the center of the right side so that the curve follows the shape of the rudder more closely.

17. At the place where the rudder contacts the bottom of the hull, select the control handle that points down and move it so that it points almost straight down, as seen on the right side of the following screenshot:

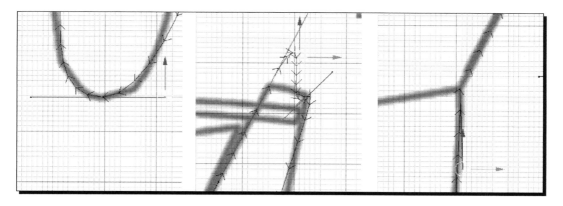

18. Select the left-hand control point at the bottom of the rudder. Move it slightly to the right so that the curve aligns with the outline of the rudder on the template.

19. In the 3D View header, set the **Viewport Shading** menu to **Solid**.

20. In the **Properties** window, select the **Object Data** button in the header. It's the button with the curve and control points on it, as shown in the next screenshot.

21. In the **Shape** subpanel, select the **2D** button to highlight it in blue, as shown in the following screenshot. In the **Geometry** subpanel, set the **Extrude:** value to 0.080, as shown in the bottom-left corner of the following screenshot:

22. Next, select the **Object** panel from the **Properties** window header, the one with the orange cube. Name the object **Rudder**.

23. Move the cursor to 3D View, and then press the *Tab* key to get back into **Object Mode**.

24. Save the file with a unique name.

What just happened?

You used the Bézier Curve to create the rudder for the sloop. First, you made the control points, and then closed the Bézier Curve.

Next, you adjusted the control points and control handles. You discovered that the commands to model with a Bézier Curve are the same as the commands to modify Bézier Curves in the Graph Editor. You may have noticed that when using a Bézier Curve, they can be a little messy at the beginning, but they are also very flexible, so you want to use the absolute minimum number of control points possible.

Finally, you made the curve into a solid object and set the extrusion to `0.080` to make a rudder with the correct thickness.

 For your reference, the file `4909_07_sloop - bcurve_rudder1.blend` has control points laid in, but not closed; `4909_07_sloop - bcurve_rudder2.blend` has the path closed and the top adjusted; and `4909_07_sloop - bcurve_rudder3.blend` has the completed rudder.

Using multiple Bézier Curves to make an object

In addition to using Bézier Curves like a cookie cutter, you can also combine them to make objects. One Bézier Curve controls the shape of an object and the other creates a path to follow.

Time for action – making the path and cross section for the tiller

First, you will create a path that describes the length of the tiller, and then you will create the shape of the cross-section of the tiller. Execute the following steps:

1. With the cursor over 3D View, press *M*, *2*, and *Enter* to move the rudder to Layer 2.

2. Adjust 3D View so that you can see the entire length of the tiller on the template (the tiller is the handle that controls the rudder).

3. Press *Shift + S* and select **Cursor to Center**. Move the mouse cursor to the vertical center of the right end of the tiller and use the mouse to move the 3D Cursor there.

4. Press *Shift + A*, and then select **Curve** and **Bezier** from the menu to make a Bézier Curve.

5. Press *R*, *Y*, *90*, and *Enter*.

6. Press the *Tab* key to get into **Edit Mode**. Move the top control point to the center of the left tip of the tiller. Move the other control point to the 3D Cursor's position.

7. Adjust the control handles so that the curve goes along the center of the tiller outline in the template and is graceful.

8. Select the **Object** panel from the **Properties** window header, the one with the orange cube. Name the curve **Tiller Path**, as shown in the following screenshot, and then press *Enter*:

9. With the cursor over 3D View, press the *Tab* key to change to **Object Mode**, and press A to deselect everything.

10. Press *Shift + A*, and then select **Curve** and **Circle** from the menus to make a Bézier Circle.

11. Select **Align to View** in the **Add Bezier Circle** subpanel of the Tool Shelf.

12. Press *S* and use the mouse to scale the circle until it is approximately the same diameter as the base of the tiller on the template, as seen on the left side of the next screenshot. Use the mouse to release the scaling.

13. Press the *Tab* key to go into **Edit Mode**, as seen in the center of the following graphic.

14. Press A to deselect all the control points and control handles. Press C for the **Circle** select. Select the control handles, but not the control points. Press the RMB to end the selection.

15. Press *V* and select **Vector** from the menu so that the circle becomes a diamond, as seen on the right side of the following screenshot.

16. Press A twice to select all control points and control handles. Then press *R, 45*, and *Enter*.

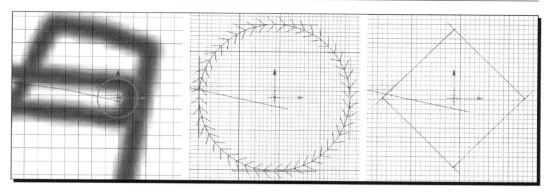

17. Press the *Tab* key to go into **Object Mode**.

18. In the **Properties** window, select the **Object** button from the header (the orange cube, fifth button from the left). Name the object **Tiller Shape**.

19. Select **Tiller Path** with the RMB. In the **Properties** window header, select the **Object Data** button with the two control points on it connected by a curve. In the **Shape** subpanel, make sure that the **3D** button is highlighted in blue.

20. In the **Geometry** subpanel, click on the box below **Bevel Object:** and select **Tiller Shape** from the menu. Then, click on the **Fill Caps** checkbox in the lower-left corner of the **Geometry** subpanel, as seen in the following image.

21. Save the file with a unique name.

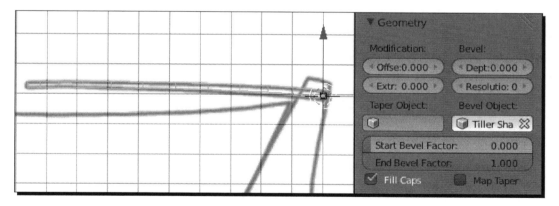

What just happened?

You just discovered another way to build with Bézier Curves, very similar to the way that Pierre Bézier had in mind when he first started to use them. You created a gentle, curving path and a shape, and put them together to make the tiller. Well done!

 For your reference, the file `4909_07_sloop - bcurve_tiller1.blend` has the path for the tiller, `4909_07_sloop - bcurve_tiller2.blend` has the shape for the tiller, `4909_07_sloop - bcurve_tiller3.blend` has the completed tiller.

Have a go hero – making the keel

This will be a good exercise in building items using a Bézier Curve. Remember to move the 3D cursor to the place where you want to begin your keel. The following steps will guide you to build the keel:

◆ The keel is the blade on the bottom of the sloop. Use a Bézier Curve to make the keel. It's very similar to building the rudder.

◆ When it's done, save it with a unique filename.

 For your reference, the file `4909_07_sloop - rudder_tiller_mast_boom_gaff_bowsprit.blend` has all the miscellaneous parts for the sloop.

Keeping everything organized

With all the booms, rudders, oars, and other parts, you are starting to get quite a collection of 3D objects here. You need to make sure they are well organized so you can find them in the future. This is what we will look at next.

Everybody organizes their files in different ways, and there are many good ways to do it. What you want to do is organize your files so that you can find them a year from now, when you've forgotten nearly everything about the project on which you are working. Projects that are hot now can be history in 20 minutes, and then come back in six months. You just never know.

A Blender project won't just be the Blender file. It also includes graphics that you have used to make textures and special plugins for Blender, such as the Bolt Factory that automates making bolts, screws, text, and Python language files, as well as the finished files you render. There's a lot to organize.

There are two ways to specify the locations of files. One is called **absolute addressing**; the other is called **relative addressing**. Absolute addressing specifies the location of a file using a specific path such as C:\blender\graphics\coolgraphic.png or http://www. blender.org/download/. Relative addresses specify where a file is in relation to where it is being called. This provides flexibility, because the root directory is not important; it's just the relationship between any two files that is important.

With Blender, once you save the Blender file on which you are working, it uses a relative path to identify all linked files. If the Blender file has not been saved, then Blender must use an absolute path. By using the relative paths, Blender allows you to set up a directory structure that makes your project modular.

This is pretty straightforward; you establish a root directory to contain all of the files, and then create subdirectories for different kinds of files, as seen in the next figure. I use a Blender subdirectory for all the Blender files, the Images subdirectory for textures and background images, and an Audio subdirectory for sound files. When my Blender file looks for an image file I have assigned it, it looks in the Images subdirectory that is in the same root directory that the Blender subdirectory is in. I can change the name of the root directory, but as long as there are both a Blender subdirectory and an image subdirectory, my Blender file will find the images that it needs. Blender can find them even if you change the name of the root directory as long as the relative paths between the Blender subdirectory and the Images subdirectory are maintained. The folder structure is shown in the following screenshot:

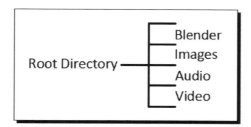

Making an index of your files

Another thing you may want to do is include a text file or spreadsheet file that lets you know what files are needed and which files are what. It can be as simple or as complex as you want, but it will pay you back for the time needed to set it up and maintain many times over. Blender has a text window, which was described in *Chapter 2, Getting Comfortable Using the 3D View*. You can use the text window to make a list of all the files you need, and the list will always be handy when you open the Blender file. You can also make text files for a particular setting that you may need, or a checklist to track your progress in completing your project.

Planning your animation

You've done a bit of modeling now, and you're doing great. However, it's time for a little break, time to think ahead about animation again. In addition, now that you are organized to never lose a Blender file or image of your animation, you are ready to focus on what you want to do. You want to tell a story.

Discovering the story you want to tell with your animation

Whether you are setting up a game, doing scientific visualization, or making an animation to show on YouTube, odds are that there's a story involved. In addition, I'm sure you want it to be a good one. I can't give you all the rules here. According to Gene Deitch, director of Tom Terrific, Tom and Jerry, and Krazy Kat cartoons, you start with a premise or an idea. The premise breaks down into three parts—a character, a conflict, and a resolution. Think about how your favorite animation breaks down into these three parts.

There are plenty of books and online sources, and the following is a list of a few of these.

Sources to create stories for animation

- *Story - What's it All About?* available at http://www.awn.com/ genedeitch/gene-deitch-how-succeed-animation/ part-one-how-you-should-do-it/chapter-7-story- whats-it-/page/1%2C1.
- *How to Write for Animation* available at http://www. jeffreyscott.tv/HTWFA.htm.
- *How to Write an Animation Script* available at http://www.ehow. com/how_2102588_write-animation-script.html.
- *Animation Scriptwriting: The Writer's Road Map* available at http://www.awn.com/mag/issue5.11/5.11pages/ demottanimation.php3.
- *How To Learn To Write Like An Animator* available at http://www. squidoo.com/writingforanimation.
- *Robert McKee Story Seminar* available at http://mckeestory.com/.

However, we've all been listening to stories, watching stories, and telling stories all our lives. Therefore, I'm willing to bet that you can make a good start with what you know now. The issue here is to get your ideas out where you can use them to plan your animation. Here are a few tips that will help you plan your animation:

◆ Work fast and loose. What you want to do is make a bunch of animations and learn a little more with each one. You're not going to win an Oscar for your first animation, so don't be a perfectionist, have fun!

◆ Sketch out your ideas on paper. Get a story down, but be willing to let it grow, as it will. In *Toy Story*, the character *Buzz Lightyear* started out as a toy one-man-band character named *Tinny*, and the character *Woody* began as a sarcastic ventriloquist's dummy.

◆ Look around you for inspiration.

◆ Keep it simple, short, and easy-to-make.

◆ Planning is not locking yourself into something. It starts as an exploration of the possibilities and morphs into figuring out the best way to present the best of your ideas.

Bringing your story to life with storyboards

Storyboards are like a comic strip where you lay out the sequence of events in quickly drawn panels that let you get an idea of the visual flow of the animations

This is how *Sam Chen* tackled the problem when he was planning his short film *Eternal Gaze* that won the *Siggraph Best of Show* award and the *Student Academy* award. He drew his storyboard on Post-it® notes. Post-it® notes are about the right size and shape for a storyboard panel, and you can rearrange them any way you want.

Once Sam was happy with the story, he scanned them in to his computer, and used the images to create an animatic to guide his animation. The story of *Sam Chen* and *Eternal Gaze* available at `http://www.independent-magazine.org/node/156` is an inspiration for the independent animator, and is worth your time to read.

Making a storyboard

We are not going to go in depth on how to make great storyboards, we will just deal with the most fundamental level; this level is an excellent method to think your animation through before you begin it.

Millionaire *Howard Hughes* first used storyboards to plan the aerial shots in the 1930 movie, *Hell's Angels*, about combat pilots in World War I.

You need storyboards because of the following reasons:

◆ They help you think out your shots and experiment before committing yourself to a shot

◆ They help you discover the continuity problems between shots

◆ They help you develop the visual style of your shots

◆ They help you communicate to other people what you intend to do

◆ They help you incorporate suggestions from others into your animation without the cost of modeling, animating, rendering, and compositing

Storyboards are notes for your camera work. They can be as simple as rough shapes and stick figures, but you want to give a feeling of scale and how much of the screen an object or character fills.

One thing you will notice is that storyboards love incorporating rectangles and arrows. We discussed camera moves in *Chapter 3, Controlling the Lamp, the Camera, and Animating Objects*. The following figure shows how a camera zooms:

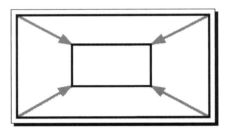

The following figure shows a camera dolly-in:

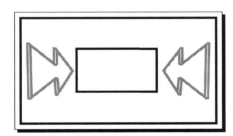

This graphic shows two ways to indicate a pan, you can use an arrow or you can show the starting and ending framing of the pan and connect them with smaller arrows, as shown in the following figure:

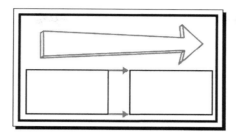

Note that there are two styles of arrows, namely stick-like arrows and 3D arrows. The stick-like arrows are generally used to show that the camera is being moved. The 3D arrows suggest motion within the scene. Then again, this is art. There are no hard and fast rules. Do it as you like, but make sure that it communicates your intent. The best way to see how others have done storyboards is to look up the word `storyboards` on Google, and then look at images that you get in the results.

Here are some links for more information on creating storyboards

- *Thoughts on drawing for storyboards-PT 1* and *Thoughts on drawing for storyboards-PT 2* are excellent sources on drawing and communicating with drawing, available at `http://drawingsfromamexican.blogspot.com/2006/11/thoughts-on-drawing-for-storyboards-pt.html` and `http://drawingsfromamexican.blogspot.com/2006/11/thoughts-on-drawing-for-storyboards-pt_27.html`, respectively.

- *Storyboards* available at `http://accad.osu.edu/womenandtech/Storyboard%20Resource/`.

- *Storyboards and What is a Storyboard Artist?* available at `http://www.wildsound-filmmaking-feedback-events.com/storyboards.html`.

Post-it®s are good for storyboarding because they come in a variety of sizes and colors. They are cheap and sticky, so you will be encouraged to work fast and loose. You need not make your sketch so beautiful that you fall in love with how it looks, and you can include the frame into a storyboard as soon as you finish drawing.

Start by drawing a rectangle that's as wide as the Post-it®. Give the rectangle the proportions your animations will be. The proportions of your animation will most likely be 16:9 HD or 4:3, standard for videos or banner ads on the Web. Make the rectangle's proportion match the proportions you will use.

Say you're doing a ghost story involving a boat. All you have in the scene is a boat sitting on the lake. How do you tell the story?

In the establishing shot, the boat is in the middle of a lake, like the first frame of the following storyboard screenshot. The camera is far from the boat so that the viewer can see that the boat is isolated, away from the shore, and without an operator:

If you want to show your boat lying idle in the middle of a lake as an opening shot, you will have to draw it so that it fills only a small part of the frame. At the bottom, put a little text that describes the shot.

Next, the boat is obviously the center of interest, so you want to investigate it. You want the camera to zoom in to the boat. As shown in the center frame of the preceding storyboard, you draw a similar frame, but you put a rectangle around the area that will be shown at the end of the zoom. You also put lines from the edges of the beginning of the zoom to the end of the zoom, and put arrowheads on the lines to show which direction the zoom is going, in or out.

Now, observing the boat closely, you can see that it is drifting in a slow circle. This tells the viewer that though the boat is empty, something has apparently happened to cause the boat to move on its own on this placid lake. In the storyboard, the top arrow shows the camera panning, and the two inner frames show where the pan starts and stops. The arrow by the boat shows which direction the boat is turning to.

As you make your storyboard, you may want to use a large board or an unused wall to tack up all your shots from left to right so that you can see the visual flow of the animation.

Technology changes every day

If you have a graphics tablet and a graphics program that you are very comfortable using, you may want to make your storyboards on your computer. However, there are some things to consider. Working completely digitally allows you to do cleaner work, trace pictures downloaded from the net, and makes creating an animatic very easy.

Using pencil and paper offers you the spontaneity of quick sketches. Being away from the computer encourages you to dig deeper into your imagination; it lets you spread all the images out where you can see them all at once.

Have a go hero – making your own storyboard

There is no better way to understand the power of a storyboard than to make one of your own. Give it a try. You'll find how flexible this method can be. Professional drawing skills are not required. However, try to make your figures occupy the same amount of room as they will in the camera. The following steps will guide you to make your own storyboard:

◆ Get yourself a pad of Post-it® notes.

◆ Make a storyboard for an animation about a haunted boat detailing the following:

❑ What has just happened?

❑ Why and how is the boat haunted?

❑ Get creative about the camera angles you use. Could the camera be in the water, about to be run over by the boat?

❑ Would the oars become bloody battle-axes or become limp and rubbery?

❑ How do you use pacing and perspective to tell a story?

Using animatics to plan the timing of your animation

If you read the article on *Sam Chen*, then you know that he scanned his Post-it® notes and made an animatic of his animation from them. Animatics are a combination of slide show, rough animations, and maybe a rough sound track. This gives you a surprisingly good feel of how your animation will work. It will help you establish the pace and timing of the scene before you animate it. The animatic video can even be used as a template for animation. With Blender, you can drop your graphics into the Video Sequence Editor and spread them out over time to give yourself a rough idea of how everything will look after it's animated. You will be introduced to using the Video Sequence Editor to edit animation clips in *Chapter 12, Rendering and Compositing*.

Links on animatics

- *Using Blender for Animatics* available at `http://www.freesoftwaremagazine.com/articles/creating_storyboard_animatic_blender`.

- *Sintel, the Animatic* available at `http://www.sintel.org/news/1st-minute-animatic/`.

- *Create an Animatic* available at `http://www.computerarts.co.uk/tutorials/create-animatic`.

- Watch the following two clips together, the animatic and the finished animation of Dirty Harry by Gorillaz. See how they changed their ideas between the animatic and final animation.

- *Gorillaz Dirty Harry Animatic* available at `http://www.youtube.com/watch?v=M1uRncKY8DU`.

- *Gorillaz Dirty Harry Finished Animation* available at `http://www.youtube.com/watch?v=gonPVgjIF6w`.

Using charts and guides to help you plan your animation

When planning your animation, it's good to make use of guides to help you save time and work. Here are some to help you establish where your animation should happen on screen, how long the actions should take, and plan what work is required to create the animation. You have already seen the Composition Guides to help you compose your shots, but here are some to help ensure that what you plan to do gets seen by your audience.

Staying in TV limits with Safe Title zone, Safe Action zone, and Lower Third

The **Safe Title zone** and **Safe Action zone** originated in the black-and-white days of television. They were created to make sure that what was put on the screen got seen.

Early TV was very imprecise. It was decided that only the inner 80 percent of the image was likely enough to be seen, and that it could be trusted to display titles and sponsor logos. Only the inner 90 percent was likely enough to be seen, so critical action could be shown. The outer 10 percent was not to be trusted at all. Sometimes, in local TV ads, you see text and images chopped off where unskilled artists fail to observe these guidelines.

The **Lower Third** is a convention for advertisers. It reserves about the bottom one-fourth to one-third for the sponsor's logo and contact information for ads. This varies with every sponsor, so contact the station or agency that is in charge of the client if you have any questions.

The following screenshot shows where these areas will appear. It is included in your download pack as 4909_07_03.png for your use. The white area is the **Safe Title** zone. The light gray area and the white area is the **Safe Action** zone. All the area in the **Safe Title** zone and under the **Lower Third** line may be used for sponsor logos, and so on. You include these into your Blender file just as you would include a template graphic.

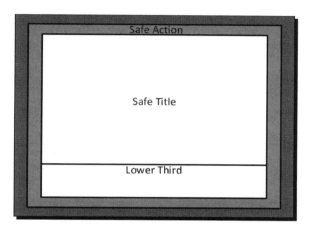

Time for action – using Blender's Safe Title/Safe Action guide

Blender has its own Safe Title/Safe Action guide included. Using it is just like using Blender's Composition Guides. The following steps will guide you to use Blender's Safe Title/Safe Action guide:

1. Save and close the Blender file that you were using to make the sloop. Save it with a unique filename that you will remember in six months.
2. Open a new Blender file.
3. Press *0* on the NumPad to get the **Camera** view.
4. Click on the border between the image area and the passe-partout to select the **Camera** view.

5. Select the **Object Data** button on the **Properties** header, it has the movie camera on it and is highlighted in blue, as seen in the following screenshot.

6. In the **Display** subpanel, check the **Safe Areas** checkbox.

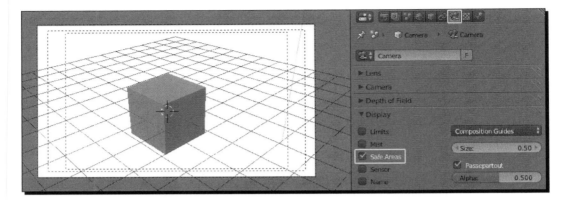

What just happened?

You discovered Blender's built-in Safe Action/Safe Title guides. They are pretty easy to set up. Just choose the camera and check the **Safe Areas** checkbox under the **Data Object** panel. Remember that the outer checkbox is the Safe Action zone, and the inner checkbox is the Safe Title zone. They don't have a Lower Thirds guide though.

Transitioning from a Standard Definition TV to a High Definition TV

Normally, Safe Title zones and Safe Action zones aren't necessary for HD. Viewers are going to see the entire image. However, during the transition from Standard resolution to HD resolution, many studios make ads at HD resolution and also release a Standard resolution version because TV stations in small markets may still broadcast at Standard resolution. Therefore, the Safe Action/Safe Title zone to work in this situation look as shown in the following figure:

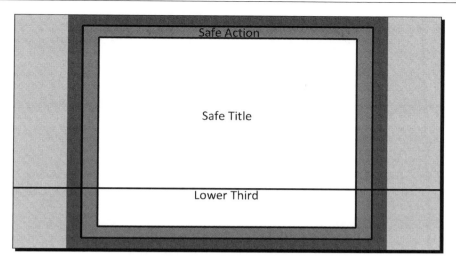

A guide similar to this will help you if you are in this situation. You set it up just as a standard template and assign it to the **Camera** view. If you are working in HD resolution, but it you want it be in standard resolution, then just put all the important action, titles, and so on within the Safe Action/Safe Title zone. Make sure that your backgrounds extend all the way to the edge of the image.

HD is a much more stable signal. You may need to reserve the lower third for the sponsor's graphics, but you do not need to worry about Safe Action and Safe Title if you are making animation strictly for HD.

The preceding graphic is available in your download pack as 4909_07_04.png and can be used with dimensions of HD NTSC 1080p or HD PAL 1080p in the same way as the the templates you added earlier.

For your reference, the file 4909_07_SafeTitle_SafeAction_NTSC_4-3.blend is set up with the Safe Title/Safe Action zone templates for a standard NTSC screen. The file 4909_07_SafeTitle_SafeAction_ PAL_4-3.blend is set up with the SafeTitle/SafeAction zone templates for a standard PAL screen. The file 4909_07_SafeTitle_SafeAction_ NTSC_HD_16-9.blend is set up with the SafeTitle/SafeAction zone templates for an HD NTSC screen. The file 4909_07_SafeTitle_SafeAction_ PAL_HD_16-9.blend is set up with the SafeTitle/SafeAction zone templates for an HD PAL screen.

Laying out your motion with Timing

There is just too much to show, but the following diagrams may help you to plan out your animation:

- **Animation bounce diagrams**: Bounce diagrams are good to analyze your motion, see how it breaks down frame-by-frame, and see how traditional cel animators get their results (check http://www.animationbrain.com/timing-2d-animation-principle.html).

- **Eadweard Muybridge photographic series**: Eadweard Muybridge invented motion capture and his photographs amazed Victorian audiences. His zoopraxiscope was one of the earliest animation display devices. His books *Muybridge's Complete Human* and *Animal Locomotion* are still in print, and are valuable references to animators. I used one of his flying bird sequences as the basis for an animation in an encyclopedia (check http://inventors.about.com/od/weirdmuseums/ig/Eadweard-Muybridge/The-Horse-in-Motion.htm).

- **Walk cycle charts**: As you saw from your rowing examples, there are many ways for a human to do any given action. The first link shows you a page of different walk cycles from *The Animation Book by Kit Laybourne* a classic that has recently been reissued to include digital animation. The second shows horse walking, with a diagram describing which feet are on the ground. The final is a collection of animations of various human motions. Check http://minyos.its.rmit.edu.au/aim/a_notes/04_walkcycle_project.html and http://blaine901.files.wordpress.com/2011/01/horse-walking600.jpg.

- **Preston Blair Phoneme Mouth**: Preston Blair was the man who animated Mickey Mouse in the *Sorcerer's Apprentice* section of *Fantasia*. His book *Welcome to Cartoon Animation* is a bible for animators and his mouth shape phoneme charts that show the position of a mouth for a certain sound are animation institutions. Check http://www.garycmartin.com/mouth_shapes.html, http://minyos.its.rmit.edu.au/~rpyjp/a_notes/mouth_shapes_01.html, and http://minyos.its.rmit.edu.au/~rpyjp/a_notes/mouth_shapes_02.html.

Planning what work must be done to make an animation

In addition to helping you plan the exact motions you want to create, there are also guides to help you plan the whole animation. They are as follows:

- **Exposure sheets**: Exposure sheets, as shown in the following image, are prepared by the animator as a way to plan their shots and to let the cameraman know what to photograph. However, with the advent of digital methods, this has changed a bit. In the action column, you can write about what is happening on that frame, for example, oar dips into water. The sound might be "oar splash". You then draw an arrow downward in the column to include any frame that this action includes. An example of exposure sheet is shown as follows:

ANIMATOR													
PRODUCTION													
SCENE NO:		SEQ NO:			LENGTH:						SHEET NO:		
NOTES:													

FRAME	ACTION	SOUND	6	5	4	3	2	1	BG	CAMERA
0										
1										
2										
3										
4										
5										
6										
7										

The columns **6**, **5**, **4**, **3**, **2**, **1**, and **BG** originally relate to the layers of cel art. The top layer is represented by **6** and **BG** stands for background. You can put the frame numbers of the artwork for each particular layer. This is useful when you get to compositing layers in the Video Sequence Editor.

Originally, the **CAMERA** column contained instructions for the cameraman, but now you can use it to mark which camera in Blender you shot a particular sequence with or what changes you made to the camera's settings.

In the **NOTES** section, you may want to write down the names of the files you are using. You may also want to develop a method that uses the scene number and sequence number to tell you which section of the animation on which you are working.

 For your reference, a copy of this exposure sheet for you to use and modify is included with the code bundle as an Excel file named `4909_07_ExposureSheet 30FPS.xls`.

- ◆ **Bar sheets**: A bar sheet is the audio equivalent of an exposure sheet. They are filled out by the director to tell everyone in the production exactly what is happening on any given frame. Nowadays, with digital methods, bar sheets are less commonly used. You should know what they are though, in case a director mentions them. More information is available at `http://www.michaelspornanimation.com/splog/?p=711`.

- **Sound as a planning guide**: Since it is so easy to create the audio track, animations are often made using the sound track as the production guide. With an audio track in their 3D program, the animators can just scrub along the timeline and know where every word or sound begins. More information on it is available at `http://academic.evergreen.edu/curricular/eat/pdf/Sound.pdf`.

Guiding animation production with an audio track

With the switch to digital animation production, one method that's getting used more and more is to just use the audio track as the basis for animation. Blender is set up to let you do this. You can drop the audio track into Blender and use the dialog, sound effects, or music to guide your animation.

Time for action – adding an audio track to Blender

Now, it's time for an introduction to the Video Sequence Editor, ironically, by adding an audio file. You will learn how to position the audio file on the timeline and display a representation of the waveform to help you in timing your animation in the following steps:

1. Put your cursor on the boundary between **3D View** and the **Timeline** windows and get to the double arrowhead. Use your mouse and hold it while you move the boundary up so that the **Timeline** window is about three times as tall as usual.

2. With the cursor over the **Timeline** window, press *Shift* + left-arrow key to go to **Frame 1**.

3. Put the mouse in the lower-left corner of the **Timeline** window, over the diagonal lines. Press the LMB and drag the mouse up to create a new window.

4. Click on the leftmost button on the upper **Timeline** window header.

5. Scroll up in the **Current Editor Type:** menu, and select **Video Sequence Editor**, as shown in the following screenshot:

6. In the **Video Sequence Editor** header, first select **Add** and then select **Sound** from the pop-up menu. Get the `4909_07_WalterRoland jookitjookit_excerpt.wav` file from the download pack's `Audio` directory, as shown in the following screenshot. When you have selected the file, press the **Add Sound Strip** button in the upper-right corner of the window.

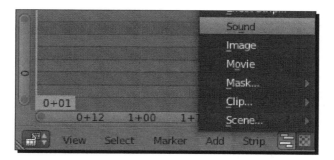

7. Press *Ctrl* + MMB and scroll the mouse up to maximize the height of the audio strip. You may also want to use *Shift* + MMB to adjust the location of the audio strip.

8. Select **View** on the Video Sequence Editor header. Uncheck the box in the pop-up menu that says **Show Seconds**.

9. Note that there are a couple of new controls that can be seen in the previous screenshot. On the left and the bottom of the Video Sequence Editor window, there are a couple of scroll bars with gray dots on the ends. The vertical one shows you which video layers are displayed. The horizontal one helps you control what portion of the time you see. Both are adjustable. Click on them to slide them. Click on the dot at the end to resize them.

10. With the cursor in the Video Sequence Editor, press *N* to open the **Properties** panel. Scroll down to the **Sound** subpanel. Check the box marked **Caching** to load the sound into the RAM for smooth playback, and check the box marked **Draw Waveform**. You should now see the waveform of the audio track within the audio strip, as shown in the following screenshot:

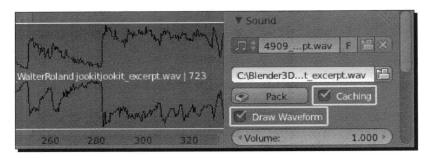

11. Go down to the **Timeline** window header and click to open the **Playback** menu. At the top of the menu, check the **Audio Scrubbing** box, as shown in the following screenshot:

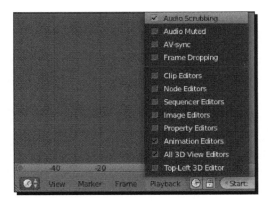

12. Now, if you scrub the **Current Frame Indicator** along the timeline, use the **Timeline** window playback controls, or press *Alt + A* over the 3D View window to preview the animation; the audio track will play in sync with the animation.

13. Save this file with a unique name that you will still remember in six months.

What just happened?

You set up Blender so that you can have an audio file to use to guide you in creating animation. After adding in the audio file, you made it so you can see the audio waveform. Seeing the audio waveform makes it easier for you to know which part you are playing at the present moment. In addition, you set Caching and Audio Scrubbing to make it easy for you to hear what is happening.

Have a go hero – animating to a boogie woogie beat

Animating to music is an old tradition going back as far as the *Felix the Cat* cartoons that you studied in *Chapter 1, Introducing Blender and Animation*. It's a good way to see the power that comes from mixing visual and acoustic rhythms. The following steps will help you to mix visual and acoustic rhythms:

◆ There is a Walter Roland tune from 1933, called *Jookit Jookit*. You have the music, now make the cube dance to it. This excerpt is 30 seconds long, so you may change the length of the animation in the timeline as we discussed in *Chapter 3, Controlling the Lamp, the Camera, and Animating Objects*.

◆ The easiest way to start is to use the controls in the timeline to play a section and acquaint yourself with a particular phrase of the music. Then, when you have a particular section in mind, use the Current Frame Indicator to scrub the timeline for frame-by-frame control. The waveform in the audio strip will help you identify important points in the audio.

◆ Once you have a section of the music identified, create the location, scale, and rotation keyframes to shake, rattle, and roll the cube to the music. If you get inspired, you can add any other object and animate it as well. Use the Graph Editor if you want. Check in the key function table to refresh your memory or how to move around in the Graph Editor and Timeline. Be sure to stay within the Safe Title and Safe Action zones.

◆ Press *Alt + A* to preview your animation.

 For your reference, the file 4909_07_Audio_Timing_jookit.blend is set up with *Walter Roland's* song *Jookit Jookit*. It is inserted into the Video Sequence Editor and a sample animation. Also included is the 4909_07_ WalterRoland jookitjookit_excerpt.wav file.

Well done! This chapter had new hands-on modeling techniques and animation mixed with some more academic organization instructions. Just to make sure you didn't forget about the organization while you were rocking to Walter Roland; let's see what you learned.

Pop quiz – organizing Blender files

Assume that you save a blender file named `MyBoat.blend` in the `C:\Boat_Project\Blender` directory and you save the textures for the deck in the `C:\Boat_Project\Images` directory location.

Q1. If you copy the `MyBoat.blend` file to a directory named `C:\NewBoat`, where will Blender look for the textures of the deck?

1. `C:\Boat_Project\Images`
2. `C:\NewBoat\Images`
3. `C:\Blender\Boat Textures`
4. `http://www.NewBoat.com/Images`

Q2. By which filename will you be able to best recognize what a Blender file is in six months?

1. `My new project.blend`
2. `Boat1.blend`
3. `Sloop of War_USS Constitution_1854 version.blend`
4. `Sloop_version 3_done.blend`

Q3. When is the best time to save your Blender file?

1. At the end of the work day.
2. Every couple of hours.
3. Right now

The key-function table

Well, I hope you enjoyed making this animation and discovered a new musician at the same time. Here is a table of keyboard commands and their functions:

Key	Function
Home	In 3D View, it zooms back to display all the visible objects in the scene.
fn + left arrow	On a Mac, it zooms back to display all the visible objects in the scene in 3D View.
V	In 3D View, this brings up the **Set Handle Type** menu for Bézier Curves.
Ctrl + MMB	In the Video Sequence Editor, use this to zoom in and out.

Summary

This chapter covered a lot. You practiced setting up a template in Blender to guide your modeling. You used the template to help model the mast, boom, gaff, and bowsprit. You learned about using Bézier Curves to model the rudder, keel, and tiller.

You got tips on planning your animation, creating a story, using storyboards to plan what you are going to do, and using animatics to get the timing of an animation right before you animate.

You looked at some charts and guides that can help you create your animations, including Safe Title/Safe Action/Lower Third guides, timing diagrams, exposure sheets, and bar sheets. Finally, you had a little fun using a sound track to guide your animation timing.

In the next chapter, you will be making the sloop itself. You will use Subdivision Surfaces to model the hull and learn how to optimize the number of faces you create. You will learn to use edge loops and edge rings for more detailed modeling. You will punch holes in your boat with Boolean objects and use Spin tools and DupliVerts to make the ship's wheel turn.

Let's go!

8

Making the Sloop

In the last chapter, you learned a lot to help you make the modeling and animation process easier by planning out what you would do. You created templates for the top view, the front view, and the camera. You also began building your sloop by modeling some of the parts, including the mast, boom, gaff, and bowsprit. You learned a new use for Bézier curves, modeling, and you used it to make the rudder, keel, and tiller. For a change of pace, you finished off by making a short animation to the rumbling piano work of Walter Roland.

In this chapter, you will have the chance to continue to improve your modeling skills by mastering more advanced modeling techniques, including the following:

- ◆ Using Subdivision Surfaces to model the hull and learning how to optimize the number of faces you create
- ◆ Adding detail to the model with edge loops and edge rings
- ◆ Punching holes for windows in the sloop's cabin with Boolean objects
- ◆ Using Spin tools and DupliVerts to make the ship's wheel

Let's get started!

Modeling with Subdivision Surfaces

With **Subdivision Surfaces**, you start with a regular mesh object, similar to the boat you made, and to use its vertices to control another smoother surface. This makes modeling smoothly curved objects and animating changes of shape easier because there are fewer points that need to be modified by you.

Time for action – making a simple Subdivision Surface

Subdivision Surfaces are popular because they make it easier to build and animate organic objects. They also let you make shapes that would be difficult with standard box modeling. Let's try one executing the following steps:

1. Open `4909_08_templates_set_up.blend` from your download pack.

2. Locate `4909_08_01.png`, `4909_08_02.png`, and `4909_08_03.png` in the `Images` directory for this chapter. If you wish, you can use the templates that you created for the last chapter. Make sure you can see the templates in the background; if you can't, redo your background images and map `4909_08_01.png` and `4909_08_02.png` to the proper views.

3. Select the reference block that you used to set the scaling of the sloop template in *Chapter 7, Planning your Work, Working your Plan*.

4. Press the *Tab* key to get into **Edit Mode**.

5. In the Properties window header, select the **Modifiers** button. It's the button with the wrench on it and is highlighted in blue in the next illustration.

6. In the **Modifiers** subpanel, click on the **Add Modifier** button, scroll down the menu, and select **Subdivision Surface**. The reference block now looks more like a ball.

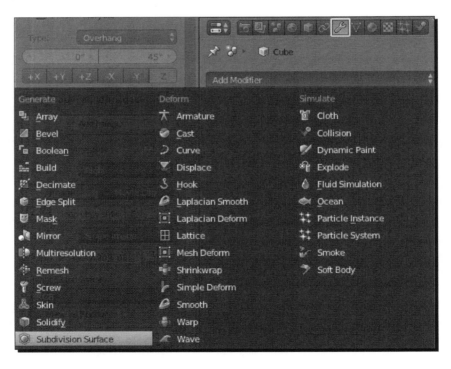

7. Go to the menu below the **Add Modifier** button. Click over the left arrow on the end of the **View:** button. Click down until **View:** is **0** (zero). Click on the arrow at the right end of the button until **View:** is **6**. Notice how the reference block responds, as shown here:

What just happened?

Well, the reference block is no longer a block. It is going to become your sloop. The **View:** button controls how many subdivisions there will be when you look at it in the 3D View header. As you drop the Subdivisions value to 0, you see a cube. As you raise the Subdivisions value to 6, it becomes a very smooth sphere. The **Render:** button just below it controls how many subdivisions of the reference block there will be when you render it. For both, the number of subdivisions changes, but the number of control points doesn't change.

The control points are similar to the control points of the Bezier Curve, but the surface does not have to go right through the control points for a Subdivision Surface. It's similar to a puppeteer controlling a marionette from a distance.

You cannot touch the edges and faces of the Subdivision Surface. The control points are the only thing you can modify. This might seem limiting at first, but it lets you control complex shapes with just a few vertices.

Did you notice the **Catmull-Clark** button? You are using the `Catmull-Clark` method of Subdivision Surfaces. It was developed by the same Ed Catmull, who is now President of Pixar. Woody, Buzz, and Jessie are all just Subdivision Surfaces.

Using Edge Tools to make modeling easier

Edge Tools are new tools that you will explore. Edge Tools can be used on any mesh object, such as the boat or the oars. They provide easier ways to subdivide edges. You will use them to help you control the form of your Subdivision Surface in this chapter.

Modeling with Subdivision Surfaces is a little like playing with clay. So, the modeling here will be a bit more art than science. We will refer to the shape of the Subdivision Surface as the surface, and refer to the mesh object with all the control points that control the surface as the control object.

Time for action – turning a reference block into a sloop

Since you have the templates scaled, you don't need the reference block any more. So, it's time to recycle it into the hull of the sloop. Using the Edge Tools, you can stretch and recontour the cube into the sloop. Perform the following steps:

1. In the **Modifiers** subpanel of the Properties window, set the **View** button to **2**.

2. Make sure that the **Limit Selection to Visible** button in the 3D View header is light gray so that you are moving all the control points, and not just the ones in front.

3. Press *A* to deselect all the control points. Select the left-hand control points. Press *G*, *Y*, and use the mouse to move them until the front end of the Subdivision Surface is at the same place as the bow of the sloop in the template. Then, press the LMB.

4. Did you notice that as you moved to the left side, the right side also moved a little? When modeling Subdivision Surfaces, you get things close, and then work them closer till they are just right.

5. Press *A* to deselect all the control points. Select the right-hand control points. Press *G*, *Y*, and use the mouse to move them until the rear end of the Subdivision Surface is at the same place as the stern of the boat in the template, as seen here. Then, press the LMB.

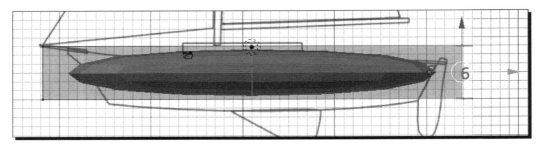

6. Now, it's time to establish some key control points.

7. Press *7* on the NumPad to get the **Top** view.

8. Now, it's time to discover the **Loop Cut** tool. Move the mouse cursor to the top edge of the control object.

9. Press *Ctrl + R*. Now, move the mouse across the side edge and back to the top edge several times. Notice that the magenta line appears in the middle. It may be horizontal or vertical. When the magenta line is horizontal, press the LMB.

10. The line turns orange and the surface changes shape. Now, move the mouse up and down and watch what the surface does.

11. Move the orange line over the front of the cabin area and click on the LMB. Check the side view briefly if you are unsure of where this is.

12. Now, move the mouse above the orange line and press *Ctrl + R* again. When you get the horizontal magenta line, press the LMB. Move the orange line until it is over the rear of the cabin and press the LMB.

13. Now, repeat this and move the orange line to the rear of the cockpit and press the LMB.

14. Move the mouse back to the center of the control object. Press *Ctrl + R*. Select the horizontal magenta line and press the LMB. Move the orange line to where the sloop is widest and press the LMB as seen in the next screenshot.

15. Now, press *3* on the NumPad to get the side view. You'll notice that the surface is longer than the sloop.

16. Press *Ctrl + R* and create a vertical orange line where the bottom of the hull starts to go up to the bow in the template.

17. Press *A* to deselect all control points. Press *B* and use the mouse to select the control points on the left edge. Press *G*, then use the MMB to limit the motion on the *Y-axis*. Move the end of the surface back to where the bow is. Press the LMB to release the motion.

18. Press *A* to deselect all control points. Select just the control points on the right edge and move the end of the surface to where the stern is, as shown in the following screenshot:

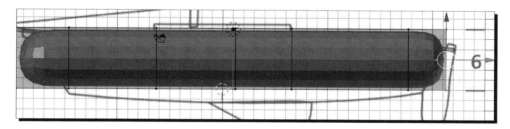

19. Save the file with a name you'll remember in 6 months.

What just happened?

Well, the sloop is starting to come into shape. You have been using a tool called the Loop Cut. It's pretty simple, but as you can see, it is very powerful because it allows you to cut a face anywhere along one of the object's edges. However, you also notice that it does not just work on one face. It works on what is called a ring of edges.

You noticed that the shape tends to move around, but you'll get it to move gently into the form you want by making smaller adjustments.

Time for action – making selection easy with Edge Loops and Edge Rings

You've got the sloop to the proper length and set up the edges you'll need to control the shape of the sloop's hull. Now, you'll learn some new tools that will give you the control you need to complete the job, as described in the following steps:

1. Use the MMB to rotate the view so you see some of the top, side, and end of the control object.

2. Choose **Edge Select Mode** from the 3D View header.

3. Put the cursor over one of the vertical edges on the side.

4. Press *Alt* + RMB to select **Edge Loop**. It will choose a loop of connected edges, as shown in the following screenshot:

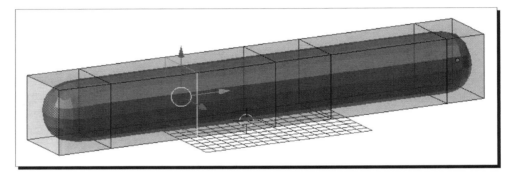

5. Move the mouse over to the edge between the top and the side. Now press *Ctrl* + *Alt* + RMB to select **Edge Ring**. It will select a ring of edges connected by their faces.

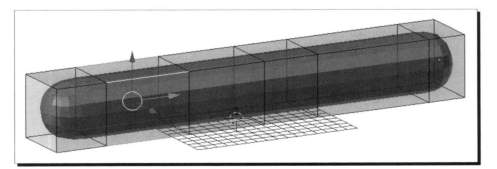

What just happened?

Edge Loop and Edge Ring are handy tools to choose multiple related edges and can speed up your modeling.

Adjusting control points to make the hull of the sloop

It's time to begin the use of Edge Loops and Edge Rings to adjust your control vertices to make the Subdivision Surface resemble a sloop.

Time for action – creating the shape of the sloop from the top

Now, you will learn to use Edge Loop to select the edges and gain experience in adjusting the control points of the Subdivision Surfaces from the following steps:

1. Press *7* on the NumPad.

2. Press *Z* to change from solid to wireframe shading.

3. Move the cursor over the horizontal edges at the widest part of the sloop. Press *Alt + RMB* to select an Edge Loop.

4. Press *S*, *X*, and use the mouse to scale the surface until it is as wide as the boat in the template, and then press the LMB. The control edges will be wider than the width of the boat image in the template. For the most precise control of scaling, remember to move the mouse away from the center of the 3D View header before you start scaling.

5. Repeat this with the horizontal edges at the front of the cabin where the hull begins to narrow toward the bow, as seen in the next screenshot.

6. The Edge Loop command will not work at the ends of the sloop. Press *A* to deselect the edges, and then press *B* and select the edges at the bow.

7. Press *S*, *X*, and use the mouse to scale the end of the surface inward until it is as wide as the bow in the template, and then press the LMB.

8. Repeat this with the horizontal edges in the rear of the sloop; work from the widest section to the stern.

9. Just as the length of the surface changed as you added vertices to the control object, the entire surface changes when you change a vertex. So, now that you have the size close to what it should be, look at each of the horizontal edges and scale them in X again as needed. Don't worry about squaring off the stern. Just get the general contours of the sloop correct. Work from the widest portion to the narrowest ends.

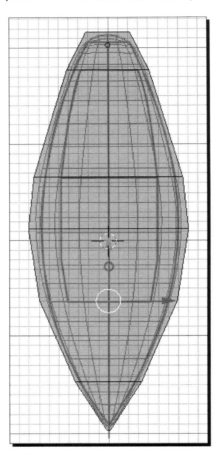

What just happened?

You worked on getting the shape of the sloop correct as seen from the top. You discovered that you can operate on the control object in **Edit Mode**, just as you modify any other object. You also discovered that Subdivision Surface is a bit unpredictable, and that you have to gently work the surface into the shape you want. The cool thing is that you are making the shape of a sloop with only 28 vertices.

Time for action – giving the hull a hull shape

You've got the top view of the hull in good shape. Now, it's time to work on the shape as seen from the side. Check the following steps:

1. Press *1* on the NumPad to get the **Front** view.

2. Notice that the hull is still oval shaped. As seen on the left of the next screenshot, the top is not flat.

3. Check that all the control points are level vertically. All of the upper points should be at the same height in Z. All of the lower points should be at the same height in Z. If any control point is higher or lower than what it should be, you can select it and scale it in Z, or move the vertices in Z.

4. Press *Ctrl + R* to activate the **Loop Cut** tool. Select the horizontal magenta line.

5. Move the orange line until it is almost all the way up to the top of the control object, as seen in the following screenshot on the right. This will control how tall and curved the deck is. There is an **Edge Slide** readout in the 3D View header. Move it till the **Edge Slide** is about **-0.85**. Use the *Shift* and *Ctrl* keys to give you better control when sliding.

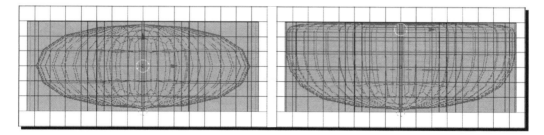

6. Press *3* on the NumPad to get the **Right** view and you can see the effect these new control points have all along the length of the shape, as shown in the following screenshot. The top is neatly pinned, and the bottom has a graceful curve at the end.

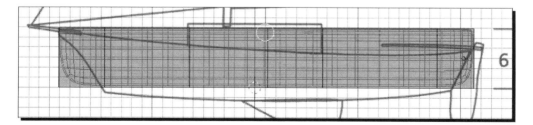

7. Choose **Vertex Select Mode** from the 3D View header.

8. Press *A* to deselect all vertices.

9. Press *B* and use the mouse to select the top two control points in the center.

10. Press *G*, *Z*, and use the mouse to move the control points down, so that the lower of the two control points is on top of the deck line in the template, as shown in the following screenshot. Then, press the LMB.

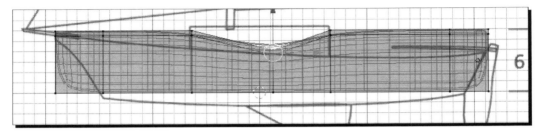

11. Repeat this on the other upper control points until they are aligned with the top of the deck, as shown in the following screenshot:

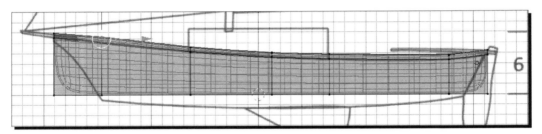

12. Press *A* to deselect all the control points. Press *B* to select all of the control points on the bottom of the hull. Press *G*, *Z*, and use the mouse to move the bottom control points down until the bottom of the surface is as low as the bottom of the hull, as shown in the following screenshot, and then press the LMB.

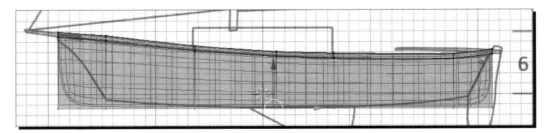

13. Press *1* on the NumPad to get the **Front** view.

14. Press *S, X*, and *0.8* to make the bottom of the hull a little narrower, as seen here, and then press *Enter*.

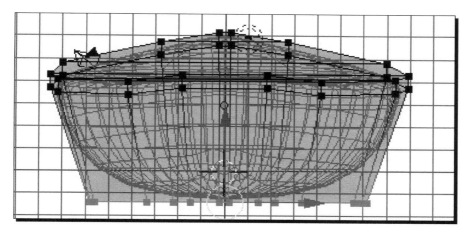

15. Press *3* on the NumPad to show the **Right** view.

16. Press *A* to deselect all the vertices.

17. Press *B*, and then use the mouse to select the vertices on the stern.

18. Make sure the **Pivot Center** button on the 3D View header is set to **Median Point**. It's the second button to the right of the **Edit/Object Mode** button.

19. Press *R, X*, and *-27* to rotate the rear control points so that they are parallel with the angle of the stern in the template, and then press *Enter*.

20. Press *G, Y*, and move the rear control points so that the stern of the sloop matches the template as closely as possible. Press the LMB to release the motion.

21. Press *A* to deselect all the vertices.

22. Press *B*, and then use the mouse to select the vertices on the bottom of the stern.

23. Press *G, Z*, and use the mouse to move the vertices up to the bottom of the hull, and then press the LMB.

24. Press *A* to deselect all the vertices.

25. Press *B*, and then use the mouse to select the vertices on the bottom of the control points just to the left of the stern, as shown in the following screenshot. Press *G*, *Z*, and use the mouse to move the vertices up to the bottom of the hull, and then press the LMB.

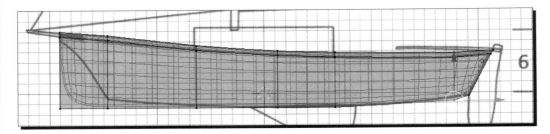

26. Now, move the other bottom control vertices up, except the ones on the very left, as shown in the following screenshot:

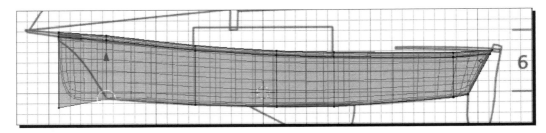

27. Finally, select the lower vertices on the left. Press *G* and move them up and over so that the curve of the bow approximates the curve seen in the template, as shown in the following screenshot. Then, press the LMB.

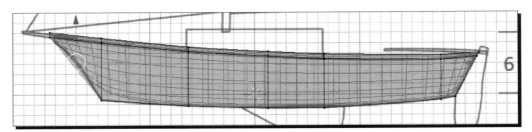

28. Select **Solid** in the **Viewport Shading** menu in the 3D View header. You can also press the *Z* key to toggle between **Wireframe** and **Solid shading**.

29. Press the MMB, use the mouse to rotate the hull of the sloop, and inspect your work.

30. Press *3* on the NumPad to return to the **Right** view.

31. Save the file with a unique name you will remember in 6 months.

What just happened?

You made the hull. Well done. You learned to gently move the surface into a complex shape by moving and scaling the vertices of the control object. It took a bit of work, but nothing was too difficult.

Finishing the shape of the hull

Now, you just have a few more steps to finish shaping the surface. You need to flatten the transom, the rear end of the sloop, so you can put a name on the stern. You need to make the bow sharper. You need to finish scaling the width. You need to make sure that the cabin and cockpit will meet where you want them to.

Time for action – flattening the transom

It's now time to flatten the transom. By setting control points very close to each other, you can make pretty sharp corners. Try it by executing the following steps:

1. Press *A* to deselect all vertices. Press *B* and use the mouse to select the control vertices for the transom on the right side of the control object.

2. Press *E* to extrude. Press *Enter*. Then, press *S, 0.95*, and *Enter*.

3. Press *Tab* to go into **Object Mode**.

4. Press the MMB and use the mouse to rotate the view so you can see that the transom of the sloop has been flattened.

What just happened?

By extruding the control points and pressing *Enter*, you put two sets of control points in the same place. This flattened out the transom. Then, you scaled in the new points just a little.

Time for action – making the bow sharper

Just like you put a corner on the stern by putting the control points close together, you can make the edge of the bow sharper as well. Execute the following steps:

1. Press *3* on the NumPad to see the **Right** view.

2. Press the *Tab* key to get back into **Edit Mode**.

3. Press *A* to deselect all the vertices. Press *B*, and then use the mouse to select the control points at the bottom of the bow, as shown in the following screenshot:

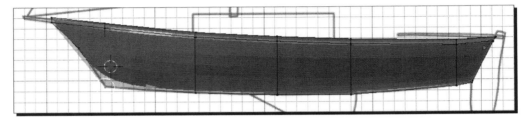

4. Press *Ctrl* and *7* on the NumPad to get the **Bottom** view.

5. Press *S, X*, and use the mouse to scale the control points in X until they are as far apart as the other control points in the bow, as shown in the following screenshot. Then, press the LMB.

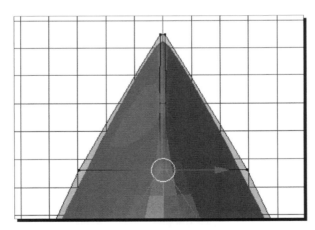

6. Press the MMB and use the mouse to rotate the view so you can see that the bow of the sloop is more pointed.

What just happened?

By scaling the control points at the bottom of the bow, you brought the point of the bow down to the bottom of the hull.

Time for action – finishing the hull

The hull is pretty close to its final shape. Now, it's time to check the shape and tighten up the dimensions using the following steps:

1. Press *7* on the NumPad to get the **Top** view.
2. Press *Z* to toggle from **Solid** to **Wireframe**. Press the *Tab* key to go into **Object Mode**.
3. Look carefully at the outline of the sloop as compared to the template, as shown on the left of the next screenshot. The boat is wider than the template shows it should be. Making the hull taller apparently made it a little wider too.
4. Press the *Tab* key again to return to **Edit Mode**. Press *A* to deselect all the control points.
5. Press *B*, and then use the mouse to select the three center sets of vertical control points, as shown in the following screenshot:

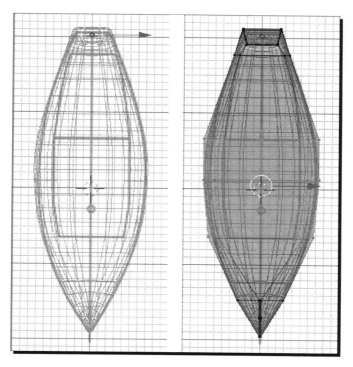

6. Press *S*, *X*, and use the mouse to scale them to the same width as the template shows the boat should be, and then press the LMB.

7. Increment the filename and save the file. In the filename, note that this file is the higher detail version of the hull.

What just happened?

Well done! Making smooth shapes like this is sometimes called organic modeling. It took a little extra care because you are manipulating the control points, not the vertices themselves, but you did it.

Now, the surface of the hull is complete.

For your reference, the 4909_08_Subdivision Surface 1.blend file has the reference block with the subdivision surface applied. The 4909_08_Subdivision Surface 2.blend file has the control object with all the vertices. The 4909_08_Subdivision Surface 3.blend file has the initial top shape. The 4909_08_Subdivision Surface 4.blend file has the initial sides finished with the angling of the bottom of the hull. The 4909_08_Subdivision Surface 5.blend file has the bow raised up. The 4909_08_Subdivision Surface 6.blend file shows making the cabin cockpit boundary.

Getting the most of your rendering time with Levels of Detail

For games, and also for video animation, models are quite often made at different levels of detail. At the beginning of this chapter, you looked at how changing the number of **Subdivisions:** changed the detail in the default cube. This allows you to have the detail when you need it, or to reduce rendering time by reducing the detail when possible. It was good for you to start out with a higher level of detail hull so that you know what the ideal lines will be. However, to keep the number of polygons down now, we have to make a lower detail version.

Time for action – making the boat simpler

Every time you make a model, you have to decide how much detail you need and balance that against how many faces and vertices you use. For now, you will make a simpler version using the following steps:

1. Press *A* to deselect all the control points.

2. Press the MMB and rotate the view so you can see the top and side of the sloop, as shown in the following screenshot. Look at how complex the surface is:

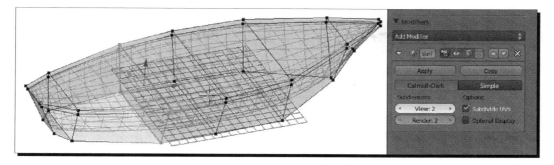

3. In the **Modifiers** subpanel of the Properties window, set **Subdivisions View** to **1**, as shown in the following screenshot. Note how much simpler this surface is compared to the preceding screenshot.

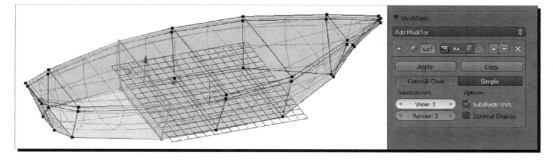

4. As usual, there is a little more massaging to do. The simpler surface does not have a subdivision in the correct place.

5. Press 7 on the NumPad to get the **Top** view.

6. Look at where the template shows the edge between the cabin and the cockpit to be, as shown in the following screenshot. You can see that the control points lie over the boundary between the cockpit and cabin, but the edge of the Subdivision Surface itself is a little further up.

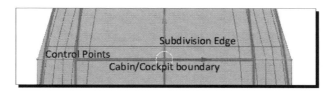

7. Select the control points on the cabin/cockpit boundary. Press *G*, *Y*, and use the mouse to move the control points down so that the subdivision edge is on the boundary between the cabin and cockpit, as shown in the following screenshot, and then press the LMB. It will be easier to see it as you move the control points.

8. Press *S, X*, and use the mouse to make sure that the width of the hull at that point is correct, and then press the LMB.

9. Press the *Tab* key to go into **Object Mode**.

10. Save the file with a unique name that you will remember in 6 months. Note that it is the lower detail version.

What just happened?

In the beginning of the chapter, you looked at the **Modifiers** subpanel of the Properties window, and at what happened to the object when you changed the number of subdivisions. You set the **Subdivisions: View:** value to **2**, which gave great smooth results. However, the price to pay is that the hull will have 736 faces after conversion. However, if you set the **Subdivisions: View:** value to **1**, the hull, when converted will have only 184 faces. For now, this will be enough and will make it easier to continue the project rather than having to hunt through lots of faces and vertices. If you want a prettier version and your computer is fairly powerful, you can come back and redo it with a higher setting for **Subdivisions: View:**.

Have a go hero – adjusting the rear of the cockpit

This is more subtle, but the back of the cockpit in the template does not line up exactly with one of the subdivision edges, as explained in the following steps:

1. You adjusted the front of the cockpit; now adjust the subdivision edge to the rear boundary of the cockpit, and adjust the width of the control points so that they match the template, as shown in the following screenshot:

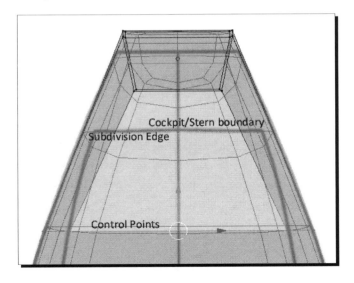

2. Now, double check the cabin/cockpit boundary again and adjust it, if necessary.

3. Look at the stern, and make sure it is the same width as it appears in the template.

4. Save the file.

 For your reference, the 4909_08_Subdivision Surface 7.blend file has the hull ready for conversion from surface to mesh.

Modeling the hull as a mesh

The Subdivision Surface was great to shape the hull. However, you need to use different methods to create the cabin and the cockpit. You need some sharper corners and straight edges to define the cockpit and the cabin. For this, you'll shift back to modeling the mesh object. First, you need to convert the surface to a mesh object, and then you can create the cockpit and use it to build the cabin.

Time for action – converting the surface to a mesh

Make sure that you saved the file at the end of the previous *Time for action – making the boat smaller* section. You are going to convert your Subdivision Surface to a mesh object using the following steps:

1. Make sure you are in **Object Mode**. Rotate the hull so you can see it well.

2. Press *Alt + C* to convert the surface into a mesh object. Select **Mesh from Curve/ Meta/Surf/Text** from the menu with the LMB, as shown in the following screenshot:

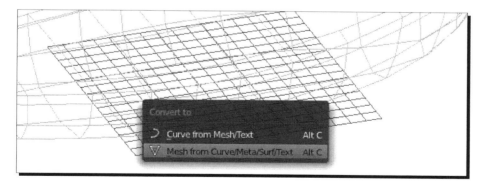

3. Press *Tab* to go into **Edit Mode**. The control points are gone. You now have a boat hull.

4. Press *A* to deselect all selected vertices.

What just happened?

This was a short but important step. Objects can be changed from one type to another. You should save your work before doing this because you cannot convert the object back.

Time for action – making the cockpit

Building the hull will be similar to building the boat because you will be using extrusion and scaling. Execute the following steps:

1. Press *7* on the NumPad to get the **Top** view.

2. Select **Face Select Mode** on the 3D View header.

3. Press *C* and use the mouse to select the faces over the cockpit and cabin on the template, as shown in the following screenshot. Press the RMB to stop selecting.

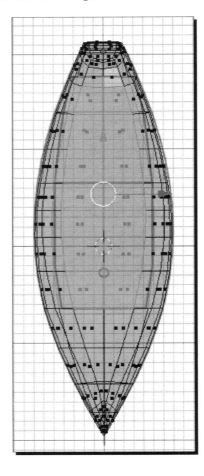

4. Press *3* on the NumPad to get the **Right** view.

5. Press *B*, and then press the MMB and use the mouse to deselect the faces on the bottom of the hull that were previously selected, as shown in the following screenshot. Leave only the faces on the top of the hull selected.

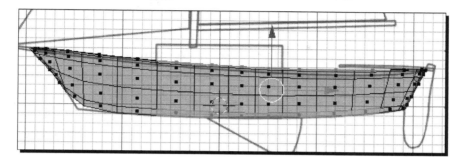

6. Go to the Properties window and select the **Object Data** button, which has three edges and three vertices on it.

7. In the **Vertex Groups** subpanel, press the plus sign to create a new vertex group. Double-click on the LMB over where it says **Group** to rename the group **Cockpit**, as shown in the following screenshot, and then press *Enter*. Press the **Assign** button to assign the selected faces to the group.

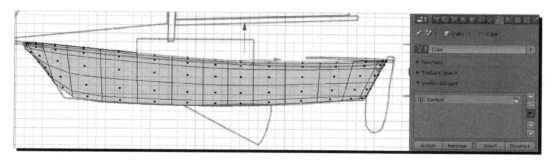

8. Press *E* to extrude the cockpit and use the mouse to move the cockpit floor down, as shown in the following screenshot:

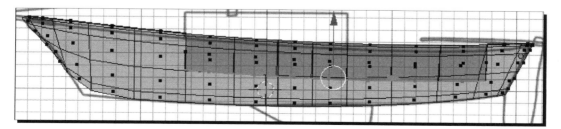

9. Press *S*, *Z*, *0*, and *Enter* to flatten the cockpit floor.

10. Move the cockpit floor up so that the front of the floor is in level with the edge between the second and third faces from the bottom, as seen in the following screenshot:

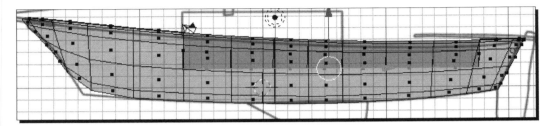

11. Press the *Z* key to toggle **Viewport Shading** to **Solid**.

12. Press the *Tab* key to go into **Object Mode**.

13. Press the MMB and use the mouse to inspect the sloop's hull.

14. In the Properties window header, select the **Object** button. It's the one with the orange cube. Rename the hull to `Sloop Hull` and press *Enter*.

15. Save the file with a unique name that lets you know it is the completed hull.

What just happened?

This was very similar to how you created your jon boat. You had a solid hull, and you selected the faces and extruded them. Next, you will use the faces you grouped to create the cabin.

Time for action – making the cabin

The cabin is made with extrusions, as was the boat. By copying faces from the hull as the basis for the cabin, you will make sure that the cabin will fit snugly on the hull. Execute the following steps:

1. Press *Z* to toggle **Viewport Shading** to **Wireframe**.

2. Press the *Tab* key to go into **Edit Mode**.

3. Press *Shift + D*, and then press *Enter* to copy the cockpit floor. Press *P* to separate the duplicated faces. Choose **Selection**, as seen in the following screenshot:

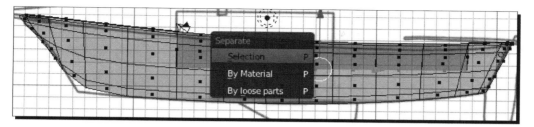

4. Press *3* on the NumPad to return to the **Right** view.

5. Press the *Tab* key to go into **Object Mode**. With the RMB, select the copy of the cockpit floor that you have just made.

6. Press *M, 2,* and then press *Enter* to move it to layer 2.

7. Press *2* to go to layer 2, or use the **Layers** controls in the 3D View header.

8. Press *7* on the NumPad to get the **Top** view. Press the *Tab* key to get into **Edit Mode**.

9. Press *A* to deselect all faces, if needed.

10. Press *B* and use the mouse to select the faces that are in the cockpit area and not in the cabin area.

11. Press *3* on the NumPad to get the **Right** side view.

12. Press *X* to delete the selected faces. Choose **Faces** from the pop-up menu, as shown in the following screenshot:

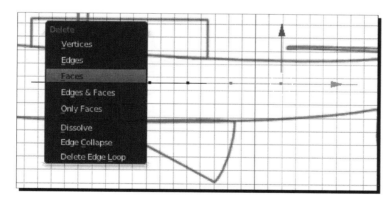

13. Press *A* to select all the faces.

14. Zoom in to where the cabin is on the template.

15. Press *E* and extrude the faces up until they are level with the roof of the cabin in the template.

16. Press *A* to deselect all the faces. Press *B* and use the mouse to select all the faces on the bottom of the cabin.

17. Press the MMB and use the mouse to get a better view of the bottom of the cabin, as shown in the following screenshot:

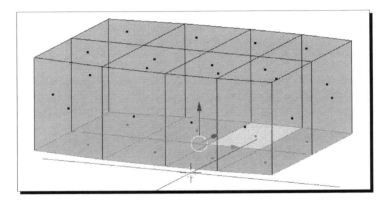

18. In the 3D View header, press *N* and open the **Display** subpanel of the Properties Panel. Uncheck **Grid Floor** for a better view of the bottom of the cabin.

19. Press *E* to extrude the bottom face and press *Enter*.

20. Press *S*, *0.95*, and then press *Enter*.

21. Press *3* on the NumPad for the **Right** view.

22. Press *E* and move the faces up so that there is an equal gap at the top and at the sides, as shown in the following illustration. Then, press the LMB.

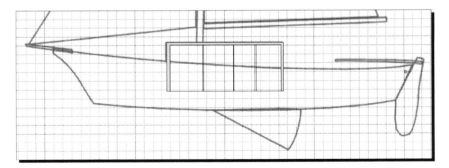

23. Press *1* on the NumPad for the **Front** view.

24. Change to the **Vertex Select** mode.

25. Press *A* to deselect all the vertices. Select the vertices in the center of the roof of the cabin.

26. Press *G*, *Z*, and use the mouse to raise the center peak about **0.6** units up. Press the *Shift + Ctrl* buttons as you move it. Then, press *Enter* or the LMB to create a peak on the cabin roof, as shown in the following screenshot:

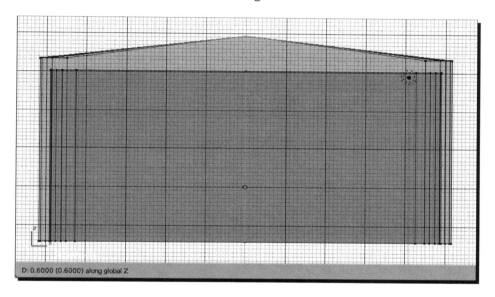

27. Press the *Tab* key to go into **Object Mode**.

28. In the Properties window, select the **Object** button, which is the one with the orange cube. Rename **Sloop Hull.001** to `Cabin`. Then press *Enter*.

What just happened?

All the recent steps should have looked familiar from earlier chapters. You did extrusions, scaled, and moved vertices. Also, using parts of the sloop to make the cabin, you ensured that they will fit together exactly.

Preparing to add openings to the cabin

You have the basic shell of the cabin finished. Now, it's time to put some openings for portals and a door into it.

Time for action – creating objects for use in Boolean operations

While preparing to cut holes out of the cabin, you must first create the shape of those holes. Follow the listed steps:

1. With the cursor over the 3D View header, press *A* to deselect the cabin.

2. In the **Layers** button of the 3D View header, select **Layer 1** with the LMB, then select **Layer 2** using *Shift* + LMB. So, you can see the hull of the sloop as well as the cabin and **Layer 2** is the active layer.

3. Press *3* on the NumPad for the **Right** view.

4. Press *Shift* + *S*. Select **Cursor to Center** from the menu.

5. Put the 3D Cursor in the center of the rear panel of the cabin, as shown in the following screenshot:

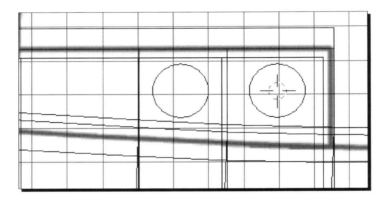

6. Press *Shift* + *A*, and make **Cylinder** from the **Mesh** menu.

7. In **Tool Shelf**, set the number of **Vertices** to **18**. Set the **Cap Fill Type** to **Triangle Fan**.

8. Check the **Align to View** checkbox so that it is properly oriented.

9. Press *S*, *0.8*, and *Enter* to scale the cylinder down in size.

10. Press *S*, *X*, *7*, and *Enter* to make the cylinder longer than the cabin's width.

11. In the Properties window, select the **Object** button on the header. It's the one with the orange cube. Rename the cylinder to **Portal Boolean**.

12. With the cursor over the 3D View header, press *Shift* + *D* to duplicate the Portal Boolean. Press the MMB after you start to move it forward to the next panel so it remains at the same height as the original Portal Boolean.

13. Look at whether the portals are centered vertically between the cabin roof and the deck. If you need to center them better vertically, hold the *Shift* key and select the original Portal Boolean so both are selected. Press *G, Z*, and use the mouse to recenter them between the deck and the cabin roof, and then press the LMB. The positions should be similar to the preceding screenshot.

14. In the **Layers** buttons in the 3D View header, select **Layer 2**.

15. Press *A* to deselect everything.

16. Press *Shift + A*, and then select **Mesh** and **Cube** from the menu.

17. Press *S, Z, 3*, and *Enter*.

18. Press *S, X, 1.5*, and *Enter*.

19. Press *1* on the NumPad for the **Front** view.

20. Press *G, Z*, and move the cube with the mouse so that the top of the cube is between the Portal Boolean and the inner roof of the cabin, as seen on the left in the next screenshot. Then, press the LMB.

21. Press *G, X, 2.5*, and *Enter*. It should be positioned as seen on the left in the next screenshot.

22. Press *3* on the NumPad for the **Right** view.

23. Press *G, Y*, and use the mouse to move the cube so it is centered on the back wall of the cabin, as seen on the right in the following screenshot, and then press the LMB.

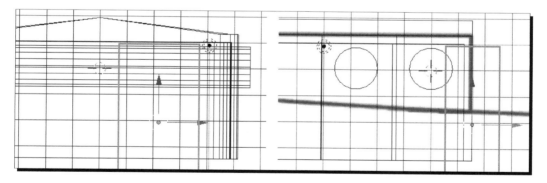

24. In the Properties window, select the **Object** button on the header. It's the one with the orange cube. Rename the cube to Door Boolean, and then press **Enter**.

25. Save this file, and remember to increment the file number before saving.

What just happened?

You just built cylinders and cubes, and you gave them the Boolean names to indicate that you will use them in Boolean operations. Next, you will discover how to use them. Note that all the objects with Boolean in their names were placed so that they cross as few edges of the cabin as possible. This makes the Boolean modifier's work easier and cleaner.

Using Boolean modifiers to cut holes in objects

Booleans are a 3D extension of the Venn diagrams taught in an algebra class. Named after George Boole, Boolean is pronounced "Bool-ee-in" with emphasis on "Bool". Bool rhymes with tool.

There are three kinds of Boolean operators: **Difference**, **Intersection**, and **Union**. The following figure shows that the circle **A** represents the object to which you add the Boolean modifier and the circle **B** represents the object added by the Boolean modifier.

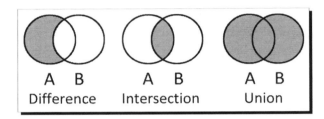

The **Difference** operation leaves all of object A that is not part of object B. With the **Intersection** operation, only what is common to both objects A and B is left. The **Union** operation combines the two objects.

Time for action – detailing the cabin using the Boolean modifier

You made the cabin, the two portal Booleans, and the door Boolean. Now, you will combine them to make the portals and door openings in the cabin. Execute the following steps:

1. Select the cabin.

2. Select the **Modifiers** button in the header of the Properties window. It's the button with the little wrench.

3. In the **Modifiers** subpanel, press the **Add Modifier** button with the LMB. Then, select **Boolean** from the pop-up menu.

4. When the **Add Modifier** subpanel appears, press the button with the cube below the word **Object**. Choose **Door Boolean** from the pop-up menu. Set **Operation** to **Difference**, as shown on the right of the next graphic.

5. You have just made the door frame.

6. Press the **Add Modifier** button with the LMB again. Then, select **Boolean** from the pop-up menu.

7. When the second **Add Modifier** subpanel appears, choose **Portal Boolean** as **Object**. Set **Operation** to **Difference**, as shown on the right of the next screenshot.

8. You have just made the rear portals on both sides of the cabin.

9. Press the **Add Modifier** button with the LMB. Then, select Boolean from the pop-up menu.

10. When the third **Add Modifier** subpanel appears, choose **Portal Boolean.001** as **Object**. Set **Operation** to **Difference**, as shown on the right of the next screenshot.

11. You have just made the forward portals on both sides of the cabin.

12. Press *7* on the NumPad.

13. Select **Door Boolean** with the RMB. Hold the *Shift* key and use the RMB to select **Portal Boolean** and **Portal Boolean.001**. Press *M*, *3*, and *Enter* to move them to **Layer 3**.

14. Press *Z* to toggle **Viewport Shading** to **Solid**.

15. With the MMB, rotate the view so you can see the cabin better, as shown in the following screenshot.

16. Increment the filename and save the file.

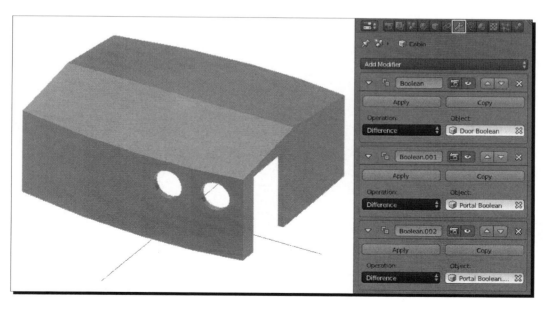

What just happened?

As you can see, creating Boolean modifiers allowed you to use the Door Boolean to punch a hole into the cabin, and you did the same with the Portal Booleans. However, you are not quite finished yet. The modifiers should be applied to the object.

Time for action – applying the Boolean modifier

This is a pretty easy step. It takes the Booleans you have made and converts the Boolean operations to a mesh model, just as you converted the Subdivision Surface to a mesh model. Check the following steps:

1. Select Cabin. In the top **Add Modifier** subpanel, click on the **Apply** button. This will make the Boolean modification permanent.

2. Now, repeat this for the other two **Add Modifier** subpanels.

3. In the **Layers** buttons of the 3D View header, select **Layer 1** and **Layer 2**.

4. Use the MMB to inspect your sloop.

5. Increment the filename and save the file.

What just happened?

Congratulations, the sloop is well on its way. You have completed making the hull and the cabin. Making the basic shape of the cabin was very similar to how you made the jon boat. The big change was using **Boolean** modifiers. They made quick work out of cutting out the portals and the door.

So, with your model, the Difference operation left the entire cabin that was not part of the Door Boolean and the Portal Booleans. Cutting holes in this manner is probably the most commonly used feature of the Boolean modifier.

If you used the Intersection modifier, you made the cabin door and the portal windows because it leaves the cabin that is part of the Door Boolean, and also part of a Portal Boolean.

The Union modifier is not used much because it is usually easier to just join the objects. It will leave the cabin and the Door Boolean as a single object.

Now, the Boolean may seem like a miracle tool, but use it with caution. You'll notice that you used pretty simple shapes, and the Portal Booleans were centered within the face they were cutting a hole out of. They did not cross the boundaries between polygons.

With more complex Booleans, you might not get the results you were hoping for and it may take a long while. They can be unpredictable and give very bad results when done wrong, which is why you should always save your files before attempting a Boolean.

Have a go hero – making doors and portal windows

Open the file you saved just before applying the Boolean operations. Make two copies of the cabin object.

Use the Boolean objects to create a door, and four portals. Use the **Intersection** operation instead of the **Difference** operation.

Can you figure out why you cannot use the intersection operation to make an object with both the Door Boolean and a Portal Boolean?

For your reference, the 4909_08_Subdivision Surface 8.blend file has the hull converted to a mesh. The 4909_08_Subdivision Surface 9.blend file has the cockpit created, and the mesh to build the cabin from separated. The 4909_08_Subdivision Surface 10.blend file has the cabin extruded. The 4909_08_Subdivision Surface 11.blend file has the door and portal Booleans created. The 4909_08_Subdivision Surface 12.blend file has the Booleans done but not applied. The 4909_08_Subdivision Surface 13.blend file has the Booleans applied.

Adding materials and textures to the sloop

With the boat in *Chapter 5, Building a Simple Boat*, and the oars in *Chapter 6, Making and Moving the Oars*, you're getting to be an old pro at adding textures, so these should be pretty easy.

Blender has a quirk when it comes to creating materials. The default cube comes with a default material. Other objects do not.

Time for action – coloring and texturing the sloop hull

The hull has two textures: a painted texture for the outer hull and the cockpit and a wooden texture for the deck. Execute the following steps to color and texture the sloop hull:

1. Reopen the file you just made in the last Time for action section that has the cabin with holes for the door and portals applied.

2. Press *3* on the NumPad to get the **Right** view. Make sure you can see the entire sloop.

3. Select **Layer 1**. Select the hull with the RMB.

4. Press the *Tab* key to go into **Edit Mode**.

5. In the 3D View header, choose the **Face Select** mode.

6. Make sure that the 3D View shading is set to **Solid** in the **Viewport Shading** menu on the header.

7. Make sure that the **Limit Selection to Visible** button is dark gray and that you cannot see through the surface of the sloop.

8. In the Properties window, make sure that the **Object Data** button is highlighted in the header. It's the button that has three edges and three vertices on it forming a triangle. Make sure that the **Vertex Groups** subpanel is open.

9. In the 3D View header, press *A* once or twice to deselect all faces. Now, you want to select the faces for the deck. They are the top row of faces as seen from the side.

10. Press *C* and start out by selecting the faces on the top with the LMB. Then, go back and press the MMB to deselect any face accidentally selected. Press the RMB when you have the faces on the top selected.

11. Press *Ctrl* and *3* on the NumPad to see the other side of the sloop.

12. Press *C* and start out by selecting the faces on the top with the LMB. Then, go back and press the MMB to deselect any face accidently selected. Press the RMB when you have the faces on the top selected.

13. Press the MMB and rotate your view of the sloop. Check the bow and stern, and select any face of the deck area that is still unselected. Press the RMB when you have all the deck faces selected or need to change your view. If needed, resume selection by pressing *C* again.

14. When you have selected all the faces of the deck, as shown in the following screenshot, create a new vertex group in the **Vertex Groups** subpanel of the Properties window. Select the plus sign to create a new group, name the group Deck, and click on the **Assign** button to assign the selected faces to the group.

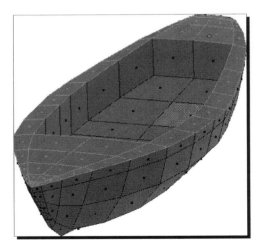

15. With the cursor over the 3D View window, press *A* to deselect all the faces.

16. In the Properties window in the **Vertex Groups** subpanel, select the **Cockpit** vertex group with the LMB, and then click on the **Select** button. Are all the faces of the floor and sides of the cockpit selected? If not, reselect them and reassign them.

17. If there are faces selected that are not part of the cockpit, deselect all of the faces that should be part of the cockpit, leaving only faces selected that are not in the cockpit, and then click the LMB over the **Remove** button in the **Vertex Groups** subpanel to remove them from the **Cockpit** vertex group.

18. With the cursor over the 3D View header, press *A* to deselect all the faces.

19. In the Properties window, go to the **Vertex Groups** subpanel, select the **Deck** vertex group with the LMB, and then click on the **Select** button. Are all the faces properly selected? If not, reselect them and reassign them. Now, in the **Vertex Groups** subpanel of the Properties window, select the **Cockpit** vertex group. Now, both vertex groups are selected.

20. In the 3D View header, choose **Select**, and then choose **Inverse** from the pop-up menu.

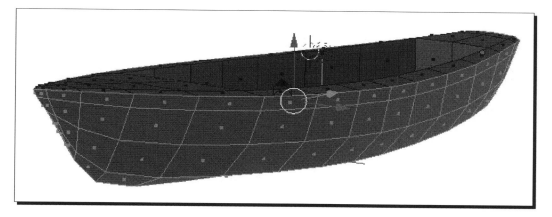

21. Create a new vertex group in the **Vertex Groups** subpanel of the Properties window. Name it `Hull`, and use the **Assign** button to select faces to the group.

22. Save the file to a unique name.

23. Select the **Materials** button on the Properties window header. It's the button with the chrome ball on it.

24. In the **Diffuse** subpanel of the Properties window, click on the white box and set the diffuse color to **0.5** Red, **0.5** Green, and **1.0** Blue, as shown in the following screenshot. Rename the material to **Hull Material**. You can check *Chapter 5, Building a Simple Boat*, if you need to refresh your memory on how to do it. Click on the **Assign** button to assign the Hull material to the Hull vertex group.

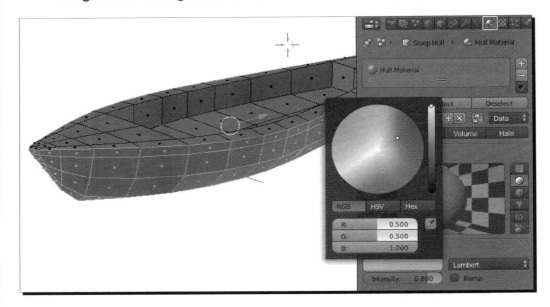

25. In the Properties window, make sure that the **Object Data** button is highlighted in the header. It's the button with three edges and three vertices on it. Make sure that the **Vertex Groups** subpanel is open.

26. In the 3D View window, press *A* to deselect all the faces. In the Properties window, highlight the **Deck** vertex group, and then click on the **Select** button.

27. Select the **Materials** button on the Properties window header. It's the button with the chrome ball on it.

28. Create a new material by pressing the LMB over the plus sign at the top right of the **Materials** panel in the Properties window. Then, press the **New** button.

29. Name the material Deck Material.

30. Select the **Texture** button on the Properties window header. It's the button with the checkerboard pattern on it. Use the MMB to slide the header to the left if you don't see it.

31. Press the button labeled **New**. Name the new texture `Deck Texture`.

32. Where it says **Type:**, press the button with the checkerboard and select **Image or Movie** from the pop-up menu, as shown in the following screenshot.

33. Go down to the **Image** subpanel. Select **Open** and get the image `4909_08_03.png` from the download pack.

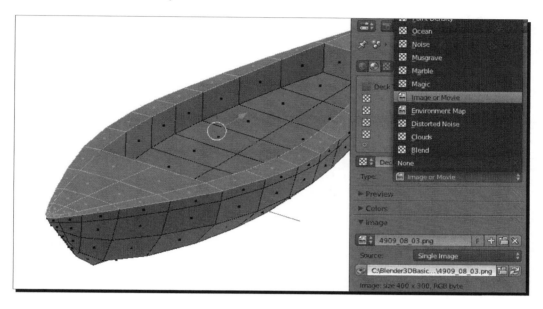

34. Select the **Materials** button from the Properties window header.

35. With **Deck Material** highlighted, Assign the Deck Material

36. In the 3D View window, press the *Tab* key to go to **Object Mode**.

37. Select the camera.

38. Press *0* on the NumPad to get the **Camera** view. Press *G*, *Z*, *Z*, and then use the mouse to back the camera up so you can see the entire sloop. Then, press the LMB.

39. Press *7* on the NumPad. Select the lamp and move it nearer to the camera. In the Properties window, change the **Lamp** type to **Hemi**.

40. Press *F12* to render the image.

41. Press *Esc* when you are done looking at the image.

42. Select the sloop again with the RMB.

43. Press the *Tab* key to go into **Edit Mode**.

44. Press *A* to deselect all the faces.

45. Select the **Object Data** button on the Properties window header. It's the button with the triangle on it.

46. In the Properties window, highlight the **Hull** vertex group and select it.

47. In the 3D View window, if you do not see the Tool Shelf on the left, press *T*. Find the tab labeled Shading/UVs, as seen in the following screenshot. Left-click on it. In the **Shading** subpanel, select the **Smooth** button under the word **Faces:**. Press the *Tab* key to return to **Object Mode**.

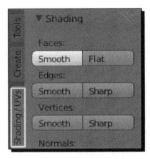

48. Press *F12* to render it. It should look similar to the following screenshot. Press the *Esc* key when you are finished looking at it.

49. Save the file with a unique name.

What just happened?

This wasn't too difficult. It was very similar to how you added textures to the boat in *Chapter 5, Building a Simple Boat*. The vertex groups made it easier to make your texture selections. You chose the **Cockpit** and the **Deck** vertex groups, and then you inverted the selection to create the **Hull** vertex group. Then, you used the vertex groups to assign the materials to the parts of the hull.

Have a go hero – creating vertex groups for the cabin

The next step is to add textures to the cabin. As you can see in the following screenshot, you will be using the same textures. However, you need to create vertex groups for the cabin.

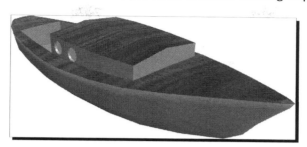

The cabin needs two vertex groups, **Cabin** and **Cabin Roof**. Go to **Layer 2**. Delete the **Cockpit** vertex group left over from separating the cabin from the hull using the minus sign. Select the faces for Cabin Roof, make a group for them, and then invert the selection and make the Cabin vertex group.

Time for action – using the same materials for two objects

Materials in Blender can be reused. This keeps files smaller and lets you easily modify materials throughout a scene. Perform the following steps:

1. Select the **Materials** button on the Properties window header.

2. In the **Material** panel, notice that **Hull Material** is already there. One clue to why that is can be found next to the box where you input the material's name. Notice that it has the number **2**, as seen in the following screenshot. The number represents how many objects use the material. Both **Sloop** and **Cabin** were made from the default cube, and the **Hull Material** started out as the default material. So, Blender has already been reusing the materials.

3. With the cursor over the 3D View window, press *A* to deselect all the faces.

4. Select the **Object Data** button on the Properties window header.

5. In the **Vertex Groups** subpanel, highlight the **Cabin Roof** group in the menu and press the **Select** button with the LMB.

6. Select the **Materials** button on the Properties window header.

7. In the **Material** panel, click on the plus sign to the right of the menu that lists **Hull Material**.

8. Press the chrome ball to the left of the **New** button. Select **Deck Material** from the drop-down menu, as shown in the following screenshot:

9. Click on the **Assign** button.

10. Press the *Tab* key to get into **Object Mode**.

11. Select both **Layer 1** and **Layer 2** in the 3D View header.

12. Press *F12* to render the image. Press *Esc* when you are done looking at it.

13. Save the file with a unique name.

What just happened?

Materials in Blender can be used over and over again. You took the materials from the hull and applied them to the cabin. Modifying a material will alter its appearance on every object that uses it.

For your reference, the 4909_08_Subdivision Surface 14.blend file has the cockpit, hull, and deck vertex groups. The 4909_08_ Subdivision Surface 15.blend file has the hull and deck materials applied. The 4909_08_Subdivision Surface 16.blend file has the cabin and cabin roof vertex groups. The 4909_08_Subdivision Surface 17.blend file has the hull and cabin textured.

Making the ship's wheel with the Spin tool and DupliVerts

There are four parts to the ship's wheel: the rim, the hub, the spokes, and a circle to put the spokes on. You will make them in that order. The Spin tool is like a 3D lathe that creates circular objects. **Dupliverts** uses the vertices of an object to control the placement of copies of a second object.

Time for action – using the Spin tool to make the rim of the ship's wheel

The Spin tool is a very handy tool to make circular objects. It operates in a way similar to extrusion, but instead of making a single extrusion in one direction, it creates a series of extrusions around a point. You can specify how many degrees you go around and how many extrusions it takes to do it. You'll use the Spin tool to make the rim of the ship's wheel. Use the following steps:

1. Select **New** from the **File** menu.
2. Press *7* on the NumPad to get the **Top** view.
3. Press *X* to delete the default cube.
4. Press *Shift + A*, and then select **Mesh** and **Plane** from the menu.
5. Press the *Tab* key to get into **Edit Mode**.
6. Press *S, X, 0.125*, and *Enter*.
7. Press *S, Y, 0.08*, and *Enter*.
8. Press the *Tab* key to return to **Object Mode**.
9. Press *N* to open the Properties Panel in the 3D View header.
10. Press *R, X, 90*, and *Enter*.
11. In the **Transform** subpanel of the 3D View Properties Panel, change the **Location** of **X** to **1**, as shown in the following screenshot, to offset the rim away from its center.

12. Use the MMB and your mouse to rotate the view, similar to what is shown in the following screenshot:

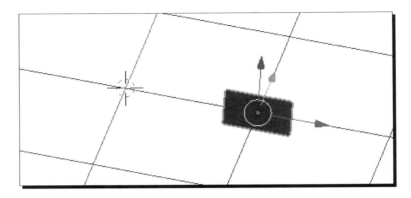

13. Press the *Tab* key to get into **Edit Mode**.

14. If Tool Shelf is not visible in the 3D View header, press *T* to make it appear.

15. In Tool Shelf, scroll down to the **Add** subpanel. Click on the **Spin** button with the LMB.

16. In the **Spin** subpanel, set the Steps to 18, the Angle to 360, and the Axis to **X: 0.000**, **Y: 0.000**, and **Z: 1.000**, as shown in the following screenshot. You can use the *Tab* key to move from button to button.

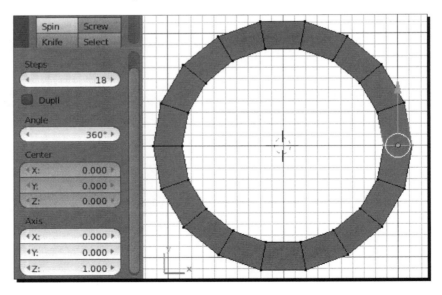

17. Press *X* to delete your original plane. Select **Faces** from the pop-up menu.

18. Press *A* to select all the vertices. Press *W* to get the **Specials** menu and choose **Remove Doubles** from the menu.

What just happened?

You just used the Spin tool. It's a very powerful tool to make objects. Think of it as a lathe. You moved the plane away from the center and sized it. Then, with the Spin tool, you spun it 360 degrees in Z around the (0, 0, 0) point, making the rim of the wheel. You deleted the original plane and removed the duplicate vertices to make the geometry smoother and the rim watertight. Doing this also made the rim **Manifold**, which means that no edges have more than two faces attached; 3D Printers cannot handle edges with more than two faces.

Making the parts for the wheel

You have the rim, now you need the rest of the parts—the hub, spokes, and a circle to hang the spokes on. The hub and circle are easy, the spokes, however, may surprise you in the way that they are made.

Time for action – making the hub

Making the hub is easy. It's simply a cylinder. Perform the following steps:

1. Press *7* on the NumPad to get the **Top** view.

2. Press the *Tab* key to get into **Object Mode**.

3. Press *Shift + A*, and then create a cylinder from the **Mesh** menu.

4. In the **Add Cylinder** subpanel in the lower half of Tool Shelf, set the number of Vertices to 18. Set the **Cap Fill Type** to **Triangle Fan**.

5. Press *S, 0.25*, and *Enter*.

6. Press *M, 2*, and *Enter* to move the hub to **Layer 2**.

What just happened?

That was easy. You put the hub in **Layer 2** so that it won't interfere with your work in making the spokes for the wheel. You will start by making a circle to control the placement of the spokes of the ship's wheel.

Time for action – making the circle

The circle is unseen, but important. It provides the basis on which to place all the spokes for the ship's wheel. Execute the following steps to make the circle:

1. Press *Shift + A*, and then select the circle from the **Mesh** menu.
2. In the **Add Circle** subpanel of Tool Shelf, set the **Vertices** to **8**.
3. Set the **Radius** to **0.25**.
4. Press *A* to deselect all objects and press 5 on the NumPad to put 3D View into Ortho mode.

What just happened?

It doesn't look like much, but you will use the circle to control the placement of the spokes of the ship's wheel. There are eight vertices in the circle, so your wheel will have eight spokes. Blender has a method called DupliVerts that lets you put a copy of the spoke at each vertex of the circle. These copies are called instances. The difference between regular objects and instances is that whatever change you make to one instance is made to all of them. This is exactly what Ivan Sutherland was talking about when he spoke about master drawings and instances.

Next, you will make a spoke for the ship's wheel.

Time for action – making the spoke

There are two stages of making the spoke. In the first stage, you will make the outline of the shape of the spoke. In the second stage, you will turn the silhouette into a 3D object using the Spin tool. Check the following steps:

1. Press *Shift + A*, and then make a **Plane** from the **Mesh** menu.
2. Press the *Tab* key to get into **Edit Mode**.
3. Press the *A* key to deselect all the vertices.
4. Press the *B* key and use the marquee to choose the vertices on the left side.
5. Press *X* and select **Delete Vertices** from the menu.
6. In the **Pivot Point** menu, in the 3D View header, select **3D Cursor**.
7. Press *A* to select all the vertices.
8. Press *S*, *X*, *0*, and *Enter* to flatten the vertices along the *X-axis*.
9. Press *W* to choose the **Specials** menu and select **Subdivide**. Then, in the **Subdivide** subpanel of Tool Shelf, set the **Number of Cuts** to **7**.

10. Press *G*, *Y*, and use the mouse to move all of the vertices up until the bottom vertex just touches the top of the eight-sided circle. Then, press the LMB to release the vertices.

11. In the 3D View header, select **Active Element** from the **Pivot Point** menu.

12. Now, you want to set a vertex as the Active Element. Press *Shift* + RMB, and then select the bottom vertex so it goes black. Press *Shift* + RMB, and then select the bottom vertex so it goes orange again. Now, all of the vertices are selected, but the bottom vertex is now the active element. The **3D Manipulator** shows you the **Active Element**.

13. Press *S*, *Y*, and use the mouse until the vertices are scaled down to about 0.7, and then press the LMB. Don't forget to use the *Shift* + *Ctrl* buttons for precision.

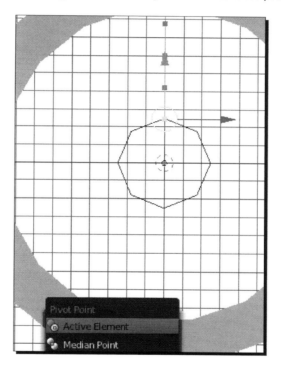

14. Press *A* to deselect all the vertices.

15. Press *B* to border select all the vertices, except the top and bottom vertices.

16. Press *G*, *X*, *0.08*, and *Enter* to move the selected vertices to the right.

17. Press *A* to deselect all the vertices.

18. Press the RMB to select the second to the bottom vertex, and then press *Shift* + RMB to select the bottom vertex so it will be the **Active Element**.

19. Press *S, Y, 0*, and *Enter*.

20. Press *G, Y*, and use the mouse to move the two vertices down until they are within the eight-sided circle, and then press the LMB.

21. Select the second to the top vertex with the RMB. Press *G, Y*, and use the mouse to move the vertex up until it is close to the top vertex, and then press the LMB.

22. Press *Shift* + RMB to select the fourth to the top vertex. Press *G, X, -0.02*, and *Enter*.

23. Select the third from the bottom vertex with the RMB. Press *G* and use the mouse to move the vertex down and to the right until the bottom part of the spoke has a nice shape. Then, press the LMB, as shown in the following screenshot:

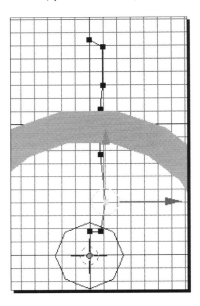

24. Next, put the center of the spoke right at the vertex of the circle in the manner described in the next steps.

25. Press the *Tab* key to get into **Object Mode**.

26. Select the eight-sided circle and press the *Tab* key to get into **Edit Mode**.

27. Select the top vertex of the circle with the RMB.

28. Press *Shift* + *S* and choose **Cursor to Selected** from the menu.

29. Press the *Tab* key to go into **Object Mode**.

30. Select the outline of the spoke.

31. In the 3D View header, select **Object**. Then, choose **Transform** and **Origin to 3D Cursor** from the pop-up menus.

32. Press the *Tab* key to get into **Edit Mode**.

33. Press *A* once or twice to select all of the vertices.

34. In the **Add** subpanel of Tool Shelf, select **Spin** with the LMB.

35. In the **Spin** subpanel of Tool Shelf, set **Steps** to **8**, **Angle** to **360 degrees** (don't move the center), and **Axis** to **X: 0.000, Y: 1.000**, and **Z: 0.000**.

36. Press *A* to select all the vertices. Press *W* to get the **Specials** menu and choose **Remove Doubles** from the menu.

37. With the cursor over the 3D View window, press the *Tab* key to go into **Object Mode**.

38. Press *Shift + S* and choose **Cursor to Center**.

39. Press *Shift + S* and choose **Selection to Cursor**.

What just happened?

You created the outline for the shape of the spoke with the vertices. It turns out that using the Active Element as the center can be a handy way of scaling vertices because it lets you move vertices towards a specific vertex, and it is handier when you are modeling complex surfaces.

You used the Spin tool again, but with very different results than when you made the rim. This time, the center of the object was within the vertices, and there was no hole in the center when they were spun. The object looked more like it was made on a lathe. The Spin tool is great to make table legs, wine glasses, and other round objects.

When you get to using DupliVerts, a copy of the spoke will be created at each vertex of the circle. The origin of each spoke will be at the vertex of the circle and rotated appropriately. You originally built the spoke in the location where it will be after using the DupliVert method. Then, you moved the spoke's origin to the location of the circle's vertex so that the spokes will be at the right locations after everything is done. Finally, you moved the spoke so that its origin is at the scene's origin so that the DupliVerts can offset it properly.

Using DupliVerts to assemble the ship's wheel

Now, it's time to use DupliVerts to turn one spoke into eight spokes and position them properly in relation to the wheel.

Time for action – assembling the ship's wheel

When using DupliVerts, Blender starts with a **pattern mesh** object, which in this case is the spoke. It makes an instance of the pattern mesh object and moves the copy to the location of a vertex on the **base** object, in your case, the circle. DupliVerts can also rotate the DupliVerted copy with respect to the center of the base object, as described in the following steps:

1. Select the circle with the RMB.

2. In the Properties window header, click on the **Object** button. It's the one with the orange cube.

3. In the **Duplication** subpanel, select the **Verts** button in the center. A **Rotation** checkbox will appear. Check it.

4. Select the spoke with the RMB. Then, select the circle again with *Shift* + RMB. Press *Ctrl* + *P* to parent the circle to the spoke. Choose **Set Parent To Object** in the menu.

5. You now have all eight spokes, but the original spoke is still there. It can be seen in the following screenshot. Press *F12* and render it, and you will see that the original spoke does not render. Press *Esc* when you are finished looking at it.

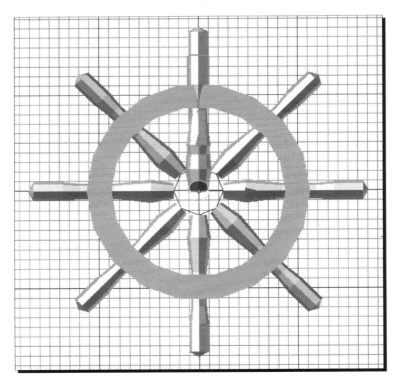

6. In the 3D View header, select **Layer 2** with *Shift* + LMB so you can see the hub.

7. Press *1* on the NumPad to get the **Front** view.

8. Select the hub with the RMB. Press *G, Z*, and use the mouse to move the hub down until the top of the hub is level with the top of the spokes, as shown in the following screenshot. Then, press the LMB.

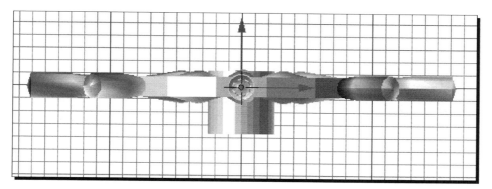

9. Save the file with a unique name.

What just happened?

DupliVerts is a Blender tool that allows you to use multiple copies of an object. This object is referred to as the pattern mesh. Their placement is controlled by another object known as the base object. In this case, you had a spoke that was your pattern mesh and a circle that was the base object.

When you parent the base object to the pattern mesh and set the duplication mode of the base object to Verts, an instance of the pattern mesh is located at each vertex of the base object. Blender will render all of the instances, but it will not render either the base object or the pattern mesh. If you need to make changes to all the instances, just make the changes to the pattern mesh. If you want to turn the instances of the pattern mesh into their own objects, select the base object, in this case, the circle, and then press *Ctrl* + *Shift* + *A*. Then, delete the pattern mesh and the base object.

For your reference, the 4909_08_Ships wheel 1.blend file has the rim completed. The 4909_08_Ships wheel 2.blend file has the spoke outline completed. The 4909_08_Ships wheel 3.blend file has the spoke and circle completed. The 4909_08_Ships wheel 4.blend file has all the parts finished. The 4909_08_Ships wheel 5.blend file has ship's wheel assembled.

Pop quiz – remembering Edge Tool commands

Now, a quick question to help you remember the Edge Tool commands:

Q1. Which of the following three statements is false?

1. To choose edges that are end to end in an Edge Loop, press *Alt* + RMB.

2. To choose edges that are connected by shared faces in an Edge Ring, press *Ctrl* + *Alt* + RMB.

3. To choose edges for a Loop Cut, press *Ctrl* + *L*.

The key-function table

These are key shortcuts you may want to remember.

Key	Function
Ctrl + *R*	Loop Cut
Alt + RMB	Edge Loop
Ctrl + *Alt* + RMB	Edge Ring
Z	Toggles between Solid and Wireframe display
Alt + *C*	Converts a surface to a mesh object
Ctrl + *Shift* + *A*	Converts DupliVert instances to independent objects

Summary

In this chapter, you learned some advanced modeling techniques. You modeled a sloop with Subdivision Surfaces, and then you grabbed some of the geometry to make a cabin that fits precisely together with the hull. You saw how you can control the quality of the model and optimize the number of faces you create depending on your needs. You discovered how to use the Loop Cut tool, Edge Loops, and Edge Rings. You learned how to use Boolean objects to punch holes and shapes in other objects. You made the ship's wheel using Spin tools and DupliVerts.

In the next chapter, you will finish the sloop. You will add the boom, mast, spar, bowsprit, gaff, rudder, tiller, and keel that you made. You will make sails for her from the NURBS surfaces. You will learn how to use text to give the sloop whatever name you want. You'll use choice of font, letter spacing, shearing, extrusion, and beveling to make it look sharp.

Let's go!

9

Finishing Your Sloop

In the previous chapter, you learned many advanced modeling techniques. You modeled a sloop with Subdivision Surfaces, and then copied some of the geometry of the hull to build a cabin that fits precisely together with the hull. You saw how you can control the quality of the model and optimize the number of faces you create depending on your needs. You discovered how to use the Loop Cut tool, Edge Loops, and Edge Rings. You learned how to use Boolean objects to punch holes and shapes in other objects. You made the ship's wheel using spin tools and DupliVerts.

In this chapter, the sloop is going to come together and look great:

- ◆ You'll add the boom, mast, spar, bowsprit, gaff, rudder, tiller, keel, and the ship's wheel that you made
- ◆ You'll discover how to use text by creating a name for your sloop
- ◆ You'll learn to add, delete, and edit text
- ◆ You'll use the choice of font, letter spacing, Bézier curves, extrusion, skewing, beveling, and materials to make it look sharp
- ◆ You'll use NURBS surfaces to make some sails
- ◆ You'll get a line to control the sails, a door, and a detailed window for the portal in the download pack that you can add to your sloop

Let's get started.

Making sure you have the files you'll need in this chapter

Make sure you have loaded the following files from your download files into the `Blender` subdirectory of this chapter's directory, or use the parts of the sloop you have made:

- `4909OS_09_sloop_hull_cabin.blend`
- `4909OS_09_sloop_rudder_tiller_mast_boom_gaff_bowsprit.blend`
- `4909OS_09_sloop_ships_wheel.blend`
- `4909OS_09_sloop_Miss_Blender_Nassau.blend`
- `4909OS_09_sloop_line.blend`
- `4909OS_09_sloop_door_window.blend`

Make sure you have loaded the following files into the `Images` subdirectory of this chapter's directory:

- `4909OS_09_01.png`
- `4909OS_09_02.png`
- `4909OS_09_03.png`
- `4909OS_09_04.png`

Finishing the sloop's superstructure

Well, you've done a lot of good work and it's time to bring it all together. The next step is to combine all the bits into a single file and finish your sloop. I have made kits of the parts that have been made so far, plus a few bonus items such as sails, a line, a door, and a glass portal. Since your sloop may vary slightly, you can either use what you have made or take parts from the kits. The parts I made are in the download pack. If you've forgotten any of the names of the sloop's parts, check the illustration in *Chapter 7, Planning Your Work, Working Your Plan*.

Time for action – setting up the boom and gaff so they swing

In addition to bringing all the parts into the same file, there are a couple of other things that need to happen to create the sloop. Some of the parts need to have the materials from the hull and the cabin added to them, and all of the parts must have their relationship to the hull defined. Objects that are fixed to the sloop, such as the cabin, will be joined to the hull to create a single object. Objects that move, such as the rudder, will have the hull parented to them.

Let's start by attaching the mast, the boom, and the gaff to the hull:

1. Open `49090S_09_sloop_hull_cabin.blend` or the file with your hull and cabin.

2. Select the hull with the RMB.

3. Press *Shift + S* and choose **Cursor to Center** from the menu.

4. Select **Object** from the 3D View header, and select **Transform** then **Origin to 3D Cursor** from the pop-up menus.

5. Select the cabin with the RMB, and then select the hull using *Shift + RMB*. Press *Ctrl + J* to join the cabin to the hull.

6. Press *1* to go to layer 1. If you are emulating the NumPad, you will need to use the layer control in the 3D View header instead.

7. In the **File** menu, select **Append**.

8. Find `49090S_09_sloop_rudder_tiller_mast_boom_gaff_bowsprit.blend`, or your file(s) containing the boom, gaff, mast, and bowsprit.

9. Open the **Object** folder.

10. Select **Boom**, **Bowsprit**, **Gaff**, and **Mast** using *Shift + LMB*, as shown in the following screenshot:

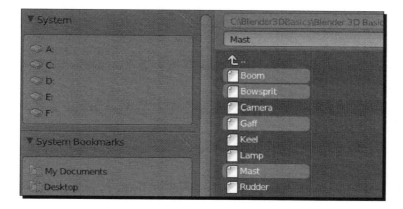

11. Press the LMB with the cursor over the **Link/Append from Library** button in the upper-right corner, as shown here:

12. In the 3D View, press *A* to deselect everything.

13. Use the RMB to select the mast.

14. Select the **Material** button in the Properties window header. It's the button with the chrome ball.

15. Now, click on the silver ball next to the **New** button. Then, choose **Deck Material** from the menu, as shown in the following screenshot:

16. Select **Boom** and repeat the steps to apply the **Deck Material** to it.

17. Select the gaff. It's near the top of the mast. Repeat the steps to apply the **Deck Material** to it.

18. Select the bowsprit and repeat the steps to apply the **Deck Material** to it.

19. Press *F12* to render it. Press *Esc* when you are through with looking at it.

20. Select the mast with the RMB. Select the bowsprit using *Shift* + RMB. Then, select the hull with *Shift* + RMB. Press *Ctrl* + *J* to join them.

21. Press the NumPad *3* key to get the **Right** view.

22. Center your view on the mast, between the boom and the gaff, then zoom in until you can no longer see the boom or the gaff, only the mast.

23. With the LMB, put the 3D Cursor just to the right side of the mast as close as you can. In the **3D Cursor** subpanel that is in the 3D View Properties panel, set the **X** value to **0.000**.

24. Press *Shift* + *A* and select **Empty** from the menu. Choose **Plain Axes** from the menu.

25. Press *S, 20, Enter* to scale out the axes of the Empty. The long axes make the Empty easier to select.

26. Move the cursor to the outer limits of the 3D View window. Press *R* and *X*, and rotate the Empty with the mouse, until its Z axis is parallel to the mast, as shown here. Press the LMB to release it.

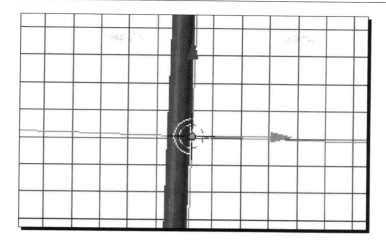

27. Select the mast with *Shift* + RMB. Press *Ctrl* + *P* to parent the mast/hull to Empty. Select **Object** from the pop-up menu.

28. Zoom out so you can see both the boom and the gaff.

29. Select the boom with the RMB. Select the Empty using *Shift* + RMB. Press *Ctrl* + *P* to parent the Empty to the boom. Select **Object** from the pop-up menu. You'll see a dotted line between them, as shown in the next screenshot.

30. Select the gaff with the RMB. Select the Empty using *Shift* + RMB. Press *Ctrl* + *P* to parent the Empty to the gaff, as shown here. Select **Object** from the pop-up menu.

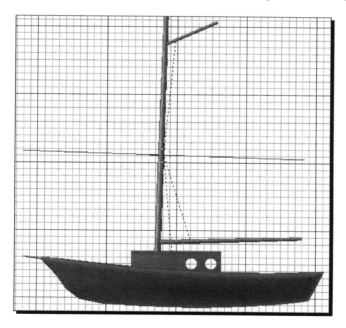

31. Select **Empty**. Press *R*, *Z*, and *Z* to rotate in the Empty's local axis. Then, use the mouse to swing the gaff and the boom back and forth. Press the RMB to release **Empty** without disturbing its position.

32. Save the file with a unique name.

What just happened?

A lot of important work happened here. After bringing the hull and the cabin in, you made sure that the origin of the sloop was in the right place. Then, you joined the cabin to the hull. You brought in the mast, boom, gaff, and bowsprit. The mast and bowsprit won't move, so they were joined to the sloop. Then, you made an Empty. An Empty is an object that has no vertices, edges, and faces, just some visible axes. However, it is good to join one or more things and control them. You rotated it so that its local *Z-axis* is parallel with the mast and then parented it to the boom and the gaff. They will swing when it does and they will swing parallel to the mast. Later, the mainsail and line will also be childed to the Empty so that all will move together.

Time for action – adding the rudder, tiller, and keel

Without the rudder, tiller, and keel, the sloop would drift aimlessly. They are simple objects, but they need a little special handling to fit correctly onto the sloop:

1. In the **File** menu, select **Append**.

2. Make sure that you are in the **Object** folder.

3. Select the **Keel, Rudder, Tiller Path**, and **Tiller Shape** by pressing *Shift* + LMB.

4. Press the LMB on the **Link/Append from Library** button.

5. In the 3D View, press *A* to deselect everything.

6. Use the RMB to select the tiller. Check to see that the tiller does not intersect with the sloop's deck. If it does, move it up so that it does not intersect.

7. Select the **Material** button in the Properties window header.

8. Click on the silver ball next to the **New** button as you did with the mast.

9. Choose the **Deck Material** from the menu to apply it to the tiller.

10. Select the rudder and repeat the steps, but choose **Hull Material** to apply. Select the keel and repeat the steps to apply **Hull Material** to it.

11. Press *Alt* + *C* to convert the keel from a Bezier Curve object to a Mesh object. When the dialog box appears after pressing *Alt* + *C*, select **Mesh from Curve/Meta/Surf/Text**.

12. Select the hull with *Shift* + RMB. Press *Ctrl* + *J* to join the keel to the hull.

13. Use *Shift* + MMB and *Ctrl* + MMB to zoom in to the rudder.

14. Select the rudder with the RMB. Make sure that there is a little gap between the rudder and the stern of the sloop, as shown in the next image. Move the rudder if necessary.

15. Choose **3D Cursor** from the **Pivot Point** menu on the 3D View header.

16. Place the mouse cursor so that it is between the rudder and the sloop, as shown on the left side of the next illustration. Click the LMB to move the 3D Cursor to that position.

17. In the 3D View Window Properties panel, find the **3D Cursor** subpanel. Set the **X** location value of the 3D Cursor to **0.000**.

18. Choose **Object** from the 3D View header. Pick **Transform** and then choose **Origin to 3D Cursor** from the pop-up menus. Press *R* and use the mouse to rotate the rudder and make sure that it rotates around the 3D Cursor. Press *Esc* to release it.

19. Next, you are going to change the local axis of the rudder so that it swings parallel to the stern of the sloop. First, you will rotate all the control points in one direction. This rotates the rudder shape, but not the axis. Then, you rotate the entire object to change the axis, and the rudder shape goes back to where it started. When you made the hull of the sloop in *Chapter 8, Making the Sloop*, you angled the stern at 27 degrees. So now, you will adjust the local axis of the rudder to match this.

20. Press the *Tab* key to get into **Edit Mode**.

21. Press *A* once or twice to select all the control points.

22. Press *R, X, 27*, and *Enter*. It will look like the following illustration on the right.

23. Press the *Tab* key to get into **Object Mode**.

24. Press *R, X, -27*, and *Enter*.

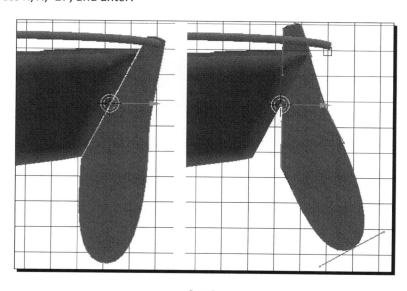

25. Select the tiller with the RMB and then select the rudder with *Shift* + RMB.

26. Press *Ctrl* + *P* to parent the rudder to the tiller and select **Object** from the menu.

27. Select the rudder with the RMB. Press *R, X, X*, and use the mouse to test the rotation of the rudder and ensure that the rudder is parented to the tiller. Press the RMB to release it without any change when done.

28. Press *F12* to render it. Press *Esc* when you are done looking at it.

29. Now, select the rudder with the RMB and then select the hull by pressing *Shift* + RMB. Parent the hull to the rudder as you parented the rudder to the tiller.

What just happened?

This was very similar to adding the mast, boom, and other parts to the hull. However, you may have wondered why you opened the rudder in **Edit Mode**, rotated the control points 27 degrees, and then rotated the object -27 degrees in **Object Mode**. This seems kind of redundant. The rudder is right back where it started.

By rotating all the control points in **Edit Mode**, you rotated them without affecting the local axis. Then, you got back into **Object Mode** and rotated the entire rudder, so the local axis was rotated by -27 degrees to match the angle of the stern. Now, the rudder swings properly in alignment with the stern, instead of just rotating horizontally as it did before you made this change.

Detailing the sloop

Good, you have the superstructure of sloop completed. The hull, cabin, mast, gaff, bowsprit, keel, rudder, and tiller are all finished. Next, we can complete other important items, the ship's wheel, a name and you will build a set sails for her.

Time for action – adding the ship's wheel

Now, it's time to add the ship's wheel. You may be surprised by an effect of the DupliVerts as you add materials:

1. Press *2* to go to layer 2.

2. In the **File** menu, select **Append**.

3. Find `4909OS_09_sloop_ships_wheel.blend` or the file you saved with the spokes rim and hub still separate.

4. Open the **Object** folder.

5. Press *A* to select all of the objects.

6. Press the LMB on the **Link/Append from Library** button.

7. Press the *Home* key to zoom into the wheel. If you're using a Mac without a *Home* key, press the *fn* + left arrow.

8. Use the MMB to rotate the view so that you can see the ship's wheel better.

9. Use the RMB to select a spoke, as shown on the left of the next screenshot.

10. Make sure you have the **Materials** panel open in the Properties window. Click on the silver ball next to the **New** button.

11. Choose the **Deck Material** from the menu.

12. Use the RMB to select another spoke. Note that it already has the Deck Material. All the spokes are instances of each other.

13. Select the rim. Assign the **Deck Material** to it.

14. Select the hub of the wheel. Assign the **Deck Material** to it.

15. Press *B* and use the mouse to select all the parts of the ship's wheel.

16. Press *Ctrl + J* to join them into a single piece.

17. Press the **Object** button in the Properties window header. It's the one with the orange cube. Name the object **Ships Wheel**.

18. Press *M*, *1*, and *Enter* to move the ship's wheel to layer 1.

19. Press *1* to go to layer 1.

20. Press the NumPad *3* key to get the **Right** view. Press *Ctrl + MMB* and use the mouse to zoom out so you can see the sloop.

21. Press *G* and move the ship's wheel up and to the right so that it is over the cockpit. Press the LMB to release it.

22. In the 3D View header, select the **Pivot Point** button and choose **Median Point** from the pop-up menu. Press *Z* to toggle from **Solid** shading to **Wireframe** shading.

23. Press *R*, *X*, *-90*, and *Enter* to orient the wheel properly.

24. Press *G* to move the wheel towards the cabin. Make the hub of the wheel touch the cabin, as shown on the right of the following screenshot. Press the LMB to release it.

25. Press *Ctrl + NumPad 1* to get the **Back** view.

26. Press *G* and move the wheel to the right side of the cabin. Press the LMB to release it.

27. Press *Shift* + RMB and select the hull. Press *Ctrl* + *P* to parent the hull to the ship's wheel. Select **Object** from the pop-up menu.

28. Save the file with a unique name.

What just happened?

Adding the ship's wheel was pretty straightforward. The surprise was that since you created the spokes by the process called DupliVerts, when you applied the material to one of them, all of them got the material applied. This is because the spokes are instances of each other. Remember *Chapter 1, Introducing Blender and Animation*, where I talked about master objects used by Sketchpad; here is one place where Blender uses them. There is really only one object, but Blender uses its object data as many times as needed.

Naming your sloop

Naming the sloop is an important task for any sloop owner. Also, it's a good reason to explore using text objects in Blender. So that's what is next.

Let's consider the first concept related to text objects, that is, the **font**. A font is a collection of letters in a particular size and style. Blender uses **TrueType** and **Adobe 1** fonts as the basis for text objects. They are widely available for download and come in a wide range of styles.

Using the proper font

Most fonts fall under a number of basic categories listed in the following table. Samples have been provided in the following graphic so that you can see the differences. The exact fonts that you have available to you will differ depending on the particular computer you are using:

Style	Features	Representative Font
Serif	Feet or decoration at the ends of characters	Century Schoolbook
San Serif	Plain letterforms	Helvetica
Slab Serif	Thick feet or decorations	Rockwell
Display	Fancy letterforms to catch attention, often all caps	Goudy Stout
Script	Letterforms that simulate cursive handwriting	Edwardian Script
Symbols	Sets of symbols instead of letters	ITC Zapf Dingbats

Each font has a certain feel, and you decide which font is best for a given situation. In general, it is best to stick to one or two fonts at most, and use the controls available to you in Blender such as boldness, italics, size, weight, and color to create variety and a proper feeling with your text. You may find that for 3D animation, you will tend to use San Serif fonts just because they are simpler, so they read well in many situations.

Understanding the parts of letters

While you may not need to know a whole lot about fonts to use them well in Blender, it's good to know a little bit about what makes up a letter. The following graphic shows the most important terms:

- ◆ **Baseline** is the line on which letters sit
- ◆ **Cap Height** is the height of the letter from the baseline to the top of the upper-case letter
- ◆ **X Height** is the height of the letter from the baseline to the top of a lower-case X
- ◆ **Serif** is a small embellishment of the stroke at the end

- **Terminal** is the end of a stroke that doesn't have a serif
- **Kerning** is the method of adjusting spacing between letters to achieve an appealing regularity
- **Ascender** is the upward stroke on lower-case letters that goes above the X height
- **Descender** is the downward stroke that goes below the baseline

Finding the fonts on your computer

Blender uses TrueType and Adobe 1 fonts that are already on your computer. This is the same location from where programs such as Photoshop and Word retrieve the fonts they need. Blender does not have a preview function, so you may want to use another graphics package such as Paint or Gimp to help you choose which font to use.

You will need to know where to find the fonts to bring them into Blender. Here is a chart of likely locations. For more help for the Mac, consult the Apple documentation for OS X at http://support.apple.com/kb/HT2435.

System	Folder or directory	Alternate locations
Windows	C:\Windows\Fonts	
Mac	/System/Library/Fonts	/Library/Fonts
		/System/Fonts
		/usr/lib/fonts
		/usr/lib/X11/fonts
		/usr/share/local
Linux	/usr/share/fonts	/usr/local/share

Deciphering names of font files

The font file names can be confusing. The **Edwardian Script** font is named ITCEDSCR.TFF. In Windows, if you use Windows Explorer to get to the directory where the fonts are stored, it will display the internal font name as well as the external font file name.

Here is a chart of fonts you are likely to find in your computer:

Platform	Serif Font	San Serif Font
Windows	Times New Roman, Palatino Linotype	Lucida, Arial
Mac	Times, Lucida Bright	Lucida, Helvetica
Linux	Century Schoolbook, URW Bookman L	URW Gothic L, Nimbus Sans L

Some more resources about fonts and how to use them

This PDF is a great introduction to fonts and their use:

`http://www.fontshop.com/education/pdf/fsfinalbook_spread.pdf`

Here is a good general background on fonts:

`http://en.wikipedia.org/wiki/Font`

The Smashing magazine is a good reference for using fonts:

`http://www.smashingmagazine.com/2010/12/14/what-font-should-i-use-five-principles-for-choosing-and-using-typefaces/`

The following are the places to get fonts:

`http://neatfonts.com/`

`http://www.dafont.com/`

Naming the sloop with a text object

According to the World Marine Partnership, many boat owners spend more time figuring out a name for their boat than for their children. It's an important task. So the best idea is to have several choices. We'll give you that by making up three different names for the sloop and you can pick the one you like best:

Time for action – creating a text object

Our first suggestion for a boat name is MySloop it's out of Papeete, Tahiti:

1. Create a new file.
2. Press the NumPad *7* key to get the **Top** view.
3. Press *X* to delete the default cube.
4. Press *Shift + A* and choose **Text** from the menu.
5. Press the *Tab* key to go into **Edit Mode**.

6. Press the *Backspace* key to delete the letters as shown here. On a Mac, use the *Delete* key.

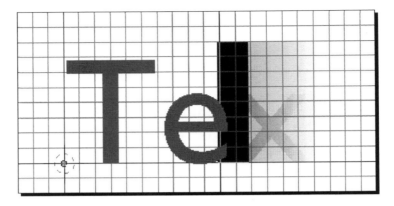

7. Type in MySloop, a carriage return, and Papeete.

8. Press the Object Data button in the header of the Properties window. It's the button with the letter **F** on it.

9. In the **Geometry** subpanel, set **Modification: Extrude** to **0.1** and set **Bevel: Depth** to **0.04**, as shown in the following image.

10. Press the MMB and rotate your view to see the text from front and back.

11. In the **Paragraph** subpanel, change **Spacing: Line:** to **1.50**, as shown here.

12. Change **Spacing: Letter:** to **1.30**, as shown next.

13. Press the **Center** button under **Align:** as shown here.

14. In the **Font** subpanel, click on the **Shear:** button and set the value to **0.300**, and then press *Enter*.

15. In the Properties window header, select the **Materials** button.

16. Create a new material with the plus sign. Press the **New** button.

17. Select the **Texture** button on the header. It has the checkerboard on it.

18. Press the **New** button. Select **Type:** of **Image or Movie**. In the **Image** subpanel, open the file **4909OS_09_03.png** from your download pack.

19. Press *F12* to render your new boat name. Press *Esc* when you have finished looking at it.

20. In the Properties window header, select the **Object** button.

21. Name the Text Object as `MySloop Papeete`.

22. Save the file with a unique name.

What just happened?

As simple as text is, there are a lot of controls you can use to affect the look. There is the size; the font; beveling the edges for a chiseled look; extruding the text to give it depth; changing the spacing between letters, words, and lines; and shearing it to create an italic look. You experimented with several of these.

Time for action – making the second sample

The second suggestion for a name is the Faceboat out of Monte Carlo. This time, you will use the **Text Editor** to help you input the text:

1. Create a **New** Blender file.

2. Look at the window below the 3D View. This is the Timeline window. In the lower-left corner of the Timeline window, click the LMB on the Editor Type menu. Select **Text Editor**, as shown in the left side of the next graphic.

3. In the **Text Editor** header, select **Text**, and then choose **Create Text Block** from the pop-up menu, as shown here on the right.

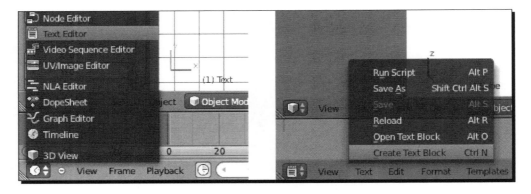

4. In the Text Editor, type in `Faceboat`, a carriage return, and `monte carlo`.

5. In the 3D View, press the NumPad 7 key to get the **Top** view.

6. Press X to delete the default cube.

7. Press *Shift + A* and choose **Text** from the menu.

8. Press *Ctrl* + MMB and use the mouse to zoom in a bit so that you can see better.

9. Press the *Tab* key to go into **Edit Mode**.

10. Press the *Backspace* key to delete the letters. Notice that as you do it, in the Tool Shelf, the lower subpanel displays the **Previous or Selection** button to show that you are deleting characters.

11. Press the Spacebar to create a space character in the Text object.

12. Note that in the Tool Shelf, the lower subpanel provides a box to enter the text, as shown in the next illustration.

13. Go to the Text Editing window. Click the LMB next to **F** in **Faceboat**. Hold the LMB down as you roll the mouse to the right until the entire word **Faceboat** is selected, and then release the LMB. Press *Ctrl + C* to copy the text **Faceboat**. You can also copy it via the **Copy** command in the **Edit** menu on the Text Editor header:

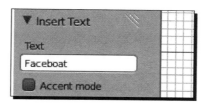

14. Move the mouse up to the Tool Shelf in the 3D View window. Click the LMB over the text input box.

15. Press *Ctrl + V* to paste the **Faceboat** text into the text input box, as shown in the previous illustration. Press *Enter*.

16. Select the Object Data button in the Properties window header. It's the button with **F** on it.

17. Look at the **Font** subpanel in the Properties window. There are four rows of controls, which are labeled **Regular**, **Bold**, **Italic**, and **Bold & Italic**, as shown here. You don't have to take these labels literally. Look at them as the opportunity to use four different fonts in one text object.

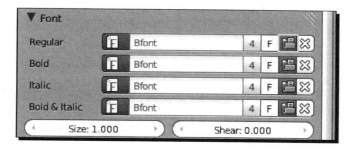

18. Click on the folder symbol to the right of where it says **Regular**. Now, using the File Browser window that popped up, navigate until you reach the place where your computer stores your fonts. Use the table of font locations provided earlier to guide you in your search. Select a serif font. Consult the preceding table for fonts that you should have on your computer if you need to.

19. Notice that the font that **Faceboat** is in has changed in the 3D View.

20. Repeat this with the Bold font. Select a San Serif font.

21. Repeat this with the Italic font. Select a display font.

22. Repeat this with the Bold & Italic font. Select a script font.

23. In the 3D View window, press the *Enter* button and then the Spacebar.

24. At the bottom of the **Font** subpanel, there is a checkbox for **Small Caps**. Press the LMB over it to check it, as shown on the right side of the next image.

25. In the Text Editor window, select the **monte carlo** text and press *Ctrl + C* to copy it.

26. Move the mouse up to the Tool Shelf in the 3D View window. Click the LMB over the text input box.

27. Press *Ctrl + V* to paste the **monte carlo** text into the text input box, as shown here. Press *Enter*.

28. With the cursor over the 3D View window, press the *Shift* key and the left arrow key until you select all of the **monte carlo** text.

29. There are three buttons labeled **Bold**, **Italic**, and **Underline** in the Text Tools subpanel of Tool Shelf in the 3D View, as shown in the left of the next image. Click on the **Bold** button several times. Notice that the words **monte carlo** change font, and notice that in the **Font** subpanel of the Properties window, there is a **Bold** checkbox that gets checked and unchecked, as shown here:

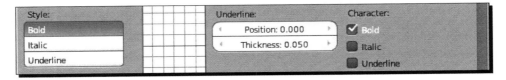

30. Click on the **Bold** button so that the **Bold** checkbox is unchecked, and then click on the **Italic** button.

31. Now, click on the **Bold** button again. Note that both the **Bold** and the **Italic** checkboxes are checked, and that the font is different than when either the **Bold** or the **Italic** checkbox is checked.

32. Finally, click on the **Italic** button so that only the **Bold** checkbox is checked.

33. In the Properties window, go down to the **Text Boxes** subpanel. Set the **Dimensions: Height** button to **4**. Press the LMB on the **Dimensions: Width** button and drag the mouse to the right as shown in the following screenshot. Notice that MONTE and CARLO move onto two different lines and that there is a dotted line that moves, as shown in the next image.

34. If you cannot see the dotted line, use the *Ctrl* + MMB to move your view backwards until the grid in the background is less busy, as in the next image. Then, keep moving the dotted line by moving the mouse over the **Dimensions: Width** button until MONTE and CARLO are on the same line again, and then release the LMB.

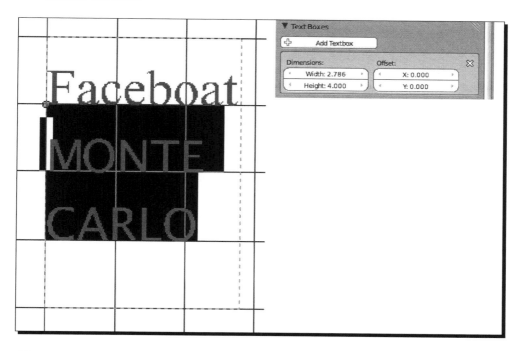

35. Move the dotted line to the left until it is next to the **t** in **Faceboat**, as shown in the previous screenshot.

36. To the left of the **Small Caps** checkbox in the **Font** subpanel of the Properties window, there is a **Small Caps: 0.75** button. Press the LMB over it and move the mouse to the left until MONTE and CARLO are on the same line, and then release the LMB.

37. In the **Paragraph** subpanel of the Properties window, press the **Spacing: Line:** button and move the mouse until the space between the lines is at about **0.50**.

38. In the **Geometry** subpanel of the Properties window, set **Modification: Extrude** to **0.1** as you did for the MySloop text. Set **Bevel: Depth** to **0.01** and **Bevel: Resolution** to **4**.

39. In the Properties window header, select the **Materials** button, with the chrome ball.

40. Press the **New** button to create a new material. Make it red. Press the **Assign** button.

41. In the 3D View, press the up arrow key to move the cursor. Press the *Shift* key and the right arrow key to select the word **Faceboat**.

42. Create a new material with the plus sign and the **New** button. In the **Diffuse** subpanel, set the color. I chose **R** as **0.234**, **G** as **0.358**, and **B** as **0.600**. Press the **Assign** button.

43. Press *F12* to render it, as shown here.

44. In the Properties window header, select the Object button.

45. Name the Text Object **Faceboat MONTE CARLO**.

46. Save the file with a unique name.

What just happened?

That was quite an accomplishment. You opened the **Text Editor**, which can be a handy scratch pad just like you used it. It's also good for making notes about your project, and can even be used to do Python programming.

You learned that the Tool Shelf has buttons to help you work with the text and gives you feedback on what is happening. You were introduced to how you can use up to four fonts in any Text Object and how to control them interactively. You learned how to move the cursor around within a text object and select portions of the text. You checked out the use of a textbox to control the wrapping of a line of text.

While you cannot resize just part of the text, you learned that if you make it into small caps, you can. And to make a part of the text small caps, you must check the checkbox before you enter the text. You can't do it just by selecting it, as you can when you change fonts with the buttons in the Tool Shelf. Finally, you learned that you could apply different materials to different characters in the Text Object and give the edges of the letters a fine edge by adjusting the Bevel Resolution.

Time for action – making the third sample

The third suggestion for a name is the Miss Blender out of Nassau. We will use the Text Editor as a resource and put the text on a curve:

1. Create a **New** Blender file.
2. Look at the Timeline window below the 3D View window. In the lower-left corner of the Timeline window, click the LMB on the Editor Type menu, which is the button farthest to the left, and select **Text Editor**.
3. In the **Text Editor** header, select the **New** button next to the plus sign.
4. Type in `Miss Blender`, a carriage return, and `Nassau`.
5. In the 3D View, press the NumPad *7* key to get the **Top** view. Press *5* on the NumPad to get the Ortho projection.
6. Press *X* to delete the default cube.
7. Select **Edit** from the Text Editor header. In the popup menu, scroll up to **Text to 3D Object**. Select **One Object Per Line**.
8. With the mouse over the 3D View window, press *A* to deselect everything.
9. Press *Shift + A*, and select **Curve** and then **Bezier** from the pop-up menus.
10. Press *Tab* to get into **Edit Mode**.
11. Press *G* to move the handle on the right-hand control point so that the path is an even arc. Press the LMB to release it.
12. Move the right control point so that it is at the bottom of the "r". Move the left control point so that it is at the bottom of the M.

13. Move the inner two control handles up so that they are of the same height and at the same distance from their respective control points, as shown here:

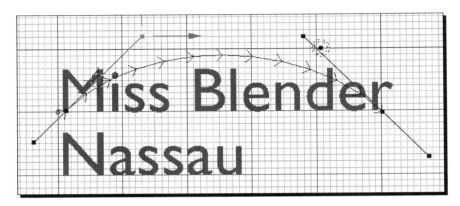

14. Press the *Tab* key to return to **Object Mode**.

15. Select the **Miss Blender** text.

16. Select the Object Data button in the Properties window header. It's the button with **F** on it.

17. In the **Geometry** subpanel of the Object Data panel in the Properties window header, set **Modification: Extrude** to **0.1**.

18. In the **Font** subpanel, select a serif font for the **Regular:** font.

19. Go down to where it says **Text on Curve:** in the lower-right corner of the following graphic. Click on the gray button and select **Bezier Curve** from the menu, and Miss Blender will follow the Bezier Curve.

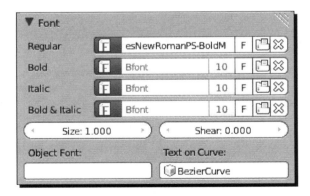

20. Use the RMB to select the Bezier Curve.

21. Press the *Tab* key to go into **Edit Mode**.

22. Select the right-hand control point. Press *G* and move the mouse left, pressing the MMB to lock in the axis of motion.

23. Move the control point left until it is under the base of the "r". Press the LMB.

24. Press *A* to deselect the control point and press *B* to select both of the inner control handles.

25. Move them down until the top of the letter B is at the major grid line. Press the LMB.

26. Press the *Tab* key to get out of **Edit Mode**.

27. Select Nassau with the RMB.

28. In the **Geometry** subpanel of the Object Data panel in the Properties window header, set **Modification: Extrude** to **0.1**.

29. Move Nassau so that the top of the lower case characters (the X line) is level with the bottom of the Bezier Curve. Center Nassau horizontally under Miss Blender so that "N" and "u" are equidistant from the Miss Blender text.

30. Select the **Miss Blender** text with the RMB.

31. Select the **Material** button in the Properties window header.

32. Create a new material and name it Gold.

33. In the **Diffuse** subpanel, set the color to **R** to **1**, **G** to **0.75**, and **B** to **0.150**, and to the right of the color, set the shade to **Lambert**, and set **Intensity** to **0.800**, as shown here.

34. In the **Specular** subpanel, set **Intensity:** to **0.500** and **Hardness** of **16**, as shown in the next graphic.

35. In the **Shading** subpanel, set the **Emit:** value to **0.075**. Set **Ambient:** to **0.175**. Set **Translucency** to **0.25**, as shown on the right of the following illustration.

36. In the **Mirror** subpanel, check the checkbox, and set the **Reflectivity** to **0.400** and the color to **R** as **1.000**, **G** as **0.750**, and **B** as **0.500**, as shown in the following screenshot:

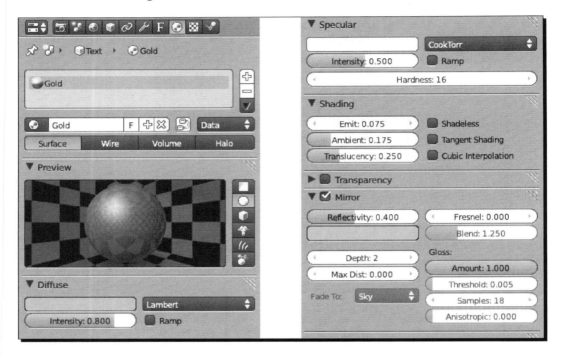

37. In the Properties window header, select the **Object** button.

38. Name the Text Object **Miss Blender**.

39. Select the Nassau Object.

40. Select the **Material** button in the Properties window header.

41. Press the plus sign to create a new Material, and then press the **New** button.

42. Name the material `Black Lacquer`.

43. In the **Diffuse** subpanel, set the color to **R** as **0.000**, **G** as **0.000**, and **B** as **0.000**.

44. In the **Specular** subpanel, set **Intensity** to **1**.

45. Set **Hardness** to **350**.

46. Press *F12* to render it, as shown here. I added a textured plane behind the camera to test the reflections as shown here. Press *Esc* when you are done looking at it.

47. Save the file with a unique name.

48. Select the **Miss Blender** object and the **Nassau** object.

49. Press *Alt + C* and then choose **Mesh** from **Curve/Meta/Surf/Text** to convert the Text Objects.

50. Press *Ctrl + J* to join them.

51. In the Properties window header, select the Object button.

52. Name the object `Miss_Blender_Nassau`.

53. Save the file with a unique name.

What just happened?

You discovered a new way to create Text Objects using the **Text To 3D Object** command in the Text Editor. You put each line of text into a separate Text Object. Next, you learned to put a Text Object onto a curve, and you could change the curve interactively to position the Text Object just the way you want. You learned to make a reflective material and adjust the specularity to create sharper highlights. Since two text objects cannot be joined, you converted them to regular mesh objects and joined them.

Want to know how to make other materials?

Here's a web page with lots of suggestions:

`http://en.wikibooks.org/wiki/Blender_3D:_Noob_to_Pro/`
`Every_Material_Known_to_Man`

For your reference, the `49090S_09_Text_MySloop.blend` file has the file for the MySloop name. The `49090S_09_Text_Faceboat.blend` file has the Faceboat name. The `49090S_09_Text_Miss_Blender.blend` file has the Miss Blender name.

Have a go hero – make your own name

You've done several examples of creating a name for your sloop. You may have better ideas for a name and a home port and some creative ideas on how you want to do it. Give it a try.

Adding the name to the boat

Adding the name to the boat is pretty straightforward, similar to adding the other parts.

Time for action – adding the boat name

Now, it's time to add the boat name and affix it to the stern of the sloop:

1. Open the file of the sloop that you saved before working on the boat names.
2. Press *Z* to get Solid shading. Press *A* to deselect all objects.
3. Press *Ctrl* + NumPad *3* to get the **Left** side view.
4. In the **File** menu, select **Append**.
5. Find `4909OS_09_sloop_Miss_Blender_Nassau.blend`, or the file you made with your favorite boat name.
6. Open the **Object** folder.
7. Select **Miss_Blender_Nassau** or the name you chose for your boat with *Shift* + LMB. Choose the name from the Object directory.
8. Press the LMB on the **Link/Append from Library** button.
9. Press *G* and move the name to the stern of the boat where you can see it, and then press the LMB to release it.
10. Press *R, Z, 180,* and *Enter*.
11. Press *S, 0.4,* and *Enter*.
12. Now, the name needs to be rotated into the proper orientation. Minus 90 degrees would turn it straight up, but if you recall in *Chapter 8, Making the Sloop*, we angled the stern of the sloop -27 degrees. So, add -90 and -27 to get -117. Press *R, X, -117,* and *Enter*.
13. Press *Ctrl* + NumPad *1* to get the **Back** view.
14. Move the name to where you want it on the stern, as shown in the center of the following image.
15. Press *Ctrl* + NumPad *3* to get the **Left** view. Move the view so you can see the stern of the sloop.

16. Press *G* and *Y*, and use the mouse to move the name to the sloop, as shown on the right. Press the LMB to release it.

17. If you have used a name other than Miss Blender Nassau, make sure it has been converted to a mesh object. Press *Alt + C* if you need to convert it.

18. Press *Shift* + RMB and select the hull. Press *Ctrl + J* to join the name to the hull of the sloop.

What just happened?

You just assembled your sloop, added all the parts you made, and added materials to them. It took a little work, but it was pretty easy. You've handled quite a variety of modeling methods now. Well done.

Time for action – using a NURBS surface to make the mainsail

You have used Subdivision Surfaces to model the sloop's hull and Bézier curves to make the rudder and keel. Now, you will use a NURBS (Non Uniform Rational B Spline) surface to make the mainsail:

1. Press *Ctrl* + NumPad *3* to see the **Left** view. Zoom out so you can see the whole sloop.

2. Press *Shift* + *S* and select **Cursor to Center**.

3. Put the cursor between the boom and gaff in the middle of where the sail will be.

4. Press *Shift* + *A*. Choose **Add Surface** and then **NURBS Surface**.

5. In the Tool Shelf's **Add Surface Patch** subpanel, check the **Align to View** checkbox.

6. Press the *Tab* key to get into **Edit Mode**.

7. In the Properties window, select the Object Data button; it has two dots that hold up a surface at one end.

8. In the Properties window, the **Active Spline** subpanel appears; check the checkboxes for **Endpoint: U** and **Endpoint: V**.

9. In the 3D View, zoom into the area between the boom and the gaff. Press *A* to deselect all the control points. Press *C* and select the bottom row of control points. Press the RMB to finish the selection.

10. Move the selected control points near to the boom. Press *A* to deselect all of the control points.

11. Select and move each bottom corner control point to its respective end of the boom, as shown on the left side of the next graphic.

12. Space the other two bottom control points evenly between the ends of the boom, as shown in the following graphic on the right.

13. Press *A* to deselect all control points. Press *C* to select the top row of the control points. Press the RMB to finish the selection.

14. Move the selected control points near to the gaff.

15. Move the top corner control points to the ends of the gaff.

16. Space the other two top control points evenly between the ends of the gaff, as shown here on the right.

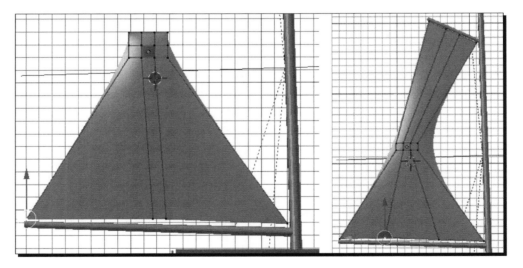

17. Now, work with the control points in the center of the sail. Move the right-hand ones so that they are evenly spaced between the boom and the gaff, by the mast. Move the left-hand ones so that they are evenly spaced between the tips of the boom and the gaff, as shown here. Then, move the center control points so that they are evenly spaced across the mainsail, as shown on the left side of the next image.

18. Press *A* to deselect all control points. Press *C* and select all four central control points. Press the RMB to complete the selection.

19. Press MMB and rotate the view until you can see the curve in the sail, as shown here.

20. Press *G* and *X*, and move the control points to -3.000. Then, press the LMB to release it.

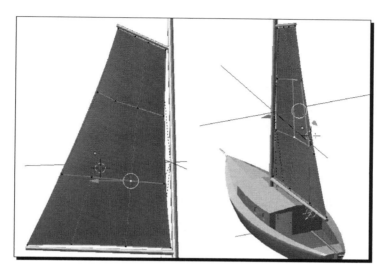

21. Press the *Tab* key to leave **Edit Mode**.

22. In the Properties window header, press the **Object** button. It's the one with the orange cube. Name the sail `Mainsail`.

23. Select the **Material** button in the Properties header. Make a material for the mainsail. Name it `Sail Material`.

24. Select **Empty** by pressing *Shift* + RMB.

25. Press *Ctrl* + *P* to parent the Empty to the mainsail. Select **Object** from the pop-up menu. Select just the Empty. Press *R*, *Z*, *Z*, and use the mouse to test that **Empty** is parented to the sail. Press *Esc* to release **Empty**.

What just happened?

The sail is a NURBS (Non Uniform Rational B-Spline) curve. A NURBS surface is similar to a Subdivision Surface in that it uses control points to control a surface. The NURBS surface gives a more accurate control, but is a little harder to use. Like Subdivision Surfaces, you can add control points to extend the surface. Blender can animate the control points of the sail, so the sail can be filled with wind. The mainsail was parented to the Empty so that it will move along with the boom and gaff.

Have a go hero – making the jib

Making the jib is very similar to making the mainsail, with one little twist; it only has three corners.

Add the NURBS surface, just as you did in the previous *Time for action - using a NURBS surface to make the mainsail* section.

To make the corner near the bowsprit, grab all the control points on the vertical edge nearest to the bowsprit and scale them all to zero. Then, move them near to the end of the bowsprit.

Next, move one corner near the mast across from the boom and one corner near the mast across from the gaff. Then, adjust all the control points evenly, as shown here:

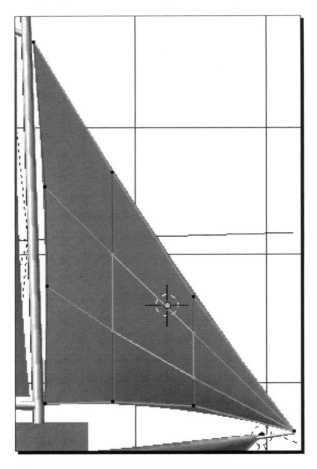

Now, add some curve to the jib as you did for the main sail. When you are done, parent the hull to the jib.

Apply the material you made for the Mainsail to the jib.

Save the file with a unique name.

Detailing the sloop, and adding a door and portals

This book cannot cover everything. It would be neat to add an interior, an anchor, and other details. However, there is still much to cover. So here are a couple of bonuses for your hard work and persistence: a line for the mainsail, which you can copy and use to create other lines for the sloop; the door; the portal window; and a nice brass portal frame.

 For your reference, the 4090OS_09_Portal_and_Door_Assembly. blend file has all the parts, textures, and instructions in the Text window on how to create the door and a glass portal window.

Time for action – adding a line to control the mainsail

You can't control the sail without a line. Made just like the tiller, it shows the flexibility of this technique:

1. Press *A* to deselect all objects. In the **File** menu, select **Append**.
2. Find 4090OS_09_sloop_line.blend.
3. Open the **Object** folder.
4. Press *A* to select the line and the line shape.
5. In the 3D View, select the line as shown in the following screenshot:

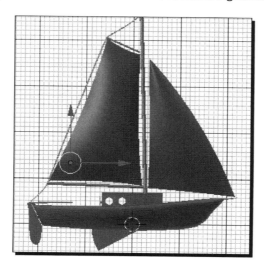

6. Press the *Tab* key to get into **Edit Mode**. You see the control points of the Bezier Curve that creates the line. Press the *Tab* key to re-enter **Object Mode**.

7. In the Properties window header, press the Object Data button. It has two dots connected by a curve. The line is made just the same way as the tiller. In the **Geometry** subpanel, you will see **Line Shape** listed as the Bevel Object, as in the following image.

8. Press *Shift* + LMB to select **Empty**. Press *Ctrl* + *P* to parent the Empty to the line.

9. Select **Empty** and press *R*, *Z*, and *Z* to do a test rotation. Press the RMB when you are done.

What just happened?

The line was made in the same way that the tiller was, with a Bezier Curve to control the shape of the length and a Bezier circle to control the shape of the cross-section. Like the sail, its control points can be animated.

Time for action – adding the door and a portal

Now, you will bring in the cabin door and the portal. You will put the cabin door together with the portal window, and separate a copy of the portal window to use on the cabin:

1. Press *A* to deselect everything. Choose **Append** from the **File** menu. Find 49090S_09_sloop_door_window.blend. Append **Cabin Door** and **Portal Window**.

2. Make a copy of **Portal Window**, and move it aside.

3. Select **Cabin Door** and **Portal Window**. Press *M*, *2*, and *Enter* to move the door and window to layer 2. Press *2* to go to layer 2.

4. Press the NumPad *3* key to get the **Right** view. Move the mouse cursor so that it's centered on the door. Click the LMB to move the 3D Cursor there.

5. Press *Ctrl + 1* to get the **Back** view. Check that 3D Cursor is on the left side of the door.

6. In the 3D View Header, select **Object** and then **Transform** from the pop-up menu and the **Origin to 3D Cursor** option.

7. In the Properties panel, click the **Materials** button. Add **Deck Material** to **Cabin Door**. The **Portal Window** does not need any material.

8. Select **Portal Window** with the RMB. Select **Cabin Door** by pressing *Shift + RMB*. Join **Portal Window** to **Cabin Door** with *Ctrl + J*.

9. Press *M*, *1*, and *Enter* to move **Cabin Door** back to layer 1. Press *1* to go to layer 1. Select the hull with *Shift + RMB*, and then press *Ctrl + P* to parent the hull to the door.

10. Don't do anything to the copy of **Portal Window** that you set aside. We will use that to cover the other portals on the sides of the cabin.

What just happened?

You appended the **Cabin Door** and **Portal Window** objects to the sloop file. You made a copy of **Portal Window** for later use. You finished with the **Cabin Door**, giving it a material and adjusting the origin of the door. Finally, you combined the **Cabin Door** and the **Portal Window** into a single object.

Time for action – adding the portals

Adding the portals to the cabin is the final touch. The cabin is not rectangular, so you will have to rotate the portals to match the angle of the walls:

1. Press *7* on the NumPad to get the **Top** view.

2. In the **Viewport** shading menu on the 3D View header, select **Wireframe** shading.

3. Select **Portal Window.001** that you set aside earlier.

4. Press *R*, *Z*, *90*, and *Enter*.

5. Press *G* and use the mouse to move the portal next to the left side of the cabin. Press the LMB to release.

6. Use *Ctrl + MMB* and *Shift + MMB* to zoom in so that you see the portal and the portal holes on the left side as well.

7. Press *G* and use the mouse to get the portal aligned as closely as possible to the forward portal hole. Press the LMB to release the portal.

8. Zoom into the forward portal hole. The portal window is a little larger than the portal hole. Aligning the dot that marks the center of the portal window with the outside wall of the cabin will help to get started. Then, make sure that the sides of the portal window extend on either side of the portal hole.

9. Press *Ctrl* + NumPad *3* to get the **Left** view. Zoom out until you can see both the portal hole and the portal window.

10. Press *G* and *Z*, and move the portal window so that it is aligned with the portal hole.

11. Use *Ctrl* + MMB and *Shift* + MMB to zoom in so that you see the portal and portal hole very well. Press the *G* key and use the mouse to align the portal with the portal hole. The edge of the portal hole will be between the two edges of the portal window, as shown in the following illustration. For finer control, press the arrow keys instead of using the mouse. Press *Enter* to release the portal in place.

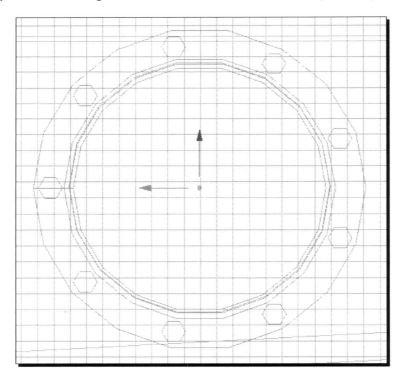

12. Press *Shift* + *D*, make a copy of the portal, and move it to the rear portal hole. Press the MMB when you move to keep it in level with the original portal. Press the LMB when it is over the portal hole.

13. Press *G* and use the left and right arrow keys to do the final alignment. Press *Enter* to release it.

14. Press the NumPad *7* key to get the **Top** view.

15. Press *G* and *X*, and move the portal next to the portal opening. Use the dot in the center of the Portal Window to guide you. Press the LMB to release it.

16. Press *R* and *Z*, and use the mouse to rotate the portal so it is flush with the side of the cabin, then press the LMB to release the rotation, as shown here. The bolt heads should be facing outward.

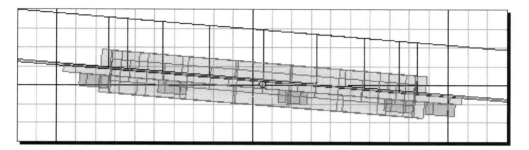

17. Zoom out so you can see both portal windows. Select the forward portal window with the RMB.

18. Press *R* and *Z*, and use the mouse to rotate the portal so it is flush with the side of the cabin, and then press the LMB. Remember to start with the cursor at the edge of the 3D View for the best control.

19. In the 3D View header, select the **Pivot Point** button and choose 3D Cursor from the pop-up menu.

20. Press *Shift + S* and choose **Cursor to Center**. Enter **Edit Mode**. Press *A* once or twice to select all the vertices.

21. Press *Shift + D* and *Enter* to duplicate the portal. Press *S, X, -1*, and *Enter*. This creates a mirror copy of the portal on the other side of the cabin. Press *Tab* to return to **Object Mode**.

22. Select the rear portal with the RMB. Enter **Edit Mode**. Press *A* once or twice to select all the vertices.

23. Press *Shift + D* and *Enter* to duplicate the portal. Press *S, X, -1*, and *Enter*. Press *Tab* to return to **Object Mode**.

24. Use *Shift* + MMB to move to the other side of the sloop. Make sure you see the portals and the portal holes well. Check that all portals fit snugly, as shown in the following screenshot. If necessary, go back into **Edit Mode** and move and rotate a portal that is not properly placed.

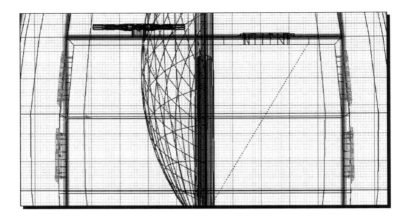

25. Make sure you are in **Object Mode**. Select both of the portal windows. Select the hull with *Shift* + RMB. Press *Ctrl* + *J* to join the portal windows to the hull.

26. In the **Viewport** shading menu on the 3D View header, select **Solid** shading.

27. Press the *Home* key so you can see the entire sloop, and use the MMB to rotate your view.

28. Press *F12* to render it. Press *Esc* when you are done viewing it.

29. Save the file with a unique name.

What just happened?

Congratulations! You have finished the sloop. That's quite an accomplishment. In this last exercise, the tricky part was getting a tight fit between the portal holes and the portal windows. You learned that the arrow keys could be used with the *G* key to move objects in small precise amounts. Just in case you didn't get a chance to check out 4909OS_09_ Portal_and_Door_Assembly.blend, the frame of the portal window was created with the same methods as the ship's wheel; the rim was made with the spin tool, the nuts are DupliVerts, and the glass windows were done with a Boolean operation. The door was also a couple of Boolean operations to cut out the door and then a portal hole in the door. Well done!

Pop quiz – fonts

These questions about the parts of a font will come from the next image.

Q1. If the **X Height** is the distance between the baseline and the top of a lower case letter, what is the **Cap Height**?

1. The distance to the baseline of the row above.

2. The height of an upper case letter.

3. The distance from the top of the ascender to the bottom of the descender.

Q2. Which statement is true?

1. The san serif font does not have any little feet on the terminals of the letter.

2. The serif font does not have any little feet on the terminals of the letter.

3. The san serif font looks like it was written by hand.

Pop quiz – rotations

Q1. When you were adding the rudder, you first had to get into **Edit Mode**, select all the vertices, and then rotate them by 27 degrees. Next, you went into **Object Mode** and rotated the whole rudder by -27 degrees. Why was this necessary?

1. The splines were oriented incorrectly when the rudder was built.

2. The axis was changed when you rotated the vertices. It had to be counteracted by rotating the rudder.

3. This was done to rotate the local axis of the rudder so that it would swing along the angle of the stern.

For your reference, the 49090S_09_sloop_build_1.blend file has the hull, cabin, mast, boom, gaff, and bowsprit as separate pieces. The 49090S_09_sloop_build_2.blend file has the boom and gaff parented to the empty, and the cabin, mast, and bowsprit joined to the hull. The 49090S_09_sloop_build_3.blend file has the rudder, tiller, and keel textured. The 49090S_09_sloop_build_4.blend file has the keel joined to the hull and the rudder re-oriented and parented to the hull. The 49090S_09_sloop_build_5.blend file has the ship's wheel added. The 49090S_09_sloop_build_6.blend file has the sails added. The 49090S_09_sloop_build_7.blend file has the ship's name. The 49090S_09_sloop_build_8.blend file has the line added. The 49090S_09_sloop_build_9.blend file has the door and glass portal added. The 49090S_09_sloop_build_10.blend file has the right-hand portals in place. The 49090S_09_sloop_build_11.blend file has all the portals in place. The 49090S_09_sloop_build_12.blend file has the completed sloop.

The key-function table

The following table shows the keyboard commands used in this chapter:

Key	Function
A	In the file browser, this selects all the files to append.
Backspace	In **Edit Mode** for a Text Object, this deletes a character. On a Mac, use the *Delete* key.
Ctrl + C	This copies text in the Text Editor or in the text entry box in the **Insert Text** subpanel of the Tool Shelf.
Ctrl + V	This pastes text in the Text Editor or in the text entry box in the **Insert Text** subpanel of the Tool Shelf.
Left arrow	In **Edit Mode** for a Text Object, this moves the cursor to the left.
Right arrow	In **Edit Mode** for a Text Object, this moves the cursor to the right.
Up arrow	In **Edit Mode** for a Text Object, this moves the cursor up one line.
Down arrow	In **Edit Mode** for a Text Object, this moves the cursor down one line.
End	In **Edit Mode** for a Text Object, this moves the cursor to the end of the line.
Home	In **Edit Mode** for a Text Object, this moves the cursor to the beginning of the line.
Shift + left arrow	In **Edit Mode** for a Text Object, this selects one character to the left.
Shift + right arrow	In **Edit Mode** for a Text Object, this selects one character to the right.
Shift + up arrow	In **Edit Mode** for a Text Object, this selects one row upwards.
Shift + down arrow	In **Edit Mode** for a Text Object, this selects one row downwards.
Shift + End	In **Edit Mode** for a Text Object, this selects all the characters from the current character to the end of the line.
Shift + Home	In **Edit Mode** for a Text Object, this selects all the characters from the current character to the beginning of the line.
Ctrl + Alt + NumPad 0	This matches the **Camera** view to the **Current** view.
Ctrl + J	This joins two objects together.
fn + left arrow	On a Mac without a *Home* key, this accomplishes the *Home* key command.
Left arrow	Used after the *G* key is pressed, this moves in small increments to the left; the motion is aligned to the screen.
Right arrow	Used after the *G* key is pressed, this moves in small increments to the right; the motion is aligned to the screen.
Up arrow	Used after the *G* key is pressed, this moves in small increments upward; the motion is aligned to the screen.
Down arrow	Used after the *G* key is pressed, this moves in small increments downward; the motion is aligned to the screen.

Summary

In this chapter, you added the boom, mast, spar, bowsprit, gaff, rudder, tiller, keel, and the ship's wheel that you created. You learned how to create a local axis for motion that is not on the global X, Y, and Z axes. You discovered how to incorporate text into your model. You created sails with NURBS surfaces, and added a line, a door, and a detailed window for the portal in the download pack.

In the next chapter, you will learn how to create organic forms, oceanic surfaces, and terrain. You will populate your world with simple buildings and build a pier for your sloop.

Let's go!

10

Modeling Organic Forms, Sea, and Terrain

In the earlier chapter, you finished off the sloop. You added the boom, mast, spar, bowsprit, gaff, rudder, tiller, keel, and the ship's wheel that you made. You learned how to create a local axis for motion that is not on the global X, Y, and Z axes. You added the bonus sails, line, a door, and a detailed window for the portal in the download pack. You created several possible names for your sloop. Choosing font, letter spacing, extrusion, Bézier curves, and beveling, you made it look sharp.

This chapter will help you create a world for the sloop and boat. You'll learn a lot of cool new ways to model. In this chapter, you will perform the following tasks:

- ◆ Use texturing to create an oceanic surface
- ◆ Use the ANT Landscape addon to create an island
- ◆ Use proportional editing to finalize the land form
- ◆ Use Blender paint to color the land form
- ◆ Create an entire pier with just four objects using arrays, DupliFrames, and bevel objects
- ◆ Make trees with the Sapling tree generator addon
- ◆ Use your organic modeling skills to model rocks and boulders
- ◆ Complete the world by appending houses, rocks, trees, boats, and the sky

Let's get started!

Getting ready to make the island

The following are the files that you should copy from the downloaded code bundle and into your Chapter 10/Blender directory:

◆ 4909_10_Boat.blend

◆ 4909_10_Boathouse.blend

◆ 4909_10_Five Rocks.blend

◆ 4909_10_House Kit.blend

◆ 4909_10_House Kit_Sample 1.blend

◆ 4909_10_House Kit_Sample 2.blend

◆ 4909_10_Island_Ocean_Pier.blend

◆ 4909_10_Port and Breakwater Templates.blend

◆ 49009_10_Sky_Cloudy.blend

◆ 4909_10_Sloop.blend

◆ 4909_10_Tree_Sample_Large.blend

◆ 4909_10_Tree_Sample_Small.blend

The following are the image files that you should copy from your download pack into the Chapter 10/Images directory:

◆ 4909_10_01.png

◆ 4909_10_02.png

◆ 4909_10_03.png

◆ 4909_10_04.png

◆ 4909_10_05.png

Creating the ocean

First, you will create an ocean for the sloop to sail on, using a texture to create a wave-like surface.

Time for action – making a surface for water

You will make your surface seem rougher using a texture map to modify the normals of the face to control the appearance rather than creating a lot of vertices. The following steps will guide you in making a surface for water:

1. Create a new file and delete the default cube.

2. Press *Shift + S* and choose **Cursor to Center**. Press *Shift + A* and select **Mesh** and then **Plane** from the menus.

3. Press *S, Shift + Z, 800*, and *Enter*. This scales the plane in both the *X* and *Y* axes.

4. Press *S, Z, 1.5*, and *Enter*.

5. In the Properties window, select the **Object** button from the header, it's the button with the cube on it. Rename the object from **Plane** to Ocean, and then press *Enter*.

6. In the Properties window, select the **Material** button from the header; it's the button with the chrome ball on it.

7. Select the **New** button.

8. Name the material Sea Material.

9. In the **Diffuse** subpanel, click on the white button and set the **Diffuse color** to **R:** 0.000, **G:** 0.015, and **B:** 0.035.

10. In the **Specular** subpanel, click on the white button and set the **Specular color** to **R:** 0.185, **G:** 0.500, **B:** 1.000.

11. In the Properties window, select the **Textures** button from the header; it's the button with the checker board on it.

12. Select the **New** button with the LMB.

13. Name the texture Sea Texture.

14. Set the texture **Type:** to **Clouds**.

15. In the **Clouds** subpanel, click on the **Greyscale** button so that it turns blue, and set the value of the **Noise:** button by clicking on the **Hard** button so that it turns blue, as shown on the left-hand side of the next screenshot.

16. In the **Mapping** subpanel, set the **Size** to **X:** 1 0 0, **Y:** 1 0 0, **Z:** 1 . 0 0, as shown in the following screenshot.

17. In the **Influence** subpanel, uncheck the **Color:** checkbox in **Diffuse:**. Make the Properties window wider if you can't tell which checkbox is for **Color**.

18. Check the **Normal:** checkbox in **Geometry:** and set the value to - 0 . 7 5 0.

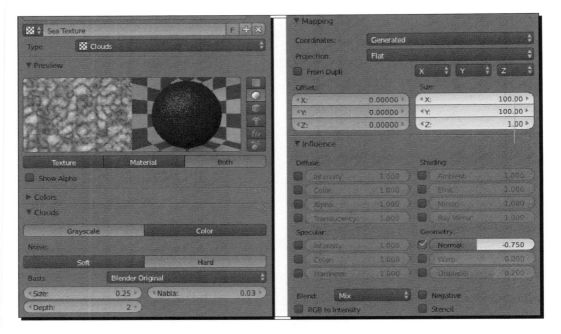

19. Select the Lamp with the RMB.

20. In the Properties window, select the **Object data** button from the header; it's the button with the sun symbol surrounded by four arrowheads on it. In the **Lamp** subpanel, change the lamp type to **Sun**.

21. With the cursor over the 3D View, press NumpPad *7* to get the Top view.

22. Press *R, Z*, and rotate the lamp 1 2 5 degrees. Use the *Ctrl* button while rotating, for finer control. Press the LMB to release the rotation.

23. Press *F12* to see the surface. It should look similar to the following screenshot. Press *Esc* when you have finished looking at it.

24. Save the file with a unique name.

What just happened?

This was pretty simple. We talked about normals in *Chapter 5, Building a Simple Boat*. They show the way that a face is pointing. The plane is flat, and there is only one face in a plane and one normal. It figures that it should look flat. All the lumpiness that you see is caused by the texture that you assigned to the Ocean object. It creates more than one normal per face.

When scaling up the plane, in addition to learning a new trick about how to scale in two dimensions at once, you may have wondered, "Wait a minute, this is a plane. It has no thickness, why am I scaling it in the Z axis?". Well, since this is a 3D space and not reality, adding scaling in the Z axis to a textured plane makes the waves appear to be higher. It's an optical illusion.

When you made the cloud texture for the Ocean object, you saw that it was shades of gray. Then, you set that texture to influence the normals of the face. So, the direction that the normal points to is then controlled by the brightness of the pixel in the texture map. The red channel controls how the normal points in the X axis, the green channel controls how the normal points in the Y axis, and the blue channel controls how the normal points in the Z axis. Blender calculates this for each point in the texture. Therefore, instead of one normal per face, there can be thousands. Just like the ocean makes waves from a flat surface and the surface of the water tilts one way or another, the texture map is tilting the surface of the face.

As this will be an outdoor scene, you selected the sun for your lamp type, and it lit the entire Ocean object evenly. The camera is pretty close to the Ocean object right now, which is why the waves look so sculpted. Once you use it in the scene, the ocean will look like calm water with just a little chop to it.

Making an island

There are several steps toward making your island paradise. First, you will create a basic landform with the *ANT Landscape* generator. Next, you will edit the finer details to make it the way you want it. Then, you will paint it.

Using the ANT Landscape addon

The ANT Landscape addon does procedural modeling. You make the object by assigning mathematical settings, and it allows you to set factors, such as the height and size of a landscape and use other settings to control the contours of the terrain. You don't have to manipulate vertices as you did with the boats. You can make flat landscapes or spherical planets.

Time for action – using ANT Landscape to make the island

The ANT Landscape uses mathematical algorithms to create a nearly infinite variety of surfaces, but by working in an ordered manner, as given in the following steps, you can achieve the results you want:

1. Select the Ocean object with the RMB. Press *M* and *2* to move the Ocean object to **Layer 2**.

2. Choose **File** and then **User Preferences** from the drop-down menu. Select **Addons**. Pick **Add Mesh** from the menu on the left-hand side. Find **Add Mesh:, ANT Landscape** on the right-side menu, and put a checkmark in the box on the right-hand side, as shown in the following screenshot:

3. Click on the **X** button in the upper right-hand corner of the Blender **User Preferences** window and close the window. If you are using a Mac or Linux, use the red dot in the left-hand corner of the Blender **User Preferences** window.

4. Press *Shift + S* and select **Cursor to Center** from the pop-up menu.

5. If your **Tool Shelf** is not visible in 3D View, press *T* to make it visible.

6. Press *Shift + A*. Select **Mesh** and then **Landscape** from the menus.

7. Zoom in to look at the landscape, as shown in the next screenshot. Use the MMB to rotate your view so that the *X* axis points down and towards the right, and the *Y* axis points up and towards the right.

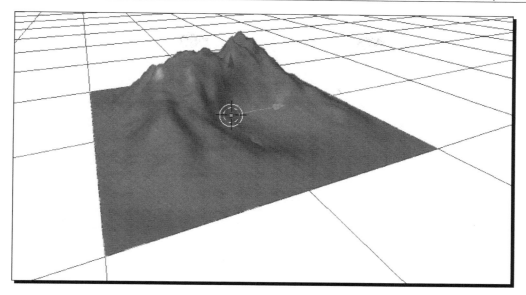

8. In the **Tool Shelf**, put the mouse over the top edge of the **Landscape** subpanel so that you get the double-headed arrow. Move the border of the subpanel up so that you can see all of the sections.

9. In the second section within the **Landscape** subpanel, there is a button labeled **Random Seed**. Change the **Random Seed** number from **0** to 5269.

10. Now, click on the arrow on either end of the **Random Seed** button several times and watch the landscape change.

11. Then, click on the arrow on the other end of the button until you are back to **5269**. The landscape with **Random Seed** number **5269** will be the basis of your island.

12. In the top section within the **Landscape** subpanel, set the **Mesh Size:** to 800.

13. Press the *Home* key on your keyboard to see the entire island again. This is not the *Home* key on your NumPad. If you are using a Mac, press *fn* + the left arrow key. It looks flat. This is not surprising; it just got 400 times larger without getting taller. Notice that the ends look a bit cut off.

14. Press *N* to open the 3D View's Properties panel. In the **View** subpanel, set the clip end to 3000 by navigating to **End** in **Clip**. The **Clip** control cuts off any detail past a certain distance to reduce work for Blender. The ocean and islands are bigger models than the sloop. Setting the Clip distance lets you see them in their entirety.

15. In the **Landscape** subpanel, set the **Height** to 400. Not much appears to have changed. This is because there is another button that affects the height.

16. Put the cursor in the center of the **Plateau** button. Hold down the LMB and move the mouse slowly to the right. Watch how the landscape slowly rises as you move the mouse. You can see the plateau on top where everything is flat. If you raise the plateau above the height that you set, then nothing changes any more.

17. Set the value of **Plateau** to 235. The landscape looks a bit pointy now, as shown on the left-hand side of the next screenshot.

18. Set the **Noise Size** to 400. The shape looks much more as it did before you enlarged it. The **Size** button in **Noise** is in the second section of the **Landscape** subpanel.

19. Scroll down and change the **Offset** to -117.

20. Now, set the **Sealevel** to -3 so that it goes below the ocean's surface.

21. Use the **Layer Controls** in the **3D View** header. Select Layer 2 with *Shift* + RMB.

22. Press the MMB, and use the mouse to rotate the view so that you can see the island in the ocean, as shown on the right-hand side of the following screenshot:

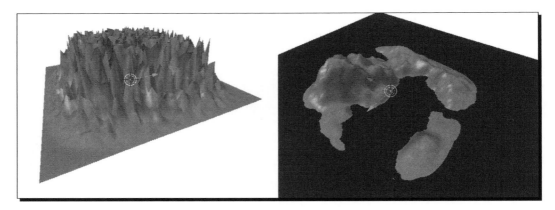

23. Save the file with a unique name.

What just happened?

ANT Landscape is a powerful addon to create landforms.

The **Subdivisions** button sets how complex your terrain will be. The setting of 64 makes a 64 x 64 grid with 4096 vertices. You can change this by selecting more subdivisions for greater detail with a larger file size, or fewer subdivisions for a smaller file size with less detail.

The **Mesh Size** button specifies how large the model will be physically.

The **Height** button specifies the maximum possible height.

The **Plateau** button flattens any details above a certain height. You might wonder why you have two controls. Setting the height higher places more of the detail higher up. Therefore, a tall height with a low Plateau will create a mesa. The same value Plateau with a lower height might only round off the tallest peak.

The **Noise Size** button controls the size of the noise. As you saw, a value of zero gives very small distances between peaks and valleys, so the landscape is jagged. The larger the value, the more the distance between the peaks and valleys and the more gentle the landscape tends to be.

The **Random Seed** button affects the entire shape of the landscape. You try different Random Seeds until you find one that suits your purposes. Your other settings are kept intact when you change the Random Seed values. For instance, the Plateau will always be at the height you set it, no matter what the Random Seed is.

There are 10,000 different Random Seeds, so you are likely to find one that will give you the kind of landscape you are seeking. In this case, I was looking for a tall peak with a large low spot that could become a sheltered cove. I also wanted a low set of hills on the far side of the cove. The Random Seed number **5269** provided this, and I liked how one of the hills became a separate island. The smaller coves on the back side of the island were a bonus, and gave it a nice shape.

Changing **Offset** raises or lowers the vertices of the terrain with respect to **Sealevel**.

Have a go hero – playing with ANT Landscape

ANT Landscape uses a series of random numbers to create landscape objects. It gives you the incredible power to make mountains, hills, and islands in Blender.

Make sure that you have saved the file. Make a new file. Load the ANT Landscape generator again if you didn't save it as a default because you don't need it that often. You can save it as a default if you wish; my philosophy, though, is to keep it simple.

Create a landscape, play with it, and see what you get. Try using the settings you created earlier as a basis and change them. One thing that will help is to keep the scale of your settings consistent. For example, in the default landscape, **Mesh Size** was **2** and **Noise Size** was **1**. When you made the island, **Mesh Size** was **800** and **Noise Size** was **400**. The ratio of mesh size to noise size stayed the same.

More subdivisions will give you a better detailed model, but it may slow things down, as it takes time to process all that detail. You may even want to back down to 32 subdivisions to speed things up while you play. If you like what you have done, save it for later reference. Also, take notes of what settings you have changed and what values each setting has when you have a terrain you like. You can write it down or type it into the Blender text editor. Once you finish playing with it and you make a change to the object in 3D View and not in the Tool Shelf, the landscape will be turned into a mesh. Also, you will not be able to go back and see what the settings were or change them.

Detailing the island

Now, it's time to discover the power of proportional editing. With proportional editing, when you move one vertex, the vertices near it are also moved so that you get a nice smooth transition between polygons. You are going to use this to finish the island.

The island is nice, but not perfect for your needs. There is no good area to add buildings, a pier, or trees. You need a **Port**. The main entrance to the harbor is so large that it offers no protection from large waves. You also need a **Breakwater**. The backside of the island is smooth and square, so it needs to be a little rougher to look more natural, as shown in the following screenshot:

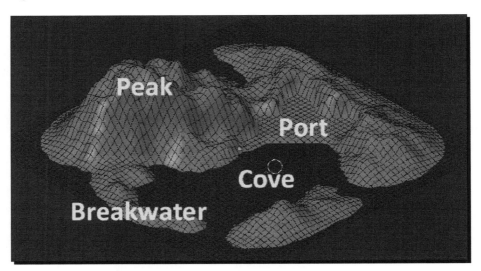

Time for action – understanding the Proportional Editing control

Proportional editing allows you to move one vertex, and all the vertices around it are affected to varying degrees. Depending on your needs, you can choose from seven different falloff patterns. Here, you will learn to set up the Proportional Editing controls using the following steps:

1. Reopen the landscape that you made before the previous section.

2. In the **Layers** control of the **3D View** header, select **Layer 1**.

3. Select the island and press the *Tab* key to go into **Edit Mode**.

4. In the **Mesh Display** subpanel, under the word **Normals:**, click on the **Faces** button with the orange parallelogram. Set the **Size:** button to 10.

5. Use the MMB and the mouse to rotate the island and inspect the normals. Be sure to check the bottom of the island. They will stick through the ocean if they are pointed down.

6. If the normals are pointing downward, press *A* to select all the faces. Then, select **Mesh** from the **3D View** header. Choose **Normals** and then **Recalculate Inside** from the pop-up menu.

7. In 3D View's Properties panel, in the **Mesh Display** subpanel, click on the **Faces** button under the word **Normals:** again to turn the Normals display off.

8. On the right-hand side of the **3D View** header, there is a button with a small gray doughnut and up and down arrowheads next to it. This is the **Proportional Editing** button. Press it with the LMB and choose **Enable** from the pop-up menu, as shown in the next screenshot.

9. On the right-hand side of the **Proportional Editing** button is the **Proportional Editing Falloff** button. Click on it, and you will see a pop-up menu of different falloff styles, as shown in the following screenshot. For now, the default **Smooth** style is fine.

10. Press *A* to deselect all the vertices. Use the MMB to rotate your view until you can see the flat area that will become the cove in-between the mountains.

11. With the RMB, select one vertex in the center of the flat area. Press *G, Z,* and *60,* but don't press *Enter*.

12. Press the *Page Up* key (on Mac, press *fn* + up arrow) and hold it until you see a circle appear around the vertex, as shown in the following screenshot. That circle shows the extent of proportional editing. Press the *Page Up* and *Page Down* (on Mac, press *fn* + down arrow) keys, and you can see how the sphere of influence grows and shrinks. You can also control this with the mouse wheel.

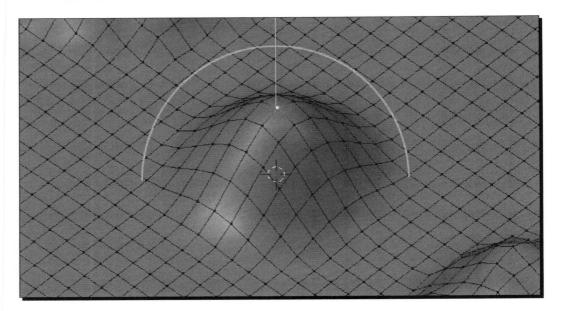

13. Make the circle very large and the whole island will be affected. Make it small again so that only a small area around the vertex is affected. Set the **Proportional size:** to about 72. You can see the readout in the **3D View** header.

14. Press the *Esc* key or the RMB to release the vertex without affecting it.

15. In the **3D View** header, click on the **Proportional Editing Falloff** button. Choose **Sphere** from the pop-up menu.

16. Press *G, Z,* and *60,* but don't press *Enter*. When you are done looking at 3D View, press *Esc*.

17. Repeat this with the other settings of the **Proportional Editing Falloff** menu and familiarize yourself with how they affect vertices near the selected one.

18. When you are done, return the **Proportional Editing Falloff** setting to **Smooth**.

19. Press the *Tab* key to return to **Object Mode**.

What just happened?

You found the controls for proportional editing. You learned how to change the circle of influence for proportional editing and how to change the falloff profile that gives you even more control over how you can move the vertices.

Detailing the island using the Proportional Editing tool

Now that the island is made and you know how to use proportional editing to make smooth contours, its time to level the port area, finish the breakwater, and detail the backsides of the island.

Time for action – using proportional editing to create the port

Now that you have a good basis for your island, it's time to tailor it to your needs. The first step is creating an area to put houses, trees, and the pier:

1. In the **Layers** control in the **3D View** header, select **Layer 2** with the LMB, and then select **Layer 1** with *Shift* + LMB.

2. I have provided a template that will help you in selecting the faces for the port and for the breakwater. Append the **Port and Breakwater** object from the `4909_10_Port and Breakwater Templates.blend` file in this chapter's download kit.

3. You'll now see two flat objects floating above your island, as shown in the following screenshot:

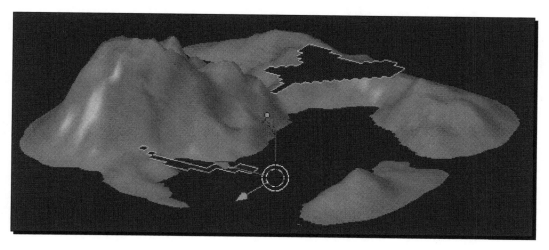

4. Select the island with the RMB.

5. Press *7* on the NumPad to get the **Top** view. Make sure that 3D View is in Ortho mode.

6. Press the *Tab* key to get back into **Edit Mode**.

7. In the **3D View** header, choose the **Face Select** mode.

8. Set the **Limit Selection to Visible** button to a lighter gray.

9. Press *A* once or twice to deselect all the faces.

10. Use *Shift* + MMB to center your view on the lower part of the template.
    Use *Ctrl* + MMB to zoom in so that part of the template fills most of 3D View.
    The template shows you the faces that you will need to select.

11. Press the *C* key, and select the faces under the template to create a flat area to add buildings, trees, and a pier, as shown in the next screenshot. This area will be the port.

12. The template will appear to be flat blue, and the unselected faces of the island will be black on gray. The selected faces will be orange lines and dots, as shown in the following screenshot. Select all of the faces under the blue template area. Use the template to guide you. As the island is the active object, the faces you select will only be faces on the island.

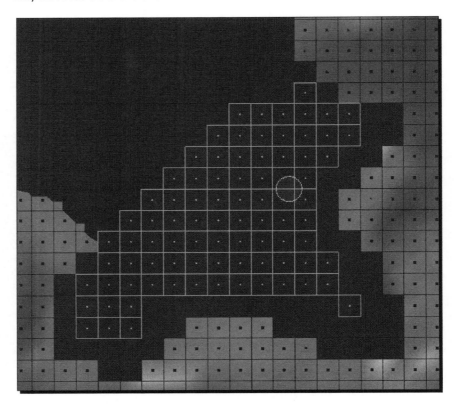

13. Use the MMB, and rotate your view so that you can see the selected port faces underneath the template.

14. Set the **Pivot Point** menu in the **3D View** header to **Median Point**.

15. Press *S*, *Z*, and *0*, but not *Enter*.

16. Press the *Page Up* or *Page Down* keys until the Proportional Editing Circle is about 25 according to the readout in the **3D View** header.

17. Press *Enter*.

18. Rotate the view with the MMB so that you can see the distance between the port and the water line well, as shown in the following screenshot:

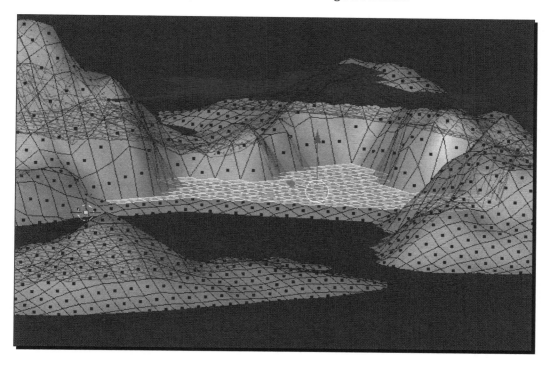

19. Press *G*, *Z*, and then use the mouse to move the selected vertices down about 11 units. Press the LMB to release the motion.

What just happened?

Well, you put proportional editing to good work now. You used proportional editing to ease the transition between the area you were flattening and the surrounding landscape. Now, you have enough room on the island to set up some buildings, some trees, and a pier.

Time for action – building the breakwater

A port needs protection from waves. The opening to the sea is too large, so you will be extending the little jetty and adding contours, using the following steps, so that it looks like a natural part of the island:

1. Press 7 on the NumPad to get the **Top** view.

2. The breakwater will be at the top of the island. Press *Shift* + MMB and use the mouse to move to the top of the island.

3. Press *A* to deselect all the faces. Press *C* to select the faces for the breakwater using the template as your guide.

4. When you are done, press the MMB and rotate around so that you can see the faces you've selected.

5. Press *G*, *Z*, and then move the selected faces up 8 units to create the base of the breakwater. Use the *Ctrl* key to round off the units. Use the *Page Up/Page Down* keys to set the **Proportional size:** to about 25. Press the LMB to release the motion.

6. Deselect some faces, as shown in the following screenshot. Press *C* and then use the MMB to deselect faces. Press the RMB to end the selection.

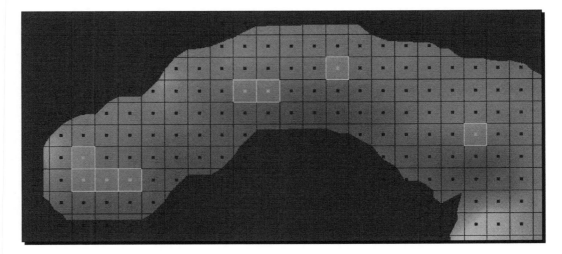

7. Move the remaining faces up 8 units to add some hills on the breakwater.

8. Repeat, but deselect the faces so that only two remain, as shown in the following screenshot:

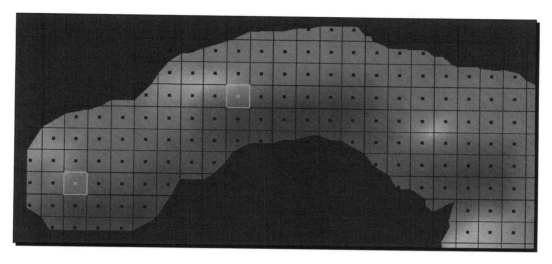

9. Move the remaining faces up 8 units to finish off the crests of the hills.

10. Press the *Tab* key to go into **Object Mode**.

11. Select the **Port and Breakwater** template with the RMB. Press *X* to delete it.

12. Save the file with a unique name.

What just happened?

In this exercise, we built a breakwater, and then kept reducing the number of vertices selected and moving them up a bit to build up a complex terrain.

Time for action – adding contours to the back side of the island

It's a small point, but the back side of the island is too smooth and flat. So next, you will add a few contours to make it look more realistic, using the following steps:

1. Select **Layer 2**, and then select **Layer 1** while holding the *Shift* key.

2. Select the island with the RMB. Press the *Tab* key to go into **Edit Mode**.

3. In the **3D View** header, choose the **Vertex Select** mode.

4. Press *A* to deselect all of the vertices.

5. Select a vertex in the center of the cove with the RMB.

6. Press *Shift + S* and choose **Cursor to Selected** from the menu.

7. In the **3D View** header, set **Pivot Point** to **3D Cursor**.

8. Press *7* on the NumPad. Press the *Home* key on your keyboard to see the entire island. This is not the *Home* key on your NumPad. If you are using a Mac, press *fn* + the left arrow key. Then, use *Ctrl* + MMB to zoom in.

9. The bottom and right sides of the island are unnaturally smooth. You need to put in some small variations to make them look right.

10. Press *C* and select some of the outer edges of the island, as shown in the following screenshot. Yours doesn't have to be an exact copy. Press the RMB when done selecting.

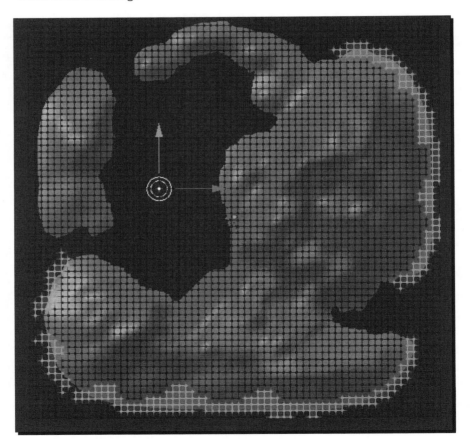

11. Press *S, Z, 0*, and then set the **Proportional size:** to about 35. Then, press *Enter*.

12. Save the file with a unique name.

What just happened?

You did just a little final detailing; adding some curves to the coastline. You started out by selecting a vertex from the cove, which is at sea level, and then moved the 3D Cursor to that location. You set the pivot center to the 3D Cursor. This way, when you scaled all of the other vertices that you selected along the edge of the island, they got scaled down to the sea level you had established when you made the island. The shape of the island is complete. Now, it's time to color it.

Painting the island

Blender has a built-in painting program. While not as fully featured as some dedicated paint programs, it will get you started and allows you to complete the painting steps without leaving Blender. By starting the painting in Blender, you can easily match the details of the painting to the details of the object.

Time for action – painting the island

Now, it's time for an introduction to using Blender paint. It takes a while to detail the landscape realistically, so here you are going to use some broad brush strokes just to get an idea of how Blender paint works. It's a idea good to go online and look at images of islands, like the one you want to make, for ideas on how the soil should look and what the plants and trees should look like. The satellite view of Google maps can give you ideas too. The following steps will help you paint the island:

1. Go down to the **Timeline** window below the 3D View window. Select the **Current Editor Type** button from the lower left-hand corner. Choose **UV/Image Editor** from the menu.

2. Move the mouse to the boundary between the **UV/Image Editor** window and the 3D View window. When you get the double arrowhead, move the boundary up so that you can see the grid background in the **UV/Image Editor**. You can also use *Ctrl* + MMB to zoom out to see the whole grid.

3. If you see a rendered image in the **UV/Image Editor** window, delete it by clicking on **X**, which is to the right of where it says **Render Result** in the **UV/Image Editor** header.

4. With the cursor in 3D View, press the *A* key once or twice to select all the vertices.

5. Open the **Mesh** menu from the **3D View** header. Select **UV Unwrap** and then **Unwrap** from the menus, as shown on the following screenshot. It may take a moment or two for this.

6. In the **UV/Image Editor** header, choose **Image**. Select **New Image** from the pop-up menu. In the **New Image** dialog box, set the name to IslandTexture. Set the **Color** to a nice sandy brown; I used **R:** 0.350, **G:** 0.200, and **B:** 0.100, as shown in the following screenshot. Uncheck the **Alpha** checkbox, and click on the **OK** button.

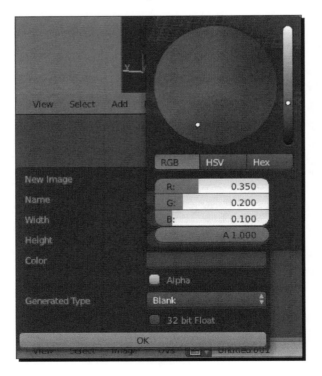

7. In the **3D View** header, click on the button that usually says either **Object Mode** or **Edit Mode**, and select **Texture Paint** from the pop-up menu.

8. Now, in the **Tool Shelf**, you have the Blender paint controls. Move the **Texture Paint Toggle** subpanel down so that you can see the entire **Brush** Tool panel.

9. At the top of the **Brush** subpanel, there is an image of a grey ball with a squiggle. Put the cursor over the image and press the LMB.

10. Choose **FBrush** from the pop-up menu. Set **Color** to a medium green. I used **R:** 0.300, **G:** 0.600, and **B:** 0.300. Set **Radius** to 35 and **Strength** to 0.5.

11. The LMB controls your paintbrush. The MMB works as usual, allowing you to rotate. With the *Shift* and *Ctrl* buttons, you can pan and zoom respectively. If you need an eyedropper tool to pick up color, click on the color swatch and then select the eyedropper from the pop-up menu.

12. Press *1* on the NumPad to get the **Front** view. Paint the top half to two-thirds of the island green. If you look at the **UV/Image Editor**, you will notice that it records your painting.

13. Press *3* on the NumPad to get the **Right Side** view and paint.

14. Press *Ctrl* + NumPad *1* to get the **Back** view and paint.

15. Press *Ctrl* + NumPad *3* to get the **Left Side** view and paint.

16. Press the MMB and rotate the view so that you can see from a high angle. You will notice gaps in the painting. Reduce the radius of your F Brush. Touch them up, but not all areas need to be colored green. Look for the valleys; as they collect water, they should be greener. Areas where the surface is indented will tend to track the water, so make that a little more green. Imagine the water flowing down the sides of the island, as shown in the following screenshot:

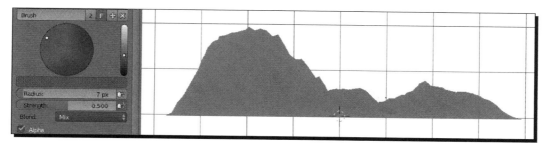

17. Now, it's time to add a darker green for areas growing better. In the 3D View **Tool Shelf**, change the brush **Color** to a darker green. I chose **R:** 0.200, **G:** 0.400, and **B:** 0.200. The easy way to do this is select the **HSV** button and set **V** to 0.4. A brush **Radius** of 9 is good. Set the **Strength** to 0.2 so that you can build up the darker green in a little bit of time and have a little more variation.

18. Use the brush to fill in the valleys; imagine water running down them, watering the plants. As **Strength** is 0.2, you can take several passes, making the color more solid with each pass and getting gentle gradations of color.

19. Now, paint the Port. In the 3D View **Tool Shelf**, change the brush **Color** to **R:** 0.000, **G:** 0.600, and **B:** 0.000. Increase the brush **Radius** to 15 and increase **Strength** to 1.

20. Use the brush to paint the port, as shown in the next screenshot.

21. Choose the **F Smear** brush from the **Brush** menu in the 3D View **Tool Shelf**. Set **Strength** to 0.4 and set **Radius** to about 25. Move the brush up or down across the border between the green color of the port and the brown color of the hills above it, as shown in the following screenshot:

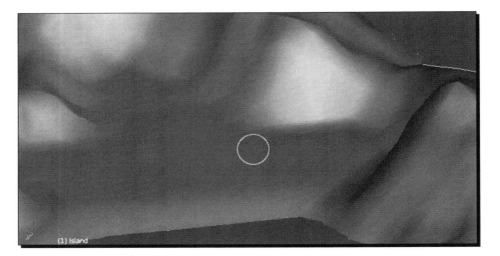

22. Make any changes or touch ups that you want to.

23. When you are done, scroll down to where it says **Texture Paint** in the **3D View** header. Select **Object Mode**. The colors will disappear.

24. In the **3D View** header, select the **Viewport Shading** button and choose **Texture** from the pop-up menu.

25. Use the MMB to get a nice view of your island.

26. Go down to the **UV/Image Editor** window, and choose the **Image** button on the header. Select **Save As Image** and put the image in your Images subdirectory. Then, click on the **Save As Image** button in the upper-right corner of the **File Browser** window. As with saving your basic Blender file, do this frequently while you are painting your terrain. The image file is not saved as part of the Blender file.

27. The image is also not automatically added as a texture for your object. While you can see it in 3D View, if you want it to render, you must add the texture to the material in the Properties window, just like you have added other textures to materials.

28. In the Properties window, select the **Material** button from the header; it's the button with the chrome ball on it.

29. Click on the **New** button and create a new material. Name it Island Material.

30. In the **Specular** subpanel, set the **Specular** color to a nice light-sandy color. I chose **R:** 0.500, **G:** 0.400, and **B:** 0.200. Set the **Intensity:** to **0.015**.

31. In the Properties window, select the **Textures** button from the header; it's the button with the checker board on it.

32. Click on the **New** button and create a new texture. Name it Island Texture.

33. Select the texture **Type** to **Image** or **Movie**.

34. In the **Image** subpanel, click on the **Open** button and select the image you saved a few steps earlier.

35. In the **Mapping** subpanel, set **Coordinates:** to **UV**.

36. Press the MMB and rotate the view so you can see the scene.

37. Press *Ctrl + Alt* + NumPad *0* to set the camera to match the view you are seeing. If 3D View goes blank, don't worry.

38. In the **Outliner** window in the upper-right corner of the Blender window, select the **Camera** with the LMB.

39. In the Properties window, select the **Object data** button from the header; it's the button with the movie camera on it.

40. In the lower-right corner of the **Lens** subpanel, the lower button below **Clipping** is the **End** button.

41. Move the cursor from left to right over the button. As the value of the **End** button goes up, the white wall recedes. The **End** button saves Blender work by not displaying anything beyond the far clipping plane, as shown in the following screenshot:

42. Now that you've seen **End** in action, set **End** button of **Clipping** to 3000 so that it will not cause you problems.

43. Press *G*, *Z*, *Z*, and then use the mouse to zoom out. Press the LMB to release the motion.

44. Press *F12* to render the scene.

45. Save the file with a unique file name.

What just happened?

You painted your island. First, you created a UV map so that Blender could map a color to a particular part of your island. Then, you made a graphic that Blender used to record the painting you made in the **Texture Paint** mode. Next, you painted your island using various brushes similar to programs such as Photoshop or Gimp. Finally, you saved the graphic and made it into your texture map for the island.

Restarting texture painting

If you have to interrupt your Blender activity and you save the file and close Blender, you may be surprised that when you open it up, your precious hand-painted texture may not there. Unless you have specifically saved the image, it is gone. However, we know that you are wise and you saved the image. When you wish to resume work on the texture, if you don't see the texture, go into **Edit Mode** in the 3D View window and select the vertices you are working on, all of them in this case. Open **UV Image Editor**, select **Image** on the header, and open the image you were working on. Then, in 3D View, choose the **Texture Paint** mode.

Have a go hero – painting your island

Well, the island still looks a little rough. So now, put me to shame and paint the island better. Explore the tools in the Blender paint Tool Shelf, and check out the references I mentioned earlier.

Making the island ready for habitation

The island is looking good. However, now, you need to add a pier, a boathouse, houses, trees, and rocks so that it will be ready for the sloop and boat.

Building the pier with just four objects

The pier will use a tool that you have already learnt, bevel objects. You will also use DupliVerts' cousin, DupliFrames, and use arrays to create the pilings for the pier.

Time for action – creating the pier frame rails with Bézier curves

It may be hard to believe that you can make an entire pier with a rectangle, a Bezier Curve, a cube, and a cylinder, but that's what you are going to do next. The first step is to create a frame to carry the planks of the pier:

1. Select **Object Mode** from the **3D View** header.
2. Press 7 on the NumPad to get the **Top** view.
3. Zoom in to the edge between the port and water.

4. In the **Layers** control in the **3D View** header, select **Layer 1** with the LMB and then select **Layer 2** with *Shift* + LMB.

5. Press *Shift + S* and select **Cursor to Center** from the menu.

6. Click the LMB over the edge between the water and port.

7. Press *A* to deselect any object.

8. Press *Shift + A*, and select **Mesh** and then **Cube** from the pop-up menus.

9. Press *G, Z, 6*, and then press *Enter*.

10. Press *S, Y, 60*, and then press *Enter*.

11. Press *R, Z, 45*, and then press *Enter*.

12. Move the cube so that it is two-thirds over the water and one-third over the port. Center it along the waterfront, as shown in the left-hand side of the next screenshot.

13. Zoom into the lower-right corner of the cube, as close as possible. If you have trouble zooming in, make sure you are in the Ortho mode; then, press Home and try again.

14. Press the *Tab* key to enter **Edit Mode**. With the RMB, select one of the vertices in the lower-left corner of the cube. Press *Shift + S*. Choose **Cursor to Selected**. Press the *Tab* key to return to **Object Mode**.

15. If 3D View's Properties panel is not already open, press *N* to open it. In the **3D Cursor** subpanel, set the 3D Cursor **Location** to **Z:** 6.000.

16. With the cursor over the 3D View window, press *A* to deselect the cube.

17. Press *Shift + A*, and select **Curve** and then **Bezier** from the menus.

18. In the Properties window, select the **Object** button from the header; it's the button with the cube on it. Rename the **BezierCurve** to Pier Railing Path.

19. Zoom in until you can see the Bezier Curve.

20. Press the *Tab* key to go into **Edit Mode**.

21. Look at the Bezier Curve. There are a series of arrowheads pointing from one Control Point to the other. The arrowheads point from the first point to the last point.

22. On the **3D View** header, click on the **Proportional Editing** button, that little doughnut, and select **Disable** from the pop-up menu.

23. Select the right-hand control point with the RMB. It's the last control point. The arrows point toward it. Zoom out so that you can see the whole length of the cube. Press *G* and move the control point to the leftmost corner of the cube over the water. Press the LMB to release the control point. Zoom into the end of the cube over the water. Move the control point right onto the leftmost corner of the cube.

24. Select the control handle on the right-hand side. Move it counter clockwise so that the control handle points out toward the cove in the same direction the long edge of the cube is going. You will see that all the arrows now point in the same direction.

25. Next, go back to the end over the land and select the other control point, the first control point. Move that control point over the lowest corner of the cube.

26. Now, the first control point is at the beginning of the pier, and the last control point is at the end. Choose the control handle on the left-hand side. Rotate it -90 degrees.

27. Press the *Tab* key to get into **Object Mode**.

28. In the **3D View** header, select **Layer 2** so that the island is no longer in view.

29. Press *A* to deselect any objects.

30. Press *Shift + A*. Select **Curve** and then **Circle** from the menus.

31. Rename **BezierCircle** to **Pier Railing Shape**.

32. With the cursor over 3D View, press the *Tab* key to go into **Edit Mode**.

33. Press *V* and select **Vector** from the pop-up menu to make a diamond out of the circle.

34. Press *R, Z, 45*, and then *Enter* to rotate it so that the diamond is a square.

35. Press *S, X, 0.12*, and then *Enter* to squish the sides.

36. Press *S, Y, 0.35*, and then *Enter* to scale the top and bottom, as seen on the right-hand side of the following screenshot:

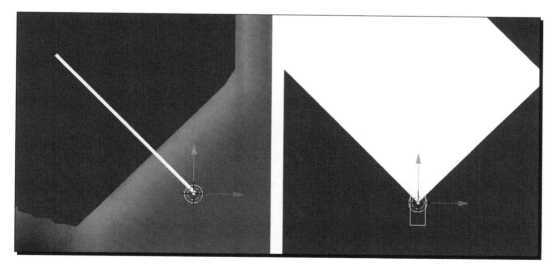

37. In the **3D View** header, set **Pivot Point** to **Median Point**.

38. Press *Shift + D* and then *Enter* to duplicate the control points. Press *G, X, 6,* and then *Enter*.

39. Press the *Tab* key to get into **Object Mode**.

40. Press *R, X, 90*, and then *Enter*.

41. Press *R, Z , 45*, and then *Enter*.

42. Now, to make the Pier Railings as you made the tiller, select the Pier Railing Path with the RMB. You know where it is; keep clicking and watch the bottom-left corner of the 3D View window until it says **Pier Railing Path**.

43. In the Properties window, select the **Object data** button from the header; it's the button with the curve and control points on it.

44. In the **Geometry** subpanel, select the **Pier Railing Shape** as the **Bevel Object**. Check the **Fill Caps** checkbox. Check that both railings are straight. If they are not, check the Pier Railing Path to make sure that it is straight.

What just happened?

This was very similar to making the tiller. However, this time, by duplicating the control points in the Pier Railing Shape and shifting one set to the right by 6 units, you were able to make both rails for the foundation of the pier at the same time.

Time for action – adding planks to the pier with DupliFrames

DupliFrames are the stronger cousin of DupliVerts. It will take one plank and make dozens out of it and use the same object that you made to control the rails of the pier. The following steps will help you to add planks to the pier with DupliFrames:

1. Now, with the RMB, select the cube you made to establish the length of the pier. In the Properties window, select the **Object** button in the header. It is the button with the cube on it. Change the name from **Cube** to **Plank**.

2. In the 3D View's Properties panel in the **Transform** subpanel, set the **Dimensions** to **X:** 8.00, **Y:** 1.000, and **Z:** 0.150.

3. Zoom out so you see the plank. Press *G* and move the plank to the land end of the rails.

4. Press *Shift* + RMB and select the Pier Railing Path.

5. Press *Ctrl* + *P* to parent the rails to the plank. Select **Object** from the pop-up menu.

6. Zoom in to the plank. Select the plank and move it so that it is beyond the right end of the rails. Center it between the rails, as shown on the left-hand side of the next screenshot. Release the motion with the LMB. If you need to, press *R*, *Z*, and rotate it so that it matches the ends of the rails. Release the rotation with the LMB.

7. Press *1* on the NumPad for the **Front** view. Use *Shift* + MMB and *Ctrl* + MMB to move your view so that you can see the plank and the rails.

8. Press *G*, *Z*, and use the mouse to move the plank up or down until it rests on top of the rails. Release the plank with the LMB.

9. In the Properties window, select the **Object** button from the header; it's the button with the cube on it.

10. In the **Duplication** subpanel, press the **Frames** button with the LMB. Uncheck the **Speed** checkbox as seen on the right-hand side of the next screenshot.

11. Select the **Pier Railing Path** with the RMB.

12. Use the MMB to rotate the view so that you can see the top of the pier.

13. In the Properties window, select the **Object data** button from the header; it's the button with the curve and control points on it.

14. In the **Path Animation** subpanel, put the cursor over the **Frames** button, press the LMB, and use the mouse to change the number of planks on the pier. Watch as the gaps between the planks change. A value of 93 for **Frames** is good.

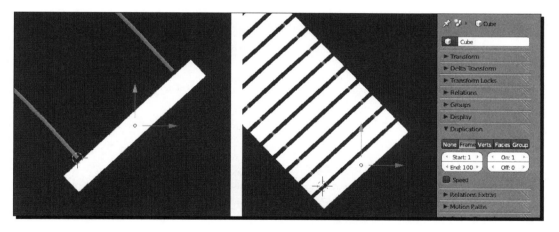

15. Save the file with a unique name.

What just happened?

Now, you got more use out of the Pier Railing Path. By reusing the cube that you made to measure out the length of the pier, you made one plank for the top and then used DupliFrames to create copies that run the entire length of the pier. The Pier Railing Path has the Path Animation ability, and you used it to control the spacing of the planks.

The DupliFrames method, while similar to DupliVerts, has some additional power. You may have noted that DupliFrames uses a Bezier Curve for its basis rather than a mesh object as the DupliVerts method does.

If you then select the Bezier Curve, the Pier Railing Path in this case, and open up the **Object data** panel, you will see the **Path Animation** subpanel. When you change the number of frames the animation covers, the number of planks changes. This is more flexible than the DupliVerts object, which sets the number of copied objects equal to the number of vertices that its parent mesh had.

If you were to check the **Speed** checkbox in the plank's **Duplication** subpanel, you would see just one plank. However, Blender would animate the plank travelling along the Pier Railing Path by making keyframes of the Evaluation Time in the **Path Animation** subpanel of the Bezier Curve.

Think of it like a roller coaster. If you make a Bezier Curve in the shape of a roller coaster track, you can use a Bevel object to create the rails as you did with the pier. If you make a cross tie, you can use parenting and DupliFrames and turn the speed off to make cross ties to support the roller coaster rails, as you did with the planks on the pier. If you make a roller coaster car and use parenting, when the speed is turned on, your roller coaster car would ride along the rails.

You can freeze the planks into individual objects with the same *Ctrl + Shift + A* command, as you did with the DupliVerts to convert the spokes of the ship's wheel. If you are making changes and you want to clear the parenting with DupliFrames, you must select the child object and press *Alt + P*.

Have a go hero – changing the shape of the pier

Select the Pier Railing Path and get into **Edit Mode**. Use the control handles to change the shape of the Bezier Curve that controls the Pier Railing Path. What other changes do you see?

Time for action – using arrays to create the pilings for the pier

Arrays are similar to DupliFrames and DupliVerts. However, instead of depending on objects to control the distribution of copies, arrays use mathematical formulas that list the number of copies and the kind of spacing that is put between copies. They are great to make pier pilings. The following steps will help you to create the pilings for the pier using arrays:

1. Reload the file you were working on before the last `Have a go hero` section.

2. Press *A* to deselect all objects.

3. Press *Shift + A*, and select **Mesh** and then **Cylinder** from the menus. Name the cylinder `Piling`.

4. If you do not see the **Add Cylinder** subpanel in the Tool Shelf, look for a small plus sign at the bottom of the **Tool Shelf**. Click on the plus sign, and the **Add Cylinder** subpanel will appear.

5. In the **Add Cylinder** subpanel of **Tool Shelf**, set the **Vertices** to **15**. Set the **Cap Fill Type** to **Triangle Fan**.

6. Move the cursor over the 3D View window. Press *S, 0.650*, and then *Enter* to make the cylinder narrower.

7. Press *S, Z, 8*, and then *Enter* to make the cylinder taller.

8. Press *7* on the NumPad so that you get a **Top** view.

9. Press *G*, and use the mouse to move the cylinder so that it is on the outside of the rail as shown in the left-hand side of the next screenshot. Release the cylinder with the LMB.

10. Press *G, Z, -3.5*, and then *Enter* to move the piling down with respect to the dock.

11. In the Properties window, select the **Object Modifiers** button from the header; it's the button with the wrench on it.

12. In the **Modifiers** subpanel, click on **Add Modifier**. Select **Array** from the menu. Set **X** to 0 in **Relative Offset** and set **Y** to 5.7 in **Relative Offset**.

13. Zoom out so that you can see both pilings.

14. With the cursor over 3D View, press *R, Z, 45*, and then *Enter*.

15. Zoom out so that you can see the entire pier. Press the MMB, and use the mouse to rotate the view so that you see the pilings better.

16. In the Properties window, increase the **Count** value until the pilings reach the end of the dock, as shown in the following screenshot. If they shoot past, then decrease the count.

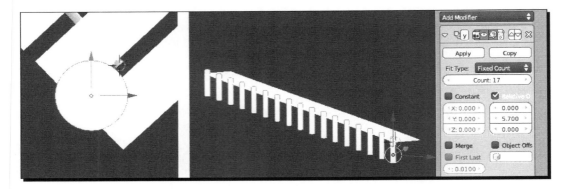

17. In the **Modifiers** subpanel, click on **Add Modifier**. Select **Array** from the menu. Move down to the second **Array Modifier** section. (Not the one that you set to **Y:** 5 . 7.) Set **X** to 6 . 0 in **Relative Offset**. Leave the **Count:** at 2.

18. Save the file with a unique name.

What just happened?

Well, you just made a pier out of a Bezier Curve, a Bezier Circle, a cube, and a cylinder. Well done!

The Array is a new technique. The **Array Modifier** allowed you to take the piling and make copies of it. The modifier took a count of how many copies you wanted, how far apart they should be, and in what direction they should go. With the first modifier, you did this to make all the pilings on one side of the pier.

The second modifier modifies the first modifier, not the original object. So, it makes a copy of the entire line of pilings that the first modifier created and moves the copy of the line of pilings in the specified direction, in this case, just across the pier. If the second modifier had worked on the original object, there would be only one piling on the other side of the pier.

This worked well. However, with Blender, there are often many ways to do something. Can you imagine using an Array to create the planks, or DupliVerts to make the pilings? Maybe, even modify a cube to the shape of a piece of lumber that would be used to frame a house, make copies of it, and move them around by hand to make the rails of the dock.

Appending the boathouse

You learned a lot about appending in the previous chapter when you finished the sloop. This will be similar, but the boathouse will need to be fitted to the pier.

Time for action – appending the boathouse and building pilings for it

In addition to bringing the boathouse into the scene, you have to place it and create some more pilings to support the backside of the boathouse. The following steps will guide you in building the boathouse and building the pilings:

1. Press *7* on the NumPad to get the **Top** view.
2. In the **3D View** header, select **Wireframe** from the **Viewport Shading** pop-up menu.
3. Select **Append** from the **File** menu.
4. Find `4909_10_boathouse.blend`.
5. Open the `Object` folder.
6. Press *A* to select the **Boathouse**, **Door Front**, **Door Garage**, and **Door knob**.
7. Press the LMB on the **Link/Append from Library** button.
8. Press *Ctrl* + MMB and zoom out of the scene so that you can see the boathouse and the pilings of the pier.
9. Press *G* and use the mouse to move the boathouse to the left of the pier. Press the LMB to release the boathouse.
10. Press *R*, *Z*, *135*, and then *Enter*.
11. Press *G* and use the mouse to move the boathouse to near the center of the pier, as seen on the left-hand side of the next screenshot. Press the LMB to release the boathouse. Leave room for a boat to dock at the end of the pier before being moved into the boathouse.

12. Zoom in and make sure that the boathouse door is located between two pilings, as seen on the right-hand side of the following screenshot. Put the right-most corner of the boathouse next to a piling. The outer line of the boathouse is the edge of the roof, and the wall is the line inside of that. Put the wall next to the pier.

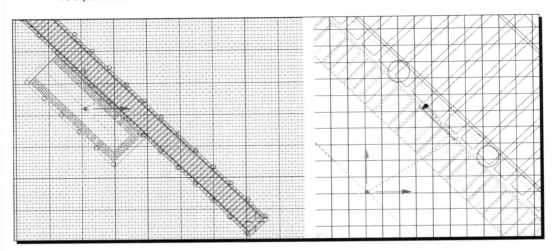

13. Press *1* on the NumPad, and press *Ctrl* + MMB to zoom in to the scene so that you can see the bottom of the boathouse and the top of the planks of the pier.

14. Press *G*, *Z*, and then use the mouse to move the bottom of the boathouse until it's level with the top of the planks of the pier. Press the LMB to release the boathouse.

15. Press *7* on the NumPad to get the **Top** view.

16. Select the pilings with the RMB.

17. Press *Shift* + *D* to copy the pilings. Move the copies to the left of the boathouse. Press the LMB to release them.

18. In the Properties window, select the **Object Modifiers** button from the header; it's the button with the wrench on it.

19. Under **Add Modifier**, there are the two **Array** modifiers that you created. Delete the lower one by clicking on **X** in the upper–right corner of the modifier section at the bottom. Now, there is just the one long row of pilings in your copy.

20. Press *Ctrl* + MMB and zoom in to the scene so that you can see the boathouse and the pilings of the pier well.

21. Press *G*, and move the copy of the pilings so that the first piling is touching the lower back corner of the boathouse. Press the LMB to release the pilings.

22. In the **Modifier** panel of the Properties window, change the **Count** to 6.

23. In the **3D View** header, set the **Viewport Shading** mode to **Solid**.

24. In the **3D View** header, press the *Shift* key and select **Layer 1** so that you can see **Layer 1** and **Layer 2**.

25. Press the MMB and rotate the view so that you can see the scene.

26. Press *Ctrl + Alt* and *0* on the NumPad to set the camera to the view you are seeing.

27. To select the camera, in 3D View, click on the edge between the camera view and the passepartout with the RMB.

28. Press *G, Z, Z*, and then use the mouse to zoom out so that you see the whole pier. Press the LMB to release the motion.

29. Press *F12* to render the scene.

30. If necessary, select the lamp; press *R* and *Z*; and then use the mouse to rotate the lamp as you did when building the ocean, about -60 degrees, so that you get the light going the way that creates nice shadows.

31. Save the file with a unique name.

What just happened?

This was pretty straightforward. What you should know is that both the door and the garage door are hinged so that you can open and close them. The door swings on its *Z* axis. The garage door swings on its local *X* axis.

Copying the piling had interesting results. When you removed the array that created the second row of pilings, you still had a row of pilings that was as long as the original one. Therefore, you reduced the count of copies until it was just as long as the boathouse.

Building modular houses

Sometimes, you will need to use files that you did not create and modify them to suit your purposes. In this case, it's a kit with which you can make a variety of modular houses.

Time for action – assembling a house from a kit

I included a kit for you to make houses. I used this kit to make the boathouse and sample houses. The kit is modular. There are eight wall sections that you can mix and match. The following steps will guide you while assembling a house from a kit:

1. Open the `4909_10_Housekit.blend` file.

2. Read the instructions in the text included with this file.

3. Look at all the wall sections available. Select them and use the offsets listed in the image in the bottom–right corner of the Blender window to guide you.

4. In the UV/Image window, there are **0_View - Rear** and **0_View - Front** images with the placement info you need.

Creating trees with the Sapling addon

Blender has a great addon for generating trees. Better than the old days when you had to stick every leaf on a tree one by one. Be careful, Sapling can make a lot of faces very quickly. The Info window header at the top gives you a read out of how many vertices, edges, and faces you have. Watch it!!

Time for action – adding trees to the landscape

Like ANT Landscape, Sapling uses mathematical algorithms to create organic forms. This is called procedural modeling. You'll step through the menus to make a tree:

1. Open the default Blender startup file.

2. In the **File** menu in the upper-left corner of the Blender window, select **User Preferences**, as you did earlier in this chapter to use the ANT Landscape addon.

3. The **Blender User Preferences** window will pop up.

4. Select **Addons** from the **Blender User Preferences** menu. Select **Add Curve** from the left-hand menu. Put a checkmark in the box for **Add Curve** and select **Sapling** in the right-hand menu.

5. Close the **User Preferences** Window.

6. Delete the default cube.

7. Press *Shift + A*, and select **Curve** and then **Add Tree** from the menus.

8. Press *1* on the NumPad to get the **Front** view. Press *5* on the NumPad to get Ortho mode. Press *Shift + MMB* and move the tree into view. Pull the right-hand side of the **Tool Shelf** to the right so that you can see the full text of the buttons. Move the upper border of the **Sapling Add Tree** subpanel up so that you can see the entire **Setting** subpanel. Watch the tree as you make changes to it.

9. In the **Geometry** subpanel perform the following steps:

1. Check the **Bevel** checkbox.

2. Set the **Ratio** to 0.02, as seen on the left-hand side of the following screenshot.

3. Click on the **Settings** button at the top of the **Sapling Add Tree** subpanel, which currently says **Geometry**. Scroll up the pop-up menu and select **Branch Splitting**.

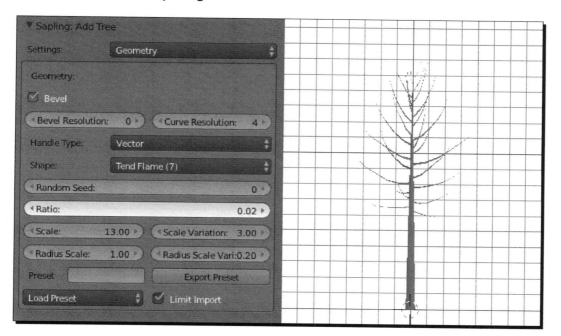

10. In the **Branch Splitting** subpanel:

❏ Set **Levels** to 3

❏ Set **Base Splits** to 3

❏ Set **Base Size** to 0.17

> ❏ Set the top row **Split Angle** to 20.00
>
> ❏ Set the top row **Split Angle Variation** to 5.0, as shown in the following screenshot:

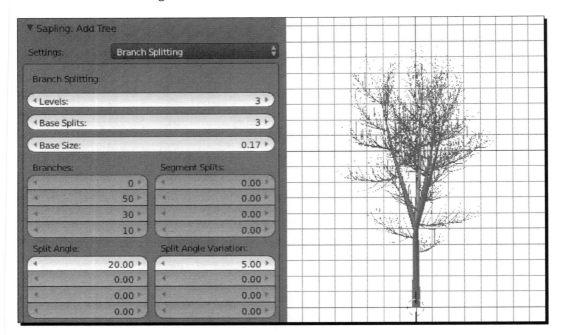

11. Click on the **Settings** button in the **Sapling Add Tree** subpanel, which currently says **Branch Splitting**, and select **Branch Growth**.

12. In the **Branch Growth** subpanel:

   ❏ Set the second row **Length** to 0.40

   ❏ Set the second row **Length Variation** to 0.30, as shown in the left-hand side of the following screenshot.

   ❏ Click on the **Settings** button in the **Sapling Add Tree** subpanel, which currently says **Branch Growth**, and select **Pruning**.

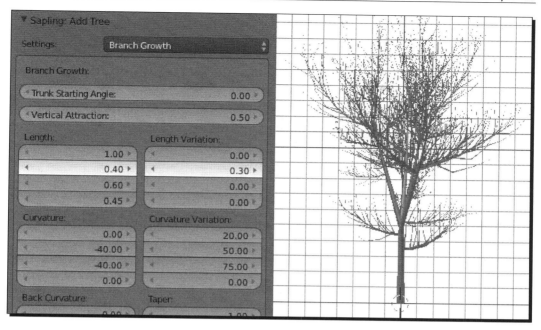

13. In the **Pruning** subpanel:

- ❑ Check the **Prune** checkbox
- ❑ Set **Prune Width** to 0.30
- ❑ Set **Prune Width Peak** to 0.50, as shown in the following screenshot:

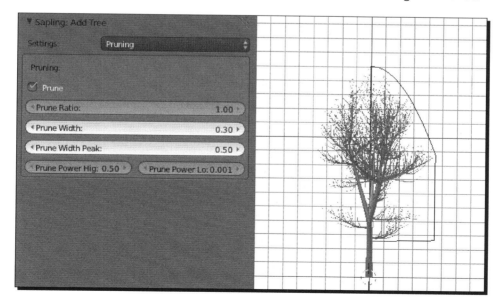

14. Click on the **Settings** button in the **Sapling Add Tree** subpanel, which currently says **Pruning**, and select **Leaves**.

15. Look at the readout of the number of vertices and faces above the right-hand side of the 3D View window. **Verts** shows the number of vertices. **Faces** shows the number of faces, as seen in the following screenshot:

16. In the **Leaves** subpanel:

- ❏ Check the **Show Leaves** checkbox
- ❏ Look at the number of vertices and faces readout at the top of the Blender window
- ❏ Set the **Leaf Shape** to **Rectangular**, as seen on the left-hand side of the next screenshot
- ❏ Look at the number of vertices and faces readout

17. You now have two objects, the leaves and the tree.

18. Put the mouse over 3D View and press *A* twice to finish making your tree.

19. Select the leaves with the RMB.

20. In the Properties window, select the **Material** button from the header; it's the button with the chrome ball on it.

21. Select the **New** button with the LMB.

22. Name the material **Leaves Material**.

23. In the **Diffuse** subpanel, set the **Diffuse** color to a dark green. I used **R:** 0.006, **G:** 0.060, and **B:** 0.000, as shown in the following screenshot:

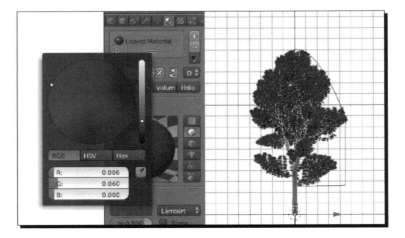

24. Select the tree with the RMB.

25. In the Properties panel, select the **New** button with the LMB.

26. Name the material **Tree Material**.

27. In the **Diffuse** subpanel, set the **Diffuse** color to a nice reddish brown; I used **R:** 0.075, **G:** 0.0035, and **B:** 0.009.

28. In the **Specular** subpanel, set the specular **Intensity:** value to 0.030.

29. Press *0* on the NumPad to select the **Camera** view.

30. Select the camera; press *G, Z, Z*; and then use the mouse to back it up so that you can see the entire tree through it. Press the LMB to release the motion.

31. Press *F12* to render the scene. Press *Esc* when you have finished viewing it.

32. Select the tree with the RMB. Press *Alt + C* to convert the tree to a mesh object. Choose Mesh from Curve/Meta/Surf/Text from the popup menu.

33. Select the leaves with the RMB. Select the tree with *Shift* + RMB. Press *Ctrl + J* to join the leaves and the tree.

34. Save the file with a unique file name.

What just happened?

Now, you're making trees! You added **Bevel** to give the tree a little girth and make round branches. **Ratio** lets you adjust the diameter of the tree. If you wanted a strange shape for the branches, you could make a shape out of a Bezier Circle and apply it as a **Bevel Object** in the **Object data** panel of the Properties window instead.

Next, you set up the basic branching. **Base Splits** controls how many main branches there are, and **Base Size** controls how tall the trunk is before there are any branches. **Levels** control manages the number of times a branch will split into smaller branches, which split into yet smaller branches. Be careful with this control, as you can make a lot of branches. Now, with the controls for **Split Angle** and **Split Angle Variations**, there are four rows of buttons. The top row affects the top order branches, the second row affects the second order branches, and so on. Setting a value for the **Split Angle Variation** adds a little randomness to the angles that they branch at.

In **Branch Growth**, **Length** controls how long a branch grows, and **Length Variation** allows for some variation in growth.

Pruning allows you to limit the size of the tree. **Prune Width** sets some basic boundaries on girth. **Prune Width Peak** lets you set where the maximum width of the tree will occur, high or low.

With the **Leaves** subpanel, choose rectangular or hexagonal leaves and modify their sizes. I chose rectangular leaves to reduce the number of faces per tree. You could see this difference when you looked at the readout of vertices and faces.

Trees are very expensive objects with regard to the number of faces they create and how they affect the rendering time. Therefore, you want to make them as simple as you can.

Have a go hero – making your own trees

Use the Sapling addon and make some more trees. Play with the settings and see what you get. Join the tree to the leaves for easy use in other scenes.

Making rocks

Rocks might seem mundane, but they have an infinite variety of shapes and sizes and offer great practice in modeling smooth organic forms.

Have a go hero – making rocks with subdivision surfaces

What would an island be without rocks? They are easy to make. Create a cube and apply a subdivision surface modifier, like you did for the hull of the sloop. Use what you learned in *Chapter 8, Making the Sloop*, about Edge Tools to add and modify control vertices to create nicely rounded, yet asymmetric, rocks.

Assembling your world

It's time to put all the objects that you have made in separate files onto your island.

You can use what you have made or the following models provided in the download pack of *Chapter 10, Modeling Organic Forms, Sea, and Terrain*:

◆ 4909_10_Sloop.blend: This contains the sloop.

◆ 4909_10_Boat.blend: This contains the boat.

◆ 4909_10_Tree_Sample_Large.blend: This contains the tree made in the exercise. Rotating a tree in the *Z* axis will make it look like a different tree, and you can also scale it.

◆ 4909_10_Tree_Sample_Small.blend: This contains a lower-detail tree. I used it as a bush.

◆ 4909_10_House Kit_Sample 1.blend: This contains the house.

◆ 4909_10_House Kit_Sample 2.blend: This contains the house that has open doors.

◆ 4909_10_Five Rocks.blend: This has five sample rocks where the modifier has not been applied yet, so you can modify them if you want.

◆ 4909_10_Sky_Cloudy.blend: This contains a hemisphere with a cloud texture as a sky for your world. Add it if you wish.

Time for action – using groups to organize your scene

Groups are a good way to organize the objects in your scene. They let you move multiple objects at a time, and each object can be a member of more than one group, so you can organize them whichever way you want:

1. Open your island file that you just made or the `4909_10_Island_Ocean_Pier.blend` file from the download pack.

2. Select the **Pier Railing Path, Pier Railing Shape, Piling,** and **Piling.001** in the Outliner window with *Shift* + LMB.

3. In the **3D View** header, select the **Object** button. Select **Group** from the pop-up menu and select **Create New Group** in the second menu.

4. In the Properties window, select the **Object** button from the header; it's the button with the cube on it.

5. In the **Groups** subpanel, under the button that says **Add to Group** is a text entry button. Enter `Pier Group` into that button.

6. Now, look in the header of the **Outliner** window above the Properties window. There is a button that says **All Scenes** or **Current Scene**. Click on it and select **Groups** from the drop-down menu.

7. You will see your new **Pier Group** listed. You can use it to select all the objects of the Pier Group at one time. Click on the **+** (plus) sign to the left of where it says **Pier Group**, and you will see all the objects in the group listed.

8. Now, click on the Boathouse.

9. In the **Groups** subpanel of the Properties window, click on the **Add to Group** button. Select **Pier Group** from the drop-down menu. If you do not see **Pier Group** listed, either scroll with the mouse wheel or start typing in the name **Pier Group** next to the magnifying glass at the top of the menu. Then, select it when it appears in the menu. Add the two doors of the Boathouse to the **Pier Group** as well.

10. Look in the **Outliner** window again, and you will see the Boathouse included in your pier group with the doors shown as children of it.

What just happened?

That was a quick introduction to using groups. You learned how to create a group and how to add an object to a group. You also learned how to select all the objects of a group and how to find out the objects present in the group.

Have a go hero – putting your world together

As you are assembling your world, there are two ways to organize it. You can use groups of objects, and you can organize your world by layers.

Initially, put each of the objects from the file you are appending onto their own layer. Select the layer before appending an object. This will give you best control over selecting objects as you arrange the scene, because if necessary, you can just display one layer and select an object or objects, group them, and then select other layers as well to see where your selected objects are in relation to the rest of your world. Later, when you have everything in place, you can sort objects into just a few layers.

Save the file after you have added the objects you want.

Here is how my world turned out:

Take your time and have fun in building and arranging your world. The possibilities are endless. Don't be afraid to redo or modify any part. No one achieves perfection on the first try. Back up your world frequently. It's become a very big file, and you don't want to lose your work.

Q1. What can be done to reduce the number of faces in your final world without hurting the look?

◆   Remove the back sides of the buildings

◆   Remove the faces in the vertex group Ocean Floor

◆   Delete the back sides of the island

The key-function table

These key shortcuts should help you speed your work.

Key	Function
O	Turns proportional editing on or off.
Page Up	Enlarges the proportional editing circle.
Page Down	Shrinks the proportional editing circle.
fn + up arrow	Enlarges the proportional editing circle on a Mac.
fn + down arrow	Shrinks the proportional editing circle on a Mac.
Shift + C	Resets 3D Cursor position to 0, 0, 0, and zooms out to show the entire scene.
Shift + X	If used with scaling (S) or moving (G), it restricts changes to the Y and Z axes.
Shift + Y	If used with scaling (S) or moving (G), it restricts changes to the X and Z axes.
Shift + Z	If used with scaling (S) or moving (G), it restricts changes to the X and Y axes.
U	Gets you to the **UV Mapping** menu.
Ctrl + G	Makes a group of the selected objects.
Shift + G	Brings up a dialog box to manipulate groups.

Summary

In this chapter, you created a world for the sloop. You used texturing to create an oceanic surface. You discovered how to use the ANT Landscape addon to create an island. You used proportional editing to finalize the landform and then painted the island with Blender paint.

With DupliFrames, bevel objects, and arrays, you created an entire pier out of four simple objects. You used the Sapling addon to create trees and subdivision surfaces to make rocks. You built houses from a kit, finding creative ways to reuse parts. You appended a boathouse and a sky to complete the scene and used layers and groups to organize the scene. You're doing some impressive work.

The next chapter will concentrate on the use of lighting and camera. You'll discover how to do a standard three-point lighting setup and use lighting falloffs and shadows. We will discuss camera basics, including perspective, use of lens, depth of field, clipping, choosing shots, and critiquing them.

Let's go!

11

Improving Your Lighting and Camera Work

In the previous chapter, you created a world for the sloop to exist in. You created the ocean's surface with texturing. You built an island with the ANT Landscape add-on. You adjusted the landform with proportional editing and then painted the island with Blender Paint. You created an entire pier out of four simple objects and used the Sapling add-on to create trees and then you made rocks to practice your skills with subdivision surfaces. You built houses from a kit and appended a boathouse and a sky to complete the scene.

In this chapter, you will concentrate on lighting and camera use. You'll discover the following:

◆ How to create the standard three-point lighting setup

◆ How to use lighting falloff and shadows

◆ How to use the camera, along with perspective, lenses, depth of field, clipping, choosing shots, and critiquing them

◆ How to animate a scene, learn ways to make adjustments, and do rapid test renderings

Getting ready to do lighting and camera work

The following are the files that you should copy from the download pack and into your Chapter 11/Blender directory:

- ◆ 4909OS_11_light_test_rig_Sintel.blend
- ◆ 4909OS_11_Blender_Island.blend
- ◆ 4909OS_11_Blender_Island_Motion_Blur.blend
- ◆ 4909OS_11_Viking_ship_subsurface.blend
- ◆ 4909OS_11_Viking_ship_mesh.blend

The following are the image files that you should copy from the download pack into the Chapter 11/Images directory:

- ◆ 4909OS_11_01.png
- ◆ 4909OS_11_02.png
- ◆ 4909OS_11_03.png
- ◆ 4909OS_11_04.png
- ◆ 4909OS_11_05.png
- ◆ 4909OS_11_06.png
- ◆ 4909OS_11_07.png

 If you are reading the printed version of this book, treat yourself by downloading all of the .png files from this chapter's image subdirectory in the download pack. In this chapter, color is important.

Using lighting

In *Chapter 3, Controlling the Lamp, the Camera, and Animating Objects*, and the bonus chapter *Chapter 5A, Lighting a Small Boat*, we looked at the lights, and you got a chance to play around with them. Now, we will take a more in-depth look at using light.

Lighting with three lights

The three-point lighting method provides a simple and easy-to-use method to light a scene. It's the basis for many professional lighting setups, and when you understand it, you will have a solid foundation for creating more complex lighting setups.

The three lights represent the three stages of setting up the lighting, listed as follows:

 ◆ Setting up the general brightness.

 ◆ Controlling the shadows so everything is well lit. This does not mean bright, but rather that critical details are not lost in shadows.

 ◆ Adding in highlights to pop the subject of the shot out from the background.

Each of the three lights has a specific name and function. These three lights are as follows:

 ◆ **Key Light**: This is placed between 15 to 45 degrees from the camera. It provides the main light for a scene.

 ◆ **Fill Light**: This is placed at about a 90-degree angle to the key light. It is dimmer and often more diffused. Its purpose is to control many of the shadows created by the key light.

 ◆ **Back Light**: This is about 180 degrees from the camera. It is used to provide a highlight on the edges of the person or object.

Time for action – introducing the three-point lighting system

I've prepared a simple lighting rig. The model is a statue of Blender Foundation's Sintel character. The rig has four layers. Layer 1 has the key light, Layer 2 has the fill light, Layer 3 has the back light, and Layer 4 has Sintel, the camera, and an Empty. Putting the lights on different layers lets you turn them on and off easily. I have set up 3D View as a QuadView window, as discussed in *Chapter 2, Getting Comfortable Using the 3D View*. This will let you adjust the lights in all axes without changing the windows.

In 3D View, the lamps are in black. You can see their location on the left side of the next screenshot, and the cones of light that are coming from them. As the active object, the camera is highlighted. The following steps will show you the three-point lighting system:

 1. Open the file `49090S_11_light_test_rig_Sintel.blend` from the download pack.

2. Press *F12*. Can you see where the lights are coming from, as shown in the following screenshot? Use the *F11* key and the *Esc* key to alternate between the image and 3D View to help you study the lighting:

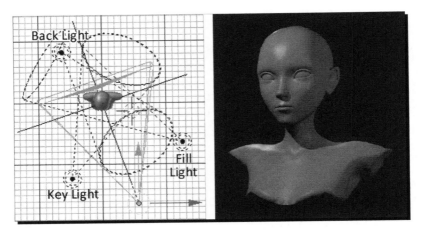

3. Select Layer 1, and then press the *Shift* key while selecting Layer 4 so that the key light, the camera, and Sintel are visible.

4. Press *F12*. The image should look similar to the next image. Press *Esc* when you have finished looking at the image.

5. What differences do you see between the previous image with all the lights and the following image with just a key light?

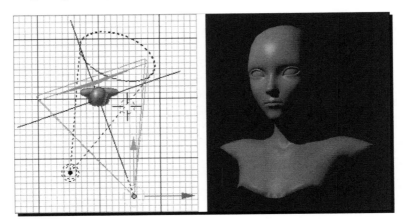

6. Select Layer 2, and then press the *Shift* key while selecting Layer 4.

7. Press *F12*. The image should look similar to the next image. Press *Esc* when you have finished looking at the image as shown in the following graphic.

8. What differences do you see between the image with all the lights and the one with just the fill light?

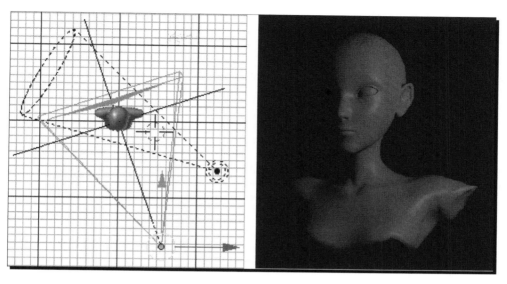

9. Select Layer 3, and then press the *Shift* key while selecting Layer 4.

10. Press *F12*. The image should look similar to the following image. Press *Esc* when you have finished looking at the image as shown next.

11. What differences do you see between the image with all lights and the image with just the back light?

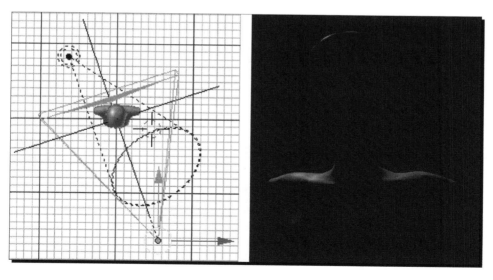

What just happened?

First, you saw all three lights. The light on Sintel was immersive, varied, and balanced. No part of her has too much light, so that you can see all the details. Both the highlights and the shadows have details.

Then, you lit her with only the key light, which is to the left of the camera and at a high angle above Sintel. The shadows are strong especially between the lips and under the nose. You saw a highlight on her forehead and at the top of her chest. However, Sintel is not overexposed; that is, too much light does not result in loss of detail. The purpose of the key light is to do the main lighting for the scene. However, the side of her head is in darkness, so more light is needed.

Next, you saw only the fill light, which is to the right of the camera. The light is dimmer by about one half to one quarter of the value of the key light. It is also placed lower, so you saw the highlights of the fill light come off the sides of her head and body. The purpose of the fill light is to reduce and soften shadows created by the key light. You can see that the fill light will give important details about Sintel's left ear and the shape of her neck.

The back light is about 180 degrees from the camera. With only the back light, you saw highlights on the top of the head and the shoulders. Like the key light, the back light is high. Its job is to create highlights that define the subject with a rim of light.

Investigating light and color

You now understand the fundamentals of lighting, setting the overall lighting level, filling in any shadow areas with light, and creation of highlights to separate objects from the background. However, this is just the beginning. Next, you'll check out colored lights and use lights to create patterns and images.

Time for action – using color to separate what you see

You've seen each lamp by itself. Now, use color to see how they work together. The color will help you see how the lights work together. The following steps will guide you to use color to separate what you see:

1. Select Layer 1, and then press the *Shift* key while selecting Layers 2, 3, and 4.

2. Select the **Spot_Key** lamp, which is to the left of the camera in the **Top** view, with the RMB. In the Properties window header, select the **Object Data** button. It's the button with a drafting lamp on it.

3. In the **Lamp** subpanel, select the white **Light Color** button below the row of buttons that define the kind of lamp you are using. In the pop-up color wheel, set **G** to 0.000 and **B** to 0.000 so that the lamp is red.

4. Select the **Spot_Fill** lamp, which is to the right of the camera in the **Top** view, with the RMB, or select it from the **Outliner** window in the upper-right corner.

5. In the **Lamp** subpanel, select the white **Light Color** button. In the pop-up color wheel, set **R** to 0.000 and **G** to 0.000 so that the lamp is blue.

6. Select the **Spot_Back** lamp, which is opposite the camera, with the RMB.

7. In the **Lamp** subpanel, select the white **Light Color** button. In the pop-up color wheel, set **R** to 0.000 and **B** to 0.000 so that the lamp is green.

8. Press *F12*. The image should look similar to the image in the following screenshot. Press *Esc* when you are done looking at it.

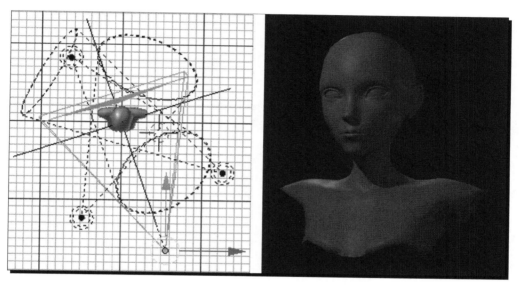

9. Save the file with a unique filename.

What just happened?

Now, you used all three lights at once, but you gave each one a different color so that you could see how the lights interact. You studied light color and how it mixes in *Chapter 3, Controlling the Lamp, the Camera, and Animating Objects*.

You can see where the key and fill lamps both illuminate Sintel on the left side of her face and body, because her skin is magenta, not red or blue. The back light is green, but the highlight on her neck becomes cyan briefly on her left-hand side where the fill and back light mix. In the center of her right shoulder, the key and back lights mix, making the color a bit more yellow. Under her chin and nose and where her lips meet, there is no light, so you have dark shadows.

Have a go hero – changing light intensity

There is only one good way to know how the intensity of the light affects the scene; try it out. Try these different light intensities.

Open `49090S_11_light test rig_Sintel.blend` again. Press *Ctrl + Alt + Q* to toggle the Quad View, so you only see one view, and set that view to the Camera view. Set the Viewport Shading to **Rendered**. Select the **Spot_Key** lamp in the Outliner Window. Set the **Energy** levels of **Spot_Key Lamp** to `0.25`. Repeat this with **Energy** levels of `0.50`, `1.00`, `2.00`, `4.00`, `8.00`, `16.00`, and `32.00`, and note the changes.

Adding shapes and patterns to your lighting

Blender allows you to attach graphics to your lights, allowing you to create any pattern of light from what looks like light filtering through a stained glass window to Batman's signal. The next exercise will show you how.

Time for action – using cookies

Mmmm. Cookies. Well, these are not the oatmeal, raisin, chocolate chip, or even the Internet kind. In films and Blender, a cookie is a screen put up in front of a lamp to create a pattern within the light. The following steps will help you in using cookies:

1. Open the file `49090S_11_light_test rig_Sintel.blend` from the download pack again.

2. In the 3D View window, select the **Spot_Key** lamp with the RMB. You can also select it in the Outliner window.

3. In the header of the Properties window, select the **Textures** button. It is the button with the checkerboard on it.

4. Press the **New** button to create a new texture.

5. Click on the button to the right of **Type**, and choose **Image or Movie** from the menu.

6. In the **Image** subpanel, click on the **Open** button and select `49090S_11_05.png` from the `Images` directory of the `Chapter 11` folder you had created.

7. Press *F12*.

8. In the **Mapping** subpanel, click on the button to the right of **Coordinates**. Select **Object** from the pop-up menu.

9. Press *F12*.

10. Click on the button to the right of **Object** text. Select **Spot_Key** from the pop-up menu as shown in the following screenshot:

11. Set the **X** and **Y** values of **Size:** to `0.50`.

12. Press *F12*.

13. In the **Influence** subpanel, set **Color** to `0.250` to provide a softer effect, as shown in the following screenshot:

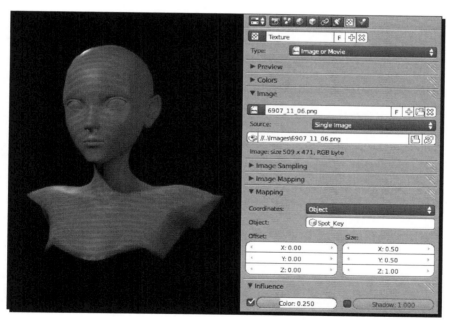

14. Press *F12*. Press *Esc* when you have finished looking at Sintel.

15. Save the file with a unique name.

What just happened?

Just as objects can have textures, lamps too can have textures. This can be very handy while suggesting details, such as a venetian blind that indicates a window, a leaf pattern that suggests a tree, or a stained glass image that suggests a church. You discovered that you can change the size of the image and its strength. You can also change the mapping; the default global mapping created a wild pattern. If you choose **View** instead of **Object** in the **Coordinates** button, the texture will suggest a pattern generated in the camera, not in the lamp.

Time for action – preparing to adjust falloff

Now, you are going to prepare a scene to investigate falloff from a light:

1. Open the file `4909OS_11_light_test_rig_Sintel.blend` from the download pack.

2. Select Sintel with the RMB.

3. In the Properties window header, select the **Object Modifiers** button; it is the button with the wrench on it.

4. In the **Modifiers** subpanel, select **Add Modifier** and choose **Array** from the menu.

5. In the **Array Modifier** subpanel, set **Relative Offset** to **X:** `0.000`, **Y:** `1.300`, and **Z:** `0.000`.

6. Set the **Count** value to `7`.

7. Select the camera with the RMB.

8. Press *G*, *X*, and move the camera 15 units with the mouse while holding down the *Ctrl* button. Finish the move with the LMB.

9. Press *G*, *Y*, and move the camera 5 units with the mouse while pressing the *Ctrl* button. Release the move with the LMB.

10. Press *R*, *Z*, and rotate it with the mouse so you can see all the Sintels in the **Camera** view. Release the rotation with the LMB. Move the camera in the *Z* axis until you can see all the Sintels at eye-level, individually, with their shoulders overlapping just a bit in the **Camera Persp** view. Release the rotation with the LMB.

11. Select Layer 1 with the LMB. Press *Shift* + LMB and select Layer 4.

12. Press *F12*. Do you see all the Sintels? Press *Esc* when you have finished looking at the image.

13. Select the **Spot_Key** lamp.

14. In the header of the Properties window, select the **Object Data** button. It is the button with the drafting lamp on it.

15. In the **Spot Shape** subpanel, set **Size** to `45` degrees.

16. Press *G*, *X*, and move the lamp 20 units with the mouse while pressing the *Ctrl* button. Release the move with the LMB.

17. Place the cursor over the **Front Ortho** window. Press *G*, *Z*, and move the lamp -6 units in the *Z* axis (down) with the mouse while pressing the *Ctrl* button. Release the move with the LMB.

18. Press *R*, *X*, and rotate the lamp in the **Right Ortho** view so that all the Sintels are within the cone as shown in the following screenshot. Press *R*, *Z*, and rotate the lamp in the **Top Ortho** view, so that the left side of the cone touches the left side of the first Sintel. Your best guide as to whether all the Sintels should be lit may be the camera view as shown in the following screenshot:

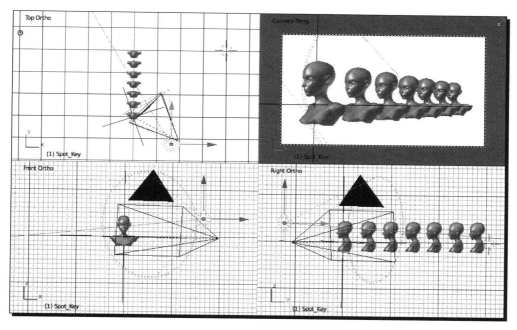

19. Press *F12*. Press *Esc* when you have finished looking at the image.

20. If you don't see all seven Sintels, readjust the lamp position and rotation.

21. If you don't see the rearmost Sintel, it's likely that the light has been clipped, just the way the camera got clipped in the previous chapter. If so, in the bottom of the **Shadow** subpanel, you can either check the **Autoclip End** checkbox, or set the **Clip End** button to 100.000.

22. Press *F12*. Note how the Sintels get darker the farther away they are. Press *Esc* when you have finished looking at the image.

23. Save the file with a unique name.

What just happened?

By setting up a number of Sintels and shining the light along them, you could see what happens as the subject is farther from the light. The light appears to be dimmer.

Time for action – adjusting the falloff

Now that the scene is set, check out how much you can vary the light without ever changing the energy that the light emits:

1. In the **Lamp** subpanel of the Properties window, click on the **Sun** button.

2. Press *F12*. No falloff will occur; sunlight does not get dimmer; only spotlights, point lights, and area lights get dimmer.

3. Click on the **Spot** button in the **Lamp** subpanel.

4. Press *F12*.

5. In the **Lamp** subpanel, change the **Distance** option of **Falloff** from **25** to 12.

6. Press *F12*.

7. In the **Lamp** subpanel, set the **Distance** option of **Falloff** to 50.

8. Press *F12*.

9. In the **Lamp** subpanel, set the **Distance** option of **Falloff** to 100.

10. Press *F12*. Press *Esc* when you have finished looking at the image. Compare what you have seen in the three renders, as shown in the following screenshot:

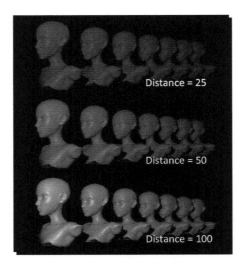

What just happened?

This section brings up a good question. If light can travel distances so far that it takes billions of years to get there, why does light get dimmer just crossing a room? Shouldn't it stay just as bright?

In real life, light gets dimmer because the farther away from the source the light travels, the greater the area it is spread over, so there is less light at any particular point.

You can see this in the following diagram. In the diagram, the light source has 90 light rays represented by the lines coming out of the center. There are four cubes that are all the same size but at different distances from the light. The closest one gets hit by 19 light rays. The next closest gets hit by **7** light rays. Farther away, the cube only gets hit by **3**, and the farthest one only gets hit by **1**. The closest cube will appear 19 times as bright as the farthest cube. Blender mimics that with falloff.

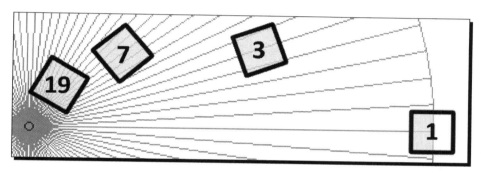

So why does the Sun lamp have no falloff? The diameter of the sun is 109 times as large as the diameter of the earth. We are small enough that for all intents and purposes, the sunlight that reaches the earth is parallel. If the sun were the size of the orange globe of light in the previous illustration, the earth would be much smaller than that single line going out to the farthest cube. All of the earth gets just about the same amount of light.

The falloff distance control specifies the distance at which an object appears half as bright as it is right at the light source.

In my example for the previous *Time for action* section, the front Sintel was 20 units from the lamp. The back Sintel was 43 units from the lamp. This is explained in more detail in the following points:

◆ When the **Distance** setting was **25**, the front Sintel was a little closer than the halfway point and was about half as bright as it would have been right by the lamp. The last Sintel was almost twice as far as the **Distance**, and the light had dimmed to almost nothing by the time it reached the last Sintel.

- When the **Distance** setting was **50**, the last Sintel was just ahead of the halfway point, and it is about as bright as the first Sintel was at the **Distance** of **25**.

- At a **Distance** of **100**, not much of the falloff has happened in the distance between the lamp and any of the Sintels. They are all brighter.

So, you can see that the effect of using the **Distance** setting is like stretching the brightness of the light as you would do to a rubber band; one end is still bright and the other is always dark, but you can vary the distance between those points.

Each lamp can have a differing **Distance**, which lets you use the light even more subtly as your key light falls off at a different rate than your fill.

Time for action – using Custom Curve to tailor light

Custom Curve allows you to tailor the falloff exactly according to your needs, as explained in the following steps:

1. In the **Lamp** subpanel, click on the button beneath **Falloff**; next, click on the button labeled **Inverse Square**, and select **Custom Curve** from the menu.

2. Set **Distance** to 47, located in the button below **Custom Curve**.

3. Scroll down to the **Falloff Curve** subpanel. Click on the triangle to the left of the Falloff curve to open the subpanel.

4. Note that there are three vertical grid lines and three horizontal grid lines. The line that goes diagonally from upper left to lower right is a Bézier curve. When you click on that line, a control point is put there, and you can move that control point to change the shape of that line.

5. Move the mouse over the diagonal line. Near the leftmost vertical grid line, press the LMB and drag the curve down so that the control point is at the intersection of the center horizontal grid line and the leftmost vertical grid line, as shown in the following screenshot as the control point numbered **1**:

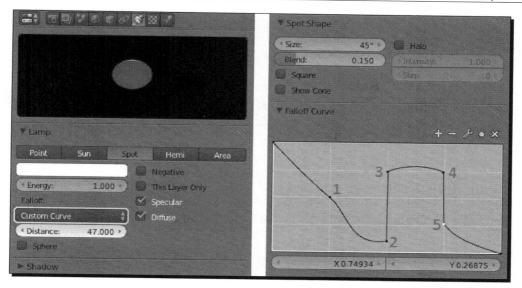

6. Press *F12*.

7. Move the mouse to the right of the control point you just created, and press the LMB over the line. Drag the point down and over, so it is on the center vertical grid at the midpoint between the lowest horizontal grid and the bottom, as shown in the preceding screenshot, at the control point numbered **2**.

8. Press *F12*.

9. Continue to put in control points at locations **3**, **4**, and **5**. Press *F12* to render an image after you put in each control point to see how it affects the lighting.

10. When you have inserted all of the control points, the final render should look as follows:

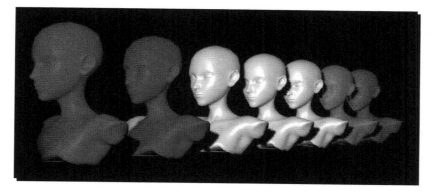

11. Save the file with a unique name.

What just happened?

The Custom Curve showed that falloff can be creative, and that in Blender, you can control the falloff into shadows exactly as you want, even if real light does not work that way.

Have a go hero – using three-point lighting

As I have said, the three-point lighting format is just a basis for lighting design. Now, try out one or more of these variations. Open the file `49090S_11_light_test_rig_Sintel.blend` from the download pack as a place to start.

Filling in from the key side lighting is an interesting twist on three-point lighting. Put both the key and fill lights on the same side at an angle of roughly 45 degrees from the camera. Keep a little space between the key and fill lights, and aim them at different parts of the face. Set the back light to 180 degrees off the key and fill.

Cameo Lighting is used to pick out a particular person in a scene. Set the key light about six Blender units above Sintel's head, shining almost straight down. Turn off the fill and back lights. Set the falloff distance to `50`.

Beauty Lighting is all about highlights. Set the key light directly in front of Sintel at eye level. Set the back light high above Sintel's head. Turn off the fill light.

Rembrandt Lighting is named after the style of painter Rembrandt van Rijn. This is very similar to three-point lighting, except that there is no backlight. The goal of Rembrandt Lighting is to create a triangle of light underneath the eye on the darker side of the face. Use **Empty** to rotate the camera so it is directly in front of Sintel. You will want the key light at a high location and the fill about level with Sintel's face. Try starting out with only the key light and get it into position, and then adjust the fill. Do a search on Rembrandt Lighting to see examples.

Film Noir Lighting is used to recapture that gritty 1940s look. Watch the video *How to Light Video Film Noir Style* by *Mark Apsalon* available at `http://www.youtube.com/watch?v=w1gMxT2R9z4`. The basic idea is to light only what you want the viewer to see. Use a strong key light and minimal fill. Use the back light to create a rim highlight. Adjust the size of the cone, the falloff, and the energy levels. Use extreme camera angles. Use cookies to give the light shapes and cast interesting shadows onto flat walls or light only the eyes.

The preceding screenshot shows what I did.

Learning more about lighting

You can refer to the following to know more about lighting:

- *Digital Lighting and Rendering, Second Edition* by *Jeremy Birn*, New Riders, Berkeley, CA 94710, 2006.
- *The Complete Guide to Light and Lighting in Digital Photography* by *Michael Freeman*, Lark Books, New York, NY 10016, 2007.
- *The Cinema as a Graphic Art* by *Vladimir Nilsen*, Hill and Wang, NY, NY, 1972.
- *How to Light Video Film Noir Style* by *Mark Apsalon*, `http://www.youtube.com/watch?v=w1gMxT2R9z4`.

The Blender camera can be used much like a film camera. A film camera has three basic controls: the lens, which controls what you see; the aperture, which controls how much light you see; and the shutter, which controls the length of the exposure. Using the aperture and the shutter together, you can control how bright the scene is and how much of the detail you can see.

Changing the field of view

The **field of view** is the area that can be seen through the camera. This can be thought of as the width of a cone in front of the camera, measured in degrees, as shown on the left side of the following screenshot.

Blender allows you to specify this angle in two ways, in degrees, or as the **Focal Length** of a camera lens that sees a scene of that width.

By default, Blender specifies the field of view as a lens of a certain focal length, as shown on the right of the following image. The focal length is specified in millimeters, in the same way as cameras do. This lets you work more easily with filmmakers because you are using the same units. For example, once I was working with a producer who needed a fire engine inserted into the foreground of a scene that had already been shot. In the scene, the camera had been trucked sideways, so it was important that my field of view settings were identical to his, so that my fire engine fitted in with the motion of all the buildings and landscape in the scene, and so that the fire engine appeared stationary in the street and undistorted.

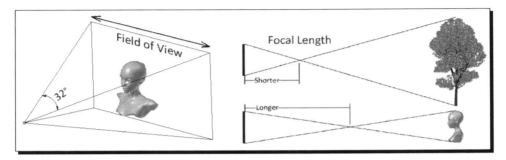

Blender uses the same lens size/field of view ratios as a professional movie camera that uses a 35 mm film or a high-quality digital camera. Both the film size/sensor size and the lens size are specified in millimeters. From now on, we will be talking about lens sizes and assuming a 35 mm film.

In the following screenshot, you see the same scene rendered from the same viewpoint with three different lens settings. The 28 mm lens shown here is a **wide-angle** lens. The wide-angle lens has a short focal length as shown in the top right of the preceding image. The 50 mm lens is a **normal** lens and reproduces approximately what people see, and the 135 mm lens is a **telephoto** lens for getting good detail from far away.

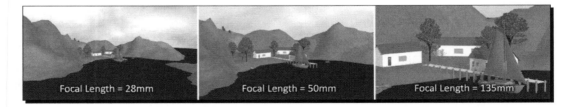

You can find out more about cameras and lenses at http://www.cambridgeincolour.com/tutorials/camera-lenses.htm.

Time for action – zooming the camera versus dollying the camera

Say you want to start out with a long shot that transitions into a close-up. Do you zoom or dolly? We studied dollying in *Chapter 3, Controlling the Lamp, the Camera, and Animating Objects*. Dollying moves the camera towards or away from the scene. **Zooming** starts with one field of view and transitions to a different field of view. You can go from a distant shot to a close-up of your subject with either method. Is there a difference in the results? Let's find out. This exercise has two identical cameras; you'll zoom one and dolly the other and see what you think. Check *Chapter 3, Controlling the Lamp, the Camera, and Animating Objects*, if you need to review the commands for navigating in the **Timeline Editor**. The following steps will show you how to zoom and dolly the camera:

1. Open the file `49090S_11_Blender_Island.blend`. **Camera.Field of View** is selected as the active camera in the upper-left **3D View** window.

2. The **Object Data** panel in the Properties window will be open. In the **Lens** subpanel, you will see a button labeled **Focal Length: 28**.

3. Move the cursor over that button and press the *I* key to create a keyframe. The button will turn yellow as shown in the following screenshot:

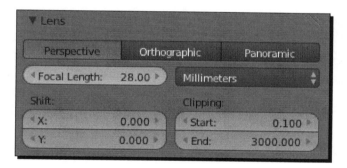

4. With the cursor over the **Timeline** window, press the *Shift* + up arrow key twice to move to frame 20.

5. In the Properties window in the **Lens** subpanel, change **Focal Length** to **135**, and with the mouse over the button, press the *I* key to create another **Focal Length** keyframe.

6. With the mouse over the **Timeline** window, press the *Shift* + down arrow key twice to move to frame **0**.

7. In the **Outliner** window, select **Camera.Dolly**. Look at the lower 3D View window and both of the upper 3D View windows. Note that the cameras are in the same place and have the same focal length.

8. With the cursor over the upper right 3D View window, press *I* and then select **Location** from **Insert Keyframe Menu**.

9. With the mouse over the **Timeline** window, press the *Shift* + up arrow key twice to move to frame 20.

10. In the lower right-hand side of the 3D View window, press *G, Z, Z*, and move the **Camera.Dolly** towards the house until the view in the upper right 3D View window is as similar as possible to what you see in the upper left 3D View window. In both cases, the house on the left will be touching the edge of the image. Press the LMB to release the move.

11. With your cursor over the lower-right 3D View window, press *I* and then select **Location** from the **Keyframe** menu.

12. Press the left or right arrow keys to progress back and forth through the 20 frames and compare the two. Do it several times and compare the two images in each frame. The zoom is on the left, and the dolly is on the right. Frame 20 is shown in the following screenshot for comparison:

13. Save the file with a unique name.

What just happened?

This shows a lot of difference between zoom and dolly. While dollying, I tried to make it match the image area of the zoom motion. In both cases, the house on the left touches the edge of the image. The zoom focuses on the house by eliminating part of the area that it sees. The dolly physically moves the lens towards the object while retaining the same field of view. They have the same image on frame one, but by frame 20, the images are different. Both images try to cover about the same area. The center of both the images is at the lower-right corner of the window of the farthest house. The left side is the outer edge of the nearer house. The differences are as follows:

- The **Camera.Dolly** is closer to the scene and it has a wider angle lens. Because the camera is closer to the house than the end of the pier is, you only see a part of the sloop's sail instead of the sloop and the pier.

- The **Camera.Dolly** image shows more perspective. The boathouse in the foreground is larger and the furthest house is smaller, and you can see the tops of the hills in the background.

- Because of the angle of the lenses, the distortion is different in each image. In the zoom image, the left side of the house looks a little smaller than the right side, whereas in the dolly image, the left side of the house looks a little larger than the right side.

Using perspective

If you took art classes in school, they probably introduced you to perspective. The following screenshot demonstrates some of the classic perspective rules. The two columns of pilings look like they would meet if you extended them out to the horizon in the background. In addition, the planks on the dock get smaller and smaller as they recede in the distance. This provides important visual clues about the structure of the scene to the viewer.

Keep the rules of perspective in mind when placing your camera. Use of perspective can affect how large or how important something appears to be in a scene. Another clue to perspective is to determine what is in focus and what is out of focus.

Using depth of field

Depth of field specifies what is in sharp focus and what is blurred in the image. It uses the **z-depth**, or calculates how far from the camera an object is, to determine what is in focus. A greater depth of field means more of the scene is in focus. A smaller depth of field means that less of the scene is in focus. By default, Blender renders everything in nice sharp focus. However, it has some tricks to fake the depth of field, as shown in the following screenshot, where you can see that the people are in focus, but the objects in the foreground and background are not.

Z-depth should not be confused with the *Z* axis. The *Z* axis describes vertical measurements, both global and local. Z-depth describes the distance between the lens and what the lens is focused on.

In addition, we just studied field of view, which can be confused with depth of field because the terms share two out of three words. Field of view is how wide the field of vision is, while depth of field is how deep the field of vision is.

Creating your own people in Blender

The two humans I am using were created in an open source program named MakeHuman. It creates fairly realistic men and women who are already rigged, and gives you a wide range of options on their appearance. Using MakeHuman is out of the scope of this book, but if you want more information, you could go to http://www.makehuman.org/.

Time for action – creating depth of field

Depth of field is a technique borrowed from film cameras to set off what is the subject and what is the background:

1. Open the file `4909OS_11_Blender_Island.blend`. In the **Outliner** window just above the Properties window, select **Camera.Depth of Field** with the LMB.

2. In the header of the upper right-hand 3D View window, select **View**, and then scroll up to **Cameras** and then select **Set Active Object as Camera**.

3. You can press *Ctrl* + MMB and the mouse to make the camera area fill the window.

4. Look at the **Layers** controls in the 3D View header. The sky is in Layer 10. Press *Shift* + LMB over Layer 10 so that all layers with objects will render.

5. Press *F12* to render the scene. It looks similar to the previous image, but without the people. Look at it and see how everything in the image is in focus. Zoom into the house to see the tiles on the roof. Do not press *Esc* to get rid of the image.

6. In the **Timeline** window, select the **Current Editor Type** button on the left end of the header and choose **Node Editor** from the pop-up menu.

7. Move your mouse to the side of the Node Editor window until you see the double-headed arrow. Hold down the mouse button and make the window bigger. Press *Ctrl* + MMB and use the mouse to zoom into the Node Editor window.

8. In the Node Editor window header, there are three buttons on the right side of the word **Node**. Click on the center button. Four checkboxes will appear as shown in the following screenshot. Select **Use Nodes**.

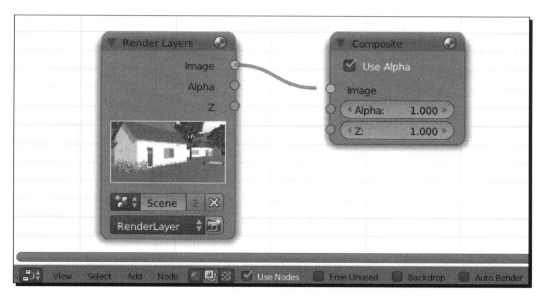

9. Two boxes connected by a cord will appear in the Node Editor. They look similar to the illustration of data blocks shown at the beginning of *Chapter 4, Modeling with Vertices, Edges, and Faces*. Each box represents a data node. The left node is the **Render Layers** node and the right node is the **Composite** node.

10. Select the yellow dot at the right end of the cord between the node boxes. Hold the LMB down, move the mouse to the left, and the cord detaches as shown in the preceding screenshot. Release the mouse button and the cord disappears.

11. In the Node Editor header, select **Add**. Choose **Filter** and then **Defocus** from the pop-up menus.

12. Select the **Defocus** node with the LMB and hold it down as you move the **Defocus** node into the center between the other two nodes. Release the LMB to release the motion.

13. Move the other two nodes apart so that there is a little space between them.

14. Now, connect the nodes. Move the cursor to the yellow dot on the right-hand side of the **Render Layers** node. Hold down the LMB and drag the cursor to the yellow dot on the bottom left-hand side of the **Defocus** node. A cord-like connection will be formed.

15. Next, in the **Render Layers** node, select the dot beside the letter **Z**. Hold down the mouse and move it to the gray dot beside the **Z** button at the bottom of the **Defocus** node, as shown in the next screenshot.

16. Click on the **Use Z-Buffer** checkbox in the **Defocus** node.

17. Now, connect the **Defocus** node to the **Composite** node on the right. Select the yellow dot on the upper right-hand side of the **Defocus** node. Hold down the LMB and move the cursor to the yellow dot on the left-hand side of the **Composite** node.

18. In the **Defocus** node, set the value of **fStop** to 3.

19. Set the **Max Blur** value to **16**.

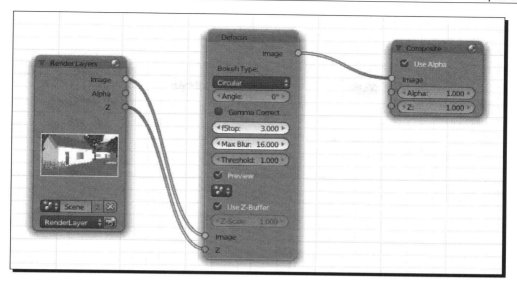

20. Notice that in the **UV/Image Editor**, the nearest building is now blurred, but parts of the trees are not.

21. If you want to save the image, with the cursor over the **UV/Image Editor** window, press *F3*.

What just happened?

Defocusing is how Blender overcomes the difference between the 3D animation camera and a real camera. A real camera is not able to keep everything in focus, but this lets the camera operator decide what the viewer should pay attention to, by giving certain portions of the image less detail.

You set up a shot and rendered it. Then, you took your first look at Blender's post-processing capability by opening up Node Editor. By default, when you add nodes in the compositing mode, as you already did, you get the Render Layers node and Composite node. You disconnected them and inserted a Defocus node in between. The Defocus node uses the z-depth information that it gets from the camera to decide how much to blur any particular part of the image.

The smaller the hole the aperture creates, the less light there is and the longer the shutter has to stay open to get a proper exposure. The longer the shutter is open, the more detail the film can capture, so you get a greater subtlety of tones and colors, and more of the image stays in focus. The larger the hole, the faster the light can expose the film, so less time is needed, but it doesn't get as much detail.

You cannot control the aperture directly, but you do it by adjusting the fStop. In a camera, the fStop is the ratio of the focal length divided by the diameter of the aperture. The aperture is the hole that lets light into the camera. The focal length was shown earlier in this chapter. So, the larger the number of fStops, the less light that gets to the camera and the longer the exposure that is needed, and with the Defocus node, the blurring is less. The smaller the number of fStops, the more light gets to the camera and the more blurring there is. You changed the fStop value from 128, down to 3, for a lot of blurring. It works out inversely; the smaller the fStop value, the more blurred the depth will be, the larger is the fStop value, the less blurred the depth will be.

The Max Blur value sets how much that blurring will be.

Adjusting the center of focus

Using the basic Z buffer was a good start. However, the center of focus was not really where you would want it. The next stage in controlling focus is to control where the center of focus is.

Time for action – controlling the center of focus

You can set how far away from the camera the focused portion of the image should be, using the following steps:

1. Look at the **Layers** controls in the 3D View header. The sky is in Layer 10.
    Press *Shift* + LMB over Layer 10 so that Layer 10 is no longer visible.

2. Press *Shift* + LMB twice over Layer 11 to make it the active layer. Layer 11 has the cameras.

3. With the cursor over the left-hand 3D View window, press *7* on the NumPad and then press the *.* (period) key on the NumPad to center on **Camera.Depth of Field** and the house. Move the cursor to where you want the center of the focused area to be. Press the LMB to put the 3D Cursor there.

4. Once again, if you want to zoom in, you can press *Shift + B* and then use the marquee to select the area that you want to zoom in to.

5. With the cursor over the 3D View window, press *N* to bring up the 3D View Properties panel. In the **3D Cursor** subpanel, set the **Z** value to `10`.

6. Press *Shift + A* and select **Empty** from the drop-down menu. Choose **Plain Axes** from the pop-up menu.

7. Press *S*, *20*, and *Enter* to make the axes visible.

8. Select the **Object** button in the Properties window header. It's the button with the orange cube.

9. Name **Empty** to `Empty.Defocus`.

10. Select **Camera.Depth of Field** in the 3D View window with the RMB, or select it in the **Outliner** window.

11. Select the **Object Data** button in the Properties window header. It's the button with the movie camera.

12. In the **Depth of Field** subpanel, below **Focus**, there is an input box with an image of a cube, as shown in the following screenshot. Click on it and select **Empty.Defocus** from the pop-up menu. If you do not see the name, scroll the mouse wheel to see other names or start typing the name into the input box.

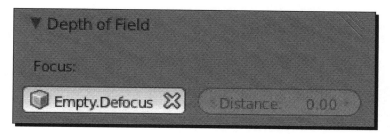

13. Press *F12* to render the scene. Press *Esc* when you have finished looking at it. Move the Empty closer to the camera or farther away, and press *F12* to re-render the image. Notice the changes.

14. Save the file with a unique name.

What just happened?

This was a little more fun. To control where the center of focus is, you created an empty object, and then set it up as the Depth of Field Focus object for the camera. With this, you can control exactly where the center of focus is. In addition, like all objects, it can be animated.

Getting variety in your camera work

Unless you are *John Ford*, the director who was famous for using medium shots almost exclusively, so that the editors had to assemble a film just as he shot it, you will probably want to cover your scenes from a variety of distances to provide rhythm and improve the storytelling. There are three basic shots: long, medium, and close-up. Anything that is not a close-up or a long shot is a medium shot. The next few screenshots show a long shot and a medium shot.

Comparing long and medium shots

Long shots are usually used as an introduction to a film or scene. As shown on the left of the following image, they give the viewer the big picture. As a computer animator, you are fortunate. You can place your camera anywhere without having to worry about how to hold it up.

The medium shot is a workhorse, often used for action shots. It is close enough to show what is going on, and also has enough room to show where that action is taking place, as you can see in the following image on the right side:

Using close-ups and two shots

A two shot, as it sounds, has two people in it, as seen on the left of this image. They can be close together or far apart. In *Forrest Gump*, when Forrest was on the park bench with the other characters, even though they sat on opposite ends of the bench, it was still a two shot.

A close-up is used to focus the viewer's attention on the subject with little background. Often, it may have only one character or a small object in it, as shown on the right side of the following image:

Applying the rule of 180

The rule of 180 helps the viewer keep track of what is happening in a conversational scene. 180 refers to 180 degrees, or a half circle. You want to draw an imaginary line through the two people having a conversation. Then, pick one side of that line to stay on. As you can see in the following two images, the camera is always on the side of the woman's left shoulder and the man's right shoulder:

Using motion blur

Motion blur can be very effective for conveying motion and gives a more realistic feel to an animation. How much blurring is needed depends on the speed of the object and how close it is to the camera.

As a director, you also have to decide what should get blurred: the object that you are interested in or the background. Here, I made an image of the sloop sailing past the pier. I chose to blur the background so that I could show that the woman was piloting the sloop. This also leads the viewer to the expectation that the sloop is the important thing in the shot, and that the next shot will show you more about the sloop.

If the sloop were blurred and the background in focus, we might expect that the sloop has sailed off, and that next, we will turn your attention back to what is happening on the island.

Time for action – using motion blur

The Motion Blur controls are pretty simple. However, they are not the same controls used for z-depth blurring. Try them out:

1. Open `49090S_11_Blender_Island_Motion_Blur.blend`.

2. Scrub the Current Time Indicator in the Timeline Window to see the sloop move.

3. Return it to frame **9**.

4. Press *F12*. Zoom in to the image and note that there is no blurring. Press *Esc* when you are finished looking at it.

5. In the Properties panel header, select the button with the still camera on it to get the Render panel. Look down until you see the **Sampled Motion Blur** subpanel. Check the **Sampled Motion Blur** checkbox. Set the **Motion Samples** button to 2, as shown in the next screenshot.

6. Press *F12*. Press *Esc* when you have finished looking at it.

What just happened?

The Motion Blur controls here were just a few settings in the Render panel. After checking out the rendering that you did after setting **Sampled Motion Blur** to 2, you probably noticed that the rendering was done twice, and then the two renderings were composited together. You could see that the pilings seemed to be doubled while the sloop and woman were clear, as shown in the following screenshot:

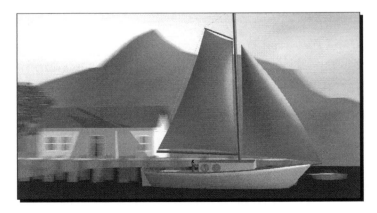

Motion blur is different than the node-based blurring that you did earlier. With node-based blurring, you render a frame and then the node compositor blurs that particular frame; the blurring is based on how far the objects are from the camera. With the motion blur, it depends on the motion of an object in relation to the camera. The camera was set to track the sloop, so the sloop did not get blurred, while the background did.

There are two controls for sampled motion blur: **Motion Samples** and **Shutter**. The shutter is like a camera shutter. It may open up for the entire duration of the frame or part of the duration of the frame. The motion samples tell you how the time is divided when the shutter is open. If a frame is like a whole cake, the shutter tells you how much of the cake is left, and the motion sample tells you how many pieces the remaining cake is cut into.

The following image shows you what happens in one frame. In this example, the motion samples are set to six. The shutter setting of 1.0 spreads the six samples evenly over the entire duration of the frame. With the 0.75 shutter setting, the six samples are taken from the first three quarters of the duration of the frame and none from the last quarter of the frame. With a 0.5 setting for the shutter, the six samples are taken from the first half of the duration of the shutter, and no samples are taken from the second half.

This also means that the more motion samples you specify, the longer it takes to render. Six motion samples take six times as long to render as one motion sample.

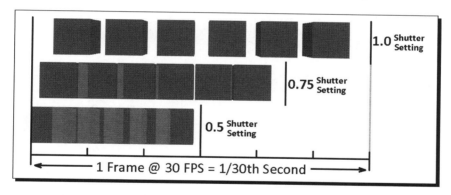

Well, you got a taste of motion blur. Now, go back into Blender and have some fun. First, try varying the number of motion samples and note the differences between the blurring. Next, vary the shutter settings. Then, vary both settings.

Then, find the **Empty.Camera** tracker object, use *Alt + P* to un-parent it from the sloop, and choose **Clear and Keep Transformation**. See how it looks when the sloop is blurred and the background remains sharp, or change the rate of travel of the sloop.

Planning your animation and making sure it comes out right

You've learned a lot, and now it's time to complete your project by animating a scene. You've learned to make keyframes, you've learned how to move objects, how to parent them, and how to change which editors are in which windows. You've studied how to plan an animation and how to time it. You know a lot!

Storyboarding your ideas

First, you need an idea. I started off with a question: what if the island got invaded by Viking raiders? I wondered what would be my initial reaction if I were in the front house when I discovered what was happening. The following is the storyboard I drew:

Have a go hero – making your storyboard

You can use your island or 49090S_11_Blender_Island.blend from the download pack. I made a Viking boat, 49090S_11_Viking_ship_subsurface.blend, which can be modified, or 49090S_11_Viking_ship_mesh.blend, which has been turned into a mesh already.

Use the sloop, any buildings, or just the haunted boat and the lagoon that we talked about in *Chapter 7, Planning Your Work, Working Your Plan*.

Laying out your animation

Now that you've got your animation planned, it's time to get back into Blender and set up the animation. For this exercise, I'll use the storyboard I drew. But you can also use your own if you like.

Time for action – laying out the animation

1. Open up `49090S_11_Blender_Island_Motion_Blur.blend` or use the world you have built.

2. What kind of lens should you use? Select the camera you will be using. Open the Object Data panel; the button has the movie camera on it. Set the lens by Focal Length or Field of View.

3. Now, time the scene. Get your stop watch. Act it out. Time each action; when you hear a shot, you run to the door, you turn the door knob, you open the door, you step through the door, you look at the boathouse, and then scan over to the right to see the sloop drifting.

4. Now, use your timings to animate the camera and door.

5. Animate the sloop. It's drifting and rotating in the water. What can you do with the sail and rudder to make it look more real?

6. Animate the Viking ship that is making a getaway, or animate the scene you have storyboarded.

What just happened?

For me, the first question was what kind of lens should I use for my camera: wide angle, telephoto, or...? I figured that I was trying to represent the hero of the animation, so choosing a camera that shows what a person would see was the best idea. I selected a 55 mm lens.

I took my stopwatch and timed out my reactions. I allowed 22 frames for the explosion sound, 5 frames to run across the room, and 3 frames of pause. While out of frame, I supposedly reached for the doorknob, and allowed 10 frames for the door to open, 9 frames of dollying the camera towards the boathouse as though I stepped out through the door, and then I rotated the camera over to the boat, ending at frame 70.

I set the sloop adrift, moving it a bit away from the dock and rotating it a little over 90 degrees, starting at frame 1 and ending at frame 120. Then, I realized that the main sail should be swinging and the rudder should be flattened to the hull as the boat drifts sideways. I remember spending time making the rudder swing along the angle of the hull, so I used the local rotations to get that to work.

The Viking ship was easy. I just laid it out behind the boat house and made a keyframe at the start of the animation. Then, I moved it so that it was almost past the breakwater at the end of the animation. Then, I found the time when it came closest to the end of the pier, put in a location keyframe, and moved it so that it missed the pier, and applied a rotation keyframe so the Viking ship rotated as it made the turn.

Some things that may help you are as follows:

- ◆ Have only the layers you need turned on.
- ◆ Right arrow and left arrow keys go one frame in the **Timeline** or **Graph Editor**.
- ◆ *Shift* + up arrow and *Shift* + down arrow keys go 10 frames.
- ◆ Up arrow and down arrow keys go to the next keyframe of the active object.

Proofing your work

There are four ways to proof your work before doing a full render:

- ◆ You can do a preview
- ◆ You can do a hardware render
- ◆ You can render just a portion of the frame
- ◆ You can tailor your rendering settings to make a quick render

Doing a preview

Once you have the rough animation laid out, it's easy to check your work. Putting the mouse over 3D View and pressing *Alt* + *A* is the easiest way. You learned about it in *Chapter 3, Controlling the Lamp, the Camera, and Animating Objects*. You can do it with **Viewport Shading** set to **Wireframe** or **Solid**. It will play more slowly and erratically the first time it loops through the animation. Watch it several times. Press *Esc* when you are done viewing the proof. If you want, you can use `49090S_11_Blender_Island_Motion_Blur.blend` to test the proofing. In the timeline window, set the end of the animation to frame `25`.

Using hardware rendering to see the motion

Hardware rendering uses advanced OpenGL commands to do a fast render without materials and textures. One unusual thing about this method of rendering is that it is window-based, not camera-based. The normal Blender render always renders what the active camera sees. The hardware render renders whatever is in the active window. One problem though, is that not all computers can do this kind of rendering. If your computer will not, you must load a newer version of OpenGL.

Here is an FAQ that may help you with any questions you have about OpenGL:

`http://www.opengl.org/wiki/FAQ`

Time for action – doing a hardware render

There are two buttons that control hardware rendering. They are on the right end of the 3D View header, as shown in the following screenshot. Unlike the regular rendering process, the hardware render will render any view, not just a camera view. It will render Texture, Solid, Wireframe, and Bounding Box shading but not full rendered shading, as given in the following steps:

1. Click on the camera symbol, as shown in the following screenshot, to render a single frame:

2. If your computer cannot do this, Blender will display the error message **Failed to create OpenGL offscreen buffer, unknown**.

3. Press the *7* on the NumPad key and then use the mouse to get a nice view. Click on the camera symbol to do another hardware render.

4. Select a different Viewport Shading mode. Click on the camera symbol to do another hardware render.

5. Click on the clapboard symbol, as shown in the preceding screenshot, to render an animation. To see the animated rendering, just press *Ctrl + F11*.

What just happened?

Hardware rendering is a separate kind of rendering with its own limitations and benefits. It's faster, and it can render the scene from any view, not just a camera view, but it won't give you a full quality rendering like Blender Internal or cycles render engines will. You learned how to use it.

Inspecting details by rendering only a part of the frame

You can save time by not rendering the entire image if you only need to check a portion of it.

Time for action – rendering only a part of the frame

It's pretty easy to render only a part of the frame, shown as follows:

1. Get a camera view in the 3D View window.

2. Press *Shift + B* and use the marquee, like the standard border select, to choose a portion of the frame in the camera image area.

3. Then, press *F12* to render it.

4. To return to rendering the entire window, press *Shift + B* and select the entire camera image area in the 3D View window. It will not change your camera settings if you select some of the passepartout area; you will just get the full camera image.

What just happened?

You learned to save time by only rendering a part of the frame. We covered earlier in this chapter that *Shift + B* allowed you to select part of a view to zoom into, using *Shift + B* in the **Camera** view lets you select a part of the whole frame to render. You can also use this trick to render animation with the *Ctrl + F12* command.

Taking a glimpse of what the animation will look like with the quick render

You also need to take a peek at the lighting and the textures. You have a couple of options: render selected frames, or do a test rendering of the animation as we did in *Chapter 3, Controlling the Lamp, the Camera, and Animating Objects*. Doing a test rendering of the animation is good. Just press *Ctrl + F12*.

After rendering about two frames though, you may begin to wonder how long it will take to do the whole render. The initial frames took about two minutes. Not too bad, but wait, two minutes times 300 frames equals 10 hours of rendering.

So what can you do to make the rendering time shorter?

Time for action – reducing render times

The basic idea here is to reduce the workload. You want to turn off everything that you don't need:

1. Move the mouse over the **Timeline** window and go to the **Current Editor type** button in the lower-left corner of the window.

2. Select **Text Editor** from the menu, as you learned in *Chapter 9, Finishing Your Sloop*.

3. Select **Text** in the **Text Editor** header and choose **Create Text Block** from the pop-up menu.

4. At the top of the UV/Image window, where the image is rendered, you will see the time that it took to render the frame. In the Text Editor, note that time.

5. In the Properties window header, select the **Render** button. It's the button with the still camera on it.

6. In the **Dimensions** subpanel, make sure that the **Resolution** percentage is no higher than **25%**.

7. In **Text Editor**, type **Reduced resolution from 100%** to 25%.

8. In the Properties window, the **Dimensions** subpanel sets the value of **Frame Step** under **Frame Range** to 2.

9. Select the **Frame Rate:** button and choose **Custom**.

10. Select the button that says **FPS: 24** and input 12.

11. In **Text Editor**, change **Changed Step** from **1** to 2, and **reduced Frame Rate from 24** to 12.

12. In the Properties window, in the **Anti-Aliasing** subpanel, uncheck the **Anti-Aliasing** checkbox.

13. In **Text Editor**, type Unchecked Anti-Aliasing.

14. If you had **Sampled Motion Blur** checked, uncheck it and note that in the **Text Editor**.

15. In the Properties window, in the **Shading** subpanel, uncheck the **Shadows**, **Subsurface Scattering**, and **Ray Tracing** checkboxes.

16. In **Text Editor**, type Unchecked Shadows, Subsurface Scattering, and Ray Tracing.

17. Save the file with a unique name. Press *F12* to test-render a frame.

18. In **Text Editor**, note the time it took to render.

19. In the Properties window, in the **Performance** subpanel, the next thing to do is to change the size of the **Tiles**. The tiles are those rectangles you see when you render an image. What setting works fastest depends on your computer and what CPU and GPU you have.

20. In **Text Editor**, note the **X:** and **Y:** dimensions of **Tile Size**. Now, you experiment. A smaller tile size will use less memory, and a larger tile size may render faster, but beyond a certain point, it will also overwhelm your CPU and / or GPU.

21. You can employ two strategies. Set the tile sizes to powers of 2; the default is 64 *x*, 64 *y*. Try going up to 128 x 128, or 256 x 256, and see what your results are.

22. Alternatively, divide your image sizes by 2, 4, 8, or 16. For me, the best result was with a tile size of 120 x 70, one-sixteenth of the original image size, or one-fourth of the 25% scale resolution we have just set up.

23. Enter the numbers, press *F12* to render the image, record the results in your text file, and see what works best for you. Try other settings and repeat.

24. When you have the lowest rendering time, save the file with a unique name.

25. Press *Ctrl + F12* to do your test-render. When it's done, press *Ctrl + F11* to view it.

What just happened?

You conquered quite a hurdle there. What started out as a 10-hour render for 300 frames, ended up taking only 15 minutes, and you still got a fairly good representation of what was going on. First, you cut the area rendered to 25 percent of the original size. This cut out 75 percent of the work. The other big thing you did was to render only every other frame and change the frame rate from 24 fps to 12 fps so that it will play at the right speed. This cut down half of the remaining work. So already, the work is reduced to 12.5 percent of the original. It also means the animation player can play the animation more easily. Then, you turned off a lot of the functions that took up computing time. You removed Anti-Aliasing that makes transitions between pixels smoother. You removed the shadows, subsurface scattering, and ray tracing, which makes the final image look better, but these are not needed now. Finally, you optimized the tile size to your computer. You are now ready to do a full test render to see what the animation will look like.

After you have done all your testing and experimenting and have the animation the way you want it, use the text in the Text Editor to guide you in putting all the settings back to what they were and do the final quality render. You will probably want to keep the tile size setting to its optimized size, though.

Reducing render times

The following are some sites with good tips on reducing rendering times:

- http://www.blenderguru.com/13-ways-to-reduce-render-times
- http://www.blenderguru.com/4-easy-ways-to-speed-up-cycles/
- http://www.youtube.com/watch?v=mbZ4PG135FM

Making corrections

Well, congratulations! Well done! Nobody makes a perfect animation the first time. However, the changes you implement will make it better. Press *Ctrl + F11* to watch the animation you have made. Watch it many times to see what you like or dislike. Remember the 12 principles of animation. Show it to your friends and get feedback. Then, make changes to your animation.

You have four basic tools to work with the animation:

- ◆ **3D View**: This window is used to reposition objects and create location, rotation, and scaling keyframes.

- ◆ **Timeline**: This window helps you maneuver through the animation timeline.

- ◆ **Graph Editor**: This window is good for adjusting the transitions between keyframes by modifying the control points and the control handles, as you learned to do in *Chapter 3, Controlling the Lamp, the Camera, and Animating Objects*.

- ◆ **Dope Sheet**: This is the best tool for changing the timing of keyframes.

You've studied the first three types of Blender editors; now, it's time for an introduction to the Dope Sheet editor.

Time for action – using the Dope Sheet

The Dope Sheet is descended from the animation timing sheets used by classic animators that we saw in *Chapter 7, Planning Your Work, Working Your Plan*. You can move, subtract, and add keyframes, but unlike the Graph Editor, you have no control of the Bézier curves that control the motion. The window controls are the same as the Graph Editor controls that you studied in *Chapter 3, Controlling the Lamp, the Camera, and Animating Objects*. The following steps will help you in using the Dope Sheet:

1. Open the file that you created when you compared dollying the camera to zooming the camera.

2. In 3D View, select the camera you dollied into the scene.

3. Move the cursor over the **Timeline Editor** window and go to the **Current Editor type** button in the lower-left corner of the window and click on it. Select **DopeSheet** from the menu.

4. Move the cursor to the border between the **DopeSheet** and the 3D View window next to it. Get the double-headed arrow, press the LMB, and use the mouse to make the **DopeSheet** editor larger.

5. You will see columns of diamonds on different layers, as shown in the following screenshot. They are the keyframes.

6. Press *Ctrl* + MMB and use the mouse to zoom in and out.

7. Press the MMB and use the mouse to pan left and right and up and down, so that you can see the keyframes well.

8. In the **DopeSheet** header, press the arrow that is to the left of the ghost. You may need to drag the header to the left to see the arrow button. Press it again and see how the channels displayed change. Press it until it only displays the keyframes of **Camera.Dolly**.

9. Select the triangle next to **Location** so that the **X Location**, **Y Location**, and **Z Location** channels become visible.

10. Press *A* to deselect all of the keyframes. The diamonds will become white.

11. Press *B* and use the cursor to select the **Y Location** keyframe and the **Z Location** keyframe on frame **20**, as shown in the following screenshot:

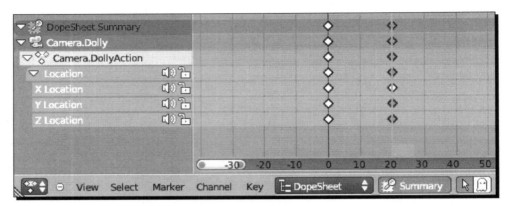

12. Press *Shift + D* to copy the keyframes and use the mouse to drag them to frame 30.

13. Press the RMB and select the **Y Location** keyframe at frame 30.

14. Press *G* and move the keyframe to frame 10. Press the LMB to release the move.

15. Select the Current Frame Indicator with the LMB. Scroll it backwards and forwards, and see how moving the keyframe has affected the camera motion.

16. Press the RMB and select the **Z Location** keyframe at frame 30.

17. Press *X* and delete the keyframe. Choose **Delete Keyframes** from the pop-up menu.

18. Move the Current Frame Indicator to a frame without keyframes and press *I*. Choose **Only Selected Channels** from the pop-up menu. You've made a new keyframe.

19. You can use *Ctrl + Z* if you didn't want those changes.

What just happened?

You were introduced to the Dope Sheet. The Dope Sheet comes in handy because often, if you have to adjust a keyframe, it's just a matter of moving the keyframe to a different frame without changing the value of the keyframe in that frame. You also saw that when you scrubbed the animation with the Current Frame Indicator, just moving the keyframe to a different frame can have dramatic results.

You played around with the Dope Sheet controls, so you know that they are very similar to the controls for other windows such as the Graph Editor window.

You may have noticed that when you copied a keyframe and moved it, there was a bar between the two diamonds. This indicates that the values of the two keyframes are the same.

Have a go hero – making corrections

One of the problems I noted when I rendered my scene was that the camera stayed on the boathouse for too long. I also found that the Viking ship started too late, and the viewer needed to be able to see a little of it as the hero runs out. I resolved the camera move by deleting some of the keyframes in the Dope Sheet to make the motion smoother. I needed to move the Viking boat closer to the shore. That meant redoing the keyframe in 3D View and then moving the timing of the keyframe in the Dope Sheet.

When making changes to the keyframes in 3D View, it's good to use the keyboard commands to navigate in the timeline, rather than dragging the Current Frame Indicator when modifying keyframes. This way, you land exactly on the keyframe. Using the Current Frame Indicator could land you part of the way through a frame, and you could make two keyframes in one frame, half a frame apart. It also ensures that all your keyframes are right on the frame, time-wise, and this will make better-looking animations.

So, go to it. Look at your test animation, analyze how you can improve it, and play with the keyframes. It's an iterative cycle, so change, preview, and repeat. Once you have implemented all the changes, go back, and using your text file as a guide, undo all the changes you made for the preview rendering and make a nice final version.

Pop quiz – lighting a scene

Here's a refresher from what you learned in the bonus chapter *Chapter 5A, Lighting a Small Boat*, to get your mind thinking about light again:

Q1. Which light controls how much light there is in a scene?

1. Key light.
2. Fill light.
3. Back light.

Q2. What is a texture added to a spot lamp called?

1. Screen.
2. Cookie.
3. Spot texture.

Improving performance

Q3. What does Tile Size refer to?

1. The size of your GPU versus the size of your CPU.
2. The area in pixels that the processor works on at any one point in time.
3. The percentage of the original resolution that you use during a test render.

The key-function table

Here are some of the keyboard shortcuts that you will find helpful in this chapter:

Key	Function
Ctrl + MMB	Using the mouse in the Dope Sheet, this zooms in or out on a range of keyframes.
MMB	Using the mouse in the Dope Sheet, this allows you to pan the range of keyframes that are displayed.
B	In the Dope Sheet, this lets you do a border select of keyframes.
RMB	In the Dope Sheet, this lets you select a single keyframe.
Shift + *D*	In the Dope Sheet, this lets you copy keyframes.
G	In the Dope Sheet, this lets you move selected keyframes.
X	In the Dope Sheet, this lets you delete selected keyframes.
I	In the Dope Sheet, this allows you to create a keyframe on the current frame.
LMB	In the Dope Sheet, this allows you to change the current frame.
Ctrl + MMB	Using the mouse in the Node Editor, this zooms in or out on the Node Editor window.
MMB	Using the mouse in the Node Editor, this allows you to pan the Node Editor window.
LMB	When holding down the LMB in the Node Editor, you can move nodes with the mouse.
Shift + *B*	In 3D View and the UV/Image editor, this allows you to do a border select and zoom in to the area selected.
Shift + *B*	In the 3D View's camera view, this allows you to select a portion of the image to render.

Summary

Well, you learned a lot on how to use a standard three-point lighting system and lots of variations of it. You experimented with falloff and got the control you need to highlight the action with light and put the rest into the shadows. You studied camera work, and discovered how to use wide-angle, normal, and telephoto lenses. You also created an animation and practiced making modifications and test renders.

In the next chapter, you will focus on rendering and compositing. With compositing, you'll learn how to use the Video Sequence Editor to edit your animation for best effects. You'll also revisit the Node Editor and learn how to create stereoscopic 3D as well as see the usage of the new cycles renderer that doesn't even need lamps.

Let's go!

12

Rendering and Compositing

In the previous chapter, you learned a lot about lighting, how to use a standard three-point lighting system, and lots of variations on it. You learned to use light to control what the viewer sees. You practiced using wide-angle, normal, and telephoto lenses. You also created an animation and practiced making modifications and test renders.

In this chapter, you will focus on rendering and compositing. You will also do the following:

◆ Edit scenes created on the island to tell a story using **Video Sequence Editor**

◆ Combine the stereographic views into a single 3D animation using the Node Editor

◆ Discover how to optimize your animations with the rendering controls

◆ Discover how using the Cycles renderer instead of the Blender internal renderer can improve and alter your 3D rendering and animation

Let's get started!

Getting ready

You will need the following files for your work in this chapter:

◆ Copy `4909OS_12_Fields.blend` from your download pack to the `Chapter 12/ Blender Files` directory

◆ Copy `Flashbang-Kibblesbob-899170896.mp3` from the `Audio` directory to your `Chapter 12/Audio` directory

- Copy 49090S_12_31.png from your download pack to your Chapter 12/Images directory

- Copy the entire Images/Video Strips directory from your download pack to the Chapter 12/Images/Video Strips directory for this chapter on your computer

- Get yourself a pair of red/cyan stereo glasses

Getting Red/Cyan glasses for the price of postage

If you do not have a pair of red/cyan glasses, you can get them for the price of postage at http://www.3dglassesonline.com/contact/free-sample-request.

You can also buy them at www.amazon.com for a little more. Just search for anaglyph glasses.

Editing with Video Sequence Editor

Video Sequence Editor is similar to many standard video editors. It allows you to combine the output from scenes, videos, still images, and audios. It also allows you to create transitions between them, apply filters, and create some special effects.

Time for action – preparing a scene in Video Sequence Editor

Now, you're going to lay in an audio track and two video tracks, and then do a dissolve between the video tracks:

1. Open a new file in Blender.

2. In the **Dimensions** subpanel of the Properties window, set **Resolution** to **X:** 512, **Y:** 512, and 100%.

3. In the Blender window header, just to the left of where it says **Default**, click on the button with the three boxes and choose **Video Editing** from the drop-down menu, as shown in the following screenshot:

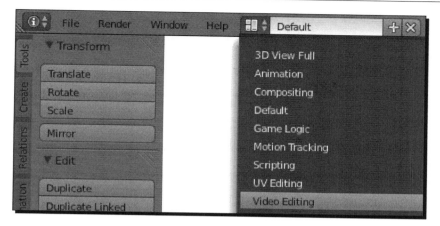

4. In the Video Editing layout, there are four windows: the **Graph Editor** window on the upper left; **Video Sequence Editor** on the upper right, set to display the video preview; **Video Sequence Editor** in the middle row, set to display the video layers; and the **Timeline** window at the bottom, as shown in the following screenshot:

5. In the header of the **Video Sequence Editor – sequencer** window, click on the **Add** button and choose **Movie** from the pop-up menu.

6. Find the Chapter 12/Images/Video Strips/ directory from your download pack and select Cam1_4909OS_12_0001-0300.avi with the LMB.

7. Click on the **Add Movie Strip** button in the upper-right corner of the window.

8. Now, there is a blue bar in the **Video Sequence Editor – sequencer** window, which represents the video track in the editor. Drag the Current Frame Indicator over the bar, and you will see the animation in the upper **Video Sequence Editor** window, as shown in the following screenshot. The Cam1 strip shows what the observer sees of the scene from the land.

9. Click on **View** in the **Video Sequence Editor – sequencer** window's header. Uncheck **Show Seconds** in the pop-up menu. Now, it displays the frame numbers.

10. Add the movie Cam2_4909OS_12_0001-0300.avi from the Chapter 12/ Images/Video Strips/ directory. The Cam2 strip shows the view from the Viking ship. Load it into **Video Sequence Editor**, the way you loaded the first strip.

11. Now, click on **Add** and choose **Sound** from the pop-up menu, and then select the audio strip named Flashbang-Kibblesbob-899170896.wav in Chapter 12/ Audio/. Click on the **Add Sound Strip** button in the upper-right corner of the window.

12. Now, to hear the explosion's sound, you have to do what you did in *Chapter 7, Planning Your Work, Working Your Plan*, when you timed the animation to the music. In the Timeline window at the bottom, select **Playback** on the header and check the checkbox next to **Audio Scrubbing** from the top of the pop-up menu, as shown in the following screenshot.

13. In the **Video Sequence Editor – sequencer** window, on the right side, is the Properties panel. Press *N* if you don't see it. Scroll down to the **Sound** subpanel and check the **Caching** checkbox to load the sound into RAM for a smooth playback and check the **Draw Waveform** checkbox. You can now see the waveform in the audio channel.

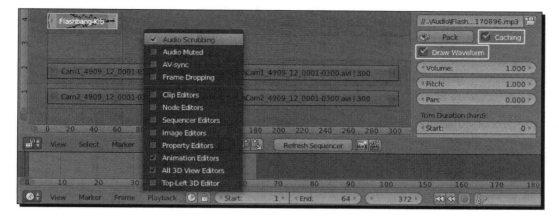

14. Move the cursor over the audio strip, press the RMB and hold it down, then use the mouse to drag the audio strip up to the fourth channel. Move the strip to the left so that its left side is at frame 1. There is a numerical readout to help you, as shown in the following screenshot. When you see the readout, you can release the RMB and just use the mouse to move the strip. Press the LMB to release the strip.

What just happened?

This should have been a little familiar to you from what you did in *Chapter 7, Planning Your Work, Working Your Plan*. But now, you also got introduced to the Video Editing screen layout and inserted video strips into **Video Sequence Editor**.

Working with video strips

Video strips are very flexible. You can stretch them, cut them in two, dissolve between them, add special effects to them, and tell stories with them.

Time for action – dissolving between video strips with Video Sequence Editor

The next stage is to manipulate the video channels, move them, trim them, and create a transition between them:

1. Move the **Cam1** strip to Channel 3.

2. Move the **Cam2** strip to Channel 1 and put its left side at frame 1. Press the LMB to release the move.

3. Move the **Cam1** strip to Channel 2. Put its left side at frame 1.

4. Select the Current Frame Indicator with the LMB and scrub it back and forth with the mouse.

5. Watch what happens in the **Video Sequence Editor – preview** window as you press the *H* key to mute the **Cam1** strip. When you press the **H** key while your cursor is over the **Video Sequence Editor – sequencer** window, the video channel is muted. With the strip muted, its image is no longer displayed.

6. Now, as you scroll the Current Frame Indicator, you'll only see the **Cam2** strip in the **Video Sequence Editor – preview** window, not the **Cam1** strip above it.

7. In the Timeline Editor window header, set the **End:** button to 64, as shown in the following screenshot:

8. Press *Alt + A* to preview the beginning of your video. Press *Esc* when you have watched and listened to it several times.

9. If you cannot see to the left of frame 0, there is a light gray scroll bar with numbers on it, on the bottom of **Video Sequence Editor**, which you can move to display different frames. Put the cursor over the scroll bar, press the LMB, and use the mouse to move it.

10. Select the **Cam2** strip in **Channel 1** with the RMB.

11. Look at the Properties panel of **Video Sequence Editor**. In the **Edit Strip** subpanel, you will see buttons that confirm that you are working in **Channel: 1** and this strip has a **Start Frame** of **1**.

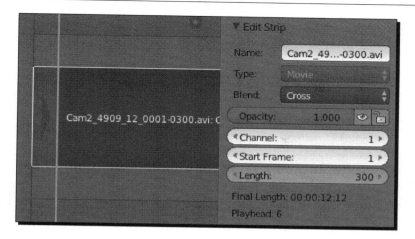

12. Press *G, X*, and use the mouse to move the left side of the **Cam2** strip in Channel 1 to frame -3. Look at the Properties panel of **Video Sequence Editor** and the **Edit Strip** subpanel for feedback on which frame the strip starts at. Press the LMB to release the move. Press *Alt + A* to preview the beginning of your video. Press *Esc* when you have watched and listened to it several times. It's just three frames, but the Viking ship seems to move in reaction to the blast now.

13. Use the **Video Sequence Editor** scroll bar, just above the header, to move the display so that you can see frame 300. On the right side of the **Cam2** strip, there is an arrow button. Click on the arrow with the RMB; hold it down till you start moving, then move that end to the left until the numerical indicator just above the arrow button says **58**. Press the LMB to release it.

14. Move the Current Frame Indicator to frame **47**, by either dragging it in the **Video Sequence Editor** window or typing 47 directly in the **Current Frame** button in the Timeline header.

15. Select the **Cam1** video strip in Channel 2 with the RMB. In the **Video Sequence Editor – sequencer** header, select **Strip** and choose **Unmute Strips** from the pop-up menu or press *Alt + H* to unmute the **Cam1** video strip. Then, press the RMB and hold it down while you begin moving it. Move it so that the left side of the strip is at frame 47. Press the LMB to release it.

16. Click on the **Cam2** video strip in Channel 1 with the RMB. Then, click on the **Cam1** video strip in Channel 2 with *Shift* + RMB to select them both.

17. In the **Video Sequence Editor – sequencer** header, select **Add** and then choose **Effect Strip** and **Cross** from the pop-up menus. The **Effect Strip** will appear in the overlap between the **Cam2** and **Cam1** strips, as shown in the following screenshot.

18. Select the Current Frame Indicator and scrub across the time with the **Cross** strip to see the transition between the two strips.

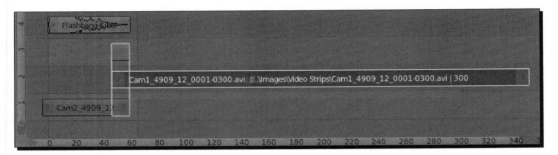

What just happened?

This is an easy method to select two video strips and put a dissolve between them. While adding an effect strip, the order in which the strips are chosen is important. While creating a dissolve, first you must choose the strip that is being dissolved from and second you must choose the strip that is being dissolved into.

If the dissolve does not behave properly, you can also try changing the **Blend** mode in **Video Sequence Editor**'s Properties panel from **Replace** to **Cross** and back to **Replace**. That should reset it properly.

Editorially, the big trick here is that when the Cam1 and Cam2 strips were animated and rendered, they actually started on the same frame, but during editing, they have been staggered 50 frames. You see the Viking ship move for the first 59 frames from the view of the ship, and then from the door, you see that the Viking Ship is just starting to move. Technically, during the transition, the Viking ship should already have moved behind the boathouse by the time you are looking from the door. But visually, this staggering of the motion gives the viewer a better idea of what is happening.

Changing Video Sequence Editor's resolution

When you edit a video, you should set **Resolution: X:** and **Y:** of your video in the **Dimensions** subpanel of the **Render** panel in the **Properties** window. Usually, this might be a setting for TV, HD, or a web banner. However, on some people's computers, Blender will only show an image in the preview window of **Video Sequence Editor** if the dimensions of the rendering resolution are powers of two, that is, **2**, **4**, **8**, **16**, **32**, **64**, **128**, **256**, **512**, **1024**, **2048**, and so on. If you have that problem, you can use **Video Sequence Editor** in one of these power-of-two settings so that you can see what is happening. Then, when you are ready to render the video out, you can change the rendering resolution to that of the original images. The videos used here were made at 512 x 512, just to avoid causing anyone problems.

Time for action – editing individual video strips

Now that you've gotten a video into **Video Sequence Editor**, you'll discover how to do some soft trims and dissolves to assemble them:

1. In **Video Sequence Editor**, move the Current Frame Indicator to frame **148**.

2. Select the **Cam2** video strip in Channel 1. Press *Shift + D* to make a copy. Move the copy to Channel 5.

3. Note that on the right-hand side of the new strip, there is a solid blue bar at the top, as shown in the following screenshot:

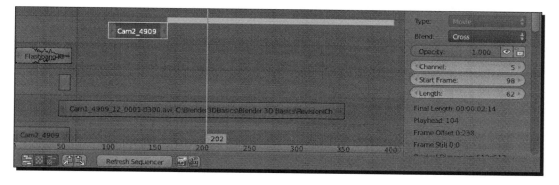

4. Use the *Ctrl + MMB* keys to scale the **Video Sequence Editor** window so that you can see the entire strip and/or the blue bar.

5. On the right side of the **Cam2** strip, there is an arrow button. Click the RMB over the arrow button on the right side of the strip. Hold it down while you start moving the mouse, and then move that end to the right until it is even with the end of the blue bar. The bar will disappear when you reach the end. Press the LMB to release it. Now, the strip is back to its original length.

6. In the Properties panel of **Video Sequence Editor**, in the **Strip Input** subpanel, note the **Trim Duration (soft)** buttons. A soft trim starts or ends a strip by hiding any frames beyond the Trim point, while a hard trim cuts the frames off. Therefore, if you think you might want to make changes at a later point, use the soft trim.

7. Press the RMB on the arrow button on the left-hand side of the strip, hold it down till you start moving, then move that end to the right until the **Trim Duration (soft)** button in the **Strip Input** subpanel reads **Start: 71**, as shown in the following screenshot. Press the LMB to release it.

8. If you cannot get frame 71 exactly, press the LMB to stop changing **Trim Duration** and use *Ctrl* + MMB and *Shift* + MMB to zoom in and pan the **Video Sequence Editor** window, and then resume with the changing of **Trim Duration**.

9. In the Properties panel of **Video Sequence Editor**, move the scroll bar up so that you can see the **Edit Strip** subpanel. Note the **Length** button.

10. Click the RMB on the arrow button on the right-hand side of the strip, hold it down till you start moving, and then move that end to the left until the **Length** button reads **90**. Press the LMB to release it.

11. Move the Current Frame Indicator to frame **148**.

12. Select the strip in its center with the RMB. Press *G*, *X*, and move the strip so that the left-hand side of the strip is at frame **148**, as shown in the following screenshot. Press the LMB to release it.

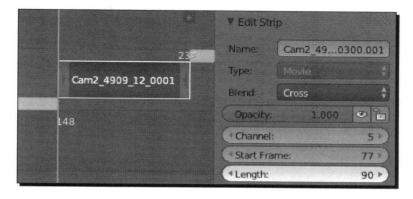

13. Press *Shift* + up arrow twice, and then press the right arrow key once to move the Current Frame Indicator by 21 frames.

14. Select the right end of the **Cam1** strip in Channel 2 with the RMB and move it so that the strip ends at the Current Frame Indicator. Press the LMB to release the movement.

15. Select **Cam2** in Channel 5 using *Shift* + RMB so that the strips in Channel 2 and 5 are both selected.

16. In the **Video Sequence Editor** header, select **Add** and then choose **Effect Strip** and **Cross** from the pop-up menus.

17. Your channels should look similar to that shown in the following screenshot:

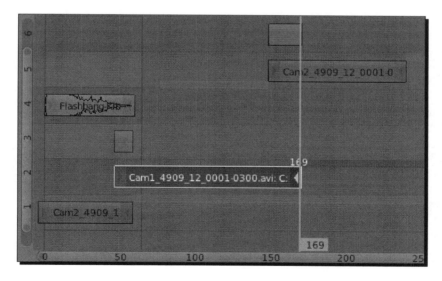

18. In the Timeline window header, set the **End** value to **238**. Press *Alt* + *A* to preview the animation.

What just happened?

You learned how to trim video segments by modifying the length of the strip in the channel. In addition, you now have an edited scene. Congratulations!

This part of the scene was done with just simple cuts, two strips of the video, and a cross dissolve. Nevertheless, it tells the story. In addition, if you watch carefully, with the camera pan and the motion of the Viking boat, the land always appears to be moving right to left, so your eye follows the flow of the motion smoothly from strip to strip.

Time for action – using K and Shift + K to make your trims

In addition to adjusting the ends of your strips, you can use the *K* and *Shift + K* commands to shorten your film strips. The command is easy to remember; just think of a knife for cutting the strips:

1. Select the **Cam1** video strip in Channel 2. Press *Shift + D* to make a copy. Move the copy to Channel 7.

2. In the **Video Sequence Editor** header, select **Strip**. Choose **Clear Strip Offset** from the pop-up menu.

3. Scroll Current Frame Indicator over the new strip. Move it with the mouse, and watch the **Video Sequence Editor – preview** window. Scroll until you see the Viking ship emerge from behind the pier and until the last shield on the far side of the ship is visible. You can use *Ctrl + MMB* to zoom into the preview image if you can't see the shields on the Viking boat.

4. With the cursor over the **Video Sequence Editor – sequencer** window, press *K* to do a soft trim. Select the strip to the left of the Current Frame Indicator and press *X* to delete it.

5. Move the Current Frame Indicator to frame 227.

6. Move the strip in Channel 7 so that the left-hand side of the strip is at frame 227. Once you start moving it, press the MMB to restrict the motion to that channel.

7. Scrub the Current Frame Indicator until you see the Viking ship touch the sloop in the **Cam1** strip in Channel 7.

8. Select the **Cam2** strip in Channel 5. Press *Shift + D* to duplicate it. Move the duplicate to Channel 8, as shown in the following screenshot:

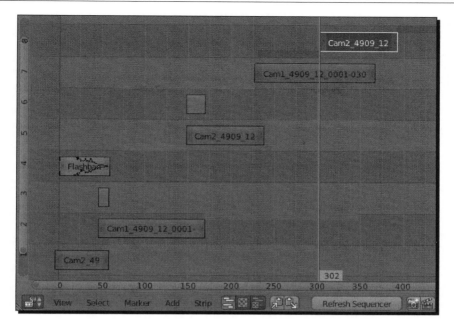

9. In the **Video Sequence Editor** header, select **Strip**. Choose **Clear Strip Offset** from the pop-up menu.

10. In the Properties panel of **Video Sequence Editor**, scroll to the **Edit Strip** subpanel and set the **Opacity** button to about 0.500.

11. Press the RMB to start moving the strip within the channel. Press the MMB to lock the motion to that channel.

12. Move the strip until you see the bow of the sloop pointing right at you in the **Video Sequence Editor – preview** window. Press the LMB to release the strip.

13. Press *Shift + K* to do a hard trim.

14. Select the portion of the strip to the left of Current Frame Indicator with the RMB. Press *X* to delete it.

15. Select the portion of the strip to the right of Current Frame Indicator with the RMB. In the Properties panel of **Video Sequence Editor**, scroll to the **Edit Strip** subpanel and set the **Opacity** button to 1.000.

16. If you want, you can see what happens when you do a hard trim. Press the RMB on the left side of the strip and move it left. It gets longer; however, if you scrub the Current Frame Indicator, because it is a hard trim, there are no more frames. Press *Ctrl + Z* a couple of times to put the strip back the way it was.

What just happened?

You discovered new ways to trim the length of a video strip. Instead of grabbing the triangle at the end of the strip, you can move the Current Frame Indicator to a certain point on a strip and press *K* to do a soft trim to achieve the same result. A strip can be restored to its original length with the **Clear Strip Offset** button. You also learned to press *Shift + K* to do a hard trim on the strip, which breaks a strip into two independent strips that share no frames, and cannot be undone with the **Clear Strip Offset** button.

You also discovered a neat trick in setting up the locations of the two video strips. You can temporarily make the upper layer partially transparent so that you can view both the layers and match up their actions.

Completing the scene in the Video Sequence Editor

With two camera angles and cross-cutting between the views, you have made an interesting and dynamic short video. Now, it's time to finish up this scene and prepare it for rendering.

Time for action – finishing the video sequence

Good. You are getting a solid understanding of how to assemble clips. Now, you'll learn to create a hold and fade the scene to black:

1. Move the Current Frame Indicator until you see the sloop centered between the last two shields of the Viking ship.

2. Select the **Cam1** video strip in Channel 2. Press *Shift + D* to make a copy. Move the copy to Channel 9.

3. In the **Video Sequence Editor** header, select **Strip**. Choose **Clear Strip Offset** from the pop-up menu or press *Alt + O*.

4. Begin to move the strip and press the MMB to keep the motion within the channel. Move the strip until the stern of the Viking ship disappears behind the sloop in the **Video Sequence Editor – preview** window. Press the LMB to release the strip.

5. Select the strips in Channel 8 and Channel 9.

6. Press *K*. Select the left-side strip in Channel 9 and the right-side strip in Channel 8. Delete them both.

7. Move the Current Frame Indicator to the last frame of the strip in Channel 9. Press the left arrow button 3 times to back up 3 frames. In the **Timeline** window header, set **End** to 440.

8. Don't move the Current Frame Indicator, but grab the right end of the **Cam1** strip in Channel 9 with the RMB and drag it to frame 440 as shown in the following screenshot:

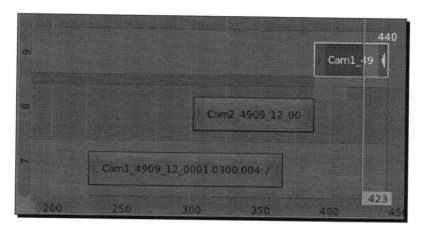

9. In the **Video Sequence Editor** header, select **Add**. Choose **Effects Strip** and then **Color** from the pop-up menus.

10. Move the new **Effects Strip** from Channel 1 to Channel 10. Move the right side of the **Effects Strip** to frame 440. Make sure that the Current Frame Indicator is still at frame 420.

11. In the **Edit Strip** subpanel of **Video Sequence Editor**, set **Opacity** to 0. With the cursor over the **Opacity** button, press *I* to create an opacity keyframe.

12. Move the Current Frame Indicator to frame **440**. Set **Opacity** to 1. With the cursor over the **Opacity** button, press *I* to create an opacity keyframe.

13. In the Timeline window, set **End** to 440. Press *Alt + A* to view the video sequence. Press *Esc* when you are done viewing it.

What just happened?

Again, you got more use out of those two video strips. However, since the action of the Cam1 strip ran out before the end of the video, you dragged the end frame to 440 and created a freeze frame between frames 423 and 440. Then, you added a color effects strip, and put keyframes at the start and end to create a fade to black.

Optimizing render settings

Most of the **Blender Internal Renderer** settings apply to the **Compositor** and **Sequencer** as well as the 3D scene. Now that you have created an animation, it's time to render it out.

Time for action – getting ready to render

We will leave **Video Sequence Editor** and return to the **Default** Blender window arrangement to set Blender to render your animation:

1. In the top row of the Blender window, select the button to the left of **Video Editing**. Select **Default** from the drop-down menu.

2. Click on the **Render** button in the Properties window header. It is the button with the still camera on it.

3. In the **Output** subpanel, click on the folder symbol on the right side of the text input box. Find the `Chapter 12` directory on your computer. Give your output file a name. Click on the **Accept** button.

4. Click on the button that says **PNG**, and select **MPEG** from the **Movie** menu.

5. In the **Encoding** subpanel, press the button next to **Format**. Set the format to **MPEG-1**. Select the button next to **Audio Codec**. Set **Audio Codec** to **MP3**.

6. If you are using a Mac, you should start with the **Quicktime** settings in the next table.

7. Save the file with a unique name. Press *Ctrl + F12* to render the sequence.

8. Press *Ctrl + F11* to play the animation you have just rendered. The Blender Player does not support audio. These settings were optimized for Windows Media Player so that you could be able to play it and listen to your work in the Windows Media Player. Other settings will make it playable in the player that you have on your system.

9. You may want to experiment with different output types. The following table has some different settings for different output types and players:

File format	Encoding format	Codec	Audio codec	Output type	Player
MPEG	MPEG-1		MP3	`.mpg`	Windows Media Player
MPEG	QuickTime	MPEG-4	MP3	`.mov`	QuickTime
MPEG	AVI	MPEG-2	MP3	`.avi`	Windows Media Player
MPEG	MPEG-4		MP3	`.mp4`	DivX
MPEG	H.264		MP3	`.avi`	Windows Media Player

What just happened?

You learned how to set up to render a video with sound to a .mp4, .mov, or .avi file.

Making stereographic 3D with the Node Editor

You've already used the Node Editor when you created depth of field in the previous chapter. Now, it's time to get a little bolder and use it to create stereographic 3D images, which will use the Node Editor's ability to modify an image.

Since red-cyan anaglyph glasses are an inexpensive way to get the 3D separation when viewing an image, you are going to turn the right and left eye images into a red image and a cyan image and then composite them.

The stereographic images were created with the boat and oars that you made in *Chapter 6, Making and Moving the Oars*. They were recorded with a stereo rig adapted from the one you made in the bonus chapter, *Chapter 6A, Using Stereographic Cameras* and were then dropped into the world created in *Chapter 10, Modeling Organic Forms, Sea, and Terrain*.

Time for action – creating the red image for the left eye

You will now use the **Node Editor** to create the Red channel, which shows what the left camera recorded and what your left eye will see:

1. Open a new file in Blender.

2. In the **Dimensions** subpanel of the **Properties** window, set the **Resolution** to **X:** 512, **Y:** 512, and 100%. Set the **End:** option in **Frame Range** to 64. Click on the **Frame Rate** button. Select **Custom** from the drop-down menu. Set **FPS** to 12.

3. In the top Blender window header, just to the right of **Default**, select the button with the three boxes and choose **Compositing** from the drop-down menu.

4. There are three windows: the Node Editor window on the top, the UV/Image Editor on the lower left, and the 3D View on the lower right, as shown in the following screenshot:

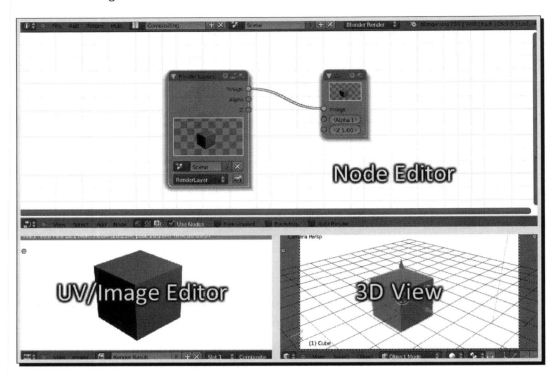

5. In the Node Editor window's header, look at the three graphic buttons just to the right of the word **Node**. They select the Node tree type that is active. Make sure the center of the three buttons is highlighted as shown in the following screenshot. It has the photo icon.

6. This is the **Compositing: tree** type. Check the **Use Nodes** checkbox as shown in the following screenshot. This displays the Render Layer and Compositing nodes.

7. In the **Node Editor** header, select **Add** and then choose **Input** and then **Image** from the pop-up menus.

8. With the mouse, move the **Image** node over to the upper left. Click the LMB to release the node.

9. Press the **Open** button at the bottom of the node and select the `boat_` `stereo_4909OS_12_L_0001.png` file from the `Chapter 12/Images/Video Strips/` directory of your download pack. Press the **Open Image** button in the upper-right corner of the **File Browser** window.

10. Select the button that is labeled **Single Image**. Choose **Image Sequence**. Set the **Frames** button to `64`.

11. If you need to zoom out or pan the **Node Editor** window, you can use the standard *Shift* + MMB and *Ctrl* + MMB commands.

12. Select the **Render Layers** node with the RMB. Press *X* to delete the node.

13. Move the cursor over the yellow dot on the right side of the **Image** node. Press the LMB and drag the connecting cord over to the yellow dot on the left side of the Composite node. Release the LMB.

14. In the **Node Editor** header, select **Add** and choose **Color**, and then select **RGB Curves** from the pop-up menus.

15. Move the new node between the **Image** node and the **Composite** node until you see the connecting cord turn orange. Blender should connect in between them automatically when you release the node.

16. Click on the shiny sphere on the upper-right corner of the Composite node to see the image.

17. In the **RGB Curves** node, there are four buttons in the upper-left, labeled **C, R, G,** and **B**. Click on the **G** button. It controls the Green channel.

18. There is a diagonal line in the graph box below those buttons. Move the cursor over the upper-right corner of the diagonal line. Press the LMB and hold it down while you move the mouse down and drag the upper-right corner of the diagonal to the lower-right corner of the graph box so it disappears, as shown in the center of the following screenshot. Notice the color change in the **Composite** node.

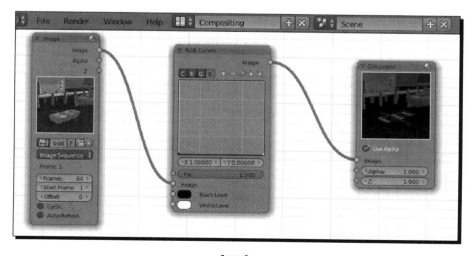

19. Click on the **B** button. It controls the Blue channel.

20. Drag the upper-right corner of the diagonal to the lower-right corner of the graph box as you did in the Green channel.

21. Note that in the **Composite** node, the image is now red, as shown in the previous screenshot.

22. Save the file with a unique name.

What just happened?

You opened up Blender and chose the **Compositing** setup. Selecting **Use Nodes** in the **Node Editor** displays the **Render Layer** and **Composite** nodes. The **Render Layer** node also links rendering and compositing.

You are not using **Render Layer**, so its node is deleted. You loaded the images of the boat being rowed, based on the animations made in the bonus chapter, *Chapter 6A, Using Stereographic Cameras*. I made them fancy by dropping them into the island scene that was made in *Chapter 10, Modeling Organic Forms, Sea, and Terrain*, but the motion is the same.

You loaded in the first frame of the sequence for the left-eye view, and told Blender how many frames there were in the sequence. Then, you added the **RGB Curves** node to process the images. The left channel is the Red channel. In the **RGB Curves** node, you modified the Green and Blue channels by adjusting their levels so that only the Red channel shows up. This can be seen in the **Composite** node.

Now, it's time to make the Cyan channel. You will use a different method to change the image from a full color to a shade of cyan, but the end result is the same as with the method you just used.

Time for action – making the right-eye view

This time, rather than adjusting the levels of a particular channel, you will just remove the Red channel:

1. Zoom out in the **Node Editor** window to allow yourself some more room to work or pan the window.

2. In the **Node Editor** header, select **Add** and choose **Input**, and then select **Image** from the pop-up menus.

3. Move the node over to the lower left. Press the LMB to release the node. Move the cursor to the right side of the **Image** node. When the double-headed arrow appears, hold down the LMB and move the mouse to the right to enlarge the node. Zoom in some if you need to.

4. Press the **Open** button and select the `boat_stereo_4909OS_12_R_0001`.png file from the `Chapter 12/Images/Video Strips/` directory of your download pack. Press the **Open Image** button in the upper right.

5. Select the button that is labeled **Single Image**. Choose **Image Sequence** from the pop-up **Source** menu. Set the **Frames** button to 64.

6. In the **Node Editor** header, select **Add** and then choose **Convertor** and **Separate RGBA** from the pop-up menus. Move it below the **RGB Curves** node.

7. Move the mouse over the yellow **Image** connector on the upper-right corner of the **Image** node. Press the LMB down and drag the connection to the **Image** connector on the lower-left corner of the **Separate RGBA** node.

8. In the **Node Editor** header, select **Add** and choose **Convertor** and **Combine RGBA** from the pop-up menu. Move it to the right of the **Separate RGBA** node and between the **RGB Curves** and the **Composite** nodes, as shown in the next screenshot.

9. Use the *Ctrl* + MMB and *Shift* + MMB controls to zoom into the **Separate RGBA** and **Combine RGBA** nodes.

10. Move the mouse over the **G** connector on the right side of the **Separate RGBA** node. Press the LMB down and drag the connection to the **G** connector on the left side of the **Combine RGBA** node, as shown in the next screenshot.

11. Move the mouse over the **B** connector on the right side of the **Separate RGBA** node. Connect it to the **B** connector on the left side of the **Combine RGBA** node, as shown in the following screenshot:

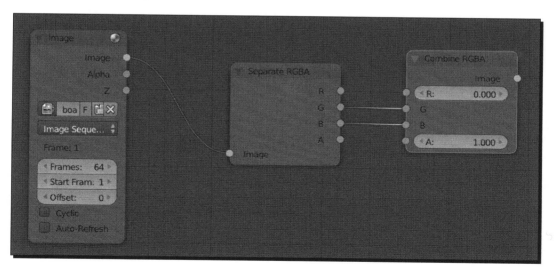

12. Do not do this for the **R** connector or the **A** connector.

13. Zoom back out so you can see all of the nodes.

14. Look at the connection between the **RGB Curves** node and the **Composite** node. Move your mouse above the connector. Hold the *Ctrl* button and the LMB down, and you will see a knife cursor. With the buttons still held down, move the cursor across the connector to cut the connector, as shown in the following screenshot:

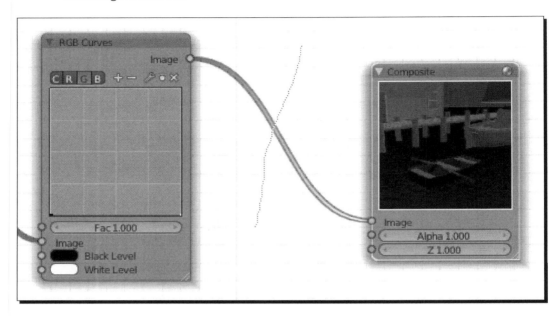

15. Connect the yellow **Image** connector on the upper-right corner of the **RGB Curves** node to the **R** connector on the upper-left corner of the **Combine RGBA** node, as shown in the following screenshot.

16. Connect the yellow **Image** connector on the upper-right of the **Combine RGBA** node to the yellow **Image** connector on the lower-left corner of the **Composite** node, as shown in the following screenshot:

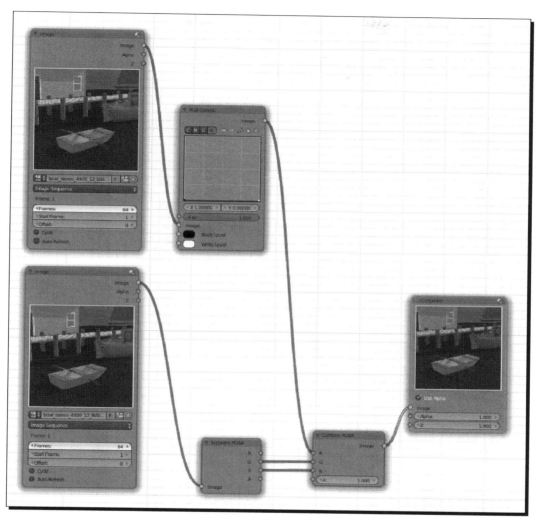

17. Press *F12*. In **UV/Image Editor**, you can see the composited image as shown in the next image. Note that you can see how the two separate images are combined and the differences between the red and cyan channels, especially with the seats of the boat and the edges of the window of the building.

18. Save the file with a unique name.

19. Press *Ctrl + F12* and render the whole sequence.

20. When it's done, pop on your red/cyan glasses. Press *Ctrl + F11* and enjoy the animation.

What just happened?

You just composited an image with the Node Editor. The Red channel of the image was created with an RGB Curves node, and you turned the Green and Blue channels down to zero. The Cyan channel, Green plus Blue, was created with a separate RGBA node, and then only the green and the blue ones were carried over and then combined with the red one by using a Combine RGBA node.

Alternatively, you could have created the Red channel by using a Separate RGBA node, or created the Cyan channel by using the RGB Curves node and turning the Red channel to zero instead of turning down the Green and Blue channels. It would work either way as long as you got the Red channel from the left camera and the Green and Blue channels from the right camera.

Time for action – making a cross-eye stereo image

Another way to do stereo viewing is the cross-eye stereo, like the image of the five Suzannes that we showed in the bonus chapter, *Chapter 6A, Using Stereographic Cameras*. You can make an animated version as well in **Video Sequence Editor**:

1. Open a new file. In the Properties window, set the resolution to `1024 x 512` and `100%`. Next, choose the **Video Editing** screen layout.

2. Add the image `49090S_12_31.png` from the `Chapter 12/Images/` directory to **Channel 1** of **Video Sequence Editor**. It's an all-black graphic of the same size as the resolution you just set.

3. Add the left-eye stereo images from the Video Strips directory to **Channel 2**. The easiest way to select them is to press *B* and do a border select of the files you want. Move the left side of the strip in Channel 2 to frame 1.

4. Check the **Image Offset** checkbox in the **Strip Input** subpanel of the **Video Sequence Editor**'s Properties panel. Set the **X** offset to `0`. Drag the right side of **Channel 1** so that it is as long as **Channel 2**.

5. Select **Channel 1** and then **Channel 2**. Add an **Effects Strip** of the type **Alpha Over** and put it in **Channel 3**.

6. Add the right-eye stereo images to **Channel 4**. Check the **Image Offset** check box in the **Video Sequence Editor**'s Properties panel. Set the **X** offset to **512**.

7. Select **Channel 3** and then **Channel 4**. Add an **Effects Strip** of the type **Alpha Over** and put it in **Channel 5**. In the timeline, set the end of the video to the length of your image strip. Press *Alt + A* to run the preview. Cross your eyes and stare at the animation until you see a third image between the two views.

8. Change to the **Default** window layout. In the **Render** panel of the **Properties** window, open the **Post Processing** subpanel and uncheck the **Compositing** checkbox. Leave the **Sequencer** checkbox checked.

9. Press *Ctrl + F12* to render a stereo animation. Then, when it is rendered, press *Ctrl + F11*, sit back, cross your eyes, and watch.

10. Save the Blender file with a unique name.

What just happened?

You learned a bit more about using **Video Sequence Editor**, and in doing so, you were able to make true color 3D animations. The black graphic established the size of the video for **Video Sequence Editor**. You had to add offsets to the left and right eye channels or Blender would attempt to spread them across the entire image.

Well done! Professional stereographic films are just in their infancy. Directors are learning to use the spacing of the lenses as they use a focal length to tell their stories. They don't just set the cameras apart and go. If you watch them carefully, you'll see that they are always changing them subtly to bring you closer to a scene or out for emotional effect.

Rendering your animations

All right, you've made a scene, you've animated it, and done your fast test renders. You're ready for a final render.

Making your computer ready to render

The first thing to do when you are ready to render is open up your file manager, and make sure you have room on your computer to do it. I can't tell you how much room you'll need for a given project, and the rule of thumb is to clear off as much space as you possibly can. It's a good time to save copies of all those projects you are no longer working on and then delete them from your hard drive. Back them up to data sticks and flash drives or one of the following:

- ◆ An external hard drive
- ◆ A CD or DVD
- ◆ Your storage on the Web

You may also want to use a program like CCleaner, for Windows, to clean up your computer's file registry and remove temporary files from browsers. Go into your Internet browser as well and manually delete the history if you don't have a program which does that. There are programs like DaisyDisk for the Mac and similar ones for Linux.

In addition, if you are running Windows, you may want to use a defragmenting program to make sure that all of your disk is as neat as possible and that the open spaces are as large as possible so Blender has room to move.

Making rendering more beautiful

In the previous chapter, you turned off a lot of things to make the rendering faster. Now, it's time to turn them back on if you need them. But, you want to know what they do.

Using Anti-Aliasing for more beautiful renderings

Aliasing is a jagged line that happens at the edge between two faces when Blender tries to display them. **Anti-Aliasing** blurs this edge for a better look. It is pronounced "An Tea A Lee SS ing".

Time for action – displaying aliasing

The best way to understand aliasing is to see it using the following steps:

1. Create a new file in Blender.

2. Press *F12*.

3. Press *Ctrl* + MMB and use the mouse to zoom into the rendered image so that you can see only the corner of the cube closest to you. It should look like the following image on the left.

4. In the **Anti-Aliasing** subpanel of the Properties window, uncheck the **Anti-Aliasing** checkbox.

5. Press *F12*.

6. Now, what you see looks like the right half of the following image, with a jagged line where different surfaces meet.

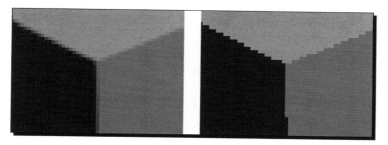

What just happened?

When you unchecked the **Anti-Aliasing** checkbox and rendered the cube, the three sides of the cube you could see were different shades, and the edge between them was jagged with no shading, as shown on the right. These jagged lines are called **Jaggies** and should be avoided. When you turned back on the Anti-Aliasing, the edges are less jagged, with lots of interim shades at the edges, as shown on the left. This looks cleaner to your eye, but it takes longer to render. That was why, in the previous chapter, you were instructed to turn off Anti-Aliasing to get quicker test renders.

Getting realism with subsurface scattering

If you've ever held your hand up to a strong light and seen the light shine through it, that's **subsurface scattering**. It's the light that bounces off layers below the surface of an object and is important for doing photo-realistic work. You'll learn more about it as you use Blender.

Time for action – using subsurface scattering

Now, Suzanne will help you learn the basics of subsurface scattering:

1. Open up a new file.

2. Select the lamp. In the Properties panel, select the **Object Data** button, with the lamp on it. In the **Lamp** subpanel, change the lamp type to **Spot**.

3. In the **Spot Shape** subpanel, change **Spot Size** to 25 degrees.

4. In the 3D View, select the default Cube. Press *X* to delete it. Press *Shift + A* to create a new object, and choose **Mesh** and **Monkey** off the pop-up menus.

5. In the **Properties** panel header, select the **Materials** button. Click on the **New** button to create a material. Press *F12* to render the image.

6. In the **Subsurface Scattering** subpanel, check the **Subsurface Scattering** check box. Open up the panel. Select the button right below the subpanel title and choose **Skin 1** from the drop-down menu.

7. Press *F12* to render the image. Press *Esc* when you are finished looking at the image. Suzanne has a nice translucent feel.

8. Save the file with a unique name.

9. In the Properties panel header, select the **Render** button with the still camera.

10. Open the **Shading** subpanel. Render the file several times, check and uncheck the **Subsurface Scattering** checkbox between renders, and notice the differences in the rendered image.

What just happened?

As a quick test, you gave Suzanne a material that included subsurface scattering settings. That had quite a profound effect. Her flat gray shading became warm, and you could see how the light passed through her head and ear.

Putting a sparkle on your animations with ray tracing

Ray tracing is a method Blender uses to figure out which objects should be lit and how much light they receive. It is especially good for rendering shiny or transparent objects. You know that real light comes from the sun and bounces around. It reflects off of objects such as cars and trees, and finally comes into your eye. Whatever object(s) the light has bounced off of has colored the light. So if you look at a car, you see the green color of a leaf, or your own reflection added to the color of the car. This is the perfect way to calculate light. It only has one problem. Most of the light doesn't go into your eye. So while it gives perfect results, it's a horribly wasteful way to calculate light for computer graphics.

To get around this, a man named *Arthur Appel* suggested doing it backwards. Follow a ray of light from your eye out into the world and see what it bounces off. You can choose how many times it bounces. If you were looking at the hood of a car, you'd see the color of the car because the light bounced off of the car, but you'd also see your own reflection because the light from the sun bounced off of you and onto the car and then back into your eyes.

Ray tracing lets Blender know what should be reflected on any given surface. It gives excellent results, but it can take a long time to calculate the scene, chasing down all these light rays. So what you do is control the time required to render a scene by limiting the light to a certain number of bounces after it leaves your eye.

Time for action – seeing ray tracing

In the following steps, you'll see ray tracing in action demonstrated with three simple spheres:

1. Open up a new file.
2. Delete the default cube.
3. Press *Shift + A*. Create **UV Sphere** from the **Add Mesh** menu.
4. In the 3D View Tool Shelf, click on the tab for the **Tools** subpanel, and set **Shading** to **Smooth**.
5. Press *0* on the NumPad to get the Camera view.
6. Press *Shift + D* to make a copy of the sphere. Move the new sphere to the right and release it next to the original.
7. In the **Properties** window, choose the **Material** button from the header.
8. Click on the **New** button and set the color in the **Diffuse** subpanel to red.
9. Select the original sphere again.
10. Press *Shift + D* to make a copy. Move the new sphere next to the original one on the left.
11. In the Properties window, click on the **New** button and set the color in the **Diffuse** subpanel to blue.
12. Select the center sphere again.
13. In the Properties window, click on the **New** button to create a new material.
14. In the **Mirror** subpanel, check the **Mirror** checkbox and set the value of the **Reflectivity** button to 0.5. Expand the panel if you don't see the button.

15. Press *F12*. You'll see the red and blue spheres reflected in the center sphere, as shown in the following screenshot:

16. Select the **Render** button in the Properties window header. It's the button with a still camera on it. Save the file with a unique name.

17. In the **Shading** subpanel, uncheck the **Ray Tracing** checkbox.

18. Press *F12* to render. The reflections are gone, as shown in the following screenshot:

What just happened?

You created three spheres and gave the center one a mirror property. When you had ray tracing on, the spheres on either side and their highlights were reflected on the center sphere because you had set its reflectivity to 0.5. When ray tracing was off, there was no reflection.

Choosing the proper number of tiles

I hope you took the time in *Chapter 11, Improving Your Lighting and Camera Work*, to test and discover which Tile settings worked best in your computer. If not, go back and discover what works best on your machine. For the fastest render times, use this setting whether you are doing a quick render or a final render.

Using alpha channels

When Blender renders a scene, it creates four channels of image data. Three of them contain the familiar red, green, and blue information for each pixel. The fourth is the **alpha channel**. Instead of telling you how red, green, or blue something is, the alpha channel tells you how transparent something is.

Time for action – exploring the alpha channel

As you have shades of red, green, and blue, you also have shades of the alpha channel. The darker the shade of alpha, the closer its value is to zero, and the more transparent that pixel is:

1.   Press *Esc* to return to the 3D View window. Select the red sphere with the RMB.
2.   In the Properties window, choose the **Material** button from the header.
3.   In the **Transparency** subpanel, check the **Transparency** checkbox and set **Alpha** to **0.4**.
4.   In the 3D View, press *Shift + D* to duplicate the red sphere. Move the duplicate sphere a bit, so that both overlap, but you can see more than half of each sphere, as shown in the next screenshot.
5.   Select the **Render** button in the Properties window header.
6.   In the **Shading** subpanel, check the **Ray Tracing** checkbox.
7.   Press *F12* and the render will look similar to the following screenshot.
8.   Press *Esc* when you are done looking at it.

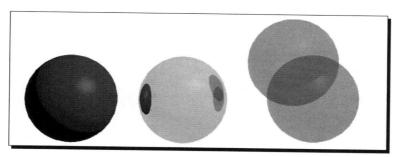

What just happened?

The alpha channel records how transparent an object is. You took one sphere and gave it a 40% transparency setting. The 100% transparency setting is solid and 0% is perfectly transparent. Then, you duplicated it and moved the copy so that the two transparent spheres overlapped and then rendered everything. Where the spheres overlap, they combine to be **80%** solid. Where they don't overlap, they are only **40%** solid. More light goes through the red spheres and doesn't bounce off. Their reflection on the center sphere is dimmer than that of the blue sphere. If you look at the glass material made for the sloop's portals and the house's windows, you will find that the transparency has been used.

Time for action – using transparency in the Video Sequence Editor

In addition to making objects transparent in relation to other objects, the transparency that you see in a scene is also used in **Video Sequence Editor** and **Node Editor**. Here is an example in **Video Sequence Editor**:

1. Move the mouse to the border between the 3D View window and the **Timeline** window. When you get the double-headed arrow, move the border up so that about a quarter of the screen height is filled with the **Timeline** window.

2. In the lower-left corner of the **Timeline** window, select the **Current Editor Type** menu button and choose **Video Sequence Editor** from the pop-up menu.

3. In the **Video Sequence Editor** header, select **Add**, and choose **Image** from the pop-up menu. Choose any of the `boat_stereo` images from `Chapter 12/Images/Video Strips/` in your download pack. You don't need the whole strip. Just select a single frame. Click on the **Add Image Strip** button in the **File Browser** window.

4. Select **Add** and choose **Scene** and then **Scene** again from the pop-up menus.

5. Press *N* to open up the Properties panel of **Video Sequence Editor**. Click on the button next to **Blend** in the **Edit Strip** subpanel and choose **Alpha Over** from the pop-up menu.

6. Move the Current Time Indicator so it is within the frames covered by both strips.

7. Select the Render button in the Properties window header. In the **Shading** subpanel, make sure that the **Alpha** is set to **Transparent**, not **Sky**.

8. Press *F12* and the composited render will look similar to the following screenshot:

9. Save the file with a unique name.

What just happened?

Now, you went into **Video Sequence Editor** and laid the scene over a background image and set its **Blend** setting to **Alpha Over**, meaning **Video Sequence Editor** uses the alpha channel of the top layer in compositing the two images. In addition, you set the Shading's Alpha to transparent so that when you rendered it, you got an image of the spheres over the island image. Since the left two spheres are solid, they completely cover the scene. The right-hand spheres are partially transparent so they let some of the boat scene image through.

Any time you want to render an image with a transparent background, you will need to set the Shading from Sky to Transparent, so remember where to find that control. You will need to make sure that, in the Output subpanel, you have selected RGBA rendering.

The following are some sources for more information on the topics we just reviewed:

Anti-Aliasing (`http://www.dpreview.com/glossary/digital-imaging/aliasing`)

Subsurface scattering (`http://en.wikipedia.org/wiki/Subsurface_scattering`)

Ray tracing (`http://en.wikipedia.org/wiki/Ray_tracing_(graphics)`)

Alpha channels (`http://en.wikipedia.org/wiki/Alpha_compositing`)

Choosing the dimensions for your animation

It's no surprise that you have to choose the size of the image. Is this animation for a banner ad on the Web, an IMAX screen, or something in between?

That's where the **Dimensions** subpanel of the **Render** panel in the Properties window comes in handy. The top button is the **Render Presets** button. If you click on it, you will find a menu of common video sizes.

Time for action – selecting render presets

Render presets can save you a lot of time, make sure you don't forget to set important settings and act as a guide for what those settings should be:

1. Press *Esc* to get back to the 3D View window. Zoom back far enough so that you can see the entire image area within the passepartout.

2. In the Properties window, choose the **Render** button from the header.

3. Look at the **Dimensions** subpanel of the **Render** panel. It shows you the **X** and **Y** resolution, the range of the frame numbers, the frame rate, and the aspect ratio.

4. Select the **Render Presets** button and choose **TV PAL 4:3** from the pop-up menu as shown in the following screenshot. Watch the 3D View window as you select it.

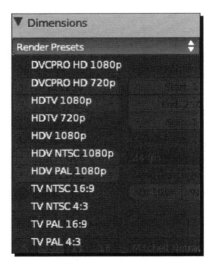

5. Note that the resolution, the frame rate, and the aspect ratio have changed.

6. Now, open up the **Post Processing** subpanel. Note the **Compositing**, **Sequencer**, and **Fields** checkboxes.

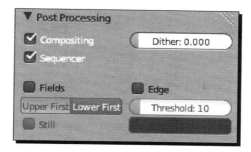

7. Make sure that the **Fields** checkbox is checked.

What just happened?

The Render Presets provide you with an easy way of setting up your animation to render. Of course, you will have to know what you are creating this animation for.

For a web banner, you will want to make the animation of the size requested by the web designer and use the slowest frame rate that still looks good. Animation, film, and video use a principle called **persistence of vision**. It means that the image is still in your brain for a short while after you see something. Bring in another image fast enough and they seem to blend together. About seven frames per second is as low as you can get and still get the persistence of vision effect that makes animations work. Films run at 24 frames per second and videos run at 25 or 30 frames per second. The reason for making web graphics low speed is to make the file size smaller and also because you don't know how powerful is someone's computer, tablet, or phone. So you have to balance the file size and animation smoothness.

Then, there is the old style TV, now known as **Standard Definition** (**SD**). The two main TV formats are **NTSC** in the U.S. and **PAL** in Europe. Earlier, TV transmitters could only send so much of the picture in the time between the start of one frame and the start of the next one, and it wasn't enough to cover a TV screen.

Therefore, they came up with a plan where they would transmit every other line of a picture from top to bottom, then go back to the top, and transmit the other lines so they could fill the screen in half the time, and this would keep refreshing the picture so the image wouldn't flicker. Each one of these sets of lines was called a **field**. Blender has a **Fields** checkbox to render videos that are compatible with TV signals.

When you check the **Fields** checkbox, the **Upper First** and **Lower First** buttons are brightened. By default, **Upper First** is highlighted. This is for the European PAL method. The American NTSC method does **Lower First**.

The advent of digital cameras has made this even more muddled; many DV formats are lower first and 1080i is often upper first. So if you have any doubts, the best thing to do is create a short animation where you move a white square on a black background from left to right. Record one version in Upper First and another version in Lower First. The correct one will look great on a TV monitor while the wrong one will look horrible.

When an image is made of two different fields, it is called an **interlaced** image. There can be one graphic or animation, but the system will read an interlaced image by displaying every other line of pixels or one field and then go back and display the other field of lines. The following diagram shows a TV screen. The even rows would be one field, and the odd rows would be another field. First, the beam moves horizontally along one row of pixels while turned on and creates a picture. Then, the lines show the beam moving to its next location while turned off. You can see it goes from one even row to another even row, not straight down. At the bottom, the beam goes up and begins the odd rows.

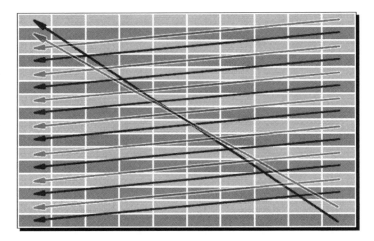

Interlacing like this is the difference between the HD formats 1080i and 1080p. 1080i is an interlaced display. With 1080p, the p stands for progressive, meaning it displays the lines in order from top to bottom.

Time for action – seeing what fields look like

I made a Blender file that has the white square on the black background for you. Looking at it in action may help you get an idea of what goes on with fields:

1. Load the program 4909OS_12_Fields.blend from your Chapter 12 download pack.

2. Press *F12*. You see a white square on a black background.

3. In the **Post Processing** subpanel of the **Render** panel in the Properties window, check the **Fields** checkbox.

4. Press *F12*.

What just happened?

When you have fields turned on, two images are rendered and merged. One image represents the time during the first half of the frame. Every other line is rendered. The other represents the time during the second half of the frame. Then, the alternating lines are rendered.

When both fields are rendered, on the computer screen, the image looks like the following screenshot. The left-hand fringe is where the square was only during the first field, and the right-hand fringe is where the square was only during the second field. The solid white area is where the square was during both fields.

The image rendered on fields may look strange in your files, but when a TV station uses them for a Standard Definition playback, they will give you a superior-looking image with extra smoothness. Again, if you have questions, supply the TV station or video production company with a sample animation like 4909OS_12_Fields.blend, one rendered out **Upper First**, and one rendered out **Lower First**, and see which one looks good.

Another thing to look out for with PAL and NTSC is the aspect ratio. There are two aspect ratios to be concerned with. One is the aspect ratio of the entire picture and the second is the aspect ratio of a single pixel, as shown in the following image. For both PAL and NTSC, the aspect ratio of the entire picture is **4** across to **3** down. Both PAL and NTSC have 720 pixels across, but PAL has 576 lines down, and NTSC has only 486. So their pixels have different shapes to achieve the 4:3 ratio for the entire picture. You can see this in the following image.

HD screens tend to have a ratio of **16** across to **9** down and normally have square pixels.

You can see what the pixel **Aspect Ratio** is when you select different rendering presets in the **Dimensions** subpanel of the **Render** panel. Look at the HDTV 1080p, TV NTSC 4:3, and TV PAL 4:3 settings:

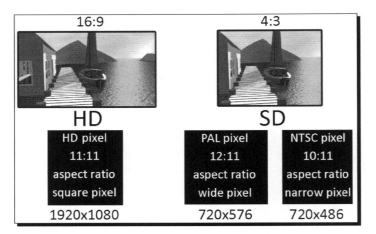

Choosing what gets rendered

In the **Post Processing** subpanel of the **Render** panel in the Properties window, there are **Compositing** and **Sequencer** checkboxes.

By default, both boxes are checked, so you don't have to worry about turning them on, but even so, if there is nothing in **Node Editor**, **Compositing** does not get activated, and if there is nothing in **Video Sequence Editor**, **Sequencer** does not get activated.

If you have used the 3D View Editor, the **Node Editor**, and **Video Sequence Editor**, Blender will go through them in order as it renders each frame:

* You link the render and/or the **Node Editor** with **Video Sequence Editor** by adding a **Scene** strip in **Video Sequence Editor** as you did earlier in this chapter. The **Scene** strip will bring the 3D View rendering output into **Video Sequence Editor**. That way, your render will be included in the compositing done in **Video Sequence Editor**, as shown in the following illustration.

* You link the render to the **Node Editor** by including a **Render Layers** node in the **Node Editor**. The **Render Layers** node brings the 3D View render output into the **Node Editor**, similar to how an **Image** node brings in an external image into the **Node Editor**. That way, your render is included in the compositing done in the **Node Editor** as shown in the following screenshot:

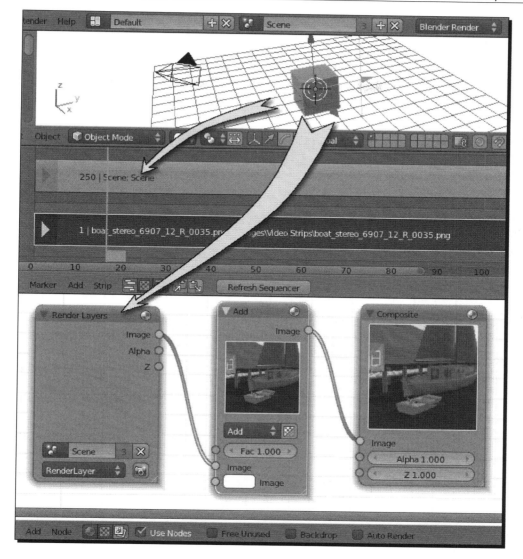

Selecting the best file format

Blender saves still images by default to the PNG format. This is a good choice. PNG files do lossless compression, which minimizes file size while not losing any detail. The PNG file also supports an alpha channel, so you can composite the images you render. It also provides the best safety if you have problems in rendering because the entire sequence doesn't have to be re-rendered, just the frames that have problems.

When you are ready for a final render, you need to decide what kind of output you want. That depends entirely on what you plan to do with the animation.

In the real world, you need to consider who you are making this video for. For example, earlier, you were given several choices of format to render out the sequence you edited. So the real world was that you needed to make it so that it would play on the video player on your computer.

If it's for YouTube, then your requirements might be a .MPEG4 or MOV file, with h264, mpeg4 video codecs and an AAC audio codec, or a .AVI file, with an MJPEG video codec and a PCM audio codec. You'd have to check on the YouTube website to find out what size your final render should be.

If you are making an animation for TV or video, then check with the people you are making it for. When I worked for an advertising agency that did TV production, most of the time they wanted a sequence of PNG images or a MOV file with PNG compression, and even though their final video was usually output to SD, they did all their work in HD. It can vary a lot, so don't be afraid to ask. Asking good questions makes you look more professional.

Major formats for video rendering are QuickTime, AVI, H.264, and MPEG. There is more information available on the following links:

```
http://wiki.blender.org/index.php/Doc:2.6/Manual/
Render/Output
```
```
http://en.wikibooks.org/wiki/Blender_3D:_Noob_to_Pro/
Output_Formats
```
```
http://wiki.blender.org/index.php/Doc:2.6/Manual/
Render/Output/Video
```

Rendering with the Cycles renderer

The Blender Internal renderer is only one of the many renderers available to the Blender user. The **Cycles** renderer has been incorporated into Blender 2.7, and development has stopped for the Blender Internal renderer. The Internal renderer is good and easy to use so it's a great way to start. However, in the long run, you will need to know the Cycles renderer.

One big difference between the Cycles renderer and the Blender Internal renderer is that Cycles simulates real light while the internal renderer does not, so Cycles gives you better results. The Cycles renderer also allows objects to be used as lights.

This makes it easy to do cool stuff like neon lights and adding a glow to the bottom of cars. Cycles also handles glass well and creates distortions of light known as caustics, like the light patterns on the bottom of a swimming pool.

Cycles does a style of ray tracing, bouncing the light around and following it to the source. This means that you get better shadows, lights, and reflections. It also means that rendering is never quite finished. It just gets better and better and you decide what is good enough.

Time for action – simulating the glow of a kiln

Cycles offers a lot of ways to use light. Here, you are going to simulate the glow of a kiln as a white sphere acts as a light source and bounces light off red faces, turning the light that bounces to red light. First, you'll build the kiln:

1. Open a new file in Blender.

2. In the center of the top header, click the LMB over the button that says **Blender Render**, and choose **Cycles Render** from the drop-down menu, as shown in the following screenshot:

3. Select the default lamp with the RMB. Press *X* to delete it.

4. Select the cube with the RMB and press the *Tab* key to get into **Edit Mode**.

5. In the 3D View header, click on the **Viewport Shading** menu button and choose **Wireframe**.

6. In the 3D View header, click on the **Face select mode** button.

7. Choose the face nearest to the camera.

8. Press *E* to extrude it, and then press *Enter*.

9. Press *S, 0.5*, and *Enter*.

10. Press *E, -1.7*, and *Enter*.

11. Press *A* to deselect all the faces.

What just happened?

This was pretty easy. You took the default cube and put a hole in it. This is very similar to building the first boat.

Time for action – creating and applying the Cycles materials

Cycles materials are very different from the Blender Internal Renderer materials. It's time for a little introduction. You are going to make a texture that is partly diffused so that it absorbs light, and partly glossy so that it reflects light. This way, you can control how much light is reflected:

1. Use the RMB and press the *Shift* + RMB keys to select only the four sides of the last extrusion you made, as shown on the left of the next screenshot.

2. Press *Ctrl* + *I* to select the inverse.

3. In the Properties window, select the **Material** button in the header.

4. If the **Material** panel looks different, as shown in the center of the next screenshot, that's because you are now creating materials for the Cycles renderer.

5. Name the material **Outside** and assign it to the selected faces.

6. With the cursor over the 3D View window, press *Ctrl* + *I* to invert the selection.

7. Click on the + sign in the **Material** panel to make a new material. Click on the **New** button.

8. Name the material **Glow**.

9. In the **Surface** subpanel, click on the button labeled **Diffuse BSDF** and choose **Mix Shader** from the pop-up menu as shown on the right of the following screenshot:

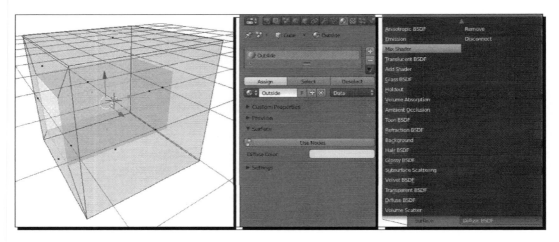

10. In the **Surface** subpanel, there are two buttons labeled **Shader**. Click on the upper **Shader** button and choose **Diffuse BSDF** from the drop-down menu.

11. Set **Color** to a solid red. I used **R 0.800**, **G 0.000**, and **B 0.080**.

12. Click on the lower **Shader** button and choose **Glossy BSDF** from the drop-down menu.

13. Set **Color** to the same shade of red. I used **R 0.800**, **G 0.000**, and **B 0.0800**.

14. Scroll up to the **Fac** button and set its value to 0.6. This sets the influence factor for each shader.

15. Press the **Assign** button.

16. With the cursor over the 3D View window, press the *Tab* key.

17. Press the *A* key to deselect the kiln.

What just happened?

First, you chose a material known as a mix shader that allows you to combine the characteristics of different shaders. Then, you chose a Diffuse BSDF material. BSDF stands for bidirectional scattering distribution function. BSDF is how Cycles calculates how much light is reflected by that material. Diffuse BSDF materials are not shiny. But, to reflect the light, a Glossy BSDF material would be better, so you chose that for the second shader to mix. Then, you set the Fac to control how much of the Diffuse BSDF and how much of the Glossy BSDF you got.

Time for action – making an emission material

Now, you have the kiln set, but you need to have a source for the light. This will be an emission material. With Cycles, your light source can be any shape:

1. Press the *3* and *5* keys on the NumPad to get the **Right Ortho** view.

2. Press *Shift + A* and create a **UV Sphere** from the **Mesh** menu.

3. Scale it down so it just fits within the central cavity of the kiln.

4. In the **Materials** panel of the Properties window, press the **+** sign to create a new material. Click on the **New** button. Name the material **Light**.

5. In the **Surface** subpanel, change the **Surface** from **Diffuse BSDF** to **Emission**. You may have to scroll to the bottom to find it.

6. Set **Strength** to 60.

7. In the **Timeline** window, select the **Current Editor Type** button, and choose **Node Editor** from the pop-up menu.

8. Use the double-pointed arrow to move the border between the **Node Editor** window and the 3D View window up a bit. Zoom into the nodes you see in the **Node Editor** window.

9. Cycles materials can be edited in the **Node Editor** as well as in the **Materials** panel of the Properties window. As an example, the nodes for the Glow material are shown in the following screenshot. The Light node is similar but simpler since it doesn't have two shaders like the Glow material does.

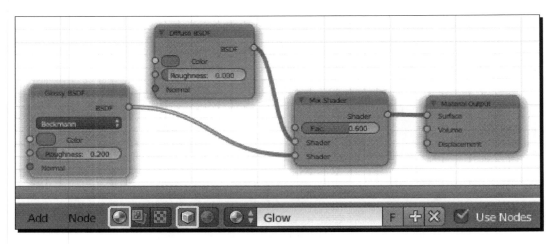

10. In the 3D View window, press the *A* key to deselect the sphere.

11. Press *Shift + A* and create a **Plane** from the **Mesh** menu.

12. Press *G, Z,* and use the mouse to move it so it is slightly below the kiln. Press the LMB to release it.

13. Press *S, 8,* and *Enter*.

14. Press *F12* to render it. Press *Esc* when you are finished looking at the image.

15. Save the file with a unique name.

What just happened?

That's kind of cool. There's no lamp, but you can see the glow, and not only do you see the light, but the color of the insides of the kiln gets picked up and reflected out as well. You noticed that the materials' settings are all different from the Internal renderer and can be edited in the Node Editor as well. The first image shown in the following graphic was a quick render with only 10 samples, whereas the second image has 1000 samples. The buttons to control this are in the Sampling subpanel of the Render panel. This makes quite a difference as you can see.

The Glow material had two portions, Diffuse BSFD and Glossy BSFD. Diffuse produces a flatter surface, and glossy produces a more highlyreflective one. Using them both allowed you to tailor exactly how glossy the inner part of the cube would be, which also affects how the light from the sphere bounces off of it. The **Fac** setting controls that balance.

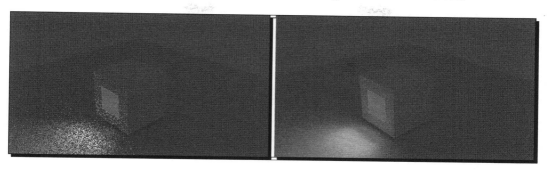

The key to improving rendering in Cycles is in the **Sampling** subpanel of the **Render** panel in the Properties window. The important thing in Cycles is time. You have to balance quality against render time.

The controls for rendering in Cycles are in the **Sampling** subpanel of the **Render** panel in the Properties window. In **Samples**, the higher the **Render** value, the better the image. Changing the **Seed** will change exactly which places are sampled.

Changing the number of bounces that the light makes can do a lot. The more **Bounces**, the more accurate the light will be. In the **Light Paths** subpanel of the **Render** panel, you can set the maximum and minimum number of bounces. And, staying within the general limits, you can customize the number of bounces for diffuse and glossy textures.

Transparency? Yes, Cycles does glass very well. Note the **No Caustics** checkbox. Caustics are the patterns of light that you see in transparent objects such as glass and water caused by the light bending. They add a lot to the realism of the render. You can include them in your rendering if you wish.

Have a go hero – adjusting render quality in Cycles

Using the current scene, make changes to the Render panel settings and see how this affects the scene and the time required to render it. Create a text file in the Blender file to make notes. Play with the materials settings too.

The following are some links to find out further information about Cycles:

`http://blenderartists.org/forum/showthread.php?232104-Blender-Cycles-Tutorial-Series`

`http://www.blendernation.com/2011/11/24/cycles-tutorial-a-thorough-introduction/`

`http://www.blendernation.com/2011/08/03/quick-tutorial-cycles-render-in-gpu-cpu/`

Pop quiz – rendering with fields

Q1. When you rendered the square without fields, it appeared square. While each field was rendering, the square appeared rectangular. Why is that?

1. A rendering bug in Blender.

2. The image in each field is blurred because it is moving.

3. When Blender renders a field, it's only rendering half of the rows of pixels, so what you see is only half as high. When they are interlaced, then you get the full height image.

The key-function table

The following table lists some key shortcut controls applicable to this chapter:

Key	Function
*	In the **File Browser** window, the asterisk acts as a wild card, allowing you to select all the images in a series if you replace the number of the frame with this in the input window.
H	This mutes a strip in **Video Sequence Editor**.
Alt + H	This unmutes a strip in **Video Sequence Editor**.
K	This does a soft trim in the Current Frame Indicator in the selected strips. This hides the other frames in the strip in **Video Sequence Editor**.
Shift + K	This does a hard trim in the Current Frame Indicator in the selected strips. This deletes the other frames beyond the end of the strip in **Video Sequence Editor**.
Left arrow	This moves one frame to the previous frame in **Video Sequence Editor**.
Right arrow	This moves to the next frame in **Video Sequence Editor**.
Shift + left arrow	This moves to the beginning of the video in **Video Sequence Editor**.
Shift + right arrow	This moves to the end of the video in **Video Sequence Editor**.

Key	Function
Shift + up arrow	This jumps ahead 10 frames in **Video Sequence Editor**.
Shift + down arrow	This jumps back 10 frames in **Video Sequence Editor**.
G	This lets you move the selected strip with the mouse in **Video Sequence Editor**.
G + X	This lets you move the selected strip with the mouse, and restricts it to the channel you are in, in **Video Sequence Editor**.
G + Y	This lets you move the selected strip with the mouse, and restricts it to the time you are at, in **Video Sequence Editor**.
MMB	Press the MMB after starting to move a strip and it locks the motion to either the X or Y direction depending on how you started moving it in **Video Sequence Editor**.
Alt + O	This removes offsets from a video strip in **Video Sequence Editor**, removing any soft trims.
X	This deletes the selected video strip in **Video Sequence Editor**.
Shift + Ctrl + S	This saves a file.
F2	This saves a file.
Ctrl + N	This creates a new file.
Ctrl + O	This opens a file.
F1	This opens a file.
L	In **Edit Mode**, this selects all connected faces, edges, and vertices.
Ctrl + Tab	In **Edit Mode**, this brings up the **Mesh Select Mode** menu.
Ctrl + I	In 3D View, this inverts the selection.

Summary

You have learned to use **Video Sequence Editor** to edit rendered scenes. You have used Node Editor to create stereographic views and composite images. You have learned to use the rendering controls to create a more finished animation and explored the Cycles renderer.

I tip my hat to you. You have done very well. You got through this book and made some awesome stuff.

You are ready to go out into the wider world of Blending. While there is much to learn yet, you've reached the point where you will be confident modeling, animating, and creating images, and you have a solid base to understand the rest of Blender. You will be comfortable on Blender websites, able to understand what people are talking about, and ready to help others. You're going to do some great work. I can't wait to see it! Happy Blending! Let's go!

Pop Quiz Answers

Chapter 1, Introducing Blender and Animation

Pop quiz – uses of Blender

Q1	1 Blender cannot be used for outputting a Flash animation.
Q2	2 Blender is not normally used by restaurants.

Chapter 2, Getting Comfortable Using the 3D View

Pop quiz – learning about Blender windows

Q1	3 Press the LMB on the diagonal lines and drag it toward the center of the window.
Q2	2 Pixels are colored rectangles that make up a digital picture.
Q3	1 To the left, farther away from you than the origin, and at the same height.
Q4	3 Press the . (period) key on NumPad to zoom in on the active object.

Chapter 3, Controlling the Lamp, the Camera, and Animating Objects

Pop quiz – working in time and space

Q1	2 Pressing the *Shift* + up arrow key, moves you ten frames forward in the timeline.
Q2	1 Put something in the foreground to bridge the gap between the end of the bench and the dancer's foot.

Chapter 4, Modeling with Vertices, Edges, and Faces

Pop quiz – making selections

Q1	2 Press *B* for Border Select
Q2	1 Press *C* + MMB to deselect with the Circle Selection Tool
Q3	2 or 3 Either of these methods would select only vertices in the eye.

Chapter 5, Building a Simple Boat

Pop quiz – extrusion, subdivision, and moving vertices

Q1	2 Pressing *W* opens the **Specials** menu that allows you to subdivide edges and faces.

Chapter 6, Making and Moving the Oars

Pop quiz – pivot points and parents

Q1	1 Average location is not a pivot point term. The term is median point.
Q2	2 The Parent object is chosen last.

Chapter 7, Planning Your Work, Working Your Plan

Pop quiz – organizing Blender files

Q1	2 `C:\NewBoat\Images`
Q2	3 `Sloop of War_USS Constitution_1854 version.blend`
Q3	3 Right now!

Chapter 8, Making the Sloop

Pop quiz – remembering Edge Tool commands

Q1	3 It is false. To chose edges for a Loop Cut, you press *Ctrl + R*.

Chapter 9, Finishing Your Sloop

Pop quiz – fonts

Q1	2 The Cap Height is the height of an upper case letter from the baseline to the top.
Q2	1 San serif means without a serif, or the little feet on the terminals of a letter.

Pop quiz – rotations

Q1	3
	The rotation was done to rotate the local axis of the rudder so it would swing along the angle of the stern. By rotating the vertices, you ensured that the rudder would be in the proper orientation even though it was rotated off the vertical axis by -27°.

Chapter 10, Modeling Organic Forms, Sea, and Terrain

Pop quiz – optimizing rendering times

Q1	2
	Removing faces from the Ocean Floor is the only way you will not delete faces that you might need. Removing the back sides of the island and buildings should only be done if you are positive that you will never need them.

Chapter 11, Improving Your Lighting and Camera Work

Pop quiz – lighting a scene

Q1	1
	The Key light controls how much light there is in a scene.
Q2	2
	The texture added to a light is called a cookie.

Pop quiz – improving performance

Q1	2
	The area in pixels that the processor works on at any one time is the tile size.

Chapter 12, Rendering and Compositing

Pop quiz – rendering with fields answer

Q1	3
	When Blender renders a field, half of the rows of pixels are rendered, so what you see is only half as high. Two fields are rendered to make the complete picture and then interlaced back together into a full height image.

Index

cockpit, boat model
  creating 278-280
color
  making, with computers 64, 65
  used, for separating view 398, 399
color depth 65
color mixing, of light
  colors, setting 79
  combinations 78
composition rules, camera
  limited palette, using 88
  negative space, using 87, 88
  positive space, using 87, 88
  rule of thirds 86, 87
Computer Aided Drafting (CAD) 60
computers
  colors, making with 64, 65
  pictures, creating with 63, 64
cones 64
constant interpolation, F-Curve 97
contours
  adding, to back side of island 363-365
controllers, Blender
  keyboard 37
  mouse 37
  NumPad 37
control points, Subdivision Surface
  adjusting 265
  hull shape, working on 267-270
  sloop shape, creating 265
cookies
  used, for creating patterns 400-402
cross-eye stereo image
  making 461
Ctrl + LMB key
  pressing, for Lasso Selection 121
  warning 121
cube
  turning, into boat with box modeling 154
Current Editor Type button
  about 40
  Header bar 40
current frame indicator 91
curves
  adding, to boat's lines by subdividing 164-167
  adding, to hull 167, 168

Custom Curve
  about 406
  used, for tailoring light 406-408
Cycles renderer
  about 476
  emission material, creating 479-481
  kiln glow, simulating 477
  materials, applying 478
  materials, creating 478
  rendering with 476
  render quality, adjusting in 481
  versus Blender Internal renderer 476
cylinder
  oar, creating from 187-189

D

DaisyDisk 462
defocusing 417
depth of field
  creating 415-418
  using 414
diagrams, animation planning
  Animation bounce diagrams 250
  Eadweard Muybridge photographic series 250
  Preston Blair Phoneme Mouth 250
  walk cycle charts 250
Difference operation 286
digital signage
  Blender, using in 32
dimensions
  selecting, for animation 470
display mode
  selecting 116
dollying 411
Dope Sheet
  about 431
  using 431, 432
driving simulators
  Blender, using in 32
DupliFrames
  about 374
  used, for adding planks to pier 374-376
DupliVerts
  about 297, 305, 316, 371
  used, for assembling ship's wheel 304, 305

E

Pan 90
Roll 90
Tilt 90
Truck 90

G

games
Blender, using in 32
global axis, camera
using 83
global coordinates 51
Goonland, Popeye cartoon animation 20
Graph Editor
animation channels, selecting 103
Bézier curve controls, working with 98
Bézier curve handles 101
channel display, controlling 106
Channel Selection Panel, using 104, 105
exploring 96
F-Curve 97
keyframes, adding 103, 104
keyframes, copying 106
keyframes for light, creating 107
keyframes, pasting 106
motion, controlling 96
squash, adding 100
stretch, adding 100
graphics, terms
Ascender 318
Baseline 317
Cap Height 317
Descender 318
Kerning 318
Serif 317
Terminal 318
X Height 317
grip, for oar
creating, box-modeling tools used 189-191
grouping 137
groups
about 389
used, for organizing scene 389
groups, of vertices
rotating 139, 140
scaling 139, 140

guard, for oar
creating, box-modeling tools used 189-191
guides, animation planning
about 246
bar sheet 251
exposure sheets 250
sound, as planning guide 252
gunwale 154

H

hardware rendering 426, 427
house
assembling, from kit 381, 382
HSV (Hue, Saturation, Value) 80
hub, ship's wheel
creating 299
hull
curves, adding to 167, 168
hull, modeling as mesh
about 277
cabin, creating 280-283
cockpit, creating 278-280
openings, adding to cabin 283
surface, converting 277
hull shape
bow, making sharper 272
checking 273
dimensions 273
finishing 271
transom, flattening 271
working on 267-270

I

ideas
storyboarding 424
image
scale, obtaining from 186
imdb
URL 20
Imperial units 158
index
making, of files 239
interactive graphics
history 24-27

U

Union operation 286
Utah Teapot 128

V

Vector handles 102
vertex by vertex
  selecting 131
vertices
  about 115
  faces, creating with 145, 146
  grouping 138, 139
  hiding 132, 133
  selecting, A key used 119
  selecting, with Border Select mode 119, 120
  visibility, controlling of 130, 131
  working with 117, 118
video
  Blender, using in 31
video channels
  manipulating 442-444
video sequence
  finishing 450, 451
Video Sequence Editor
  about 438
  render settings, optimizing 451-453
  resolution, modifying 445
  scene, completing in 450, 451
  scene, preparing in 438-441
  transparency, using in 468, 469
video strips
  editing 445-448
  working with 441-444

Viewport Shading menu 116
virtual reality
  creating, Blender used 33
virtual sets
  rendered, Blender used 33
visibility
  controlling, of vertices 130, 131

W

walk cycle charts
  about 250
  URL 250
water tight 168
web animation
  Blender, using in 31
wide-angle lens 410
window modifications, Blender
  about 45
  window header, flipping 46
  windows, creating with secret method 45
  windows, maximizing 45, 46
  windows, removing with secret method 45
  windows, tiling 45, 46
windows, Blender
  creating, with parallel edges 45
  joining 44
  resizing 42
  splitting 42, 43
  using 39
  working with 40, 41

Z

zooming 411

Thank you for buying
Blender 3D Basics Beginner's Guide
Second Edition

About Packt Publishing

Packt, pronounced 'packed', published its first book "*Mastering phpMyAdmin for Effective MySQL Management*" in April 2004 and subsequently continued to specialize in publishing highly focused books on specific technologies and solutions.

Our books and publications share the experiences of your fellow IT professionals in adapting and customizing today's systems, applications, and frameworks. Our solution based books give you the knowledge and power to customize the software and technologies you're using to get the job done. Packt books are more specific and less general than the IT books you have seen in the past. Our unique business model allows us to bring you more focused information, giving you more of what you need to know, and less of what you don't.

Packt is a modern, yet unique publishing company, which focuses on producing quality, cutting-edge books for communities of developers, administrators, and newbies alike. For more information, please visit our website: www.packtpub.com.

About Packt Open Source

In 2010, Packt launched two new brands, Packt Open Source and Packt Enterprise, in order to continue its focus on specialization. This book is part of the Packt Open Source brand, home to books published on software built around Open Source licenses, and offering information to anybody from advanced developers to budding web designers. The Open Source brand also runs Packt's Open Source Royalty Scheme, by which Packt gives a royalty to each Open Source project about whose software a book is sold.

Writing for Packt

We welcome all inquiries from people who are interested in authoring. Book proposals should be sent to author@packtpub.com. If your book idea is still at an early stage and you would like to discuss it first before writing a formal book proposal, contact us; one of our commissioning editors will get in touch with you.

We're not just looking for published authors; if you have strong technical skills but no writing experience, our experienced editors can help you develop a writing career, or simply get some additional reward for your expertise.

Blender 3D Basics Beginner's Guide

ISBN: 978-1-84951-690-7   Paperback: 468 pages

The complete novice's guide to 3D modeling and animation

1. The best starter guide for complete newcomers to 3D modeling and animation.

2. Easier learning curve than any other book on Blender.

3. You will learn all the important foundation skills ready to apply to any 3D software.

Blender 2.6 Cycles: Materials and Textures Cookbook

ISBN: 978-1-78216-130-1   Paperback: 280 pages

Over 40 recipes to help you create stunning materials and textures using the Cycles rendering engine with Blender

1. Create naturalistic materials and textures—such as rock, snow, and ice—using Cycles.

2. Learn Cycle's node-based material system.

3. Get to grips with the powerful Cycles rendering engine.

Please check **www.PacktPub.com** for information on our titles

Blender 3D Printing Essentials

ISBN: 978-1-78328-459-7   Paperback: 114 pages

Bring your ideas to life in Blender and learn how to design beautiful, light, and strong 3D printed objects

1. Design beautiful, colorful, and practical objects in Blender to print or export.

2. Master Blender's special 3D printing tools to maximize print quality and minimize cost.

3. Consider requirements unique to 3D printing such as structural integrity and stability.

Blender Game Engine Beginner's Guide

ISBN: 978-1-84951-702-7   Paperback: 206 pages

The non programmer's guide to creating 3D video games

1. Use Blender to create a complete 3D video game.

2. Ideal entry level to game development without the need for coding.

3. No programming or scripting required.

Please check **www.PacktPub.com** for information on our titles

Printed in Great Britain
by Amazon